KILLING RADICALISM

Killing Radicalism

Anti-Rape Advocacy Reimagined

Melinda Chen 陳婉怡

New York University Press

New York

NEW YORK UNIVERSITY PRESS
New York
www.nyupress.org

© 2026 by New York University
All rights reserved

Please contact the Library of Congress for Cataloging-in-Publication data.

ISBN: 9781479828234 (hardback)
ISBN: 9781479828241 (paperback)
ISBN: 9781479828265 (library ebook)
ISBN: 9781479828258 (consumer ebook)

This book is printed on acid-free paper, and its binding materials are chosen for strength and durability. We strive to use environmentally responsible suppliers and materials to the greatest extent possible in publishing our books.

The manufacturer's authorized representative in the EU for product safety is Mare Nostrum Group B.V., Mauritskade 21D, 1091 GC Amsterdam, The Netherlands.
Email: gpsr@mare-nostrum.co.uk.

Manufactured in the United States of America

10 9 8 7 6 5 4 3 2 1

Also available as an ebook

CONTENTS

Introduction: Neoliberal Normativity in the
Anti-Rape Movement 1

1. Weaving Our Stories: The Abolitionist Genealogies of
Anti-Rape Advocacy 21

2. Capitalizing Empowerment: The Culture of
Making Survivors 54

3. A Hierarchy of Advocacy: White Professional Cooptation
of the Rape Crisis Center 90

4. Our Carceral Creep: Panoptic Policing of the
Anti-Rape Community 131

5. Who Counts? Quantifying Victims in Grant Applications 167

Conclusion: An Open Letter to the Anti-Rape Movement 201

Acknowledgments 211

Appendix A: Study Design 215

Appendix B: Voices of a Movement 233

Appendix C: Terminology 237

Appendix D: Abbreviations 241

Notes 243

Index 285

About the Author 327

Introduction

Neoliberal Normativity in the Anti-Rape Movement

> Just because a person is Black, a woman, queer or transgender (or both) does not mean one is automatically radical or a revolutionary. Being radical is a choice, and it takes work.
> —Charlene A. Carruthers, *Unapologetic*

At the edge of a small rural town lies a nondescript beige-colored building with a green awning. In front of the building, a newly refurbished parking lot holds red and blue trucks and SUVs. Some spill out onto the street, breathing color into the quiet neighborhood. Electric wires surround the building, draping themselves just over treetops, and the little alleyways along the sides of the beige building scurry outwards to the back streets where quaint homes and churches rest. This building looks like every other building on the street, blending into the town.

There is a billboard next to the building. It is green like the awning, and the sides holding up the signage are faded, worn from the snowy winters and yawning sun. Posters stick to the painted plaster, offering services for the everyday American: KEYSTONE FINANCIAL, Badger Transportation, *Hair Massage Nails Body Wraps Facials Pedicures*, and Tactical Escape 101. The messages are there as if saying to some passerby, Stop by the building and see what we can do to help. And to be sure, the haphazardly constructed billboard is indeed a map, of sorts. A dentist's office and a loan company stake their claim in the building, offering everyday and necessary services. But there is another service inside the building. Embrace, an anti-violence victim services agency, finds a home there, too.

As an agency dedicated to supporting survivors of sexual violence, Embrace staff and volunteer advocates work to inspire hope of a safe and liberated world by responding to 24/7 hotline calls, providing material resources like clothing and food, and accompanying survivors as they navigate their communities after acute violence. Deep understanding of the ordinariness with which rape presents has made many of the advocates move with care: In this odd mash-up of an office and home, where plush couches are juxtaposed with wooden desks and office chairs, there is no flurry of activity, no urgent order shouting for immediate attention, no actions that imitate the places that visitors had just left for Embrace. Instead, advocates chat with each other casually, leaning over their shared table to talk. Through soft and gentle murmurs, Embrace welcomes survivors with warm, open arms.

One summer day, the advocates see protests on the news. People smash windows and light fires, calling attention to the police officers standing in riot gear in front of them. They scream someone's name and cry out to the police for their wrongdoing. They want to hear the offenders acknowledge their pain and loss of a community member. But none of the officers do. An advocate at Embrace absorbs the news for a moment. The riots are not anywhere near Embrace; they are over three hundred miles away. Yet the news chills her. She can feel the protesters' anger through the screen. She can empathize with the loss of a friend. She is scared, but not of the rioters. She is afraid of the police, who stand in defiance of justice before the protesters. The advocate turns to her neighbor and quietly asks a question. The neighbor nods her head in agreement.

Within a few hours, a sign is placed at the front desk. It reads, Black Lives Matter.

* * *

In September 2020, the sheriff of Barron County, Wisconsin, discovers the signage at Embrace. He reaches out to the advocates through the community rape response team. As an Embrace board member, he is confused and defensive about Embrace's support of Black Lives Matter, which he perceives to be a violent, radical movement. He writes, "I am struggling with this on why we have [the sign] up. While we need to advocate for domestic abuse and sexual assault—which is our mission, [it] seems we are branching out on social issues, which are divisive. From a funding standpoint this is very dangerous."[1]

Bemused, the advocates respond. They say that eliminating police brutality against Black people, as Black Lives Matter seeks to do, can reduce sexual violence. Black, Indigenous, and People of Color (BIPOC), especially those who are queer, immigrant, and disabled, are more likely to be sexually assaulted than other groups of people because perpetrators, many of whom are white,[2] cisgender, and heterosexual men,[3] weaponize their privilege through rape.[4] To eradicate sexual violence, the advocates argue, one must employ an intersectional framework. One's gender contributes to the vulnerability to rape, but so too do one's race, ethnicity, sexuality, class, skin color, ability, language, and immigrant status.[5] The advocates explain to the sheriff in an email, "Embrace can't end one form of violence without addressing the other, and we can't properly serve all survivors if we don't acknowledge and address the oppression and violence the most marginalized and oppressed survivors in our area are experiencing. Racism, police violence, sexual violence, and domestic violence all have the same root causes and they interact and compound on each other both in society and within the survivors we serve."[6] But the exchange fails. Within a few weeks, the sheriff resigns from Embrace's board of directors and circulates an email encouraging local law enforcement to do the same. One by one, fourteen of the seventeen law enforcement offices working in Embrace's jurisdiction withdraw their community partnerships with Embrace. And unlike Embrace's sign, their actions have immediate and significant negative material consequences for survivors. Law enforcement begins to drop victims off at sister agencies, even if those victims do not live in the area, and they throw into the trash Embrace's brochures and pamphlets about housing, employment, and community-based resources for victims. In public statements, officers decry Embrace for "taking the side of some of the anti–law enforcement out there" and shame Embrace for supporting a political movement that seeks to "defund the police."[7] For them, advocates' support of the Black racial justice movement crosses the line into radicalism, a kind of activism that is impermissible for a 501(c)(3) nonprofit that must be nonpartisan to receive federal and state dollars.[8] Victim services agencies should not be political, law enforcement argues, because ending sexual violence is a bipartisan issue. Because they see Embrace as supporting a partisan issue, the officers rescind their charitable donations of twenty-five thousand dollars meant for rape victims.[9]

Embrace's challenges with the bifurcation between sexual and intersecting racial justice movements are not unique. Over the last two decades, anti-violence advocates and scholars have become more vocal about the entanglements of victim advocacy with state institutions, which prevent advocates from openly participating in ongoing political events. Federal and state entities, such as the Office for Victims of Crime, as well as private agencies sponsored by the government, such as United Way, control how advocates on the ground spend money to support survivors in a phenomenon known as neoliberalism.[10] Many rape crisis centers operate as nonprofit agencies, and those that do not nevertheless draw upon significant governmental funding.[11] While anti-rape work is seemingly independent of the state, the domination of state funding in this work pushes advocates into supporting state interests over the interests of survivors.[12] For example, the sheriff and related "systems professionals," like the district attorney, held board member statuses at Embrace. Their position overseeing the distribution of money and capital resources granted them the power to reorganize victim services in ways that superseded the needs of survivors and advocates alike, in this case, complacency in the face of hostile police brutality against victims of systemic violence. Like Embrace, the vast majority of the several thousands of anti-violence agencies in the United States are entangled in these "braids" of neoliberalism.[13]

Systems professionals are granted nearly absolute power over advocates in anti-rape responses because it is assumed that the government provides advocates with sufficient financial means to carry out effective support services. Alternatives to this funding relationship with systems are usually seen as moot. Many advocates do not raise enough money from their local communities or individual donors and therefore heavily depend on federal and state grants to survive.[14] However, relying on the state to fund victim services is often contingent upon cooperation with policing, medical, and welfare systems, complexes that more often harm than help victims.[15] For example, advocates must persuade survivors to cooperate with police officers and sexual assault forensic-medical examiners in order to access Crime Victims Compensation, funds that reimburse survivors for the expenses accrued from rape victimization. Advocates must also ensure that their "community partners" are involved in rape responses even in instances in which the survivor may not want their presence. In Embrace's case, the sheriff's office demanded that advocates not participate in what the sheriff believed was a violent movement against police officers, or else the agency would lose a significant funding stream and the legitimacy that came with his membership on the board of directors. Fearful of losing resources, advocates can feel compelled to displace survivors' needs in favor of the nonprofit industrial complex (NPIC) to receive *any* funding for service provisions.[16]

Such displacement is a second rape, this time by advocates' own hands.[17] Systems professionals have repeatedly been shown to revictimize survivors by dismissing their needs in an ill-fated quest for carceral justice.[18] For advocates, however, this second rape is more subliminal; it comes from the adoption of the everywoman analysis: the belief that sexual violence affects everyone, including wealthy, able-bodied, cisgender white women, and the subsequent equation of sexual violence experienced by elite women with the experiences of violence by marginalized and "underserved" survivors.[19] The everywoman analysis presents in the anti-rape movement as the myth that social action for anything but justice for (elite cisgender) women, like Black Lives Matter, is secondary or unimportant to the agenda of ending rape.[20] Through pressures to conform to state funding demands, advocates conceptualize their work not as the abolition of intersectional violence to empower all victims but as an isolated, clinical procedure led by skilled "experts" to funnel only certain kinds of survivors toward therapeutic empowerment and all Others toward incarceration in settler-carceral prisons.[21] Advocates' use of the everywoman analysis, one that states that there is only one "normal" way to carry out victim advocacy for one "normal" victim, contradicts the very ethos of advocacy, which is to continuously reduce harm and build a safe and liberated world without any kind of violence in all communities. This *neoliberal normativity* makes advocates beholden to the values of funders (read: the hegemonic state) rather than the constituents whom advocates are supposed to help (read: survivors), killing radicalism without advocates' awareness of their own extermination.[22]

This book, *Killing Radicalism: Anti-Rape Advocacy Reimagined*, challenges the narrative that victim advocates are inherently helpful for survivors of sexual violence and instead describes the ways in which they confront collisions between mainstream funding and radical justice. Because of neoliberal policies and values that regulate their work, advocates provide normative victim services to survivors of sexual violence; in following normative neoliberalism, advocates themselves become complicit in revictimizing the survivors they seek to help. Though the violence of neoliberal advocacy appears benign in comparison to the violence of rape, advocates who labor on behalf of victims without recognizing intersectionality amplify the violence of the second rape, feeding violent systems within America's Prison Nation.[23] In sharing the stories of advocates, *Killing Radicalism* shows anti-rape activists just how efforts to bring about radical change can die in the face of normative governmental authorities and advocates' complicity in providing them with unfettered access to survivors.

The title of this book is inspired by bell hooks's "killing rage." In her essay, hooks explains that she felt a "killing rage" when a white man refused to help hooks and her Black woman friend as they encountered multiple instances of racism and sexism at an airport. She explains that the white man apologized to them but points out that his lack of intervention made him complicit in the same violence of the original perpetrators, the white airport attendees and flight attendants. The rage she felt culminated in a murderous feeling, a desire to "kill" the man next to her and "tenderly" inform him of the error of his ways.[24] *Killing Radicalism* shares the sentiment of hooks's "killing rage." While advocates may not actively harm victims, advocates abuse marginalized survivors when they are complicit in the racist, sexist, ableist, nativist, and related violence of systems.

But anti-rape activists should feel a "killing rage" every time we see violence. We have always threaded the line between helping systems or helping people; as of late, our decisions have leaned toward helping systems that subject victims to more violence. In these decisions, we stop critically evaluating the impact our work has on victims, and we therefore stop feeling the anger we should feel when faced with intersectional violence. It is this affect that is absent in our present anti-rape movement. In the spirit of hooks's "killing rage," *Killing Radicalism* awakens us to the "killing" affect that is necessary to transform advocacy. Against the backdrop of those neutral, normative actions that have "killed radicalism," *Killing Radicalism* shakes us into a "killing radicalism" that demands a different world of anti-rape advocacy.

Reclaiming Radicalism

I'm an advocate, and I've been volunteering at rape crisis centers for the past several years. When I first began this work, I thought that advocacy was the answer to rape culture. It was a way to give back to survivors and those who helped me with my own experiences with violence. But over time, I realized that marginalized survivors, mainly queer women of color just like me, were more likely to drop out of victim services than normative white, heterosexual women survivors. These attrition rates were not due to a failure on victims' parts. I saw—with hot-blooded fury—just how often my fellow advocates sided with systems even when presented with clear instances of intersecting violence. I felt a rage kindle inside of me, stirred by the problems of neoliberal advocacy. We were—are—complicit in the normative oppressions of neoliberalism when we acquiesce to systems values.

It is advocates' duty to be the defense between survivors and normative violence; we cannot dismiss and reviolate the people for whom we are responsible. This stance on advocacy is radical. As a fellow advocate who has also served victims of violence, I recognize the enormous weight of neoliberalism, and I generally presume that advocates are well intentioned when they concede to it. But I do not exculpate advocates from our responsibility to survivors of all identities and backgrounds. Advocates sometimes see themselves as already "radical" for denouncing rape culture, yet I believe that advocates must actively dismantle interlocking oppressions experienced by rape victims to be considered "radical." It is dangerous to believe that simply because we offer necessary services that otherwise would not be provided, we are immune from doing harm. The reality is that, rather than think of ourselves as already radical, we must be *more* radical, more attentive to the needs of marginalized peoples. Just because one is an advocate and challenges institutionalized patriarchy does not mean that one is automatically a radical who challenges racism, classism, ableism, and nativism. Advocates must challenge neoliberal normativity in all its faces to be considered "radical."

Nevertheless, I admit that "radicalism" invokes many meanings, from unruly protests against the "natural" order to those activist actions that challenge the neoliberal NPIC and prison systems. As an advocate-scholar, I struggle with the mutability of radicalism. Still, I want to reclaim radicalism from and for feminists. I want to strip away the misconceptions that we have about radicalism to look closely at what it is and what it can be, because I think that radicalism is the key to envisioning a transformative advocacy. To me, radicalism means the personal and political activism of feminist anti-violence advocates who strive to create a world without violence, welcoming of diverse identities and peoples. It is a messy affect that allows its wielders to create a new world order without rape.

Though I use "radicalism" in an activist manner, others who use the term generally mean something other than what I mean. Therefore, I clarify my meaning of "radicalism" here. First, conservatives may define a "radical" as someone who causes a commotion. I think of Sara Ahmed's feminist killjoy here—the feminist who *kills* the *joy* of others by raising discomfort and shattering the expectation to be happy.[25] We live in a world where any number of "good deeds" for people in need are considered "good." In contrast, an advocate who disrupts the bliss of the rape crisis center, say by calling out the racism or ableism enacted by their colleagues, also kills the joy of helping others. Think of the advocates at Embrace: It is as though the advocates say that our work is not good enough. Why insist on the negative public affects of guilt and trauma often associated with Black Lives Matter?[26] Radicalism as the killjoy seems to ignore the benefits of advocacy and willfully, or gleefully, seeks the death of empowerment. Nonetheless, a feminist killjoy "radical" is not someone who creates discomfort. That discomfort already exists for marginalized people but has simply remained unnamed in normative spaces. When I refer to radicalism that disrupts the happy affect of doing advocacy, I am speaking not to any "positive" emotions that tell us we are resilient but to the "ugly" emotions like anger, frustration, sorrow, and despair that wake advocates up to the urgent fires around us.[27] This feeling of radicalism jolts us into seeing the urgency of changing advocacy now.[28] Radicalism is an affective choice against political neutrality, an *activism* resolutely insistent upon *active* feeling and change.

Second, among well-meaning scholars, radicalism appears as "radical feminism."[29] This version of radicalism invokes an image of the white radical feminists of the "second wave" who decry the sex-class system in which cisgender women are subordinate to cisgender men.[30] Radical feminists take the premise that liberal feminist efforts to reform the patriarchal structure of US society, like suffrage movements, have largely failed to combat sexism. Thus, they work to manifest an alternative "radical" future in which structural inequities between women and men do not exist, such as establishing independent women-only collectives.[31] But though *this* radical feminism addresses structural inequities beyond liberal feminist reforms, anti-violence activists criticize "radical feminism" for its essentialism. Under many feminist interpretations of "radical feminism," womanhood is typically confined to those who have traditional women's sex characteristics, excluding trans and gender-diverse people who align with feminine or women's values.[32] It is also regularly criticized for being white feminism, that is, a feminism that believes sex is the hegemonic form of oppression, and all other identities like race are second to sexual identity.[33]

Though we might immediately reference "radical feminism" when discussing radicalism, white radical feminism is not the only form of radicalism and certainly not one that this book endorses. Radical feminism has been appropriated by white trans-exclusionary women who monopolize "radicalism" to justify their position in anti-violence spaces.[34] By saying that radical feminists created anti-violence advocacy, white radical feminists feel as though they must be central to the movement. But while white radical feminists did indeed *formalize* advocacy, white women were not responsible for radicalism. Proposing an alternate understanding of radical feminism, historian Becky Thompson has written that it is inaccurate to call white women "second wave" "radical feminists," as radicalism was not associated with them in the period from the 1960s to the 1980s.[35] Instead, radicalism was commonly associated with women lesbians of color, who understood that radicalism came from generations of activism that challenges racial, class-based, and sexual norms found within many existing white and cisheteropatriarchal US institutions.[36] Radicalism is thus not essentialist nor white. It is in fact rooted in a long history of queer of color feminisms that refuse systems and structural violence—a quality that makes radicalism (or radical feminism) highly desirable in today's neoliberal "multicultural" world that rarely recognizes systemic violence.[37]

Radicalism is a gesture to the vast responses we might have to the violence of normativity. It challenges normativity by widening our emotional bandwidth to see disparities inherent to neoliberalism. It is also not a singular act nor value. Radicalism fluctuates to meet the form of normativity present in the space and time within which it emerges, a mutable collective praxis built by the most marginalized among us for the present now. It is a trickle-up approach that creates the world as we imagine it could be.[38]

I affirm that radicalism is helpful for advocates. In a moment when we are often presented with the choice between supporting survivors and generating funding, we need a way to see beyond the binary. Radicalism shifts our attention away from this choice and toward the diverse transformative responses that are possible.[39] Through these tensions, we see that supporting survivors and generating funding are not mutually exclusive but are coconstitutive. We can think of radicalism as a utopic approach, situated on the horizon of change. We might not be able to conceptualize what it means to *do* radical advocacy, especially those of us in the trenches, until we start taking the steps to forge it.[40] Thus, we must undertake the hard and messy grunt work of being on the front lines with survivors to shape a world that abolishes all interlocking violence, starting with accepting our responsibility to feel and to make change. We who are radically inclined create radicalism, a weapon against the binary of neoliberal normativity.

The Potentiality of Advocacy

The issue of neoliberalism in anti-rape work is not new to anti-violence scholars. In the last two decades, anti-violence scholars have lambasted neoliberalism for emboldening the carceral state and plundering resources from welfare systems. In her condemnation of neoliberalism, Kristin Bumiller illustrated that anti-violence feminists consciously chose to place sexual violence on the public agenda in the 1990s, aligning with neoconservatives to mainstream anti-violence projects. These activists publicized cultural images of the rape victim to generate support for the anti-violence movement, and their work was largely considered successful by many anti-rape workers. However, contrary to feminists' expectations in which *feminism* would influence *the state*, Bumiller showed that neoliberal conservatives gradually appropriated the feminist movement in ways that disavow the movement's initial aims, normalizing only one therapeutic way of responding to sexual assault victims.[41]

Rose Corrigan built on Bumiller's work by sharing stories of anti-rape advocacy as it met with neoliberalism on the front lines of the movement. Through interviews with 167 rape crisis advocates in six states, Corrigan described the ways that feminists publicly touted the successes of anti-violence advocacy. She then contrasted these messages with advocate interviews that exemplified frustrations about the restrictions placed on them in their day-to-day work. Detailing stories of repeated abuse of survivors by carceral agents and the inability for advocates to intervene, Corrigan cautioned against believing that governmental funding has positively transformed anti-violence advocacy. Instead, she concluded that mainstreaming anti-rape advocacy has only led to increased restrictions on advocates' capacities to spark social change.[42]

For Bumiller, Corrigan, and many other anti-violence scholars, neoliberalism spelled the death of advocacy despite public messaging that anti-violence work has been successful. Their scholarship opened the gates to criticizing neoliberalism in important ways. However, as Carrie N. Baker and Maria Bevacqua explain, these critiques of neoliberalism often focus on the growing proximity of anti-rape advocacy to criminal legal and medical systems.[43] In turn, activism that looks outside carceral systems, typically the work of marginalized advocates and survivors, is given little scholarly attention. Baker and Bevacqua criticize these earlier studies: "[They focus] on one aspect of a multifaceted movement and then [draw] broad conclusions about the movement as a whole. [They] also [decline] to consider the intersections of numerous forms of identity and how these intersections inform the sexual assault experience and, therefore, services."[44]

Addressing the problems raised by Baker and Bevacqua, social workers Mimi E. Kim and Val Kalei Kanuha (Kānaka Maoli) examined the uses of restorative justice in sexual assault and domestic violence cases.[45] They noted that some survivors, many of whom are queer people and people of color, rely on restorative justice, a kind of rape response like mediation or restitution that seeks to resolve violence outside the harmful carceral state.[46] But despite growing activism in favor of noncarceral remedies, Kim and Kanuha found that restorative justice nevertheless embeds another kind of normativity within anti-rape work. Sexual violence advocacy that wields restorative justice is often insufficient to disrupt systemic violence because advocates usually carry out restorative justice only when carceral justice has been exhausted.[47] Thus, Kim and Kanuha call neoliberalism a "fatal strategy," stressing that even well-intentioned advocacy efforts to desist from neoliberal normativity have resulted in another form of abuse.[48]

The contemporary debate around neoliberal normativity in anti-rape work suggests that advocacy in the neoliberal state should be dismembered, set afire, and reborn. Anti-violence scholarship and activism continue to press for social change to support survivors, and time and again, the violence of neoliberal normativity has been made all too clear. This book on changing neoliberal advocacy, then, may be too late for the movement. Yet it is precisely the desire for change that piques my hope for the anti-rape movement. Scholars may declare a premature eulogy for anti-violence activism, but many still seek resistance.[49] For example, Campbell, Baker, and Mazurek admitted that while rape crisis centers no longer reflect the same "radical bent" as 1970s grassroots radical collectives, they still lobby for political change and provide essential postrape services.[50] Their supposed "de-radicaliz[ation]" was advocates' defense mechanism for "weathering changing political climates."[51] Baker and Bevacqua have also suggested that although radicalism within the mainstream anti-rape movement is no longer the same as it was in the 1970s, advocates—particularly grassroots activists identifying as 2SLGBTQIA+ people and BIPOC—have still made significant advancements into developing alternative remedies to sexual violence apart from the criminal legal system. These advances are important examples of social justice organizing in the face of neoliberal normativity.[52]

The latter body of scholarship hints that anti-rape advocates are still working toward a radical future, but in ways that are not obvious to the mainstream. In other words, the very changes that advocates have made to respond to neoliberal normativity are underground tactics to keep radical momentum going. Rather than die by neoliberalism's hand, radicalism resists the "no future" imposed by systems and illuminates discomforting affects in the present to stir up rage, fear, and rebellion for the future.[53] Even if the *practice* of transforming advocacy is difficult to envision now, advocates' very nature as anti-violence advocates implies that there is a radical *potentiality* still left in them. *Killing Radicalism* holds that an evaluation of neoliberal anti-rape advocacy is still necessary because advocates *feel* the need for change.

I acknowledge that mainstream advocacy—the advocacy presently entwined with the neoliberal state—no longer welcomes critical queer of color advocacy that dismantles interlocking oppressions. This normativity paints a grim future for the broader anti-rape movement. As intersectionality theorist Kimberlé Crenshaw has written of anti-violence work, "The struggle over incorporating these differences is not a petty or superficial conflict about who gets to sit at the head of the table. In the context of violence, it is sometimes a deadly serious matter of who will survive—and who will not."[54] However, I suggest that normativity can be resisted through radicalism, especially if our underground feelings are still alive. The stories of advocates in this book show that advocates are ready and willing to participate in political activism but are unsure of where to start and how successful they may be. This book, then, calls for a reradicalization of the long anti-violence movement by showing where, how, and for whom we can advocate.

Killing Radicalism

Killing Radicalism identifies the locus of neoliberal victimization and radical transformation as being in advocates' hands. This book employs two main methods to do this. First, I draw on in-depth semistructured qualitative interviews with sixty-three victim advocates who have directly worked with victims at over fifty mainstream and culturally specific rape crisis centers, domestic violence shelters, and anti-violence coalitions in twenty-five US states and tribal land. Much of an advocate's work lives in the "in-between" space between policy and practice, the community and individual survivor, and neoliberalism and radicalism.[55] Accordingly, advocates negotiate normative neoliberalism from the top at the same time that they negotiate intersectional radicalism from below.[56] Prior studies on the anti-rape movement confined their analyses to the authorities within social institutions, which left out key decisions about services provided by ground-level advocates. This book's emphasis on "direct services" advocates who work directly with victims best illustrates how funders' decisions at the upper echelons of the anti-rape movement filter down into decisions made by advocates and then survivors on the ground precisely because advocates decide the direction of the movement.[57]

Interviewees are diverse to show that, in spite of (or because of) some advocates' marginalized positionalities that make them sympathetic to the needs of marginalized survivors, neoliberalism continues to exert its power over all in the anti-violence field. Advocates shared common perspectives regarding rape response norms, detailing stories of abuse, frustration, and anger. However, many did not wish to be identified by their name and perspectives for reasons such as losing their jobs or being outed as a victim-survivor. Therefore, I describe advocates by their social identities rather than consistent name or pseudonym. Throughout the book, the chosen identity presented with the advocate's interview excerpt depended on both the participant's own self-disclosed identities as relevant to the case and my own interpretation of the case based on the reported information. There are several interview excerpts without an attached social identity reported because I have removed that information for confidentiality purposes or because the advocate and I did not attach that particular perspective to a specific social identity. Further discussion about the qualitative study design, including interview questions, sampling, recruitment, and limitations of the project, can be found in appendix A.

Second, this book draws on archival materials gathered from the Schomburg Center for Research in Black Culture, Smith College Sophia Smith collections, and Harvard Schlesinger Library's women's studies collections, along with materials sourced from online archives, including the Library of Congress, Digital Public Library of America, and miscellaneous repositories. Particularly for chapter 1, which provides historical context into present-day stories of neoliberal entanglements in victim advocacy, I chose to source primary materials and place them in conversation with secondary sources because many more recent studies about the anti-rape movement's past tended to pull earlier sources out of their contexts. For instance, scholars frequently sought to define "rape" but oftentimes did so with the belief that rape is a women's issue rather than an issue of interlocking power and oppression, specifically as it is tethered to race, sex, and skin color.[58] Consequently, scholarly framing of rape repeated advocates' mistakes: many academics assumed that rape only affected (white) women, erasing colonial and enslaved rape, and reduced advocacy only to legal reform. Drawing on primary and secondary materials and remixing them into a "third" reading was paramount to rectifying the myopia surrounding the radical genealogies of the anti-rape movement.[59] For the full list of the reviewed collections, please see the methods appendix.

On an epistemic level, *Killing Radicalism* applies an expressly queer of color lens to neoliberal advocacy. Queer of color critique is a theoretical and methodological approach that unpacks the complexity of subject and identity formations, locating and transgressing the boundaries and movement of social groupings and alliances.[60] I deployed queer of color critique by engaging with participants in discussions about the structural barriers faced by nonnormative "queers," including racial minorities, in accessing relevant and adequate postrape advocacy. I also wielded queer of color critique to assess participants' perspectives as they developed, taking care to avoid rigidifying identities and perspectives into categorizable norms.[61] My approach addresses the mutability of normativity. Normativity changes forms often, transforming every time radicalism demands presence.[62] By using queer of color critique, *Killing Radicalism* explicitly names and therefore deconstructs those advocate actions that produce norms against marginalized peoples within anti-violence work.

The way that I use "rape" in this book harkens to the queer of color backdrop of this project. My definition is flexible: I define rape as the corporeal violation of the body and mind, transgressing one's sexual autonomy through the touching or feeling of sexual organs.[63] I use the term "rape" interchangeably and liberally with "violence," including "sexual violence," "sexual assault," and "interpersonal violence," to express that rape changes definitions according to those in power.[64] Rape may include elements of domestic violence (sometimes called "intimate partner violence" or "spousal/dating violence"), though domestic violence is primarily situated in the home and/or in a domestic partnership whereas rape may occur anywhere, anytime, and with anyone. My definition is deliberately broad so as to recognize that other identity-based oppressions interwoven with sexual oppression such as racism and classism may manifest differently than we expect rape to manifest. I do not want to limit the extent of rape violation to specific forms, such as the penetration of a vagina, because limited definitions can engender and racialize who gets to be counted as a "rape victim" and what is considered "rape," expelling marginal and queered survivors out of the purview of anti-violence services. I do, however, focus predominantly on advocates whose main function is to support victims of sexual assault, not domestic violence victims, because some domestic violence situations do not involve sexual acts; some are physical-only without a violation of sexual autonomy. Because I am interested in the ways that radicalism operates within the context of seemingly anti–*sexual* violence spaces, I primarily reserve the findings of my analysis to anti-rape spaces, though I recognize that rape and domestic violence often feed one another in a mutually destructive cycle.

I also use the term "queer" in a queered application to rape. In this book, "queer" or "2SLGBTQIA+" refers to people who identify as Two-Spirit, lesbian, gay, bisexual, trans, queer, or another noncisgender or nonheterosexual identity. "Queer" might also refer to those actions, beliefs, or people that are nonnormative.[65] 2SLGBTQIA+ people are included under "queer" but so too are people who live outside of normative constructs, such as invisible disabled populations or undocumented communities outside of the "formal" economy. The latter group of people are queered. "Queered" or "queering," optionally with a slash mark ("queer/ing"), indicates those actions, beliefs, or people who are in the process of becoming or unbecoming queer, speaking to the fluidity of queer formations. For example, my use of "anti-rape" "implies the existence of some equal and opposite and explicitly *pro-rape* force."[66] Yet "anti" resistance is not a monolithic cause nor is "rape" a singular construct. They are both messy social constructs, and it is this fact that there is no binary between *rape* and *not rape* that makes my analysis of *anti-rape advocacy* a queered project.[67]

Book Plan

Killing Radicalism is a book for those of us who seek to do better for the people we care about. By situating this book on advocates' affective perspectives, I expose the minutiae of deradicalization on the ground, at the front lines, where smaller actions assemble into a more threatening enemy called "neoliberalism." Activists, social workers, and community organizers, especially those who identify as minorities and preach about equity and justice, are likely to find respite in this text. But this book is not for them alone. This book is for anyone who wishes to radically transform the way we conduct culturally responsive care in support of victims of violence.

Killing Radicalism is organized around the everyday activities of a victim advocate at a contemporary rape crisis center. We open with the initial interpersonal engagement between advocate and survivor before moving on to multidisciplinary and community teamwork. Each chapter is self-contained, engaging in specific disciplinary literature and suggesting avenues for social change in that realm of anti-rape work. Therefore, each chapter may be read on its own. Advocates pressed for time may wish to skip chapter 1, which speaks to our theoretical rather than our material work. However, while each chapter is an independent story, the chapters altogether show the interconnected nature of neoliberal normativity and the need for an integrated, radical anti-rape movement. This book moves in a cycle formation to show the slow death of radicalism in advocacy. It starts and ends with the ways advocates suppress our own voices and the voices of survivors, but, like a crescendo, caterwauls into the concatenation of neoliberal normativity. Because of the book's organizational structure, it is recommended that activists vested in radicalism read this book from front to back to fully grasp our role in shaping the anti-violence movement.

Chapter 1 shares the messy genealogies of anti-rape victim advocacy. Currently at the helm of the anti-rape movement are advocates untrained in their own ancestries. Our ignorance has led us to believe the myth that advocacy has always been attached to carceral and welfare systems, such that we no longer participate in contemporary political movements. Weaving seemingly contrasting narratives to show the potentiality of radical advocacy, this chapter rewrites past advocacy strategies to illuminate a multiplicity of possible advocate methods. By subverting the dominant story of the state in anti-rape organizing, the chapter repositions present-day survivor-advocates as powerful captains of the anti-rape movement, taking back control over our own histories for our futures.

Chapter 2 examines the construction of a capitalist NPIC logic in anti-rape work. Capitalism is often read only in economic terms; however, capitalism is also sociocultural resource mobilization. Drawing on cultural capitalist theory as theorized by Pierre Bourdieu and advanced by many cultural capitalist theorists, including Cedric Robinson and Tara J. Yosso, I show that the "crisis" of anti-rape intervention produces feelings of precarity and austerity in neoliberal rape crisis centers. These artificial restrictions on our work compel us to sever survivors from the free anti-rape market and prevent them from accessing holistic victim care. Advocates who operate under capitalist logics ultimately reify the same problems of victim valuation as in enslavement and marginal oppressions, reproducing secondary violence in our own homes.

Chapter 3 evaluates the emergence and effects of a "professional advocacy," a form of advocacy precariously tethered to state funding that produces norms about who can and should support survivors. Professional advocacy emerged when neoliberal welfare "reforms" collided with anti-violence organizing, and this abusive connection restructured formerly mutual aid–based anti-violence collectives into a bureaucratic hierarchy in which administrators favoring systems control direct services work. Administrators include boards of directors, therapists, and grant writers, who often have little stake in advancing radical agendas in anti-violence advocacy. This dominant group, led primarily by white, formally educated people, increasingly appropriates grassroots organizing historically conducted by queer, poor, and working-class BIPOC, in turn rebranding abolitionist anti-violence labor as white women's "social work" charity. The professionalization expected of advocates by neoliberal administrators contributes to the decline of radicalism by normalizing one type of advocacy, paternalistic whiteness, and stigmatizing grassroots radical advocacy of color activism.

Chapter 4 takes stock of expanded carceralism within anti-violence work. But rather than focus on police officers and lawyers who intrude on advocacy work, as other scholars have done, I consider how advocates themselves take on the role of carceralism within welfare. Nodding to the inherent relationship between carceralism and welfare under neoliberalism, I highlight the performative acts by advocates that contribute to the "panoptic policing" of marginalized survivors. I show that advocates inadvertently conduct surveillance of victims who do not fit into normative interpretations of a rape survivor by ceding authority to carceral agents and appropriating carceral logics for themselves. This ceding of advocates' responsibilities to criminal legal authorities offsets the responsibility of care onto victims themselves, forcing them—not the state—to pay for the consequences of criminalizing rape. Through the carceral neoliberalization of care, advocates become the "third party police," just like the oppressors we used to resist.

Chapter 5 analyzes how advocates record victims' identities and experiences with violence on grant applications. Funding for anti-rape services through the Violence Against Women Act and similar programs is increasingly tightened, especially those offered to support marginalized "underserved" victims. Thus, advocates feel progressively pressured to compete with one another for limited funds. This competition coerces advocates into inscribing normative assumptions of rape victims onto grant applications, and consent becomes attached to legibility to the state. Indirectly, advocates' decisions regarding state-sponsored statistical reporting violate radical interpretations of survivorship and push forth a narrative about a normative rape victim. Over time, advocates erase any acknowledgment of the malleability of identities and can no longer practice advocacy in more creative ways.

The chapters critique the interlocking ways that neoliberal advocacy isolates anti-rape activism from other forms of anti-violence organizing. However, *Killing Radicalism* does not conclude by arguing that neoliberalism has killed radicalism altogether. Rather, this book is a reclamation project for radical advocacy as intersectional anti-violence organizing, seeking to upend our current trends toward normativity. At the end of this book, I reflect on ongoing and parallel struggles for radical politics with the anti-rape movement, and the feelings of fear and rage that earmark many of these "crises." Our ugly feelings help to reignite momentum against neoliberal normativity by reshaping advocacy into a "killing radicalism." If rape is the manifestation of oppressive violence across multiple levels and identities, then anti-violence advocates can wield the violence inflicted upon them to advocate for liberation from interlocking oppression as well. Advocates are not merely beholden to state norms but are instead brave, powerful activists who may transform the anti-violence field into a violence-free utopia.

1

Weaving Our Stories

The Abolitionist Genealogies of Anti-Rape Advocacy

History is never just a method that scholars bring to bear on capitalism. History is one of the many transactions that take place within a matrix of monetized value. That is, history becomes a transaction in capitalism because that is what capitalism needs it to mean.
—Lucia Hulsether, *Capitalist Humanitarianism*

What does it mean to be an anti-rape victim advocate? Many advocates chuckled before responding, "We are the people who help survivors of sexual violence." They called an advocate a "guide" or "companion" who listens to victims in order to empower them. Some explained their role as helping victims to build a workable safety plan that they feel comfortable carrying out for themselves. Others described an advocate as a "teddy bear" in contrast to the "hard" and "clinical" police officers and sexual assault forensic examiners (SAFEs) commonly involved in rape responses. We are "soft" helpers who serve as knowledgeable "resource hub[s]" who can, with their consent, connect survivors to the "right" places. In their responses, the advocates point to a problem in the way that I phrased the question. Because rape looks different for every person, there is no one way to "be" an advocate, no standing definition that captures who we are. They hinted at the more urgent question behind my ask: What does an advocate *do*?

Upon asking this second question, I learned that many advocates couched their descriptions of advocacy behaviors in more "legitimate" systems-based rape responder terms. They described how they carried out "emotional validation" of survivors, listening to their stories without judgment, but often made the caveats, "I'm not a therapist" or "I'm not a licensed social worker." Some dismissed emotional care work as not a "real" service because "I can validate forever . . . and it can also not be helpful at all." Advocates also chose to define their work as "technical assistance," the skilled support to victims often provided in the form of community partner connections, provisions of survivor equipment, and negotiations with systems professionals. One advocate described how she liaised a survivor to a Spanish-speaking therapist, illustrating that advocacy requires "technical" knowledge about welfare systems just as much as the nursing or policing professions do.

Curiously, throughout our conversations, advocates shied away from more politicized terms like "activist" and "community organizer" and evaded topics like boycotting, picketing, and mutual aid. The rote deposition of a standardized advocacy procedure seemed to reflect how systems-based responders thought about advocates, typically as "service providers" who are there merely to help victims process their trauma in a crisis moment. The rest of advocacy—the prevention, the outreach, the long-term intervention strategies, and most importantly, the *activism*—disappeared underneath the clinical terms and institutional policies.[1] To my ears as an advocate-scholar, these depictions of advocacy were strange to hear. Excavating the histories of anti-violence advocacy through the archives and books, and with the gentle mentorship of a few advocates-turned-academics, I had learned in graduate school that our advocate forebearers included some of the most well-known radical protesters in American histories: Angela Davis, Rosa Parks, Ida B. Wells, to name a few popular examples. All of them *did advocacy* in full support of victims in their communities. Why were my fellow advocates saying that advocates acted as "service providers" representing the welfare state instead of "activists" freely supporting all victims of intersectional violence?

There are perhaps many reasons for this myopia: Individuals were simply uninterested in learning about the legacies of advocacy in civil rights; advocates did not think that it was important to promote the political nature of advocacy; or maybe advocacy is indeed different at the grassroots level than in the books I scoured during my graduate training. But the script of advocacy as just any other human service was repeated too many times to indicate that these reasons held merit. After all, advocates from across the United States, not just from one or a handful of rape crisis centers, were asked to describe their work. The similarities in sixty-three interviews were likely not due to any universal chance or a poor sampling method (though I admit I spoke primarily to intervention advocates). Instead, something else was (is) happening—something more worrisome: Someone was erasing advocates' histories in civil liberties activism.

In this chapter, I rewrite the messy genealogies of rape victim advocacy to illuminate what advocates do, and have long done. Through these descriptions, I show that it is the US capitalist-carceral settler state that is erasing our histories in order to control anti-rape work.[2] In historical explorations of marginalized or femininized political participation, scholars have found that BIPOC, women, and queers are routinely misrepresented or scrubbed from the textbooks entirely to push forth a more accommodating image of the state and its defenders. For example, in their readings of contemporary narratives of the 1960s Civil Rights Movement, Jacquelyn Dowd Hall and Danielle L. McGuire illustrated that Dr. Martin Luther King Jr. and Rosa Parks, respectively, were caricatured into a devout preacher and a "little old lady" who resisted the "bad guy" whites. These representations rendered radical Black liberation activists into domesticated (and therefore easily manipulatable) tokens while furthermore drawing attention away from the reality that most racist white people were not explicitly "bad" people but people who stood silent as white supremacist violence repeatedly harmed communities of color.[3] Contemporary representations of past anti-rape advocacy are no different. Rather than portray the anti-rape movement as complex threads that intersect and overlap, as a vibrant meld of legal and non- or extralegal organizers, the state and its interlocuters manipulate the radical stories of advocacy into a singular narrative of service provisions to assert their presence in our stories. By repeating the dominant discourse of advocacy as mere social services, advocates have manifested that reality of advocacy as mere social services—and forgotten how to write our own legacies.

This chapter sheds light on the radical genealogies of anti-rape advocacy to open pathways for transforming advocacy back to intersectional justice and healing. Setting the foundation for the remainder of this book, I begin by reflecting on our affective ties to history making, grounding our purpose in the long anti-rape movement. Then, I turn to the myriad threads of the movement to critically evaluate how advocates have long thought of themselves, a praxis that allows contemporary advocates to theorize advocacy strategies past neoliberal systems interpretations of anti-rape work. As a part of this quest, this chapter combats the dominant myth that advocacy only began in the 1970s, integrating often-forgotten advocates back into the rich multi-story of anti-rape activism. This chapter, thus, contributes to a deeper understanding of advocacy—what it is, why it has always been important, and what we can do to help each other better as we move toward abolitionist futures.

Self-Flagellation, and Other Mechanisms of Mutilation and Murder

The conventional mode of storytelling usually recounts the life story of an important figure or describes a series of events in one location or temporal period to capture the dominant scene of a movement. This mode importantly shows how fragments come together toward one divisive end. However, sharing the stories of the anti-rape movement requires a different approach, for its histories are multiple, complex, and always in the making. Dominant narratives do not simply suppress marginal voices but rework the mechanisms through which we come to know history. Thus, we cannot employ the same methods as the powerful, or else we will enact the violence of the powerful upon ourselves.[4]

To tell a story about the anti-rape movement, I ask us to deliberately feel the discomfort of returning to our pasts. Like advocacy, sharing the story of the anti-rape movement is both an emotional and a technical undertaking. Many stories of rape summon collective fear and despair; therefore, storytellers must feel rape as victim-survivors did in the past in order to remake the place and time in which violence transpired, but not so much as to entrap them in their own headspaces or revive pornographic "damage-centered" narratives.[5] Feeling rape *is* anti-rape work, and it demands that we self-flagellate, to some extent, to introspectively review our multiply assembled histories.[6] At the same time, we must be savvy enough to rescript instances of rape without composite portraits of it. Large swathes of radical advocacy histories have been scrubbed from our textbooks, erased as though they were never there in the first place in a colonial epistemicide.[7] This is murder of another kind. White men smothered subjugated voices under the presumption of cohesive linearity—that one event led to the next, and so on—to control where we understand our roots to lie and cut us off from generations of knowledge trees.[8] Moreover, women of color, and Black women in particular, have chosen to dissemble from the dominant history to survive. Dissemblance has allowed women of color to choose which aspects of themselves to publicly reveal in order to stave off dominant exploitation of their stories while still guarding their most sacred secrets.[9]

These challenges have eroded our memories, and with time, such stories are lost, unknown to our current generation. Shani D'Cruze explained of anti-rape historical research, "The kinds of questions social historians seek to ask about sexual violence (what happened? To whom? How often?) are commonly interpreted within chronological parameters that comprehend a transition from medieval through industrial to contemporary society and a conceptual framework which addresses social and economic relations in some form. But such a line of enquiry is frequently frustrated by the nature and the scarcity of the sources. Consequently historical study of this topic (perhaps more than most others) is necessarily a discourse on and around the surviving evidences, not an unmediated description of 'what happened.'"[10]

Rescripting the frayed ends of the anti-rape movement story is not an easy task. But feminist scholars have provided ways of reconstructing slippery pasts, looking underneath matter to identify the marginal.[11] Though we cannot resurrect past advocates nor victims to share their stories in their own words, we *can* imagine how resistance fighters figured in the accounts that were preserved in hallowed historical repositories. Saidiya Hartman describes this method as "critical fabulation" and writes, in application to enslaved voices, "The intent of this practice is not to *give voice* to the slave, but rather to imagine what cannot be verified . . . It is a narrative of what might have been or could have been; it is a history written with and against the archive."[12] Rewriting anti-rape advocacy stories involves imagination of what is *not* here as well as *what could have been done*. In other words, we must write our stories, with all their wondrous and frustrating affects, imagining what it must have felt like to do advocacy in diverse sociohistorical spaces, to position us as the captains of the movement once more.

This imaginative enterprise is not a piecemeal response to the "partial" fragments in the archives. Instead, as Marisa Fuentes explained in her work on reconstructing enslavement and abolitionism, we wield archival fractals to destabilize notions of linearity and objectivity persistent in the dominant historical narrative.[13] The accounts of radical advocacy may be found in normative stories, in white-led newspapers or state legislative documents, but they may also be found in the fugitive files of diaries, letters, and disjointed slips of note-taking paper that spark thought and feeling. These mutilated stories are not "incomplete"; they represent the multiplicities of consciousness that survive generations of rape. Destabilization asks us to read against the archive's "bias grain."[14] That is, what we might think of as "advocacy" might not be advocacy at all, and what we neglect might offer a new interpretation of advocacy. This collective imagination, between the advocate participants, myself, and readers, stretches the limits of anti-rape work beyond criminal legal affairs and instead enters the world in which we survive, as advocates, survivors, and radical abolitionists.

Indeed, examining sexual violence in culturally specific communities, advocates Susan Ghanbarpour and Ada Palotai explain how critical fabulation and the imagination of other(ed) stories propel the wings of grassroots social change: "What we learn from when we see *differently*, by looking from diverse standpoints, has the potential to radically transform how we support *all* survivors. When we recognize where dominant paradigms fall short, fail to reach those most vulnerable (or those who are vulnerable in different ways), or reproduce the oppressive tendencies that we purport to be against, only then we can begin to *practice differently*, in ways that can take seriously the real diversity of lived experiences of survivors as well as the histories and structures that shape them."[15]

Threads

The dominant narrative *makes* advocates into mere service workers. This is one story, and one that isolates us from feeling the radical potentiality of anti-rape advocacy. It has been effective at capturing the imagination of advocates because it makes the story linear, splicing queered ends to isolate a simple thread. This method of constructing advocacy, however, expels radical advocacy that had long existed, such as mutual aid conducted by many 2SLGBTQIA+ communities of color. It also presents past advocacy as *not* advocacy, as "uncivilized" or "unprofessional," "alien" or "illegitimate," to gaslight us into perceiving effective organizing strategies as unhelpful or unwarranted action.[16] But advocacy is not simply about supporting victims as they collide with the neoliberal state; rather, advocacy has been and continues to be about supporting victims in their needs in whatever form they feel is necessary and appropriate for their trauma.

To understand the intricacies of anti-rape advocacy, we must become writers of our own stories. I follow the abolitionist Ruth Wilson Gilmore's interpretation of storytelling, "Rather than rehearse well-known critical histories of stolen land, stolen labor, gender domination, and iron-fisted capital expansion, . . . [I construct] a series of scenes from various periods that, in sum, are designed to demonstrate the persistence and convergence of patterns and systems."[17] Similarly, I have chosen to craft scenes that demonstrate a throughline of anti-rape victim advocacy that empowered survivors across multiple spaces, places, and times. Each set of scenes constructs a unique thread of anti-rape advocacy. Threads expose the powerful impact of the neoliberal story on anti-rape advocacy by allowing us to see the same events through kaleidoscopic lenses.[18] Through this retelling, these threads become our messy "genealogies" of radicalism, simultaneously locating historically situated feminist activism at the same time that they open space for advocacy's futures.[19] We can identify which narrative comes from dominant sources and fashion our own contributions to the movement when we see advocacy not as a single thread but as a rich, colorful, and complex tapestry.

Thread 1. Rape Law Reform, or Stalking the Past (1994–Present)

The dominant neoliberal story of the anti-rape movement goes something like this. In the mid-1970s, evangelical Christian Republicans and Democratic women's liberation activists put aside their differences to raise awareness of the violence of sexual assault. Both sides practiced letter writing and hotline affirmations, and organized consciousness-raising groups to persuade the government to take action against one of the most universally abhorred and widespread crimes in America.[20]

For example, in 1975, liberal feminist Susan Brownmiller published the worldwide sensation *Against Our Will* to direct attention to the widespread violence of rape globally. This book shared the same sentiment as the Religious Right Citizens for Decency Through Law, who combated the rising tide of pornographic imagery of children in the United States.[21] Collectively, anti-rape activists successfully petitioned for bipartisan change. The Law Enforcement Assistance Administration (LEAA) in the US Department of Justice, which had been originally created as a part of Lyndon B. Johnson's War on Poverty, disbursed millions of dollars to law enforcement for training on and operations in rape responses, and the Federal Bureau of Investigation (FBI) expanded its counterintelligence arm to capture the "everyday" rapist who violently abused women behind closed doors.[22]

Federal changes to rape law, however, did not happen until two decades later. Instead, because rape law was originally premised on property rights, each individual US state was tasked with reforming its own rape laws, moving rape away from a crime of "passion" to a crime of legitimized violence.[23] Michigan led the charge. In 1973, feminist lawyer Jan BenDor formed the Michigan Women's Task Force on Rape (MWTFR), a task force with members including "politicians, lawmakers, other influential individuals, and powerful organizations."[24] Drawing on rape data collected by then-emerging nationwide anti-rape networks, including the National Organization for Women (NOW) Rape Task Force, MWTFR proposed a new model rape law that reshaped rape definitions to better protect victims on the stand and encourage heftier punishment of perpetrators.[25] Specifically, Michigan's Criminal Sexual Misconduct statute replaced the unwieldy term "rape" with "criminal sexual misconduct," implemented degrees of criminal sexual assault, made sexual assault a gender-neutral crime (i.e., women could sexually assault men), reformed the definition of coercion and instituted a policy of consent, and introduced rape shield laws that prevented victims' sexual histories from becoming known to biased juries determining the outcome of the case.[26] The reforms passed, and many states quickly followed Michigan's example, creating the first comprehensive criminal statutes against rape.[27]

In the wake of flourishing criminal codes, anti-rape activists leveraged political momentum to tackle other forms of sexualized violence in another bipartisan alliance. The new anti-rape movement had emphasized that rape was often perpetrated not by a stranger but by an acquaintance or intimate partner, a framework that gave legitimacy to rape as a violent crime and birthed the domestic violence movement.[28] While MWTFR had deleted a spousal rape clause in Michigan's criminal code to preserve the bipartisan alliance, resistance to intimate partner violence nonetheless grew in force.[29] By the late 1970s and into the early 1980s, programs originally designed to protect race-based civil rights were reworked to support underserved partnered women. In particular, the Comprehensive Employment and Training Act, LEAA, and Title XX directed federal funding toward the construction and staffing of women's shelters, enhanced training programs, and implemented mandatory arrest policies for law enforcement officers who respond to domestic violence victims. Simultaneously, newer federal offices were being built to support victims of crime. Both passed in 1984, the Victims of Crime Act (VOCA) and the Family Violence Prevention and Services Act supported individual victims and the state welfare workers who helped them by covering expenses accrued from rape, such as reimbursement for lost property or therapy.[30]

Anti-rape activists also turned to sex trafficking and pornography. Throughout the 1970s and 1980s, as a response to the sexual repression of the previous "happy housewife" era, the gaming, video, and television industries were producing massive quantities of adult pornographic media, such as the problematic anti-Indigenous video game, Custer's Revenge.[31] Both rape law reformers and feminists, most notably Andrea Dworkin and Catharine Mackinnon, deplored the content as obscene and saw it as the promotion of sex trafficking.[32] (Robin Morgan framed it most clearly when she said, "Pornography is the theory, and rape is the practice.")[33] Connecting pornography to sexual assault, anti-rape activists reframed sexual violence as civil rights violations in addition to criminal misconduct. In Minneapolis and Indianapolis, perpetrators could be taken to court for objectifying women victims and showing graphic female genitalia in public spaces.[34]

The myriad strands of anti-rape organizing came together in 1994 with the passage of the Violence Against Women Act (VAWA). The federal Violent Crime Control and Law Enforcement Act, of which VAWA is a part, was the "largest crime bill in the history of the country" and "was the first attempt to formulate a national policy" to address sexualized violence.[35] VAWA funded the first rape crisis centers as we know them today. Law enforcement concerned with the perpetuation of gender-based violence took responsibility for rape victims and established crime prevention initiatives that sponsored victim advocates.[36] Additionally, VAWA and its subsequent reauthorizations paved the road for many other federal laws and policies that help gender-based violence victims, such as the Victims of Trafficking and Violence Protection Act and the more recent reauthorizations of the Child Abuse Prevention and Treatment Act.[37] While VAWA was somewhat tempered in the following years due to a small but vocal group of late-1990s antifeminists such as Katie Roiphe and Camille Paglia, as well as the US Supreme Court case *United States v. Morrison* in 2000, which took away the civil rights bent of anti-rape legislation, women across political lines heralded VAWA as "the most significant accomplishment of the anti-rape movement" that formally moved rape from a private issue into a public crime.[38]

Despite the significant victories made possible through bipartisan alliances, tensions existed among anti-rape activist circles. In the quest for the harsher sentencing of rapists, both the National Association for the Advancement of Colored People (NAACP) and the American Civil Liberties Union (ACLU) pointed out that the defendants who were most likely to be convicted of sexual assault were Black men who had been historically lynched on the basis of false claims of rape. The NAACP Legal Defense and Educational Fund (LDF) specifically raised the question of capital punishment of rapists. LDF assistant counsel David E. Kendall illustrated, with much effectiveness, that between 1930 and 1975, 90 percent of convicted people accused of rape were Black men, fifty-eight of whom had been sentenced to death. Kendall also argued, with future US Supreme Court Justice Ruth Bader Ginsburg and her ACLU Women's Rights Project (WRP), that rape did not involve death in the same way as homicide or other lethal crimes. Together, the NAACP LDF and ACLU WRP persuaded the US Supreme Court in the case *Coker v. Georgia* that the death sentence was a disproportionate punishment for rape. But, to address the concerns raised by feminists, WRP also emphasized that due process must remain intact for effective rape law reform, a measure that allowed for heightened punishment of sex offenders without feeding into racist rape myths.[39]

The issue of harsher sentencing was not the only tension. In one of the most publicized feminist struggles, the Sex Wars divided anti-rape activists between those in support of antipornography initiatives and those in support of sex workers, particularly the LGBT community. Like the 1970s feminists who protested uncensored adult media, anti-rape activists of the 1980s and 1990s believed that "prostitutes" were unwilling participants in the sexual economy and sought to bring "johns" to civil or criminal court.[40] However, emerging 1990s queer liberation activists, including Janet Halley and Lisa Duggan, argued that pornography and other forms of deviant sex, including S/M, kink, cruising, and polygamy, were means of subverting sexual norms that produced gendered violence.[41] This debate was further complicated by the input of neoconservative women such as Phyllis Schlafly and, later, Germaine Greer, who alleged that women were biologically feminine beings who should welcome sexual relations with men. This Moral Majority spawned the belief that the state had no right to intervene in the natural affairs of intimacy, refuting rape law reform entirely.[42]

However, whether rape is an issue of crime, sex, or something else did not significantly impact the formation of anti-rape advocacy. At the height of the "war," anti-rape collectives on all sides found themselves unable to survive as small independent collectives amidst financial difficulties. Volunteers were hard to come by, and the high numbers of women in need did not abate. VAWA helped to smooth the tensions by financing anti-rape institutions through the Young Women's Christian Association (YWCA) and similar umbrella nonprofit social services agencies. VAWA also encouraged more professional entities such as police officers to get involved with victim services, filling in the gaps left by the first anti-rape activists. The federalization of anti-rape advocacy "made" advocacy into an effective social service, turning it from incoherent community organizing into legitimate work that could be sustained over the decades. Today, rape crisis centers can successfully meet survivors' needs because the US government is involved; it funds the work as an acknowledgment of the importance of anti-rape advocacy.[43]

As the dominant story goes, the US government provided critical funds to create rape victim advocacy. We are supposed to thank the anti-rape activists who contributed to VAWA and other important anti-rape legislation for consolidating anti-rape work into streamlined social services. However, the tensions raised on the axes of race (capital punishment) and sexual orientation (sex work and trafficking) illustrate the problem with the dominant narrative: anti-rape activists were themselves divided on how to best approach victim support. Is rape a biological phenomenon? Could the police adequately respond to victims? To what extent would the state interfere in intimate matters? Just beneath the surface of the dominant narrative are many uncomfortable questions poking at the linear incoherence of the state-made story.

It is clear that the US settler-carceral state is stalking our pasts. By this I mean that the state and its accessories have literally created a more forgiving narrative of the state's role in the anti-rape movement and harassed anti-rape advocates into accepting it out of gaslighting and guilt. The US state might admit to ignoring the problem of rape until the 1970s, but it leverages its confession of negligence to support a narrative of anti-rape progress, only visible through the law. A story told otherwise rebuffs the state's pity of poor rape victims and implies that the millions of dollars poured from the state's coffers into anti-rape advocacy were a "waste" of money. Stripped naked, the skeletal remains of the state-spun story lay out the shameful failures of anti-rape advocacy for all the public to see.

Thread 2. Radical Feminism, Our Heroines (1972–1994)

The dominant story is not the only story of the anti-rape movement. An easy correction is turning to "feminist" activism, specifically the nonlegal strategies employed by women's activists to abolish rape. It is presumed that this portrayal of the anti-rape movement better reflects the tough, nitty-gritty, day-to-day operations of anti-rape resistance by showing the grunt work performed by "real" advocates, not the "reforms" carried out by white-collar masculine lawyers and police captains who historically refused to address sexual violence.[44] It also captures the efforts carried out by queer and gender-diverse BIPOC anti-rape advocates, who brought an intersectional lens to anti-violence organizing.[45]

The story of the "real" anti-rape movement goes something like this. The Civil Rights Movement of the 1960s had raised early consciousness of women (of color)'s vulnerable position in US society. Specifically, in 1968, the Black Women's Liberation Committee (BWLC) of the Student

Nonviolence Coordinating Committee (SNCC) formed the Third World Women's Alliance (TWWA), comprised of Arab, Asian, Black, Chicana, Latine, Pacific Islander, and Indigenous women.[46] Taking their lead from Black radical leaders who agitated against prison and medical systems, BWLC cofounders Frances Beal, Mae Jackson, and Gwendolyn Patton showed that the vast majority of incarcerated women identified as people of color, especially Black and Puerto Rican, and an overwhelming majority of the women who died as a result of an abortion performed by an unqualified professional identified as Puerto Rican and nonwhite.[47] Furthermore, at the time, most women of color lived in communities impacted by forced sterilization and were routinely dismissed by white male physicians as "hysterical" or drug-dependent "welfare queens."[48] TWWA aimed to expose the scope of the harms committed by the masculine US capitalist-carceral empire against women of color, and members developed early theories about the intersectional nature of violence interwoven in the US state.[49]

Radicals of the 1960s importantly moved the feminist movement away from liberal "equality" reforms and toward woman-centered independence. For example, the Boston Women's Health Collective published *Our Bodies, Ourselves* in 1970 to emphasize the urgency of empowering women to take control of their own bodies in lieu of state control.[50] These radical feminist ideas about nonreformist activism bled into early anti-rape writings. In 1971, Berkeley Women's Liberation members came together to write the feminist newspaper, *It Ain't Me Babe*, which printed the first major story explicitly about rape. The story, "Anatomy of a Rape," describes how a local artist had been picked up and assaulted by two GIs while hitchhiking home from a women's event. Rather than fight for equality in the legal system as past suffragettes had done, *It Ain't Me Babe* took an explicitly nonlegal approach to remedying violence, arguing instead for the victim's choice of justice after rape, including castration and community shaming.[51]

As a demonstration of women's independence, self-defense became a major rallying activity for radical feminists. TWWA's magazine *Triple Jeopardy*, for example, was one of the first to publicly advocate for armed resistance of women of color against white men.[52] The Boston group, Cell 16, quickly joined in. Cell 16 believed that men perceive women and their bodies to be an extension of men, which led to the high frequency of men's rape against women. Therefore, to escape rape, Cell 16 believed that women should empower themselves through hand-to-hand combat. Cell 16er Betsy Warrior designed a widely disseminated poster that read, "Disarm rapists: Smash sexism," alongside an image of a woman kicking a man in his groin.[53] This poster contributed to the mass proliferation of self-defense organizing across the country and helped to legitimize activism on behalf of abused women who had defended themselves from rape. Protests grew rapidly for the release of women who were on trial for self-defense from rape, including Native American (Sinixt/Arrow Lakes Nation of the Colville Federated Tribes) woman Yvonne Wanrow in 1972, Hispanic woman Inez García in 1974, and Black women Joan Little in 1974 and Dessie Woods in 1979.[54] Their trials showed that feminists *could* change society without liberal reforms by developing their own communities of resistance.

Through and alongside these sensationalized cases, anti-rape squads sprang up across the country, connecting interracial networks with one another to forge a coalitional anti-rape consciousness. In one of the earliest anti-rape groups, and fresh off the call-out traditions started by the New York Redstockings on abortion, the New York Radical Feminists (NYRF) organized the first rape speak-out in January 1971.[55] At the speak-out, women described how they were victimized by their husbands, male classmates, and male physicians, and they demanded retribution through public shaming, castration, and capital punishment. Quickly, NYRF members realized that there were far more rape victims who were willing to speak out than they had initially thought, and three months later, in April, they enlarged the speak-out to host the first anti-rape conference, bringing together activists from all backgrounds to pool their resources in the fight against sexual violence.[56] A few years later, in 1975, NYRF members joined hands with the National Black Feminist Organization New York Chapter, the Manhattan Women's Political Caucus, NOW New York, and many other local organizations to raise public consciousness through the creation of Rape Prevention Month and to protest emerging rape myth–imbued state legislation.[57] On the West Coast, multiracial coalitions also rose to challenge rape culture. In the Viva García campaign (to free Inez García from incarceration), TWWA, Latina group Concilio Mujeres, the National Conference of Puerto Rican Women, the gay men's group Combating Sexism, the

Black Panther Party (BPP), and United Farm Workers came together to circulate information about rape, prisons, and racism; fundraise for García's legal defense; and launch political organizing against the punitive carceral state.[58] These coalitions allowed for anti-rape activists from a multitude of backgrounds to collectively support victims through the abolition of intersectional violence.

Anti-rape advocacy emerged within and from these coalitions. Encouraged by early radical feminist dialogue against rape, four, then six multiracial women formed the DC Rape Crisis Center in 1972. The first edition of their widely disseminated guidebook, "How to Start a Rape Crisis Center," explains that the cofounders had initially started a letter center, then a hotline, and finally an informal shelter for abused unhoused women who could come together in support groups to help one another.[59] This first anti-rape center was resolutely "politically minded."[60] DC advocates directed their energies to educating the public, understanding that both prevention through political advocacy and direct services intervention were necessary to address the multifaceted nature of rape. The founders also acknowledged that medical professionals, police officers, and lawyers could play critical roles in the empowerment of victims by supporting them through criminal legal procedures and preventing the rapist from accessing the victim; however, DC advocates were adamant that advocate-survivors were the prime authorities on rape. They noted that "a moderately effective service can be run on a very limited budget if there is a high level of in-services, e.g., women who freely donate transportation. . . . We want to avoid the situation that we become so dependent on a large budget, that a decrease in the money available would threaten the Center's survival."[61]

Leaning into radical feminism, the first rape crisis center eschewed systems and instead relied on its in-network connections to sustain rape victim advocacy. They built out a new nationwide network called the Feminist Alliance Against Rape (FAAR) in which rape crisis center advocates could connect and share resources with one another in a mutual aid framework. FAAR was intended to "serve as a clearinghouse for information, news, and opinion for this expanding network of rape crisis centers, hoping to aid in establishing a true grassroots alliance."[62] The *FAAR Newsletter* disseminated information about ongoing federal and state laws affecting anti-rape advocates' work, local or regional task forces that addressed survivor support, and other activities pertaining to anti-rape direct services, such as the creation of new shelters or hotlines. By 1974, the DC Rape Crisis Center reported that there were approximately one hundred rape crisis centers in the United States; by 1976, there were about four hundred.[63]

Beginning in 1978, FAAR worked closely with the domestic violence coalition, the National Communication Network (NCN), and eventually merged to form a joint anti–rape–domestic-violence network, disseminating news of FAAR-NCN through the periodical *Aegis*. The FAAR-NCN network was originally a devoutly politically feminist, not bipartisan, coalition. In a 1978 *Aegis* newsletter, for example, DC Rape Crisis Center advocate and cofounder Deb Friedman volunteered to write a piece entitled "Rape, Racism—and Reality" to challenge the growing professionalization of anti-violence advocacy. Lambasting activists who called Susan Brownmiller a "spokesperson" of the anti-rape movement (and by extension, white feminists as the leaders of the anti-rape movement), Friedman described long histories of "Black, Hispanic, Chicano, Indian, or Asian" women experiencing rape and racism, and noted that late-1970s efforts to recognize racism in anti-rape advocacy had not adequately taken a "unified analytic position on racism and rape."[64] Her position, as well as the position of many radical feminists, alluded to the growing tensions within the anti-violence movement along racial and class lines.

By the late 1970s, some advocates responded to FAAR-NCN's openly antistate position by writing letters arguing that federal support could legitimize and/or fund their work.[65] This latter group of liberal feminists saw anti-rape advocacy as too radically left in contrast to the bipartisan approach that seemed to advance the anti-rape agenda, such as the progress made by NOW.[66] According to Santa Cruz Women Against Rape (SCWAR) advocates robin mc'duff, deanne pernell, and karen saunders, this group "considered themselves service groups, who . . . felt that the criminal justice system and the anti-rape movement had a common cause, 'to get rapists off the street.'"[67] However, as SCWAR pointed out, the emphasis on working with systems professionals presents no choice to survivors *but* the carceral system, pushing the survivors who are victimized by the carceral state out of rape responses. For example, at the Women's Crisis Center of Ann Arbor, Michigan, advocates took heed of the DC Rape Crisis Center's suggestion to organize local volunteer and staff for the crisis hotline, but when describing the psychology of sexual violence, advocates only referenced sources about sexual violence that sampled from a white women population.[68] The omission of race and other social identities centered whiteness and meant that the agency's counseling program delivered only therapeutic approaches to rape trauma that did not address the perpetration of intersectional violence.[69] SCWAR remarked, "Instead [of systems], the anti-rape movement should work on community education, and on developing practical alternatives that deal with both the systems and the roots of sexism and violence."[70]

This early theorizing of transformative justice came to fruition at the 1980 Third World Women and Violence Conference. In 1976, after four years of operation at the DC Rape Crisis Center, I. Nkenge Touré was hired as the first African American rape crisis center director in the country, and she immediately hired other Black activists, including Loretta J. Ross and Yulanda Ward, to organize community-based events and identify people who could serve as network liaisons.[71] Key network members included Cherríe Moraga, Audre Lorde, Nellie Wong, and countless others who sustained the coalition through informal letters and calls with each other.[72] In 1979, Touré and Ross successfully persuaded the DC Rape Crisis Center board of directors to organize the first conference about sexual violence open only to BIPOC advocates, and in August 1980, over one hundred women and gender-diverse people of multiple races, ethnicities, and political stances arrived in Washington, DC, to discuss ways of abolishing rape and interlocking violence.[73] Emily L. Thuma recounts, "As gestures of solidarity, women at All Souls donated money, white women [rape crisis center] volunteers donated child care labor and coordinated local transportation for out-of-town attendees, and Black Panther artist Malik Edwards designed the conference logo."[74] The mutual aid framework as well as the interethnic nature of the conference led to the creation of multiple women of color publications and periodicals, including the anthologies *This Bridge Called My Back* and *Home Girls* and the transnational feminist of color journal, *Meridians*. It also led to many interethnic coalitional gatherings throughout the 1980s, including the 1981 National Coalition Against Domestic Violence National Day of Unity, 1983 Women of Color anti-violence conference, and 1985 New York Women Against Rape Inaugural Women of Color Caucus meeting.[75]

The conference, however, reflected the struggles of developing transformative anti-rape advocacy in light of growing neoliberal sentiment. During the conference, many advocates highlighted how ongoing world and national events conflicted with the timing of the conference, including the first National Asian/Pacific American Women's Conference and the ten-day protest against uranium mining and nuclear power development in the sacred Black Hills of the Lakota Nation. Moreover, the dominance of Black feminism over other Third World feminisms, particularly Latine feminisms, which had been critical to anticarceral dialogues, caused some tensions in the group.[76] These tensions illuminated that neoconservative ideas about "multiculturalism," in which all races and ethnicities are made equal, were beginning to stratify anti-violence politics.[77] At the end of the conference, Touré noted, "Within the ranks of each group, there are internal contradictions to be resolved and between Black and Latino women there remain contradictions to be resolved. These, however, are non-antagonistic in nature and through sharing self-criticism and criticism for the purpose of arriving at a comfortable unity, that gap can be bridged. The Conference must encompass the needs of as many participants as possible so that in fact not all of the emphasis is on one Third World grouping."[78]

Still, Touré's cautionary guidance was quickly eclipsed by the murder of Yulanda Ward less than three months after the first Third World Women and Violence conference. In addition to her work as a conference organizer, Ward had worked tirelessly as a housing justice worker and at the DC Rape Crisis Center as a direct services advocate. On November 6, 1980, four unknown armed men shot Ward to death in the middle of the night. Anti-rape feminists understood that Ward's death was not an accidental murder, as police reports suggested; they knew that it was a political assassination intended to kill radical anti-violence organizing in the DC Area, the birthplace of victim advocacy.[79] Although activists from FAAR, the African People's Socialist Party, the Feminist Law Collective, and the National Black United Front came together in protest and linked Ward's murder to other ongoing political struggles, including that of Assata Shakur, Malcolm X, Rev. Dr. King Jr., and George Jackson, the second Third World Women and Violence conference was delayed and the formerly interethnic coalitions gradually separated into distinct ethnic silos as a means of protecting themselves from white supremacist gun violence.[80]

Ward's death and the systems-based setbacks of feminist of color organizing opened the door for white policing and medical professionals to coopt the anti-rape movement. Intrafeminist conflicts about the direction of the movement led many rape crisis centers to reduce their community outreach programs in cultural arenas and narrow their focus to legal organizing. This reduction in political agitation corresponded with the rise of the carceral state that privatized prisons and punished the poor, exacerbating the power of policing and therapeutic systems professionals in responses to crimes like sexual assault.[81] Studying these divisions in the anti-rape movement, Mimi E. Kim laments, "The numerical and political dominance of White women within the [mainstream] anti-violence movement suppressed the potential of a more unified alternative platform and set of strategies led by women of color (Richie, 2012). Rather, women-of-color anti-violence activism taking place throughout the late 1970s and 1980s translated into more narrowly focused demands for greater representation in terms of numbers within membership bodies, task forces, and caucuses, and greater influence in terms of placement in positions of power."[82] In 1994, (neo) liberal feminists fully coopted the movement through VAWA, nailing the coffin of radical advocacy. Anti-rape advocacy would no longer be possible through independent feminist collectives; instead, through crime control initiatives, the state would sponsor and thus control victim services.[83]

This narrative of the anti-rape movement reflects the commonly held belief by anti-rape advocates that openly radical and political activism died with the neoliberalization of anti-rape work. It captures the racial diversity of doing anti-rape work and the grunt labor required to support victims at the grassroots direct services level. In doing so, it exposes how the state has coopted advocates' story by only situating advocacy as a legal service; its exposé of the non- or extralegal organizing shows how advocacy came about even without the state's intervention. Speaking on the narratives written of the anti-rape movement, Rose Corrigan writes, "This [narrative of decline] . . . is a very different picture of the community response to rape than those offered by the popular media, news coverage, or by legal and medical systems," which celebrate the feminist movement for successfully implementing anti-rape programs.[84] Instead of a narrative of success, this second thread illustrates how significant activity in defense of rape victims, especially those of color, was gradually appropriated by systems through the murders of radical activists and their values.

Although we might see this second story in a more positive light, this thread nevertheless renders advocates into affective subjects who want nothing more than to return to the past. By locating the origins of the anti-rape movement with the radical feminists of the 1960s, we contemporary advocates and scholars who feel the pain of present-day neoliberalism will look more fondly back at this thread, in nostalgia erasing the tensions inherent to radical organizing. This feeling of safety is dangerous.[85] Any narrative of success or decline, as Hall describes of the 1960s Civil Rights Movement, "distorts and suppresses as much as it reveals."[86] As illuminated in the backgrounds of these stories, anti-rape advocates have always struggled to merge anti-rape activism with anti-racist activism. Fashioning the "first" advocates as 1972 radical feminists wholly against white systems tokenizes their struggles and extols them as pure "heroines" who can do no wrong. But just as we might call rapists from the dominant story the enemies of the anti-rape movement, denouncing systems professionals or the advocates who worked with them only perpetuates the idea that there is only one "right" kind of advocate, only one "right" way to do advocacy.[87]

Moreover, the radical advocates of the 1970s did not draw their strategies of hotline calls, police and medical accompaniment, and shelters out of thin air. Rather, 1970s anti-rape advocates were trained by 1960s radical Black Freedom and Third World activists, who were themselves under the tutelage of the anticolonial, anticapitalist, and antienslavement activists of the previous centuries.[88] By seeing 1970s radical feminists as the "first" advocates, we forget to look to our ancestors who have long fought rape culture. Through this resistance narrative, we render contemporary advocates agentless, without guides or mentors who can help us move past this moment of neoliberal normativity. This second thread of the anti-rape movement is therefore a well-meaning alternative to the state's conscripted story, but one that ultimately fails to listen to radical advocacy's rich genealogies.

Thread 3. Abolition (Always in Now)

The second thread imposes another kind of dominance by suggesting that there is a "real" story to be discovered. It is worth remembering that we may too harm survivors when we perpetuate a history incongruent with the complicated legacies of violence and anti-violence resistance. In recognition of such secondary harm, anti-rape advocates have in the last few years begun to extract the histories of the anti-rape movement distinct from the US carceral state and the radical feminists of the "second wave." They attempt to show that advocacy is not a new form of activism and is, in fact, a legitimate form of work, just one that has been largely conducted by BIPOC and thus ignored by dominant movement makers. For example, in 2020, the Maine Coalition Against Sexual Assault (MECASA) developed an online module that explores the history of the anti-violence movement. In it, MECASA writes, "People have been organizing underground and grassroots supports for survivors of sexual violence throughout history. . . . The history of sexual violence, and movements to end it, dates so far back that there is often little written history on record."[89] The advocates aim to show that anti-rape advocacy, much like rape, has a long history, and they attempt to move away from the problematic narrative that sees advocacy's origins in 1970s radical feminism and toward a richer, more diverse history.

Despite the good intentions of these endeavors, any emphasis on linear cohesion falls into the trap of creating one "real" story.[90] To take MECASA's history as an example, MECASA begins by arguing that Indigenous communities had previously not experienced rape, "but that changed with the arrival of Europeans."[91] Recognizing rape as a tool of colonization decolonizes our histories by acknowledging the ways that Indigenous peoples truly produced the first advocacy. Yet Kānaka Maoli feminist Val Kalei Kanuha argued that rape existed in precolonial Hawai'i, proclaiming, "If you listen to the stories that many advocates and others talk about today concerning the different forms of violence against women that occur in our society, my guess is you will find that many of these forms of violence against women existed before outsiders came into our societies."[92] Like sex, rape must have existed prior to the arrival of colonizers, born through frictions among the varied factions within and external to each Indigenous community. A story that represents rape otherwise romanticizes precontact communities while furthermore portraying anti-rape resistance as a product of colonial times. In other words, we might come to the erroneous assumption that advocacy exists *because of* European colonizers if we believe that colonial rape was the first rape. Through the marking of linear colonial time, MECASA's story unintentionally invalidates the credibility of Indigenous rape victims who had experienced sexual violence before colonization and disturbingly attaches anti-rape victim advocacy to the colonization of Indigenous peoples.

History, it must be remembered, is not an objective act; it is actively weaponized by the US settler state to impose dominant values on marginalized radical genealogies. We cannot use the same methods of retrieving the past as in the dominant two threads, or else we will recreate "a learned and organized epistemology of ignorance."[93] Furthermore, our goal cannot be to find a "real" anti-rape movement. Heeding the words of Touré, to create a truly intersectional anti-rape movement requires not that we have one unified history but that we consider the messy range of advocacy across race, class, and gender. To break free from the violence of a dominant story, we must examine other ways in which people from all walks of life have supported rape victims over the years. This endeavor requires that we look beyond what we define as "anti-rape advocacy" and parse through the activism that nonetheless helped rape survivors and their communities. That is, we must destabilize the notion that there is "one" right way of doing advocacy itself. Wielding archival fractals in a critical imaginary project to find our advocate histories, we imagine *what isn't there* that could have supported survivors.

Critical feminist historians have begun the work of rehistoricizing rape (and, implied in such endeavors, anti-rape advocacy) in ways that escape the dominant story.[94] The dominant history of rape in the United States often focuses on analyzing rape laws that were developed by white British settler men, who relied on the infamous Sir Matthew Hale's interpretation of rape, in which Hale argued that rape was "an accusation easily to be made and hard to be proved, and harder to be defended by the party accused, tho never so innocent."[95] Hale's argument demonstrates that English men forcibly brought Indigenous and non-English European settlers under patriarchal Anglo-American rape law through the negation of rape by property law. In other words, rape could not exist as a legitimate crime, and its deviant status from the state's purview is another type of exclusionary colonial patriarchal control. While studying early rape law subverts one element of the dominant story, this reading exemplifies how the study of only legal anti-rape advocacy does not make visible the rape of enslaved Black, Indigenous, and multiracial women and girls, and even some white indentured or otherwise poor white women and girls, at the hands of white male masters. Because "rape" legally only involved white women, who were themselves property of white men, looking directly at rape law contextualizes only one kind of rape.

Given the malleability of rape forms, we need to examine rape through other social institutions not explicitly about rape, such as colonization and enslavement, to develop a more composite portrait of anti-rape organizing.[96] To take one example, colonial-era survivor-advocates often carried out raids of white supremacist towns in an effort to end rape. Beginning in the late 1400s, Spanish settlers brought enslaved African people to the Americas in search of precious gold and silver and razed Mexico City and its outposts under the guise of Catholic proselytization. They enslaved upper-class Indigenous women and girls by forcing them to marry wealthy Spanish missionaries or commanders who frequently raped, beat, and murdered them. Poor and enslaved Indigenous women and girls were forced to labor until late at night, and as many of them returned to their neighborhoods on the outskirts of the missions, Spanish soldiers kidnapped and gang raped them. Seeing rape as a form of social anarchy, military commanders and Catholic priests passed numerous ordinances to prohibit sexual violence, such as passing laws to physically separate male Spanish soldiers from Indigenous women laborers; however, this early version of rape law did not empower survivors, nor did it curtail violence.[97] Instead, reclaiming their own lands and bodies, Indigenous women survivors planned and led attacks on Spanish missions, burning settlers' homes and murdering rapists with knives and clubs. Some women, like Japchivit *ranchería* Toypurina, wielded their statuses as medicine women to influence their community members to join raids. Several survivor-advocates also actively enforced women-only parties and tortured, sometimes beheaded, rapists to demand release from domestic and marital enslavement. Antonia I. Castañeda reported that Indigenous people "were neither docile nor passive in the face of repeated assaults."[98]

Analyzing this example, I ask, Is raiding *not* anti-rape advocacy? This question prompts us to think about what *is* advocacy, if *not* raiding. Raiding was certainly not the only response taken by Indigenous people to colonial rape. Some Indigenous women invested in spiritual reclamation, burning and ingesting herbal medicine and sweating to renew their bodies after sexual assault.[99] Another few escaped to surrounding tribes, such as the Apache and Diné (Navajo) communities, to avoid surviving in an increasingly colonial environment.[100] Tribes were also not uniform in their responses to rape. Some tribal members blamed victims for rape and banished them for fear of disease.[101] Others killed or abandoned pregnant women or new mothers who had been raped by male colonizers, believing that their children would be contaminated by the blood of another heritage.[102] The high variation in rape responses indicates that early development of decolonial anti-rape advocacy was messy; there *was* no one "right" way to do advocacy, no "first" tactic that fully helped victims, only budding attempts to remedy colonial violence. Through this messiness, however, we see that there was not one "real" anti-rape movement but a spectrum of activities that supported rape victims—raiding, murder, banishment, and spiritual reclamation.

That we contemporary advocates should go out and conduct raids to be "radical" decolonial activists is not the lesson we must learn. Instead, by thinking about anti-rape advocacy *not* connected to state services, *not* directly about rape but about colonial conquest, we can reimagine advocacy as the multiplicity of actions taken in the aftermath of violence. This critical historicization of *not* anti-rape advocacy, with the humbling reminder that we have not always done right by victims, helps us to identify past strategies that could be used to support rape victims now, beyond the binary between rape law reform and non- or extralegal anti-rape justice. It also reminds us of the inherent intersectional ties between the US state and rape, and why we must protest beyond interpersonal help.[103]

Theorizing the abolition of rape through this method informs our contemporary organizing strategies. In the present day, advocates think about their work in relation to criminal legal professionals and see themselves as mediators of the state, refusing or neglecting to intervene in public, political ways. However, advocates of the past did not think of themselves in this way. In the early nineteenth century, formerly enslaved Black women survivors ran away from white male masters who raped them to create "maroon communities," fugitive sanctuaries that connected the anti-enslavement abolitionist movement with Indigenous sovereignty movements.[104] Borrowing guerilla tactics from their southwestern Indigenous and Caribbean counterparts, marooners called for the raiding of white supremacist towns, burning, poisoning, and shooting rapists.[105] Through the armed defense of kin, and unlike our contemporary ideas of a peaceful proto-advocate, marooners created safe interracial communities away from the horrors of colonial rape; their raids empowered survivors through active resistance. In the post–Civil War years, the famed Black liberationist Ida B. Wells would echo calls for armed "self-help," advocating for a Winchester rifle on the mantle of every Black fireplace.[106] Here, contemporary advocates might generate knowledge. Just as past survivor-advocates escaped their prisons of enslavement through active armed defense, contemporary advocates might empower ourselves out of the neoliberal prison by creating our own marooning sanctuaries today, escaping to transformative justice organizations armed by mutual aid practices instead of nonprofit rape crisis centers funded by the neoliberal state.

Critical fabulation also identifies the power of transformative advocacy for marginalized survivors even with practices we might initially reject, like death. During the colonial and antebellum periods, many enslaved survivors on plantations chose to engage in self-harm and self-sterilization to induce miscarriages, ingesting medicines to avoid pregnancy, which helped them to avoid childbearing by rape.[107] Others chose to commit infanticide to prevent their children from experiencing the slow death of enslaved captivity.[108] Enslaved mother of four children Margaret Garner, for example, "declared that she would kill herself and her children before she would return to bondage," and when she saw that "their hopes of freedom were vain, seized a butcher knife that lay on the table and with one stroke cut the throat of her little daughter."[109] These strategies of self-harm, suicide, and murder exemplify that, in the US state that legalizes the punishment of BIPOC, rape survivors did anti-rape advocacy by refusing the state. And, like raiding, suicide and murder are forms of advocacy because they are strategies to reclaim one's life in violent spaces.[110] While I cannot endorse this particular method of death for contemporary advocate-survivors, the example shows that, if advocacy is empowering survivors, then there are many other ways of taking back control beyond systems-based services.

Rather than limit us to legal reform or nonlegal resistance, radical advocacy has always lived in gray spaces and therefore offers much more than one strategy or set of strategies. Raiding, marooning, suicide, and murder demonstrate that we have many tactics in our toolkit that can prevent rape and support victims, if only we hold onto the same values of abolitionism. Still, the subversion of a linear thread must go beyond this period in American history. Critical scholars have already conducted the work of uncovering rape by colonization and enslavement, and many might falsely claim that this part of the anti-rape movement is irrelevant to present-day struggles. I suggest we look for other everyday violence that might not be as readily obvious to us as normative systems to create radical advocacy in the present. Otherwise, as Sharon P. Holland asks of our tendency to conflate liberalism with radicalism, "What more normativizing act can there be than to participate in *reproduction*?"[111]

We must ask how radical advocacy might look in less visibly anti-rape ways to move historic anti-rape abolitionism into the present day, now and for the future. One example of this invisible advocacy that does not at first appear to have any salience for rape victims but likely helped many of them is the late-nineteenth- and early-twentieth-century YWCA and its contributions to the Christian welfare reform movement. Most advocates' immediate reaction to religion, specifically Christianity, is to reject it; fundamental and/or evangelical Christianity has been long wielded against rape survivors of all stripes.[112] But however masochistic our analysis may be, this example moves us out of the period of explicit colonization and enslavement to show the building of yet another carceral system against survivors, this time in the form of industrialism, which is not immediately obvious to us as just another prison. It also shows us how activists who did not explicitly tackle the issue of rape nevertheless contributed to the anti-rape movement, illuminating coconspirator bedfellows with whom we could collaborate for radical social change.

The YWCA was established in the 1860s, at the cusp of the American Civil War. At the time, many Black individuals were already involved in the church, specifically the Black Baptist, Zionist, and African Methodist Episcopal churches. The church was one of the few places where Black people could commune in large public gatherings and receive an education without white mob interference. It served as a "multiple site—at once being a place of worship, theater, publishing house, school, and lodge."[113] White women also found refuge in the church, especially southern whites. From the antebellum to the post–Civil War periods, most white women tethered their sense of womanhood and thus social power to Protestantism.[114]

The end of the Civil War prompted mass migrations to the North and West and catapulted the United States into the industrial period. Many poor BIPOC and white women moved to urban slums, taking on low-wage factory jobs and domestic work that made them vulnerable to frequent sexual harassment and assault.[115] In addition, laws enforcing curfews and poverty wages for women (particularly BIPOC) workers prevented many of them from escaping enslavement under a different name, and criminal codes began to incarcerate those who failed to pay back loan-shark debts, developing a new gendered and racialized system of convict leasing.[116] These systems of incarceration were premised on white male Christian sexual norms that punished newly arriving immigrants, such as Asian (typically Chinese) workers, and formerly southern Black women who had migrated to the North.[117] Seeing the connections between capitalist exploitation and gendered violence, Protestant white women and Black Baptist women determined that there was a serious need for gender-segregated housing facilities and separate skills training for girls entering the increasingly manufacturing-based workforce. In 1860, the YWCA funded the first boarding house for female students, teachers, and faculty workers in New York.[118] This would be the first of many proto-shelter institutions, though it would be 1893 before a Y shelter accepted nonwhites and 1917 before the first Black Y association could operate semi-independently from white Y organizations.[119]

The YWCA was a part of a larger movement to reform welfare in the United States in the late 1800s, called the "settlement house movement." White woman Jane Addams saw the plight of poor women in the slums of Chicago, and she established Hull House in 1889 and many similar settlement houses to protect and safeguard them. These homes were rooted in evangelical ideas about peaceful democracies. Though she was not an openly devout Christian, Addams led education projects to create kindergartens and child play; she pioneered efforts to enhance nursing and healthcare training and services; and she was instrumental in labor unionizing.[120] The Y was responsible for developing and then adapting many of Hull House's strategies as they popularized. Though Judith Weisenfeld is careful to note that, given the longstanding presence of the church in Black communities, "For African American women ... the YWCA represented merely *one* arena in which to work," Black women led the charge to educate young girls, including offering skills training in beauty, business, English, and religious studies; hosting political celebrities such as members of the NAACP; and fundraising for young girls' home and public needs.[121] Y activism empowered young Black and white girls by giving them the skills to survive in the cutthroat industrialist period. Ida B. Wells, for her part, called Addams "the greatest woman in the United States" for her contributions to welfare.[122]

The settlement house movement and the rapid growth of the Y set the foundation for radical feminist work in the 1930s. The First World War encouraged mass migrations from Western Europe and South America to North America, drastically changing the demographics of the US workforce. Echoing sentiment similar to today's neoconservative politicians, "native" men, namely, those identifying as white, US-born Christian nationalists, believed that immigrants were "stealing their jobs" and should not receive federal aid.[123] Just over a decade later, the Great Depression put many young women out of their homes and jobs. With no one to rely on and no permanent jobs available, the growing poverty class of unemployed unmarried women turned to their "neighborhood" for support.[124] Young, mainly Black, Indigenous, Asian, and Latina women shared money, goods, and services like food, clothes, and housework with each other to survive.[125] Their networks were largely comprised of single women with children who, while experiencing significant stigma from the white public, believed in the benefits of socialist-like communal living without US state services interference.[126] Women from the YWCA and other community organizers supported interracial gatherings by teaching English to new migrants and disbursing resources to people in need.[127]

Just as before, I ask, Are the strategies employed by the YWCA *not* advocacy? Y practices were not just social services or even an early version of nonprofit work. Instead, Bettina Aptheker explains the welfare reform movement as the "instrument through which to realize the egalitarian ethic of an authentic democracy. . . . It was to provide a cultural, literary and artistic oasis for the slum dweller."[128] In essence, the Y and the broader welfare reform movement were instrumental in transforming the image of estranged single and unmarried women as prostitutes who were responsible for their troubles into survivors who needed to learn how to advocate for themselves in the white man's world. *Is this not advocacy*, to create a consciousness-raising space that empowers the disadvantaged? Moreover, the movement reignited interest in nonviolent responses to violence. While restorative justice, sometimes called peacemaking, originated with Indigenous American tribes, the movement endorsed democratic values in which responses to violence are premised on cultivating peaceful communities in which all members play equal and important roles.[129] While nonviolence was merely one out of multiple strategies in the advocate's toolkit,[130] the Y's emphasis on kinship allowed its members to see themselves *with* clients instead of as managers of clients, a key mutual aid principle that stressed sharing and community.[131] *Is this not advocacy*, to empower people—peers for and by peers—through coalitional consciousness raising?

The example of the YWCA shows another way of conducting radical anti-rape advocacy, moving past strategies into the present day. Although the early-twentieth-century YWCA did not explicitly address rape, we can critically imagine that its support of mutual aid collectives of disadvantaged women and girls deterred people from victimizing Y clients, at least as openly, and YWCA educational programs likely supported many rape victims to regain some semblance of their sexual autonomy. Importantly, the YWCA example underscores how industrialist systems or other corporate and philanthropic entities can nevertheless revictimize people and stresses our responsibility in dismantling institutionalized violence. While factories are not readily obvious as violent, industrialization pushed capitalist logics of competition onto the workforce and thus disaggregated workers across gendered and racial lines, producing intersectional secondary harm. The

YWCA example reveals that radicalism breathes through community building. Taking up the same principles of finding community with each other, in all our complexities, might better equip us to abolish today's neoliberal normativity than relying on the state or isolated collectives that merely reform rape law. The YWCA example suspends the state/nonprofit binary by illustrating the gray actions we can take that nevertheless support rape victims.

Back in the 1980s, the radical anti-violence feminist Yolanda Bako pointed out that the first formalized women's shelter was, in fact, the Sanctified Sisters Woman's Commonwealth, established in 1867 in Belton, Texas.[132] Bako disrupts the narrative that the Y or Hull House were the first "real" shelters. But whether these institutions were formal or informal, "real" or "not real," the "first" or otherwise, seem to be less important questions than asking whether these spaces were or were not carrying out *anti-rape* advocacy in their endeavor to support the queered and Othered—especially those who were poor and working-class young femme victims of color. Indeed, by asking ourselves what is not anti-*rape* resistance, we remove ourselves from the dominant gaze and find anti-rape advocacy's purpose: to support rape survivors, and abolish all forms of interlocking violence that lead to and are rape.

In deconstructing the dominant histories of the anti-rape movement, we also smash the dominant story and its control over our movement building. Any number of threads might argue that advocacy only began in 1994, 1972, or 1612. These threads might serve good intentions, to honor specific individuals or collectives who came before us. But there is no "real" anti-rape movement history. There are multiple realities, multiple agendas, and thus multiple possibilities to make a world without violence.

The anti-rape movement's genealogies are always in the abolitionist now. The abolition of rape means the abolition of racism, sexism, classism, and all the other -isms that oppress us, going backwards and forwards, sideways and otherwise in a subversion of a dominant story.[133] This movement is messy, and through its messiness, we escape to an immortal temporal plane unbound to the normative state. Unlike the first thread, which ignores the grassroots activism of the 1970s, and unlike the second thread, which erases our ugly emotions, the messiness of nonlinear, asynchronous threads helps us to feel again, to understand the complex emotions—some shame, some guilt, some joy, and some rage—of working in and out of the state. We are made to *look* at our hauntings and the disturbing attachments we still hold.[134] Though sticky to navigate, our relationships refute simple or dichotomous answers to carve another future, on the horizon of change.[135]

Is This Still Advocacy?

History is a dangerous game. As the threads reveal, anti-rape advocacy was never about providing services or working within systems. From the Indigenous and Black women who took up arms in self-defense of their lands and bodies to the multiracial Christian communities who lived with survivors, advocacy has always been about supporting people in the ways that they need. This advocacy is just as much about resisting social and institutional secondary violence through visible and invisible activist protest as it is about resisting interpersonal sexual assault through social services.

We must be cautious about having the state "think" and "speak" for us; we need to *think* and *feel* as radical anti-rape advocates and survivors did in the past and now to sustain radicalism for the next generation. We need to become our own architects, our own archivists who preserve our radical genealogies in methods that come from long generations of knowledge production. Indeed, we need to shift our question if we are to survive, moving from *is this not advocacy* toward a newer question: *Is this still advocacy?*

Herein lies one final test, then, from the words of one advocate seeking to do good.

> [The survivor] was within a community that speaks a different language, a Native language. And there was only one person, it was the [family member] of one of the victims. One person who thought that they could sit through the trial, who wanted that, who, who wanted to feel like someone witnessing what was being said, um, about their family. And this person was bilingual English and, and this other language and, I sat with them in the courtroom up until the point that . . . (quietly) the really tough stuff, images, uh, came up, you can imagine what a triple homi-

cide, what is presented to the jury. And there was this moment when she looked at me and, I said, Do you need to go? And she said, Yeah I need to go. And we were whispering 'cause you know, there's a trial going [on] and I said, do you want me to come with you or do you want me to stay? I'll tell you what is said or, I can bear witness with you, wherever we go. And she's like, I want you to stay. And I thought, I had a moment of like, is this still, is this still advocacy?

Um, but in the moment it just came out and I felt that, that's what was right, um, 'cause I know how badly she wanted someone of that family, someone to be in that room and no one was 'cause, they couldn't understand what was going on, um, and because it turns out, this is messed up but the court will only pay for an interpreter for one of the parties, like a plaintiff or a defendant? So, (increasingly raises speaking volume) that person, he had a headset on and he was having interpretation obviously, his trial. But no one else gets to [be] privy to the [interpretation]—which leaves a huge fit about what [Midwestern US state] supports it so, whatever.

The point was . . . she wanted more than anything to sit in that room all day every day to those weeks, and come back out and tell her family who were waiting in little rooms. This is what happened today. And since she wasn't able to do that I stayed, and listened to what happened and took notes or whatever and then went out to come and tell her. And, um . . . I just asked, I questioned myself if I would've done that if someone didn't speak English or, or you know how, I don't know. I just question myself all the time how that went . . .

I don't know, it just felt right and I felt so already upset that it was an injustice that, the whole family couldn't understand what was going on. Um, it felt wrong, and I felt so angry, I just thought, this is my little way of doing something you know.

* * *

Tracing the genealogies of the anti-rape movement is not a mere exercise but a practice that realizes the potentiality of radical advocacy in the present. The anti-rape movement has long been entangled with normativity, only this time we have lost sight of our purpose as advocates and slowly stopped resisting. In the following chapters, I show that neoliberalism is not a simple, unidirectional top-down force. There is no singular subject-enemy against whom we can come together and fight, nor singular action that will abolish rape and its many faces. Instead, we become the enemy by unseeing violence. I encourage the reader to ask what it means to do advocacy in the face of neoliberalism. What is *still* truly advocacy oftentimes does not look the way we think it should. We should critically inspect our work, feel our rage, guilt, shame, and perhaps even regret, to stumble along the path toward transformative justice.

2

Capitalizing Empowerment

The Culture of Making Survivors

The crisis dimensions of sexual violence constitute one of the facets of a deep-going crisis of capitalism. Even if this crisis subsides, however, the problem of rape will remain. As the violent face of sexism, the threat of rape will exist as long as capitalist society survives.
—Angela Davis, "Rape, Race and the Capitalist Setting"

At the height of "second wave" feminism, Angela Y. Davis made a bold claim about the anti-rape movement: Without active anticapitalist resistance in advocacy, the anti-rape movement will fail in its agenda to eliminate violence. Entitled "Rape, Racism and the Capitalist Setting," Davis's essay claimed that capitalist societies like the United States tended to see higher frequencies of rape than noncapitalist societies because capitalism organizes people into a hierarchy of social groups; the white, masculine, elite class rapes poor BIPOC to accumulate wealth.[1] Since the birth of the US settler-carceral state, white men have enslaved Black and Indigenous women and girls to rape them, bartering people as financially viable capital goods.[2] This exchange of money for marginalized bodies suggests that rape is a technique of the powerful to economically and socially subjugate Others.

Davis's critique of capitalism rang true in 1978 but is just as critical for anti-violence advocates today. Though the literal enslavement of marginalized bodies is now outlawed, the exchange of rape survivors for money continues silently in the nonprofit industrial complex (NPIC).[3] Advocates became implicated in the NPIC when they chose to take funding from the US state, bonding with systems to formalize rape crisis centers. Sharply contrasting with the grassroots activism of the earlier centuries, advocates at contemporary agencies calculate the value of victims based on our expenditure of state resources.⁴ We count how much labor we have exerted, the number of days we have delivered services, and the amount of clothing, food, shelter, and other resources we have given to survivors for the purposes of institutional profit.⁵ This exchange of survivors for agency funding is racialized, sexed, gendered, and able-bodied as much as it was during genocide and enslavement: We barter victims for dollars, upholding a normative social hierarchy.⁶

What is the purpose of judging rape survivors in this way? Aside from financial benefits to the neoliberal anti-rape institution, neither advocates nor survivors profit from the NPIC method of fundraising. In fact, wielding capitalist logics has only exaggerated secondary victimization. As this chapter demonstrates, advocates artificially restrict our work to only those services that are financially covered under state grants, such as medical-forensic exams and therapy appointments, in fear of state violence for misuse of funds. These quotidian acts uplift the myth of a "perfect" victim by predetermining that victims' needs can be best met with some universal victim capital.⁷ We engage with victims as though they hold some value financially, even if we show empathy and care. In turn, we forgo radical advocacy that could help survivors with complex needs outside of the state's purview simply because radical work costs us more than we as capitalists are willing to give.⁸ Support for safety and mental and emotional well-being becomes intertwined with debates about who is worth the money—or, who is rapeable and who is not.⁹

This chapter explores the relationships between capitalism and victim advocacy. I ask, In what ways does capitalism show up in our everyday advocacy? And why does this particular kind of advocacy reproduce social hierarchies that replay rape of a different kind? I focus on the ways that advocates enforce capitalist logics through their direct victim support, specifically the inventorying and distribution of victim resources. Through a critique of capitalism, we can see, with remarkable clarity, that advocates administrate, police, and violate the rules of abolition for a cutthroat chance at profit. We might think of ourselves as radical abolitionists because we respond to rape, but without an expansive, offensive strategy against the capitalist state, we cannot wholly extract ourselves from normative violence.¹⁰ We must begin our work here, at capitalism, the locus of neoliberal entanglement.

The Culture of Capitalism

What *is* capitalism? If I am arguing that capitalism drives marginalization within the state-sponsored rape crisis center, we must understand that capitalism is multifaceted, and most frequently deployed to disguise social oppressions.[11] Many of us understand capitalism to be an economic system in which private entities compete with one another to produce better and more products and accumulate wealth. Capitalism is an economic system, for sure, but it is also a racist, sexist, and oppressive system that has long structured US society.[12] The governance of economic classes often parallels and, indeed, is the subjugation of various cultures in a system known as cultural capitalism.[13] *Cultural capitalism* is the conglomerate of theories around the sociality and culture of and around capitalism.[14]

There are many forms of cultural capitalism.[15] Nominally, cultural capitalism includes racial capitalism, ethnic capitalism, settler-colonial capitalism, sexual and/or gender capitalism, and erotic capitalism, among many other kinds.[16] Each of these types of capitalism focuses on the ways that capitalist economic systems affect distinct, often marginalized individuals such as BIPOC, immigrants, women, and trans and gender-diverse people. Each of them also focuses on the ways that capitalist economic systems produce and reproduce power hierarchies across social groups. For example, racial capitalism,[17] as defined by Cedric Robinson, is the pursuit of a racial social ordering through the "development, organization, and expansion of capitalist society."[18] In contrast to believing the development narrative that Euro-American cultures moved from archaic feudal systems dependent on enslavement to democratic capitalist systems with free markets, racial capitalism argues that the capitalist system is in and of itself a form of feudalism that continues to reinforce racial hierarchies, one that subjugates and has subjugated Black people over centuries and across geopolitical landscapes.[19] The racial capitalist thesis holds true if we look at the example of enslavement. While legal, enslavement formed a critical feature of US culture in which white colonizers dealt and traded in enslaved persons.[20] As with land and physical commodities, white settlers valued and insured enslaved people who were exploited to expand white wealth.[21] Today, these bets come in the form of un(der) paid labor in the prison industrial complex.[22] Racial capitalism theory exposes the ways that white settler economic dispossession *is* sociocultural (specifically anti-Black racial) oppression against Black people and people of color.[23]

Cultural capitalism identifies the kinds of capital that increase or decrease one's overall cultural community wealth. Aside from cash or material property, which are often assigned clearly delineated values, there are other kinds of capital that make up one's wealth and thus social standing in a capitalist society: the knowledge of diverse cultures, spoken language that reflects a high educational background, and networks of support and community that expedite time and energy to complete tasks.[24] These forms of capital are not financial nor materialist in nature; rather, they are cultural capital that enhance one's social standing, generating comparative wealth. Like material capital goods, cultural capital is "priced" differently in different kinds of societies. For instance, as racial capitalism posits, knowledge about white European cultures, such as its histories of art, warfare, and business, can elevate one's wealth and thus social standing in a predominantly white or white supremacist society.[25] Similarly, in anti-rape spheres, victim capital is capital that can support rape victims, such as medicine like azithromycin and PrEP, and connections to shelters with readily available beds. Some victim capital is more valuable than others. For example, a public transportation ticket is more valuable for a survivor in a neighborhood with high road traffic than it is for a survivor in a rural area without accessible public transportation. It is the fact that the ticket is delivered to a survivor in a *high-road-traffic area* that inflates its sociocultural worth, not that the ticket costs a set dollar amount. Capital that is considered valuable is called an asset while capital that is valueless is called a liability.[26]

Reading Capitalism into Rape Studies

Although cultural capitalism has salience for many elements of anti-violence advocacy, most critiques of capitalism in anti-rape studies narrowly focus on interpersonal rape.[27] Known as the victim commodity thesis, this approach to capitalism in rape exposes the ways that rapists capitalize on victims to increase their social standing.[28] Donald Dripps, who theorized the victim commodity thesis, explained that "sexual cooperation is a service much like any other, which individuals have a right to offer for compensation, or not, as they choose."[29] In other words, all victims are assumed to carry different kinds of capital, ranging from material goods like cash and a home to more symbolic goods like knowledge about consent and sexual intercourse. For example, victims might own an automobile independently from an abuser, which is a highly valuable materialist capital good that can safely transport them to and from a rape crisis center, but they might also have intangible victim capital of worth, such as knowledge of free or low-cost welfare services in the area.[30] Proponents of the victim commodity thesis suggest that positive sexual intercourse can be read like any other commodity or service with an assigned numerical value. All people can sexually engage with another person and quantify the financial weight of the sexual act(s). Under this line of reasoning, proponents of the thesis characterize *rape* as the *theft of sexual capital*; a person who rapes has in essence stolen sexual capital, positive sexual intercourse, from a victim.[31]

The victim commodity thesis importantly shows that rape, like any other crime, is a legitimate form of violence because rapists have exploited individual rape victims for their own gains.[32] However, while anti-rape theorists who support the victim commodity thesis are usually well intentioned, the thesis problematically assumes the myth of the "ideal," or perfect, victim.[33] Originally coined by Nils Christie in relation to gender-based violence, "the ideal victim" is a weak, young, or elderly female who had been harmed by a "big and bad" stranger, often coded as Black.[34] Because the perfect victim had not instigated the rape, nor was able to fend off her attacker, the theft of *her* sexual capital, which had been so carefully guarded otherwise, is justifiably a crime that should be met with severe carceral punishment. Yet contrary to this myth, most victims are not "perfect." Most rapes are between known parties, not strangers. In the vast majority of sexual assault cases, victims engage with perpetrators before they rape, for instance, allowing the abuser into the home or indicating consent to one sexual activity, like fondling, but not another, like penetration.[35] In effect, the thesis positions positive sexual intercourse as an exchange commodity, such that sex is made equal for all parties.[36] But positioning sexual intercourse as an exchange commodity "create[s] equivalencies between what are otherwise incommensurable qualities."[37]

Just as patriarchal rape culture assumes that all victims are liabilities, the victim commodity thesis assumes that victims who are not "perfect" are liabilities in rape responses. It determines whether someone has raped on the basis of victims' social capacities to engage in sexual relations, not on whether perpetrators have hurt victims.[38] This assumption has serious consequences for marginalized rape victims because it preemptively negates the cultural violence of rape. In her critique of racial progression narratives, for example, Saidiya Hartman powerfully argued that during the colonial era, enslaved Black victims were held to property and theft codes, not under common rape law that protected white victims.[39] Though Hartman's use of property law to expose intersectional violence is reminiscent of the victim commodity thesis, Hartman brought in racial capitalism theory to argue that enslaved Black rape victims did not hold legal power to resist rape; they were preemptively valued as material capital who could partake in any sexual activities regardless of consent, force, or harm based on their enslaved and racialized status. She remarked, "Consent is unseemly in a context in which the very notion of subjectivity is predicated upon the negation of will."[40] Simply put, if the enslaved woman or girl has *no* power to consent under the law, then rape cannot be the theft of positive sexual intercourse; the paradigm of consent is prefiguratively restricted on a racialized basis. Hartman concluded, thus, that any kind of rape-as-theft argument only admits to a narrow version of the violation of rape, whose victims' "only resource was the newly acquired property in the self."[41]

Criticizing the victim commodity thesis, Robin West similarly illustrated that viewing rape as the theft of some universally positive sexual intercourse fails to consider diverse forms of sexual relations, such as those involving at least one party who engages in sexual intercourse for economic security, friendship, or fidelity.[42] Though we might assign a financial value to sex, as in the case of sex work, most sexual relations are not simply about isolated sexual behaviors, even within sex work itself.[43] For example, a single mother may wish to engage in a sexual relationship with a single man for her child to have another hetero-parental figure who can assist in elevating her social status to family and friends. The decision to engage sexually is centered not on the "cost" of sexual relations, nor on whether the single mother can afford such a price (factors that the commodity thesis would consider), but rather on whether the unpartnered mother is perceived to have preemptively fewer cultural assets than an unpartnered man, such as being a mother, single, and with a child in a patriarchal, heteronormative, and sexually active world.[44]

Theorizing victim capitalism through property and theft law illustrates that capitalism can have adverse effects on rape victims, and, accordingly, that rape should be considered a legitimate crime. However, the victim commodity thesis is insufficient to acknowledge the violence of capitalist rape: It reifies the problem of valuing the victim's worth, igniting worn conversations about victims' ability to have consented. As numerous feminist anti-violence scholars illustrate, sex and rape are not zero-sum games. A victim does not simply lose a predetermined amount of sexual capital from rape, nor do they forgo some universally valued cultural capital. Instead, the rape victim themself—as an embodied person with multiple interlocking positionalities—becomes a part of the violation.[45] We must expand our analysis of rape to contemplate the social and institutional forces that incite capitalist violence against victims.

Precarity, Austerity, Disparity

The problem with the victim commodity thesis is that it is incomplete, particularly for marginalized victims whose victimization involves violence other than sexualization.[46] To evaluate the violence of rape across intersectional contexts, I propose that we modify our approach to the capitalist *production* of rape survivors in the neoliberal rape crisis center. Examining production uncovers the striking similarities between the valuation of individual victims and their bodies, as with enslavement, and the valuation of victims in neoliberal anti-rape work, along with its intersectional problems. This shift in focus furthermore allows us to move away from conceptualizing capitalism in rape as an "outdated" relic of enslavement and toward an understanding that colonial white men's capitalistic abuse of enslaved bodies in the present day has merely transformed into contemporary advocates' secondary capitalistic abuse of rape victims seeking support.[47] Our reading departs from white Western limited frameworks of capitalism and affirms the use of a queer/trans of color lens. We examine not *who* is capital, but *how* assets and liabilities are produced and distributed throughout the neoliberal rape crisis center.

This focus on the capitalist production of victims requires that we take inventory of the resources we presently use to support survivors and our distribution of this set of victim capital. In past anti-rape collectives, advocates did not see victims as "clients" to be given material goods but as friends and neighbors who shared their values of abolition. Thus, advocates provided victims with whatever resources they had in a mutual aid network. For example, one of the founders of the DC Rape Crisis Center noted that she opened her "stable" home to fellow survivors who needed it without questioning them.[48] Contemporary advocates adopted similar language to describe their work, vocalizing that the market is "open" for distribution. An advocate explained, "I don't want you to have services that you feel like are not bringing you [to] where you need to be supported."

However, though individual advocates may have expressed "unconditional positive regard" towards victims, they also commented on how their free-market advocacy was limited by funding constraints. Without explicitly naming neoliberalism, advocates pointed out that, far from following a survivor-centered approach, state funders regulate the flow and transfer of victim capital from the public sector to individual agencies, which determine advocates' inventory of victim capital.[49] Funders can direct money to specific aspects of anti-rape work, such as financing medical-forensic exams to amplify the number of medical remedies in the market.[50] They may also place restrictions on the ways that center funds are utilized.[51] In one example, an advocate sighed at the funding conditions placed on the type of shelters available. "This is the thing about putting them in hotels because you know we have to have funding for the hotels? . . . We have to put them in two-star hotels to continue to have the funding. So the demographic of the motels aren't the greatest demographics because we're trying to make a safe place, um, but we also have to keep it within funding." These restrictions are not limited to material resources. Many advocates made a point to say that they were not "qualified" as legitimate professionals to support victims emotionally, holding little formal educational knowledge about victim services. One advocate explained her reasoning: "It's like oh thank you for trying to reach out to me. But I really don't know that much about, I mean I do know about [support], but, I don't like to be in charge of stuff like that because I feel like that's a lot more pressure added to my plate." Some advocates explained that certain victim capital was withheld because they were concerned about "liability." For example, "We give them the necessities like if they need clothes [. . .] We don't give rides but we look for the people who give them because that is a liability for us. Because transportation in the South is just horrendous down here." In this example, the advocate felt that she could not freely distribute victim capital because her supervisor was concerned about being sued by victims and losing a pool of money designated for other victims.

If survivors wanted a service that the rape crisis center was not willing to readily supply, advocates explained that they asked survivors to provide written documentation of their consent. Their request for paperwork was a tangible way of showing that survivors were "informed" that they were accepting help from a service worker outside of the state-sponsored anti-rape market. An advocate explained how consent waivers regarding the transference of victim's information were common at her agency.

> Well, and usually what we do is, um, we have them sign a release form, if they're willing to sign . . . Sometimes law enforcement will call here and ask questions. And we explain that to them. The releases are very specific of what the, um, victim wants us to tell them. We just, we don't tell them everything. We just, if they say, "Has she came in, has she followed up?" "Yes." "Can you tell me what, what you talked about?" . . . We say no, we, we don't have a consent or release to [say] that. And they're only good for thirty days.

These behaviors underscore the most significant change with the neoliberal turn. Though it calls for free markets, the state quietly controls the supply and types of capital in the anti-rape advocacy market.[52]

Restrictions on the amount and types of victim capital clearly reduce the total amount of support provided to victims overall. But these restrictions more often hurt *marginalized* survivors than those conforming to the "perfect victim" stereotype by proportionately exacerbating the percentage of unmet needs by survivors already marginalized in US society. An advocate without a criminal record gave a tangible example of this constraint on incarcerated survivors.

For incarcerated individuals, our ability to offer any services outside of a crisis intervention situation or outside of a hospital is next to nothing. Um, outside of connecting them . . . we can do some advocacy around housing unit[s]. So like, if they were assaulted, right, we can advocate that they be relocated within the jail, and for the most part, that tends . . . that is the extent to which we can . . . [that's the only] service we can provide to folks. Um, obviously once they're, if they're released or once they're released, like then we can provide services as, as any other.

The advocate is mindful about the needs of incarcerated survivors, describing how she could relocate incarcerated survivors within a jail system to reduce the possibility of lethal retribution for reporting rape. But she also exposes the transformation of free-market advocacy into conditional advocacy. Unlike in the past when advocates expressly endorsed prison abolition to support incarcerated survivors, today's advocates do not provide support to people inside prisons in the same way that they support nonincarcerated individuals.

The state-imposed market limitations absolve advocates of their duty to respond to victims of culturally diverse needs. Funders restrict the market, causing advocates to feel a need to compete with one another to show that they will use state-sponsored capital in the most efficient way possible and generate the most profit.[53] The most visible and historically "successful" method through which advocates have shown their effectiveness to the state is the survivor discourse, also called the empowerment model.[54] In this production process, advocates show the state that victims are still worth helping by inflating their value financially.[55] If "victims" are liabilities because they are traumatized and therefore cannot contribute to the US capitalist economy, then "survivors" must be assets because they are empowered people who are stronger after rape, and therefore *more* self-sufficient, *more* capable at working for state interests.[56] Describing the mainstream anti-violence movement, Paige L. Sweet explains, "[Advocates] convinced policy makers that they could respond to the 'crisis of the family' and they made themselves into the experts who could 'treat' victims—who could, in fact, *make victims into trauma survivors*."[57]

Advocates sought to produce "survivors" to convince the state to infuse capital into their specific rape crisis center. They changed "victims" to "survivors" by stressing that victims should empower themselves. As one advocate described, for example, "I empower people to tell their story. When you tell your story the more and more you tell it, you create the narrative."

Advocates' emphasis on empowerment may support victims in their healing journey. However, advocates' production of survivors *because of a fear of financial loss* creates disparities within victim services. In an unstable market, we do not think about advocacy as abolishing all violence in communities. Instead, because we are afraid of losing a funding stream, we attempt to *manage* our supply of capital.[58] Advocates told me of how they reluctantly began to triage victims instead of supporting all of them through whatever means necessary, justifying their decisions by the "limited" market. An advocate with a graduate medical degree described differences in her support of two victims with different cultural wealth.

> [Survivors] deserve empathy, they deserve understanding, they deserve connections to resources. But then you also have to like realize that like everybody is so different and because of the different identities a person has that like, maybe I'm like, too educated you know but like, Maslow's hierarchy of needs, right. You do have your survivors who come in and they are college students who are middle-class and you know they, like, drugged at a party or whatever, and you can kind of talk to them on the level of like, you know, here are some things that you can do to kind of come back from this, your school probably has a counseling center and you should consider going. But then you have people who've been on the streets for years and you know suffering from substance abuse disorders and they don't have, like, shoes. Right? So how are you supposed to do the whole like, flowery you know like, self-positive you know talk when they haven't eaten in like forty-eight hours. At that point, like, I consider my role to then be, like, trying to make their like immediate circumstances more comfortable.

The advocate explains that all survivors "deserve empathy." But she also shows that there is a difference in the degree of care that she can provide to the first victim, a "middle-class" college student, versus an unhoused person "suffering from substance abuse disorders" because she sees her role as the advocate as being to "make their ... immediate circumstances more comfortable." Contrary to previous calls in which advocates believed that they should support victims in whatever ways they feel are appropriate, the advocate inadvertently limits the scope of her advocacy to *just* "talk[ing] to them," addressing only interpersonal violence, and she does not take action to protest *social* inequities, like addressing the lack of affordable housing, when pressured into producing survivors. In turn, the first victim with fewer needs is better supported than the second, who "[hasn't] eaten in like forty-eight hours."

Triaging instead of employing free market strategies is known as "precarity," the intense fear that there is a shortage of capital to provide to victims and that therefore those strategies will create loss.[59] Widespread in capitalist economies, the precarity crisis compels workers to consistently fight one another for limited resources. The *more* capital (be it time, money, or resources) that advocates expend on a victim, the *less* valuable the victim becomes to the advocate and the state; likewise, the *less* capital advocates expend on a victim, the *more* advocates pay attention to them. For example, a survivor wishing to access Plan B will typically use more of an advocate's labor and the victim's own resources than a survivor who does not wish to obtain contraceptives. This constitutes an "extra" service because of ongoing national restrictions on reproductive care that persuade advocates to *not* take social action. One advocate mused, disappointedly, that her center would not directly dispense contraceptive pills to victims and was simply told to tell survivors to travel to their doctor's office for care, despite the fact that many do not carry health insurance. In another, more extreme example, a hotline advocate called attention to the scarcity of victim resources and offset her responsibility to support one of the most marginalized of victims.

> There was one time, where I had somebody who, um was being evicted from their home, and, basically I was walking them through all of these different homeless resources that we had, um, they even would've qualified for victim shelter but basically this person told me that they had burned bridges with all of these different programs, and had bad relationships with all of these different programs for one reason or another. And I was just trying to be really empathetic um, you know because, this person was kind of on their last leg and there wasn't really a lot for them,

um. And that's hard. But, you know I really didn't have anything to give her then, because I would refer her to places that would do rent assistance, homeless shelters, um, even our victim shelter because she really would've qualified but, she didn't wanna stay at any of those places or go through any of those programs because she'd had bad experiences with all of them. And, so I—I went down a-all the list of things that I really had or knew to refer her to. And, she expressed you know it had been a few years since she'd spoke to some of them so I said I—I would try giving them a call back maybe this person that you had an issue with has moved onto a different, you know different place or position. Otherwise there really wasn't much I could do for her, and that's always a tough feeling.

The advocate comments that the restrictions placed on the anti-rape market—the seemingly limited number of shelters to which the survivor could go—led to her inability to support the victim in the ways that she needed. But the secondary harm was not that the survivor could not go to specific shelters. Instead, the harm derives, unintentionally, from the hotline advocate and those at the shelters for refusing to help a survivor with multiple, recurring needs. By relying on the excuse of limited inventory—the myth that a survivor should only need to enter shelter once, even though most victims will take about seven attempts before leaving an abuser—the advocates artificially restricted the scope of their work to simply connecting survivors to existing programs.[60] Any other support (including long-term shelter and the call-out of the advocates for implicit victim blaming) goes beyond the scope of neoliberal advocacy.

The state's control over the anti-rape market spikes austerity, creating disparities within the rape crisis center.[61] One advocate with over a decade of experience commented on the change in affect, "You just go scared, and you just keep it moving." This artificial fear compels advocates to focus on the production of *some* survivors, namely, those who consume the fewest capital, over others. An advocate identifying as white and feminist had this to say about a colleague entrenched in the capitalist mindset.

> What we know is that, if you are, like, the intersectionality of race and resources, whatever those resources are, whether it's financial or familial, or,

um, any type of resources, we know that people are more vulnerable. And we know the system also treats people differently, um, depending on their background, um, how they behave, what they look like. And when I say what they look like, it's not always just color; it's also socioeconomic class. So, um. There was a woman I worked with . . . was a woman of color, but if somebody came in dirty or, um, unkempt, she was less interested in helping them [than] if they were clean, in need people. [. . .] Because they weren't representing well, right? Like, they should care [about their appearance].

The advocate underscores the problem with the production of survivors: conditional funding compels advocates to distinguish between worthy and unworthy victims according to the *normativity* of the survivors' needs. Her colleague was "less interested" in helping survivors who are "unkempt" because she understood that she would need to take more action to support them, to help them to care about their appearance. However, this decision was premised on judgmental ideas about survivors' class, race, and skin color, which goes against the values of anti-rape work: to support all survivors.

An Asian feminist advocate summarized the challenge with the "commercialization" of anti-rape work: "It bothered me too a lot because of the way, um, certain survivors would be kind of elevated? In the fact that like *they* succeeded, they worked hard to overcome all of their burdens. And then like what about the ones who are struggling and they do mess up. They don't have the means to pull themselves up by the bootstraps."

The transformation of advocacy from free-market support to conditional, profit-driven production reduces our capacity to support victims at both the individual and community levels. In the last two decades, many agencies have outsourced advocacy to normative systems, engorging the NPIC. Independent rape crisis centers are frequently absorbed by larger social services agencies affiliated with legal and medical complexes, such as United Way. As of 2009, 74 percent of all rape response agencies "were affiliated with multi-service agencies" compared to just 26 percent free-standing independent rape crisis centers, forcing advocates to rely on resources unsuited for marginalized sexual assault victims.[62] In addition to these institutional transformations, numerous advocates housed at both larger social services agencies and independent rape crisis centers shared that they have begun to offload the responsibility of providing direct victim services onto existing social welfare and health systems. Rather than expend resources at their disposal, hotlines, systems accompaniment, and many related advocacy functions are now performed by nonadvocate criminal legal professionals, creating a cascade of attrition points for survivor help seeking.[63]

The reliance on capital external to the neoliberal rape crisis center has allowed advocates to make up the "cost" of producing survivors, but at the expense of excusing systems-based harms. For example, one advocate who identifies as a straight white Christian-raised woman shared her reasoning for outsourcing help. For her, connecting survivors to therapy is the ultimate form of advocacy, not radical activism against the hegemonic state. Referring to a conversation with a young immigrant Muslim woman living in an intergenerational household, she said,

> I'd had one survivor who was, you know, she was raised Muslim. And so she had a lot of, um, a lot came up for her in terms of purity and the cultural aspect of it. [. . .] I don't think it's that I needed to know more about her culture, um. I've taken, you know, Middle Eastern history classes and stuff in college so I felt comfortable with understanding where she was coming from and the, the thing was more I felt very . . . powerless, I think, is a bit big for the feeling . . . and I don't know how to better fix . . . all of the problems. We can set, set someone up to feel safe. [. . .] I said the follow-up therapy would be really good for you and, you know her reaction of course was like, how do I tell [my parents] I'm going to therapy and you know it's just like, oh man that's a whole other (laughs)—you know like I've, I've been through that battle with my parents of like, being told like no, you should just pray it away and stuff and being like *errr* no I gotta, I gotta go talk to someone, this is, this is not controllable like that.

The advocate shows that she endorses the survivor discourse, and she believes attending therapy is the most efficient way to achieve empowerment. However, while the advocate relates to the survivor's experiences with faith, parents, and therapy, saying that she has "been through that battle with my parents," the advocate nonetheless stresses that "this is not controllable like that." Without meaning to, the advocate minimizes the survivor's fear of Islamophobic therapy, and the advocate later reflected on how she unintentionally pressured the victim, "That was a real moment for me too to look at my own privilege and kind of see that you know I'm, even though you know my parents tend to be maybe not super evangelical but you know religious, that [evangelical approaches to therapy] still has maybe a bit more leeway." Her heavy emphasis on outsourced therapy to attain survivorship, even when misaligned with the victim's cultural needs, dominates over the individual victim's decision.[64]

Advocates increasingly circumvent their responsibility to support all victims by excusing their agency's capitalistic inventory of victim capital or falling back on systems resources to conduct advocacy-related tasks. The issues with the neoliberalization of the anti-rape market are thus twofold. First, the capital provided by advocates to victims may not always be the most culturally relevant for them, as it is determined by state funders or systems professionals and not survivors. In lieu of supporting all victims freely, advocates in a precarious anti-rape market will lean toward helping the most normative of victims because doing so is the most "effective" demonstration of their "success." Second, advocates believe that they have fulfilled their duties to support survivors without taking the steps to address nonsexualized cultural and community-level violence. We become central in the making of disparity when we decide whom we help, especially when we judge victims according to their race, gender, class, and body. As one advocate remarked, "Just because a resource exists doesn't mean that it's gonna work out."

Mask by Multiculturalism

Neoliberal advocacy is racialized, gendered, classed, and embodied. Advocates will more often choose to support those who fit "ideal" representations of rape victims than those who do not because they are afraid of losing agency wealth. Considering the disparity in rape victim support, some advocates have called for the expansion of multicultural victim capital in the anti-rape market. Seeking to combat the disparity in numbers between normative victims and marginalized victims who are served, proponents of multiculturalism suggest that centering culture in support services helps to develop a more meaningful understanding of victimhood apart from "the perfect victim" and foster inclusivity and belonging in otherwise monolithic spaces.[65]

There have been two main ways in which advocates produce multiculturalism in anti-rape advocacy. First, culturally specific organizations primarily support "cultural minority" victims, such as Ujima, the National Center on Violence Against Women in the Black Community. These agencies often emphasize specific cultural capital that can assist marginalized victims, such as hearing aids or interpreters for hard-of-hearing or D/deaf victims, that may not be found at mainstream rape crisis centers.[66] Second, mainstream and culturally specific agencies may organize "cultural competency" trainings (CCTs). CCTs introduce advocates to various social groups such as BIPOC, 2SLGBTQIA+ people, and immigrants. They are aimed at educating advocates on ways of responding to these victims appropriately on the basis of their identities.[67] For example, a training on 2SLGBTQIA+ people might discuss pronouns and the rates of violence against queers.[68] Both culturally specific organizations and CCTs support the idea that one's culture must be central in victim support.[69]

Many advocates supported efforts to organize CCTs at their agencies. For example, a Latina advocate expressed her desire to participate in a training about African American women; "[My prevention education director] didn't have any cultural [trainings]. And I was like okay. Come on. And um right now with the whole #BlackLivesMatter, that—it should be a big factor into it as well, um, because, that, that's a movement that agencies should be behind. . . . I actually went—if you go on YouTube there is a great, great webinar about African Americans. I loved it because it gave you the numbers about how African American women are being abused." The advocate stresses the importance of learning about African American survivors, arguing that a CCT would help her to understand the high prevalence of rape against Black communities. Her position is not unique. In their systematic review of advocacy literature, Annie Wegrzyn and colleagues suggested that "there is a glaring lack of attention to diversity and multiply marginalized survivors," particularly with respect to the disparity in the receipt of advocacy services and the degree to which advocacy is being tailored to specific cultural groups.[70] Many advocates have therefore spent considerable energy discussing ways to improve these trainings, such as proposing reading groups and organizing diversity, equity, and inclusion (DEI) task forces.[71] Numerous anti-violence agencies and coalitions have also attempted to offer cultural competency model templates, for instance, the National Sexual Violence Resource Center's "Cultural Competency" podcasts and the Pennsylvania Coalition to Advance Respect's "Cultural Responsiveness" technical assistance bulletins.[72]

Although multiculturalism may be helpful for some individuals, multiculturalism merely reorganizes the portfolio of victim capital within a rape crisis center without addressing the production of survivors. This negligence, as Angela Davis cautions, ignores how capitalism produces violence.[73] Advocates who are trained to support victims through multiculturalism learn to take stock of their race, gender, or another social identity and provide them with a predetermined form and amount of capital. But this approach merely changes to whom capital should go; it continues to enforce the boundaries of the market imposed by funders rather than resist them. A genderqueer advocate described this problem. In their main training sessions, they were trained to support victims who were presumed to be perfect survivors through criminal legal proceedings. Comparatively, in their CCT, they were trained to acknowledge bias within the criminal legal proceedings but were not taught about how many cultural minorities, particularly trans and gender-nonconforming people, felt about systems.[74] Accordingly, the trainings reinforced normative interpretations of victims and did little to address systemic intersectional violence. They explain,

> I don't know how to explain this but, foundational skills [to advocacy] very much yes [it was helpful]. And then actually talking about like [the population in the rape crisis center's jurisdiction], and like the work we're doing and how it works and how [protection from abuse orders] interact with certain communities and certain folks and which parts of our community really resonate with certain spaces i-it started to turn into the like, regular norm survivor conversation of it's going to be a, twenty-year-old white girl who's going to the cops, that's when it started to mold into this same situation every time opposed to the . . . specifics of our actual like city and space.

The advocate locates the normative victim as a "twenty-year-old white girl who's going to the cops." This production of the survivor is normative, and thus marginalizing, not because the victim self-identified as "white" but rather because the victim, who can be racially white or BIPOC, chose to engage with the criminal legal system in ways that align with white normative expectations of perfect survivors. Even though the trainings described LGBT and BIPOC populations, the advocate points out that the training reverted to the normative "white girl" narrative because the victim is still expected to become a survivor—thus, advocacy even for diverse victims still looks the same when it occurs under neoliberal market conditions.

Multiculturalism also produces a particularly insidious form of invisible violence. Because we are concerned with supporting specifically "underserved" survivors, we narrow our focus to resolving issues within a singular cultural community, isolating marginalized victims from holistic care. Culture becomes bite-sized, consumable pieces instead of survivors' complex social worlds. For example, a Black advocate explained that she was trained to support Asian communities through CCTs but subliminally reinforced white supremacist perspectives about Asian people.

> Asian communities. They're very private. A lot of times they are introverts. They do not—like you know I'm, I'm telling you like you don't [know]. [Interviewer is Asian American.] (laughs) Uh, it's, it's a very private community. They're not gonna talk about their pain, they come across very strong, they don't wanna look as weak. And I talk about it. I talk about—so [my nail tech] . . . and I are really really close. And he's from Cambodia. And, I just talk to him all the time about his experiences and his family's experiences and how, um, you have to listen to your parent—the culture's just different like (laughs).

The advocate importantly recognizes that Asian survivors are underserved. She reads Asian victims as "private" and "com[ing] across very strong," and suggests that Asian victims require strengths-based remedies. However, she also collapses her work to only delivering predetermined "strong" Asian advocacy capital instead of understanding the specific structural violence faced by Asian communities.[75] In doing so, she unintentionally normalizes Asian survivors into another multicultural "perfect victim"—simply swap out the perfect victim's white race for the Asian race.[76]

A multiracial advocate scoffed, "I don't know how useful a training on a race is right? Like . . . Like I really question its utility. For a number of reasons. One, is that reinforcing that populations are monolithic? I think it does. Um like I, I really struggle with that." Because multiculturalism still stresses the production of a perfect survivor, advocates work toward the same outcome: to produce a survivor who consumes little to no capital and can return to work for the US state. We might allocate some funding for cultural minority victim capital like burning sage or T-visa assistance because we recognize the importance of culture in care, but cultural minority victim capital remains the least effective method of turning victims into survivors in the rape crisis center's overall capital portfolio. Multicultural capitalism thus repeats the problem with the victim commodity thesis. While we might speak about the disparity in rape victim services, we do not attend to the ways that marginalized survivors have fewer cultural assets than "perfect" survivors because of the normative rape crisis center market and broader US society. In turn, victims who are already marginalized are less likely to receive culturally relevant aid, marginalizing the marginal even further.

Recognizing where capitalism emerges in our work is urgently needed. Our fear of market supply and our subsequent endorsement of multiculturalism have restricted the scope of advocacy to fighting for scraps of diversity. About half of the advocates interviewed for this study reported that they did not have CCTs at their agencies, sharing that their directors either did not see the point of the trainings or used the excuse of labor shortages to avoid organizing them. An advocate coordinator explained her reasoning: "I want to include as much as possible [in a training] and, I know like we're, we run out of time, you know such that like I give people additional reading assignments and watch this video and, um. If [the prison advocate coordinator] were left to his own devices, the training that he does would be four hours long."

The other half of the interviewed advocates reported that while they underwent CCTs, most of their trainings did not prepare them to support minority victims. Local agencies were often ill equipped to discuss subjects like intersectionality or spent too few resources to make the trainings truly effective. For example, an advocate with disabilities felt that the CCTs at his agency were largely "superficial." He said,

> Like, the training... was really like a, PDF that had a paragraph about different identities. It had a lot of military survivors, it had a lot on college students, some teen survivors, um. And I think one or two other demographics but it really didn't cover immigrants, it didn't cover people of color, it didn't cover LGBT, they didn't cover like, elderly survivors that, male survivors you know like there was like, so much and there's been a long—I just did like a quick refresher course with [a neighboring rape crisis center] so I can't like, [the first time I was trained] has been a long time, but I feel like everything was kind of superficially covered.

When CCTs were routed through anti-rape state coalitions or national organizations, like the Office for Victims of Crime's Victim Assistance Training (VAT), many advocates, including those with experience working at state coalitions or federal agencies, criticized how they were not localized to service areas. An Indigenous federal victim specialist decried, "You can't just throw a book at 'em and say, hey, BIPOC, if you came in[to contact with] a BIPOC person you gotta behave this way, I mean it's gonna have to be culturally specific to the, to the jurisdiction that they're serving." The problem, according to her, was that "you're generalizing communities."

A white advocate acknowledged that there were no written guidelines at her local agency on addressing victims experiencing intersectional sexual and racial violence due to an overreliance on state guidelines and outsourcing of labor to cultural organizations that do not address gender-based issues. The absence of localized guidelines caused her to feel unprepared for non–English-speaking immigrant victims in a predominantly white area, which, she speculated, caused a downturn in the number of immigrant survivors seeking services from her rape crisis center. Her perspective echoed that of other advocates who called out coalition-led CCTs for enforcing xenophobic, racist, and colonial stereotypes. A white advocate shared one harrowing experience at a CCT intended to review diversity and discrimination policies, hosted by the state coalition.

> The, uh, diversity um, training that [the state coalition] recently put on, right, the summit, there was a director from [a neighboring city]... Literally got on and said I, I don't know how to say this to a facilitator who

identified as Indigenous, um, you're just so beautiful I would say that you're Pocahontas. [. . .] It's that kind of stuff, and if you're the leader of that organization what are your supervisees saying and doing, they're covering [multiple] counties in [this state]. Like . . . *whaaat*? [. . .] Um so, it's those kinds of little nuances—appearing to be nuanced things that are *detrimental* to community partnerships and to conversations.

A white advocate in the conservative Deep South similarly reported that her agency refused to organize CCTs, preferring instead to substitute them with VAT. But as the advocate shared,

> I think that there is . . . almost a performance of diversity in those trainings where it's clear they've thought through, well, not everyone we show in this training can be like white, right? And so there's some like racial diversity, some like age diversity, definitely no faith-based diversity. And so it's clear they thought through some of these, right, and—but there's still like this element of—it doesn't feel like with real world kind of, it feels like . . . a bunch of white people sat in a room and were like how do we make this diverse, right. I-it feels like that, it feels sort of performative and this like, well we gotta have Ricky in there.

The lack of critical CCTs has real consequences for marginalized survivors. Sounding the alarm, the aforementioned advocate expressed deep concern about the fact that her agency had seen no Black clients in months, even though they are located in a predominantly white and Black mixed service area.

Altogether, advocates collectively pooled areas that are understudied by individual rape crisis centers. Table 2.1 describes the identities that were most often discussed in either general advocacy trainings or CCTs, as well as ones that were briefly discussed or not discussed at all. Advocacy trainers should take heed of these areas, with the caveat that advocates in this study only empirically observed, and did not systematically analyze, these identities in (or not in) their trainings. For further context, trainers may wish to reference Bromley et al.'s literature review of organizational and interpersonal risk and resilience factors experienced by advocates.[77] Further, there is a high variability in the degree to which these identities were "taught" to advocates. Some trainings effectively addressed advocates' personal biases toward specific identities and localized the ways certain people were marginalized in their service areas, while others only superficially described statistics or general concerns with minority communities without attending to local variations.

TABLE 2.1. Training by Cultural Identities

Training	Identities
High Discussion: More than Ten Agencies Offered This Identity-Specific Training	Low Income
	Acquaintance or Family-Related Rape
	Unhoused
	Prison
	College and K-12 Schools, Title IX
	Race/Ethnicity
	Immigrant
	Low or No English Proficiency
	Rural
	Parental Status / Number of Dependents
	Alcohol-Related Rape
	Christian Faith
	Age
Low Discussion: Three to Ten Agencies Offered This Identity-Specific Training	2SLGBTQIA+
	STI, HIV/AIDS
	Disability
	Tribal Citizens or Descendants
	Non-Christian Faith
	Ex-Abusers
No Discussion: Zero to Two Agencies Offered This Identity-Specific Training	Out-of-State or Transient Non-Resident of Agency's Service Area
	Pregnant Before Rape or Because of Rape
	Education/Literacy Level
	With Criminal or Arrest Record
	Regular Substance Users
	Sex Workers
	Wealthy/High Income/High Socioeconomic Class
	High Social Class Occupation (e.g., medical professional, business, security)
	Other Advocates
	Political Affiliation

CCTs may offer a necessary baseline for advocates with dominant identities who are unfamiliar with certain marginalized populations. For example, one white advocate found her agency's CCT helpful: "Now they're saying it's officially politically correct to say people of color, but not colored people, you know?" CCTs might even serve as a "refresher" for advocates who have worked in the field for a long time. As one advocate said, "Training helps refresh you sometimes... because I trained a long time ago." Nevertheless, multiculturalism actively espouses diversity as it negates our capacities for intersectional social change. We focus on improving aspects of multicultural training, like extending the duration of trainings, adding more to trainings, and offering more pamphlets and infographics about rape against marginalized folx. But as this advocate pointed out, "You can't teach, like, thorough crisis intervention skills, and cultural humility, and the history of the feminist movement and like, heh! How to be an advocate, like you cannot teach that in forty hours. And, also expose someone to all the resources that they're gonna need to know... in that time." Indeed, the problems with cultural capitalism in anti-rape advocacy are exacerbated with multiculturalism. Rape crisis centers understand the need to inventory multiple types of victim capital for ease of distribution and therefore encourage their advocates to rely on a "resource book" or "resource binder." These guides typically include a list of phone numbers to local social services, such as police stations, public health centers, local housing organizations, and pro bono lawyers, but offer little other information that might be helpful for survivors or the advocates supporting them, like whether the organization can support specific individuals experiencing intersectional violence. The binders also imply that advocates' work could be helpful for marginalized victims if they only give a phone number or email address to the victim. For one advocate, "I kind of envision myself well, in one hand I have a binder of resources and people we can reach out to and my other hand is, you know, holding the hand of the survivor, literally the decisions the survivor makes I'm gonna support, I'm gonna help you and be there for you. That's kind of how I view advocacy, overall." Advocacy is rendered interpersonal social services, no longer abolitionist social change.

Equally as problematic, though resource booklets might contain specific systems professionals' phone numbers, they may also inadvertently drag systems professionals into victims' cases without adequately preparing systems professionals for the work required to support marginalized survivors. One advocate explained that espousing multiculturalism without addressing the survivor discourse actually exaggerated systems-based secondary violence: "I mean you take the, take the uh environment right now where everybody's like #DefundthePolice. [...] Cultural humility training's not useful because you've got this other issue that somebody needs to step up and do. We can give all the training in the world, but if you don't give them the resources to see it through, then it's just more work. And, that's, you know that's overwhelming for law enforcement and then you get, you know, you get cops that are ... (smiles) pissed off all the time." Redirecting capital to support marginalized victims without addressing market conditions only overburdens advocates while encouraging law enforcement to blame marginalized victims for expending limited resources on them without turning a profit.

In their analysis of ethnoracial solidarity capitalism, Jody Agius Villejo and Stephanie L. Canizales summarize the problem with multiculturalism: "The sole presence of ethnic financial institutions in minoritized communities does not remedy economic inequalities."[78] Likewise, the sole introduction of diverse cultural capital does not change the neoliberal capitalist framework of the rape crisis center. Much like the victim commodity thesis that devalues queer/ed people of color, the multicultural capitalist framework devalues cultural minority victims who are in need. We have, in essence, recycled the narrative that victims must make themselves financially worthy of aid, "consenting" to the discord of neoliberalism even as we sing for diversity in our homes. We do not fight for dismantling the capitalist system, and we are left with only liberal, not radical, strategies for change. Through the valuation of victims in a precarity crisis, we are forced to ask ourselves whether it is worth it to help someone out—or, more honestly, whom it is okay to rape.

Excess Others

Expulsion of marginalized victims from care no longer occurs through clearly delineated "black" versus "white" narratives, as in earlier centuries. Instead, rather than define oppression through skin color, place of origin, sexual orientation, and other identity-based labels, this othering in today's neoliberal rape crisis center is invisible.[79] "Perfect" survivors are not necessarily, though they are nearly almost always, white, heterosexual, and cisgender female US citizens who speak English precisely because they do not have to ask for "extra" services outside of what we currently offer in a restricted market to achieve empowerment. It is not their professed identity that causes valuation; it is their absence of need *in a precarious market* that we judge. "Othered" victims become liabilities on the basis of their legitimate need for radical advocacy. If they ask for "more"—what they truly need to become empowered—they are cast aside as "excess" Others who have asked too much of our limited inventory.[80]

This is discrimination of another kind. While we do not outright banish marginalized victims from the rape crisis center, advocates come to perceive victims as excess on the basis of how much time and resources we expend to help them. Gradually, advocates begin to think about these othered victims not as the "typical" survivor that they expect to produce but as "extra" survivors for whom they have exhausted resources. We tell ourselves that they have not turned into survivors because we have limited resources and not because we force victims who may not wish to turn into normative survivors for the capitalist rape crisis center. Mary V. Wrenn explains this social ontology of fear under neoliberalism: "System justification means that individuals support and advocate for the continuance of a system regardless of its empirical efficacy and oppose any social change. This dogmatic support of a system is more the result of a feeling of a loss of personal control rather than a response to existential anxiety."[81] We justify our self-imposed restrictions on victim capital distribution, alienating marginalized victims, because we are afraid of the consequences if we choose to do more than we have been told we can.

A hearing advocate framed D/deaf victims as excess, demonstrating the limits of neoliberal advocacy.

> I've only worked with two, um, Deaf people, um. The first one was able to read lips, but we had an interpreter anyway just to make sure. That one was a little bit harder, um, because the person like, I had to, like just the person had to use their eyes to, to hear basically. So it was kind of difficult, um, I've never had anybody really intently stare at my lips while

I talk. So making sure that I was trying to go a little bit slower and not fast, not you know, not rush through it and don't mumble, um. And, like [look] at them while I'm talking, that was a little bit harder because I don't necessarily like, make eye contact a hundred percent of the time. The person that we had to have the sign language interpreter, um. That one was a little bit easier because when I was talking I could look at the person, um. But, they were looking at the interpreter while I was talking, it was just, you know. I-it took a little bit of extra time and little bit of getting used to, um. And I don't do a lot of touching.

The advocate acknowledges that supporting D/deaf survivors "took a little bit of extra time and little bit of getting used to" because she has "only worked with two . . . Deaf people." The low rate of marginalized survivors such as D/deaf survivors accessing advocacy is itself a cause for alarm; it signals that D/deaf survivors do not feel welcomed at rape crisis centers. But it is also important to identify that the advocate positions hearing people as the norm and adapts D/deaf people around hearing. She feels that supporting a survivor with a sign language interpreter was "easier" than the situation in which she had to "go a little bit slower." The distinction illustrates that the advocate sees D/deaf support, such as talking more slowly and deliberately making eye contact, as an othered type of support in which she must execute "more" labor.

Like D/deaf survivors, survivors of color are also subjected to notions that their support requires "extra" effort on advocates' parts. Numerous white advocates explained that supporting survivors of color required "additional" work to show them that their advocacy is not "white saviorism." One white advocate explained her support of Black victims.

The people that I feel like I serve the least or I don't serve the best are [Black people]. Which those are . . . in my experience the ones with, I interact with the most actually, um, for clients . . . The fact that I am white and they are Black in this situation, heh, um . . . (exhales) I, I always straddle the line of being like you know am I being, I always wanna comfort and I mean I'm very—and like of course I ask p-permission and stuff like that, like do you want me to be close to you, do you want me to touch you etcetera. And I know that I know that culturally sometimes we're like really different in those things? [. . .]

> I also spend a lot of time explaining to Black clients like you don't have to impress me. Like you don't have to, you don't have to say yes to something because you think that I'm going to react negatively to it or say no to something and think that I'm gonna feel rejected, um. Like, I'm going to give you that, what I hope is the same level of care is for somebody that looks like me. Um. But I do I feel like I'm, I feel like I'm constantly doing this dance of being like you know, am I being too overbearing in this situation and I'm not giving enough attention, you know.

The advocate explains that she is "constantly doing this dance of being . . . overbearing" versus "not giving enough attention." This dance is the advocate's awareness that normative advocacy is too often white, which at once strengthens the image of advocacy as white and casts aside Black advocacy, *even though*, as the advocate notes, she most often supports Black survivors. The advocate's narrative also illustrates that the advocate does not wish to impose her views on the survivor, particularly if Black survivors have historically experienced negative reactions by white people and people in positions of authority, especially in care-based institutions. She is motivated by morally sound justifications to reduce white supremacy. Yet she nonetheless reifies the idea of a support service that is "excess" to mainstream advocacy, such as saying that she "[explains] to Black clients like you don't have to impress me."

Though advocates may wish to practice inclusive care, many still premise their work on normative cultural capitalist values. We place artificial limits on our advocacy for marginalized survivors because of precarity. We distance "cultural" advocacy from normative advocacy and unintentionally render marginalized cultures and services as "extra" costly, and we come to see cultural services as outside the parameters of our work. This reading of culture has consequences for both victims and our role as advocates: "Is it helping in the sense that it's like nobody is really benefiting after they leave? Um, or alternatively me being there, um, I'm actually hurting people—well I'm part of that process, you know? Talking about marginalized groups and stuff like that, I'm doing it with the best intentions but intentions don't really matter, you know, if people are still being hurt. And maybe they don't know how to tell people and maybe they, maybe they lack the language or they're *scared* to tell the only group that is helping them."

Certainly, to play devil's advocate for a moment, able-bodied, white, and otherwise normative survivors may not need sign language interpretation or a caveat about not impressing the advocate. One white advocate described her experiences with a normative victim, for example: "Well educated, great job. Caucasian, you know. Someone that society doesn't preach is going to be assaulted . . . She just didn't need the same level of . . . information, resources—not that they weren't provided but she either wasn't there yet with you know wanting to accept them or wasn't interested." However, as the advocate explained to an advocate-in-training, the problem is that capitalist logics position advocacy as *only* for normative survivors and expels culturally specific advocacy from being considered helpful. If we do not actively present diverse options to survivors at the outset—for example, showing even normative victims that we could assist with restorative mediation or queer therapy—because we fear losing capital, then we are ultimately reinforcing the perfect victim myth to the very people who seek our help. All survivors should be made aware of where we stand as advocates and what we can do to help, regardless of whether those avenues are taken by victims. Otherwise, our actions segregate advocacy tactics on the basis of market conditions, dividing victims according to their perceived value to the dominant social order.

The production of perfect survivors shows us that capitalist advocacy is as transactional and normalizing an act as the literal exchange of enslaved bodies. We weigh the extent to which our labor and resources will "help" individual rape victims to no longer seek additional resources and become "survivors" rather than offer capital that allows survivors to live as they are, freely, in liberation. Our delivery of "services" as opposed to radical activism creates a fictitious hierarchy of rape victim needs. At the top of the hierarchy are the services that do not require substantive time and energy to deliver, usually those that borrow from medical-carceral services.[82] Therapy, medical-forensic exams, and counseling are judged as fair exchanges to end rape despite the fact that they financially cost millions every year because we can outsource this victim capital to systems to "save us" money in the long run. We assume that victims who seek justice through psychotherapy and the criminal legal system will achieve survivorship more quickly than others and in turn, we assume a new neoliberal perfect survivor based on their consumption.[83] At the bottom of the hierarchy are the services that demand "excess" victim capital to adequately stop violence for victims with complex and marginal needs. Commonly, radical abolitionist strategies like social protests and movements are the first to be cut, along with services for victims marginalized by the broader US culture, including transportation for rural or transient victims, translation services for victims with limited English-speaking skills, and gender-affirming attire for trans victims. One advocate connected the loss of rural services in an agricultural area, and thus the loss of many Hispanic clients, to the precarity crisis. She explained that this service allowed her rape crisis center to reach otherwise too transient populations and bemoaned, "Unfortunately we just lost funding for that position, like right now it doesn't feel like that big of a deal since it's COVID but once, once we can be back to normal again it is, we're gonna have to figure out something 'cause we can't just, [it] grew to be a really important, really important position that would be just a shame to lose." Despite its importance, rural advocacy was the first to be cut in a precarity crisis, under the justification that we cannot afford to have diversity during financial downturns.

Neoliberalism has splintered advocacy between the normative and culturally specific. Moreover, state-driven market conditions have made us believe that culturally diverse anti-rape advocacy is un- or less important during a period of austerity. We disburse our available capital in limited quantities to the people whom we are supposed to help, choosing to focus on those victims who allow us to expend the least number of resources. Over time, we simply deliver state welfare victim services; we become subservient to the abusive (multi)cultural capitalist state.

Advocacy in Relation

Instead of investing in free-market advocacy, advocates in the neoliberal rape crisis center invest in the precarious state-run market and turn away victims without high production value. Ironically, our attempt to rectify our lack of resources has only sustained the lifeblood of precarity. We think about how we use our increasingly depleting resources to the best of our ability all while worrying about when those resources will eventually dry up. We *don't* think about how each victim has unique and complex needs or how we might expand our market options beyond the state's money. We lose sight of the radical potentiality of advocacy that can make real social change because we have chosen to comply with the rules of capitalism.

We need to re-create radical advocacy to return to our original agenda to abolish rape. But how might we challenge such a normative sociocultural economic system? Our work is tempered by the very real needs of victims.[84] Furthermore, agency assets cannot be regulated by the state because the neoliberal institution will always take precedence over survivors.[85] To return to radicalism, we must undo capitalism within the rape crisis center. As Angela Davis wrote, "If . . . the incentives for rape are not a natural product of male anatomy or psychology, but are rather social in nature, the prospects for eradicating sexual violence will depend on changes of an entirely different order."[86] That other order demands that we think creatively and in the long term, beyond immediate-gratification funding from the state. Rethinking the production of *advocacy* gives us permission to finally abandon questions of which capital—which *victim*—is worthy of help.

Our first step is to slow down and breathe through the precarity crisis. The precarity crisis was and continues to be fabricated by the state. Advocates of earlier centuries supported survivors without a capitalist oversight body.[87] We should recognize that there are many ways to mobilize resources outside of the state's capital inventory, slowing down our panic at the precarity crisis to think carefully. As a Black feminist advocate said, "When you see an ambulance hold your breath. (deep sharp inhale) How much of an emergency now do you realize that ambulance is, hold your breath. It's an emergency." Another advocate sighed, releasing the stress of precarity, "Sometimes I'm not even hearing what they're saying, and I have to slow myself and remind myself that I'm not in the business of just, throwing resources at them and going through the motions, that I need to actually hear their story and support them the best that, that I can and by what they need."

Our second step is to reenvision the anti-rape market. Capitalism anchors itself on the positive affects of production.[88] That is, we might feel that we are "doing good" by connecting victims to *any* resource. However, this happy affect of doing neoliberal advocacy scaffolds who we support. Rather than critically inspect the kinds of victim capital that we deliver, we sanctify advocacy to ease the pain of systemic violence in our communities. We need to reframe our work as activism that challenges intersectional violence, and we do that by accepting how we feel about the restricted neoliberal market. An advocate describes her troubled feelings at denying support for an unhoused survivor, accompanying us back onto the path toward abolition.

> INTERVIEWEE: This guy on Saturday I like, I was so worried and it broke my heart because like his mom wasn't gonna pay for this motel and I was like, I've never cried during a case. I haven't cried after a case, like I'm very good at like, keepin' it together, um. And at some point it was like hour seven heh, and . . . my heart was just like breaking and I called like [the rape response coordinator] and I was like can I pay for a hotel for him—like he asked me he said I have nineteen dollars, do you think that would be enough? And I'm like, I wasn't allowed to because I would you know what if I personally pay for this hotel you know like? (laughs) And I know it's not something that you can do for everyone and I know that . . .
> INTERVIEWER: So can I ask then why is it crossing a boundary?
> INTERVIEWEE: Why *is* it crossing a boundary to pay for a hotel for the person? You know, it's funny because that's something I've been asking myself.

The boundary is the edge of the neoliberal anti-rape market. Just one step outside of it can illuminate the many options that suddenly become available through mutual aid. *Mutual aid*, a political activity in which community members take care of each other, is a leap of faith into trusting our families, neighbors, friends, and strangers to take the right action.[89] Our goal becomes not to stockpile cultural minority assets at the rape crisis center in fear and defensiveness. Instead, with honest feelings of trepidation and hope, we connect with each other to create abolitionism. This is an advocacy in relation: an advocacy made by our communities, driven by our desires for a world without violence.[90]

Our disturbed affects of guilt and shame propel us toward consciousness raising.[91] Advocacy is, and has always been, "an arsenal of tools, which all have to do with different kinds of interpersonal skills." If we are to extinguish the normative rape culture we live in, we need to trust that we can always relate with each other to address a common problem. Surviving the long battle of capitalist oppression, we move toward a "continuum of prevention." Advocates intervene in the three areas of outreach, prevention, and intervention, and while advocates increasingly "silo" them from one another,[92] the three should function as a well-oiled wheel, where outreach leads to increased prevention of violence, which then decreases the need for crisis intervention.

Referrals are an effective method of creating this wheel. Because, as an advocate put it, "nobody expects someone to know everything," a "collaborative network" will alleviate the pressures on advocates to know everything about all cultures, asking our community members to step in when we, too, as advocates, need support—whether we are in immediate crisis conducting "tertiary prevention" or otherwise. These relations consist not only of medical-carceral systems and schools but also of cultural community centers and "cultural brokers," churches and faith-based organizations, barber shops and hair salons, laundromats, libraries, and recreation centers. Moreover, as another advocate explained about racial relations between herself and victims of color, "I try to be really sensitive but I never know what's gonna, um, hurt someone or make them feel uncomfortable." CCTs cannot address victim support beyond the individual because culture is unquantifiable. Comparatively, culturally informed referrals inherently tap into an existing network of coconspirators and allies who will help us to end rape, uplifting whole communities.[93]

A tribal advocate described how advocates' relations with communities build cultural wealth, and thus support individual victims.

> It just takes time and you have to constantly be willing to meet people. Like the other day, we did human trafficking, and it was COVID, so it was like, okay, how do we do outreach? So we just made a banner and um took the blue [human trafficking] campaign, um, little, uh . . . key chains, and then we did a little crystal that was blue, and we just kind of took that around to the different tribal complexes and took pictures. And so the more that we're doing things like that, the more that people are seeing, oh, they're trying to really do some things for that program. [. . .] I mean, that's said in a very, like, resource-heavy kind of way, but it is true that you are building trust from small acts of, of kindness, essentially. And then obviously, I think it, it comes back to the clients too. When the clients

say oh well I met [this person] or I met these girls. I went up there and they, they're really, they really got it going on. They really treated me with respect. I'm going to refer my sister there, or, you know? I think word of mouth is a huge . . . because if you're treated decent with respect and um, given empathy and you get your needs met, then, word of mouth is going to spread like wildfire, and I think we're starting to see that.

Another advocate connected the agenda of advocacy to eliminate rape with community resource mobilization.

> I don't get [to] judge who is a victim of violence or not. Violence is violence and violence shouldn't happen. If we're an anti-violence project we don't get to pick and choose who's a victim and who's a perp, I mean, violence is violence is violence is violence. [. . .] The phobias that drive and compel this power and control dynamic that, you know, there's a scarcity of resources, I can't let you have any of my resources so I'm gonna use this form of bullying essentially, to remind you where you stand. Right, I'm gonna yell at you, I'm gonna make you less than, blahblahblahblahblah. And we can go on for rape culture for days but, you know, and that's where if we can connect those two, like, -isms and this idea that, there's not enough to go around, right, that power and control is this, I'm wealthy I have access to resources, essentially is one way it's been defined by accessibility to resources, I'm gonna take your accessibility away because you're not worthy of that. Well quite frankly you can fuck off because who are you to decide!

These community-advocate relationships are not exploitative or exchanged. Referrals must be made without basing relationships in fear of funding loss. As one advocate remarked, a "bad referral" can "fuck up" relationships between the anti-rape agency and the community, leading to fewer survivors seeking support from rape crisis centers. Caution is especially critical for marginalized survivors and their communities. Another advocate noted, "For all our programs . . . they're understaffed, but also our culturally specific programs tend to be more understaffed." We cannot simply outsource our outreach; instead, we need to "go into their homes" and earn the trust of our people. These actions are not "us having a thousand different phone numbers" because that is "overwhelming." They are meaningful relationships, in the trust that we will help each other when we need support. As this advocate explained, her relationships with farming communities are simply being in community with one another without thinking about who is most or least valuable in a precarious market.

> It makes total sense for us to, to work with um [this culturally specific organization] which is the organization that works on behalf of farm, farm-labor justice, farm-worker justice, agricultural, heh, work. And, but the idea is that it was, like, we should, we should like go there without any intention of like getting anything you know back from them like let's just go to their, and be supportive at their, at their rallies and you know and the work that they're doing and like, heh, just build relationships and like not expect like oh this is, this is a good time for us to like, um, hand out brochures or something like that, uh, but yeah, get involved in a way that is not necessarily expecting anybody else to give anything else back to us or that we should be you know allowed to take up space but like we're going to like support your work because, your success you know, like the success of, of other agencies like that are going to increase safety for survivors ultimately.

These networks are already in place, awaiting our arrival. An advocate astutely noted, "Everybody has their own support built in already, it's already there. *We* are just now aware of it! Hello?! . . . How are we in the dark about knowing that?" With patience in the collective, ongoing struggle, we can come into the recognition of whom to contact, why we contact them, and for what resources. A queer advocate explained her gradual coming into advocacy in relation.

> I think, there are ways of maybe, like, okay, like certain populations . . . Certain cultures are more communitarian than others. Like what does that look like in the context of, I don't know, like, intrafamilial violence? Like what are some things . . . that's in cul—within cultures that tend to be a bit more like valuing a family unit and less individualistic, how do you then provide service when there's intrafamilial dynamics? Or in small immigrant communities, everyone knows everybody, right, like what are

some common things without [. . .] How do we understand and situate historical trauma within our own models of care?

Instead of squabbling over the perfect victim capital or hoarding some minority capital over others, we find ourselves rich with the resources of each other and our lived cultural capital. Understanding the process of community building fulfills an aim of CCT, why we began organizing such trainings in the first place: "The most important parts of training [are] . . . information about *why* we're doing what we're doing. They need to know *how*."

Relationships with each other restore radical advocacy for the long fight against rape culture. Our anger at the injustices of the market opens our eyes to parallel though distinct movements, empowering us with community. Community wealth dismantles the capitalist framework of the state in anti-rape work and, together, moves us into abolitionist victim advocacy.

3

A Hierarchy of Advocacy

White Professional Cooptation of the Rape Crisis Center

In Morrison's telling, the board unlawfully fired Chikoti-Bandua largely because she had not "deescalated" a range of conflicts with people who worked with and for [the coalition]—especially the fight with OCVA [the Office of Crime Victims Advocacy], without whose funding [the coalition] couldn't operate. The conflicts Morrison cited as examples all involved Chikoti-Bandua's allegations of anti-Black racism: clashes in which she refused to back down, to smooth things over, to let go of words or actions she believed were discriminatory. . . . "We did not think that there was real leadership, what we would have expected an executive director to do, to deescalate situations," Morrison says.
To Morrison, these amounted to "performance" issues; to Chikoti-Bandua, they are racial ones. "All of their responses, and the way that they behaved, was like, 'Could you just stop bringing these things up,'" she says. "What they wanted was for me to behave, basically, as a white [executive director]. What was evident in that whole process was that I was discarded."
—Madison Pauly, "How the Mainstream Movement Against Gender-Based Violence Fails Black Workers and Survivors"

Valériana Chikoti-Bandua Estes, a longstanding advocate for survivors of violence, lounges in her room as we talk about her experiences over Zoom. Her hair is wrapped back in braids and lies gently on her colorfully patterned blouse. Valériana is a proud Black and immigrant woman and a former refugee from the Indigenous Ovimbundu tribe in the Republic of Angola. She is also the former co–executive director of the Washington Coalition of Sexual Assault Programs (WCSAP, pronounced "wick-sap"), one of fifty-two state coalitions against sexual assault in the United States. Valériana and I became acquainted in the summer of 2022 after I had read about her experiences with WCSAP in an article written by white journalist Madison Pauly.[1] In the article, Valériana's struggles with anti-Blackness in WCSAP are made visible, situated in stark contrast to WCSAP's external façade as a revolutionary organization.[2]

Like any other state coalition, WCSAP offers technical support for local advocacy agencies that support survivors, and it manages state-level resources like grants, publications, and medical-welfare assistance for advocates and survivors alike. WCSAP once prided itself on racial equity, consistently publishing reports and posting on social media about the ways that institutions like corporate workplaces, schools, and immigration systems structure the lived experiences of marginalized survivors. From an outsider's perspective, WCSAP could have been considered one of the most successful of the state coalitions that have effectively tackled numerous interlocking social injustices. The organization organized keynotes on the Missing and Murdered Indigenous Women, Girls, and Two-Spirit movement, designed workshops about working with disabled and neurodivergent survivors, and even translated many of its publications into Spanish for the transient Hispanic community across the state. Yet, Valériana tells me, despite the visible performative diversity efforts made by WCSAP for the community, WCSAP has an internal historical pattern of anti-Black violence. Though WCSAP might claim to be diverse, white and some nonwhite members of the WCSAP community have, through their workplace norms, actively engaged in the oppression of Black advocates, Black leadership, Black people, and similarly situated marginalized advocates.

WCSAP unlawfully terminated Valériana on March 24, 2020, a few days after the shutdowns and a few days before the Black Lives Matter movement reentered the public scene with the lynching of George Floyd. The agency also demanded that she sign a nondisclosure agreement to prevent her and other people from historically exploited communities involved in the movement from sharing their stories. Valériana tells me that the decision to unlawfully "terminate" her was wholly unjustified and illegal, premised on an anti-Black agenda. Just the year prior, Valériana had received her green card after a lifelong struggle of navigating a series of immigration statuses: from the time she was born into this world and classified as a refugee to the time when she moved to the United States as an international student, from briefly relying on an H1b work visa to serving as a United Nations diplomat. In 2016, Valériana took it upon herself to research and begin the process of self-petitioning for a green card through the EB2-National Interest Waiver visa process, otherwise known as the "Einstein" visa. It is by far one of the toughest visas to qualify for, as it is only awarded to professionals who have an advanced degree with qualifications, credentials, and contributions that are nationally recognized and are viewed as having talents that are exceptional and beneficial to the United States. Valériana successfully obtained her green card in 2019, recognized as a distinguished professional who could make substantial nationwide social change.

Valériana's success, however, was quickly met with hard deterrence. WCSAP embodied a working environment that favored white supremacy and colonial and racist logics to argue that she was "unprofessional" for speaking out about anti-Black injustices. Despite that Valériana had over ten years of community-organizing experience and a freshly minted "Einstein" pass, WCSAP's board, funders, and sister organizations interrogated the ways that she spoke up in meetings to hold white funders accountable for their exploitation of marginalized communities. Mary Ellen Stone, the white then–executive director of the King County Sexual Assault Resource Center, went so far as to lead a coalition of executive directors to question the validity of Valériana's mere presence and leadership in the movement. Stone contacted OCVA, WCSAP's primary funder, to complain about Valériana's leadership. Valeriana describes the situation in her own words:

> I learned very quickly that the movement to end gender-based violence was actually very violent towards the presence of Black-led leadership, as none of the white executive directors even took a bold stance to interrupt Mary Ellen's anti-Black behavior. While there were instances upon instances when I felt undermined, this all came to a head when I was publicly punished and made an example of in 2020 a few days before the pandemic, when Patrick Morrison (former board treasurer), Michelle Woo (former board president), and Kyra Laughlin (former WCSAP board member) abruptly appeared at the WCSAP office to demonstrate their white supremacist authority and discard me in such a violent way.

All while Michelle Woo, who had refused to believe my experiences of anti-Blackness, led the short-lived charge of becoming WCSAP's board president and marching into WCSAP's office unannounced. Michelle Woo's behavior was cold, alarming, as my former staff members witnessed her reveling in watching me have a real-time panic attack. Michelle Woo went as far as to tell me in front of my staff members that I would need to find a new job, and enjoyed belittling me.

In comparison to Valériana's experience, white co–executive director Michelle Dixon-Wall filed a formal grievance against Valériana's leadership and was never questioned about her qualifications, nor did WCSAP ever hold her accountable. Because Valériana and Dixon-Wall were hired as codirectors, Dixon-Wall's decisions directly impacted Valériana's eligibility to serve in a leadership role. While Valériana had encouraged the movement, and specifically her non-Black staff, to examine their role in interrupting anti-Black oppression in the workplace, Dixon-Wall falsely claimed to WCSAP's board that Valériana did not know how to manage the finances of a large anti-violence nonprofit and did not connect with community partners and funders as readily as they expected, despite that Dixon-Wall had appointed herself as the financial point person. She furthermore actively used her personal friendships and connections with OCVA and the National Sexual Assault Coalition Resource Sharing Project to engage in white supremacist tendencies that emboldened Dixon-Wall to resign initially but reemerge as a leader within WCSAP from 2020 to 2022. Valériana would even later learn that one of the white board members wanted to pay Dixon-Wall a higher salary than hers, and a white staff member sneered that she was a mere "diversity hire." Board member Patrick Morrison, on behalf of WCSAP, suggested to Valériana that the decision to fire and replace her with Dixon-Wall was based on "performance" issues—but she knows it was anti-Black racism that ejected her from the mainstream anti-violence organization.

Valériana's story is unique in that, though WCSAP's board initially voted to enforce a nondisclosure agreement for the rest of her life, the board discovered that they could not enforce it because of state whistleblower laws. These legal protections made it possible for Valériana's story to serve as a cautionary warning to contemporary rape crisis centers.[3] But Valériana's tale *isn't* unique in many other ways.[4] Marginalized advocates shared that, like Valériana, they were frequently labeled as "unprofessional" for simply existing as themselves. Their skin color, communication styles, and actions in defiant support of survivors determined whether they were taken seriously as anti-violence workers. For many of them, there was an underlying expectation to be a helping "professional" that subjected them to abuse and flouted the values of grassroots radical activism.

While Valériana is careful to note that many of the concerns she had with WCSAP have specifically to do with anti-Blackness in the movement, we agree that oppressions in advocacy emerge in subtle ways. That is, it is not easy to codify precisely what makes certain workplace actions unacceptable according to the neoliberal institution. Rather, anti-rape workers reflexively self-impose "professional" workplace norms to maintain a hierarchy of white power at their agencies. These norms are not explicit. As Valériana tells me, the people who violated her trust were not always white, though a significant number were. Native American, Asian, Latine, and Pacific Islander–identified advocates also took part in subjugating Black advocates at WCSAP. They were "acting white," taking actions that would have otherwise been played by white administrators.[5] Non-Black people of color could also participate in anti-Blackness and racism at rape crisis centers because whiteness hides under the guise of professionalism.

How did advocacy get here? As Valériana's story illuminates, anti-rape workers strive to embody the normative professional advocate, and in doing so, they subject marginalized peoples—their coworkers and survivors—to abuse and discrimination. As one moves up the anti-violence institution, there are fewer and fewer radical feminists running the everyday operations of supposedly survivor-led organizations—and more white or white-acting professionals who ignore racism in their own homes. For what reasons did normative white or white-acting advocates come to replace queer(ed) advocates of color, particularly at the upper echelons of anti-violence organizing? And what are the consequences of this racial hierarchy of advocacy for anti-rape activists? This chapter explores the rise of a professional advocate workforce and its consequences for radicalism in the anti-rape movement.

Colonial Logics of Helping Professionalism

To understand the normativity of contemporary professional advocacy, we turn to the origins of helping work. The idea of a "helping profession" emerged from English Elizabethan Protestant welfare projects of the 1600s. Early Protestant women believed that poverty prevented otherwise capable citizens from participating in public life. They sought to help the "poor people in need" by providing resources to the lower classes, which they thought would uplift society.[6] While their motives may have been well intentioned, their perspectives about their "clients" carried normative assumptions about people in need. One's value depended on the extent to which one could be cultivated into a productive worker in an emerging industrialized society, or, simply put, capitalism as we know it today. For disabled people and people of color who were not legible as people, especially femmes of color, this prejudice resulted in heightened surveillance or exclusion from "helping" projects. Elizabethan welfare determined who could and should be supported according to racist, ableist, and sexist notions about people.[7]

Elizabethan welfare logics traveled to the United States in the 1800s with the settler movement westwards. As their husbands' wealth grew from the exploitation of Black people, white women directed their attention onto Indigenous children. Though some white women served in the anti-enslavement abolitionist movement, many were active in the creation of boarding schools that separated Indigenous children from their communities.[8] Using the same colonial logics of Elizabethan "helpers," white women provided educational resources with the expectation that Indigenous children would become productive laborers for the US state as adults.[9] They forced Indigenous children to learn English, practice Christianity, and present an Anglo-US appearance, such as cutting their hair and dressing them in pantsuits and dresses. This "educational" model became one of the earliest iterations of helping professionalism.[10] "Kill the Indian," they said, "save the man."[11]

In the late nineteenth century, boarding school educators collaborated with white charity workers to formally establish the "helping professions." White settler women noticed that their services had uneven impacts across different groups of people in need. In particular, Anna L. Dawes realized that the success of their work "depends upon the officer who administers its affairs, whether known as superintendent or secretary, and whether man or woman."¹² In other words, the degree to which people in need were "helped" into becoming productive workers depended on the skill set of the person helping the people in need. Dawes argued that the success of any charity program therefore relied upon the individual's training and advocated for the establishment of formal educational institutions that could reduce discrepancies across social services. "Helpers" established social work training institutes where they could earn baccalaureate degrees. But rather than empower people, these "helping professionals" learned to exploit Black and Brown people's resources, redistributing them to the people whom the white elite class believed were worthy of help.¹³

Social work became a legitimate profession through racial segregation. Formally trained, racially white social workers proclaimed that only those with the proper skills and training, namely, white people who could afford to attend higher educational institutions, should undertake administrative roles overseeing direct services workers, usually people of color with trades-based work experience.¹⁴ This perspective, however, contrasted with the growing Black social work movement that had seen the benefits of collective mutual aid.¹⁵ Founding Black social worker Forrester B. Washington noted in 1935,

> The Negro worker knows the resources of the Negro community better than the white worker. The Negro worker is in touch with the Negro community and is learning about it twenty-four hours per day while the white social worker leaves it at five o'clock when her day's work is ended. The white worker can not bring as much cooperation to her Negro cases from the Negro community as can the Negro community. The white worker cannot get into the most intimate places of Negro life as can the Negro worker. The white worker's ignorance of the Negro community is dangerous because he or she has to make quick decisions and has little time and limited means for checking on homes and institutions to which she is referring Negroes in the Negro community.¹⁶

Although Washington was careful to acknowledge that "there is no such thing as 'Negro social work' (biologically speaking)," he nevertheless highlighted a critical difference between Black and white social work:

To support people in need as social work proclaims to do, social workers need intimate knowledge of their communities, epistemologies that often lie outside the scope of formal white cultural knowledge.[17]

Yet professional social workers resisted BIPOC communities' neighborhood work.[18] By the mid-twentieth century, white social workers joined hands with medical professionals to form the National Association of Social Workers (NASW) while Black social workers drew from Black Power movements to form their own organization, the National Association of Black Social Workers (NABSW).[19] NABSW scathingly termed NASW a "white institution insofar as the members of the board and planning committee do not reflect an ethnic composition commensurate with its expressed concern" and called for NASW to "publicly repudiate the current welfare system," which they saw as punitive and anti-Black.[20] Despite the public callout, however, NASW did not respond to critiques of their social work until recently, following the Black Lives Matter movement when the organization publicly apologized for its contributions to racist practices.[21] Nevertheless, through NASW, social workers continued the tradition of colonial helping professionalism by leveraging medical and other state-based educational credentials to justify their work instead of drawing upon lived experiences.[22]

NASW's whitewashed approaches criminalized people on welfare through the medical industrial complex.[23] In the 1980s, Ronald Reagan sought to "reform" welfare programs by cutting federal income assistance, federal education spending, and federal social services. These cuts were paralleled with growing health and Social Security subsidies, aimed at supporting the expanding aging population.[24] While government welfare spending increased overall by $253 billion (36 percent) during this period, the simultaneous cutbacks for social services with the expansion of medical subsidies actually forced marginalized people, including low-income individuals, women, and people of color, to turn to the for-profit medical industrial complex for redress.[25] Instead of treating the root causes of systemic social injustice, formally educated social workers pathologized poor people, calling social problems "epidemics" and people in need "patients" who were responsible for their suffering.[26] Reaganomic "welfare reforms" were, in essence, a targeted ploy to enslave BIPOC through health "care" to continue laboring for the US state.[27]

Charity workers interjected medicalized welfare approaches in "helping" work into anti-rape victim advocacy in the 1990s.[28] The tightening of government welfare caused the "nonprofitization effect," in which social organizations adopted nonprofit statuses to fill in the gaps left by the state.[29] Loosely organized advocacy collectives chose to follow the nonprofitization trend under the assumption that they could better support victims as nonprofits.[30] But rather than this change enhancing their work, advocates found themselves a part of the "third sector," where the state could discreetly monitor their actions through rape crisis center grants.[31] Radical advocate-activists were quickly expected to serve as "qualified" "helping professionals" at these government-contracted nonprofits, similar to previous generations of white social workers who "helped" poor BIPOC.[32] Specifically, as a part of the Violence Against Women Act (VAWA), the Services, Training, Officers, and Prosecutors (STOP) program instituted a policy that at least 25 percent of state funds were to be spent on domestic and intimate partner violence and sexual assault victim services.[33] To receive government funds, advocates made the argument that they, not survivors, were the "experts" on rape trauma.[34]

This image of "rape experts" was ensconced into advocacy in the 2005 VAWA Reauthorization. In it, the Sexual Assault Services Program (SASP) sought to financially support the training of anti-rape advocates and programming for sexual assault victims.[35] SASP denoted that grants were to be distributed to sexual assault victim and community coordinators, and, as with the STOP program, SASP demanded that a legitimate authority receive the grants.[36] However, SASP did not only disburse funds to rape crisis centers; it also asked for a specific point person within the rape crisis center to receive grants, an advocate who could represent victims' interests and serve as a legitimate authority on par with systems-based rape responders, like law enforcement and medical professionals.[37] The need for a grants manager formally fissured advocacy into at least two levels, administration (those who work in nonprofit management) and direct services (those who work for/with victims).[38]

The hierarchization of the rape crisis center subtly shifted anti-rape advocacy away from its agenda to abolish rape and toward colonized social services. Advocacy has historically manifested as the validation of survivors and abolition of rape. For example, advocates in the 1975 Feminist Alliance Against Rape (FAAR) described that while many advocates longed for professional involvement to support victims, they also warned that professionals such as (formally educated) social workers, psychologists, and counselors oftentimes "deal with rape as an individual woman's problem, rather than a political issue" and "don't assume any responsibility for finding solutions to the problem."[39] However, nonprofit rape crisis centers emphasize legitimizing their work to the state, a directive that moves resources out of frontline intervention and toward sectors without significant direct contact with survivors.[40] This shift paralleled growing concerns from community partners, especially police officers and sexual assault forensic nurses (SAFEs), who demanded that there be skilled workers, not volunteers, with whom they could coordinate rape responses.[41] To address legitimacy and liability concerns, rape crisis centers created or strengthened the power of boards of directors, formalized recruitment and hiring processes, and channeled substantive funding toward therapeutic and medical-carceral services.[42] Executives also began to hire or increase salaries for paid staff advocates to execute administrative tasks, such as legal advocacy and grant writing, while allowing direct services advocates like hotline coordinators, who did not have formal relationships with grant entities, to continue serving in volunteer and entry-level capacities.[43] The administration level of rape crisis centers burgeoned rapidly, forming a top-heavy bureaucracy and creating an anti-rape nonprofit industrial complex (NPIC).[44]

Today, direct services advocates are monitored by administrators in a "cascade of supervision" (an interviewee's words) in which supervisors must authorize direct services activities. Much like the white women who "educated" Indigenous children at boarding schools, administrators control the work of direct services advocates to ensure agency benefit. This supervision has made it more difficult for advocates to take necessary expedient action with survivors. A tribal advocate gave an example of a pet deposit fee: "I had a, um, tribal administrator call me last week and said why are we paying this pet deposit? And I'm like uh because [the victim] didn't want to leave, without her pet, duh! 'Well that's just dumb. Why would you pay $250 for that?' Because that's a barrier in the victim leaving her perpetrator. How can you not [understand]? Like in my terms, I'm like that's easy to rationalize, that's easy to justify, but they don't grasp those things." While the pet fee appeared to be superficial to the administrators, it is often a barrier to leaving a perpetrator. The need to justify a pet deposit to an administrator disempowered the direct services advocate of both autonomy and time to make decisions on behalf of the survivor.

Similarly, a direct services advocate found it challenging to support survivors when forced to request authorization from her administrator for any financial action. She described,

> [The director is] awesome, I don't have like any personal issues with her, um. The one thing that kinda sucks is like when you're in that moment with the client and then you're like, well hold on one second let me go and make sure this is okay with my director, because if I go do something like say I pay for gas for a client, and then I turn in that purchase order, if it gets declined, I'm out that money. And I'm out that time. [. . .] My thinking is I only make like eighteen dollars an hour and if I go ahead and do this for a client . . . and I don't get approval first, then I—I can be out that money and that time if my director comes back and says you know, I wasn't, I wouldn't've approved this and so, I'm sorry but you're out twenty dollars or whatever it may be and it might not be a big deal. . . . It always kinda sucks to be like heh, when you're talking with a client and like the client feels like yes, you're gonna help me and then you're like just let me go run this by my director and I'll be right back and you know you can kinda tell that they're like, okay, so I'm not maybe worthy of this service.

Though she personally had a friendly relationship with her director, the required policy reporting by the direct services advocate to the administrator forced the direct services advocate to spend her own resources to quickly and appropriately respond to the survivor. Furthermore, through this cascade of supervision, the administrator implied that only survivors who require fewer resources deserve support, actions that echo the capitalist "perfect victim" narrative as described in the last chapter.

Colonial logics have clearly permeated anti-rape victim advocacy. Advocates have historically stood in solidarity with survivors. But with the neoliberalization of anti-rape advocacy, white social work with its generations of colonial tactics has supplanted radicalism. Today, many of us are not worthy of the label of "community organizers"; too many of us now serve as vanguards of the medico-carceral-welfare state.

Becoming the Professional Advocate

Neoliberal welfare reforms turned anti-rape advocacy collectives into bureaucratic social services. This change, however, does not appear at first glance to be racialized or discriminatory. After all, if one is better educated or has more experience, it only makes sense, at least in our minds trained in capitalism, that this system rewards an ethic of hard work. However, just as in the last chapter I demonstrated the pitfalls of capitalist resource management for survivors, here in this chapter, I illustrate how colonial-capitalist approaches to care work subject marginalized advocates, especially poor and working-class BIPOC, to violence. Specifically, advocacy labor is racialized through the socialization of advocates into helping professionals, a process that slowly transforms radical activists into normative mediators of the state.

Changes made to anti-rape advocates' funding streams opened the floodgates for more formally educated individuals to find their way into rape crisis centers and serve as authorities over direct services advocates who regularly work with victims.[45] This rapid expansion of credentialed professionals in anti-rape work influences advocates to believe that professionals are best suited to respond to rape victims.[46] Speaking on colonial racial capitalism, Susan Koshy et al. point out that "capital accumulation often relies on administrative procedures to abstract and obscure violence."[47] Thus, as victims are increasingly manufactured into survivors, those assigned responsibility for this production, advocates, gradually professionalize. This socialization into helping professionals is not a written procedure but is rather a product of powerful social norms about work and workers that are regulated by workers in power. Professionalism is a range. As Jennifer Wies defined in her study on domestic violence advocates, professionalism is "a pattern of behaviors and attitudes that transforms individuals with respect to their vocation . . . exist[ing] as a continuum, ranging from unprofessional to very professional."[48]

This process of transforming advocates is inherently a process imbricated with race and interrelated identities. Contrary to popular belief that one's skin color or biological traits affect workplace attitudes, the ways in which people act their race have a correlative effect on the ways that they are treated in the workplace.[49] For example, David B.

Wilkins explained that in the legal field, workers of color are pressured into dressing in specific kinds of attire worn mainly by white people and communicating using Western English-based strategies; otherwise, they run the risk of being perceived as "unprofessional" within the predominantly white legal field and therefore unworthy of promotions or higher wages.[50] It is the *expectation* to act like an assigned race (or any social identity) that shapes workers' perceptions of each other.

In the neoliberal rape crisis center, we come to know advocacy—and its embedded social norms—through advocacy trainings. Though there is no standard curriculum assigned to all anti-violence agencies, for the most part, advocacy trainings generally include the same content and are of similar form. Rape crisis centers usually mandate that incoming advocates undergo at least thirty to forty hours of in-house training before they begin working with survivors.[51] Trainings are usually "free" of charge and cover a wide variety of subjects, from the different types of abuse (e.g., physical, mental, and psychological) to the prosecutorial process for criminal legal cases. They aim to introduce advocates to rape scenarios that they might encounter while working at the rape crisis center. Some trainings take their lead from anti-violence coalitions, like WCSAP, where advocates bring back information circulated at the coalition's events to their individual agency. Other trainings bring in "experts" on sexual violence, such as detectives or survivor speakers, to provide a robust overview of the significance of advocacy for rape victims. One advocate shared the details of her training during her interview, which I recreate in Table 3.1 to contextualize the baseline training given to most advocates.

Rape crisis center trainings are *how* advocates are initiated into understanding advocacy as a kind of whitewashed professional social work. In the sample training program, students are led to believe that advocacy is rooted in systems collaboration. The training revolves around the daily operations of supporting survivors as they go through criminal legal and medical proceedings, such as touring a hospital emergency room or meeting with SVU detectives. It only adds on working with survivors of diverse identities when the work requires that advocates conduct mandatory reporting, such as with disabled and elderly victims. Students who undergo this training, as well as similar ones found across the country, learn to practice procedural advocacy with implicit expectations about survivors' needs. For example, a white advocate pursuing

TABLE 3.1. Sample Rape Crisis Center Advocacy Training

Day	Material Covered
1	Dynamics of sexual assault, domestic violence, and intimate partner violence. Included introductory "helping skills" and trauma-informed care practices.
2	Rape culture and sexual assault
3	Child sexual abuse, mandatory reporting, the role of Child Protective Services (CPS)
4	Medical advocacy, tour of hospital emergency rooms,[a] rape kit procedures, and strangulation identification training
5	Stalking, protective orders, safety planning
6	Working with Special Victims Unit (SVU) detectives (Detective brought in as guest speaker to discuss working with victims.)
7	Adult Protective Services, particularly for disabled and elderly survivors
8	Advocacy techniques, such as paraphrasing, reflecting, and asking open-ended questions
9	Role plays
10–11	Shadow advocacy (2 shifts required)

a. Some rape crisis centers do not have independent, freestanding sexual assault nurse examiner (SANE) facilities; therefore, advocates-in-training tour a hospital emergency room or a hospital-based SANE facility to get acquainted with the layout. Advocates who work at rape crisis centers that have their own SANE facility will tour the in-house facility.

a bachelor's degree in psychology described the importance of therapy for survivors, alluding to her training, but left out an important critique about understanding each survivor's unique needs outside of systems: "When we get trained, uh, with [the advocate coordinator] on the questions, for example like instead of asking yes or no questions, um, you ask for example how do you feel about that, listen, so that's the same thing that I'm learning in my therapy and counseling class about self-disclosure." While the advocate identifies the need to ask open-ended questions, the advocate equates "therapy and counseling" with advocacy. Inadvertently, she assumes that therapy, a medical systems-based approach to sexual trauma, is a core component of advocacy because of her training, when advocacy has historically eschewed formalized therapeutic services.[52]

Although some elements of systems-based training can support advocates to better help some victims, training advocates to rely on medical-carceral-welfare systems socializes advocates into supporting survivors *only* or *primarily* when they seek systems-based services. The content of the training, or the lack thereof, limits the scope of advocacy to social services instead of radical protest. It further leaves out critical epistemologies about radically supporting diverse victims. A Latina advocate expressed her dismay: "[The trainers are] not talking about what I wanna hear. . . . I wanna hear a lot of culture, and how we can break [white culture]. I wanna hear what we can do to help within each other. I want a movement for us." Later, she deplored how her supervisor did not change the training after she had raised her critique, describing her supervisor as having a "white privilege mentality."

Importantly, the foci of advocacy trainings introduce social norms about who can and should conduct advocacy. Several white advocates described themselves as "generic," "classic," or "boring" cisgender white women, with few attributes or life experiences that could help them to support victims who did not come from white European-US ancestry. They therefore praised the general advocacy trainings: "The training really helped me understand how to talk to people who are going through crisis, like I did not know how to do that before." In contrast, queer advocates and advocates of color leaned into their personal life experiences to support culturally diverse survivors. A Latina advocate explained that she relied on her husband's personal networks with local Mexican supermarkets and businesses to fundraise; an Indigenous advocate explained that she circulated agency information in private tribal social media groups to increase outreach. While some racially white advocates also dipped into their personal networks, such as one advocate who leveraged her experiences teaching at a Title I school to support a low-income survivor with little formal education, advocates pointed out that their value for the neoliberal rape crisis center was dependent on the extent to which the agency could capitalize on their "diverse" identities. Like Forrester B. Washington, the latter group suggested that a social worker who does not live in the community has less critical knowledge about supporting the community.

The fact that advocates draw on their life experiences to advocate is not problematic. In fact, previous literature suggests that personal knowledges may amplify support for marginalized survivors.[53] However, advocates reported that trainings rarely educated them on how they as helpers held implicit biases and how these internalized oppressions manifested in their advocacy. Several advocates shared that their agency policies prevented them from sharing their own identities and experiences, including victim status, faith, and sexual orientation, with survivors. Many more told me that they felt "uncomfortable" with sharing information about themselves to colleagues and victims, having had no prior exposure to reflecting on their internal biases. For one person, "[Survivors] don't get to know me other than they see that I'm white.... I become more of a two-dimensional person."

Such negation of identities produces norms about advocacy as a profession. Trainings are designed to teach a "neutral" advocate with little connection to the survivor community. For example, one advocate said that her training was effective because "not everyone knows and I didn't know that, you know, these communities [of color] are more vulnerable." While information about vulnerable communities can better support advocates in their efforts to help them, the training subliminally reinforces that the advocate-in-training has no relevant a priori knowledge—or rather, is a white outsider coming to support the poor worthy masses in need. Simultaneously, thus, advocacy trainings fail to acknowledge the specialized expertise by (prospective) marginalized advocates and uplifts ill-informed normative (prospective) advocates.

Beyond content, the structure of advocacy trainings also inseminates subliminal rules around who can perform advocacy. Even though trainings are meant to educate direct services advocates who operate at all hours of the day, trainings are often hosted by administrative advocate coordinators who operate on a nine-to-five workday schedule. As many BIPOC and working-class advocates complained, advocate trainings were therefore usually organized at times when blue-collar individuals worked at their full-time jobs and could not attend training sessions to become a volunteer or part-time staff advocate. One advocate without children or an intimate partner at the time of interviewing exclaimed, "Who has time [for] forty hours after work? It's mostly, like, white young women who don't have kids. You know, who have the money. Or have childcare or partners who can watch the kids." An advocate who worked at a large urban rape crisis center connected the advocacy training demands at her agency to social barriers for racial minority and low-income advocates in her city.

> Our volunteering program, there's a one-year contract. You have to commit to a year of volunteering, two shifts a month for twelve hours. Okay. If you have young children and work full-time, like, you're—the barriers

to you volunteering are [more]. . . . We reflect our population in that, like, the communities that we serve . . . are mostly white. . . . They come from certain neighborhoods . . . so I think that's the other, other side of, like, our volunteer core versus our staff like is also a symptom of like a larger societal issue of segregation, of geographic segregation in [the city].

Due to legacies of redlining, the advocate's rape crisis center is in a white neighborhood. Therefore, despite their interest in anti-rape work, many low-income and BIPOC trainees could not meet the criteria for the agency's training, such as committing to a high number of shifts per month. Their lack of training completion and/or their absence of continuation in the movement occurs not because advocates of color are not invested in anti-rape projects but because trainers did not design the structure of the trainings to address geographic and social discrimination, specifically, the heightened time in travel duration experienced mainly by prospective advocates of color and the high cost of childcare in that city.

The requirement of specific work shifts is an expectation largely set by advocates who are "mostly white," are middle-class, and "come from certain neighborhoods." Consequently, the normative training design blames marginalized advocates for an inability to meet systems demands instead of recognizing the neoliberal agency's inaccessible professionalization requirements. An advocate who previously worked at a low-wage job shared her reasoning for delaying participation in the anti-rape movement: "Once I met my executive director while I was working at my job and she offered me—she was looking for volunteers. And I told her how interested I was and (exhales) she offered me okay why don't you volunteer, um but at that time frame I couldn't be able [I wasn't able] while I was a single mother. I didn't have time." Though the director was well meaning, she indirectly minimized the hardships experienced by the advocate, who was a "single mother," and further exploited the advocate by asking her to labor for free because she failed to acknowledge the needs of low-income unpartnered parents.

Advocacy trainings socialize advocates into thinking about advocacy as a normative social service. Advocates learn to be "rape response professionals," limited to systems responses, and they do not learn how to support survivors in all arenas of social life. Prospective and active advocates are thus ill equipped to support racial minorities, low-income workers, and many Others. Furthermore, the people who can attend advocacy trainings are most often those who operate on a white-collar corporate workday structure. Through implied expectations of a "professional" advocacy, the trainings leave out scores of potential advocates who have lived experiences with violence and who can support victim community members. Gradually, fewer advocates with radical inclinations come to labor for anti-rape causes.

Outsourcing Politics

The norming of advocacy through trainings is paralleled by the increase in the outsourcing of anti-rape education. At the same time that personal life experiences are devalued as legitimate advocacy knowledge, advocate coordinators shared that they are increasingly pressed for time and often have little capacity to train incoming advocates, even though they are aware of the need for well-trained direct services advocates. To accommodate this need, greater numbers of rape crisis centers have recently changed their requirements around advocacy training, allowing trainees to replace some or all of their mandatory in-house advocacy training or experience with formal education, i.e., college.

Though outsourcing training to postsecondary institutions may account for the labor gap, the transfer of in-house training to formal schooling creates yet another barrier of entry for marginalized people to serve as advocates and facilitates the racist professionalization of advocacy. As FAAR noted in 1975, "Professionalism is a means of maintaining class distinctions in this society. Professional degrees are not readily obtainable by all members of society, nor are they necessarily accessible to the most capable individuals."[54] Today, college degrees are more expensive than ever before, in terms of both the cost and the time required to complete a degree. According to the Education Data Initiative, the average cost of college in the United States in 2023 is $36,436 per student per year, accounting for "books, supplies, and daily living expenses."[55] This cost has "more than doubled" in the last twenty years and reflects seismic shifts at both public and private four-year institutions.[56] The racial demographics of college students expose the inaccessibility of college for poor BIPOC, especially recent immigrants.[57] The National

Center for Education Statistics reports that on average, only 49 percent of twenty-five- to twenty-nine-year-olds have completed an associate's or higher degree. American Indian/Alaska Native, Black, Hispanic, Pacific Islander, and multiracial people within that age range or older hold fewer collegiate degrees than Asian or white people.[58] Within the field of social work, which houses one of the highest number of individuals seeking to enter anti-violence advocacy, as of 2020, 49.1 percent of baccalaureate social work students identified as white (non-Hispanic), 21.7 percent identified as African American/Black, and 17.9 percent identified as Hispanic/Latinx.[59] While racial proportions are not as drastic in social work as the overarching numbers of people attaining college degrees generally, the poverty wages and social stigma of the social work profession will likely deter many BIPOC from working in the field, ensuring the continuation of white supremacy in care work.[60]

Advocacy that leans on the broken US education system to fill positions accelerates its professionalization. Advocates reported seeing an increase in white people, specifically white "traditional" college-aged students, who seek to become victim advocates as a "stepping stone" for their longer social services careers. At one agency, a white advocate with a bachelor's degree in psychology explained that this increase could be attributed to the new training requirements set forth by her rape crisis center. Advocates without a degree, typically BIPOC and/or poor or working-class white people beyond the traditional age of college, were required to complete nine out of twelve available training seminars, but advocates who were currently in college or already held a college degree, typically white and middle-class or wealthy students, were only required to complete six out of twelve seminars. This difference in expectations meant that those who were white and privileged to attend college were assumed to already have been trained in key advocacy skills, despite that they were not trained on the radical genealogies nor strategies of anti-rape advocacy.

Several advocates underscored how little formal schooling actually taught about civic protest. In fact, several advocates denounced how most helping professional education is another form of colonization, socializing advocates into committing cultural genocide. A Native advocate shared that she once trained formally educated white advocates about the connection between boarding schools and generational sexual victimization and found that none of the attendees had ever been exposed to this history.

> I did a course one time for social workers, and I, I, it's a forty-minute course but basically what it did . . . was [. . .] I drew a town, and I drew lakes and forest areas and stuff parts on the outside of this town, and I put all of the, the main stores and stuff in the center. And I said, Where do you wanna live, where do you wanna live, and I'll mark [where] all of those people where they wanted to live. How many children do you have? Um, how many children do you have over the age of five? Okay so I'd mark all that out, and then I said okay there's a school over here [gestures with right hand] it's a hundred miles away. This area right here [gestures with left hand], this is a reservation. You can't go over there [points from the right to the left]. Any child that you've got in your home over five is in that [right hand] school. And it's like they're just shocked.

Because formal educational institutions were built upon legacies of colonization, formal education cannot substitute for experiential learning when it comes to understanding the ways that sexual violence impacts nonwhite, but especially Indigenous, communities.

Ignorance about the political roots of advocacy, as a by-product of substituting experience with formal schooling, has placed the burden of educating peers about racism and normativity on individual marginalized advocates. Angela Davis and colleagues explain, in the context of policing anti-violence justice work, "Cooptation can mean professionalization, intimately tethered to whiteness, and the disqualification of those who have been doing this work effectively without credentials or pay and the reformation of movements and mutual aid into social service agencies and charities."[61] One Native Hawaiian advocate whose highest level of education is a GED acknowledged, somewhat bemusedly, "I'm the oldest, like, seniority of everyone. Um, I've been here the longest, everybody else is kind of, like, brand new or they just, they only have, like one year under their belt." Following this comment, she pointed out that all her colleagues came to her agency fresh out of master's programs in social work, in contrast to her GED. They were all also *"haole,"* with no prior connection to the Native Hawaiian population whom they served. The advocate recalled that though she was a low-paid direct services advocate, she often trained her white colleagues on trauma-informed ways of working with local survivors and the ways that they should file government forms for survivors who are Native Hawaiian. Formal schooling did not help her colleagues to effectively support victims, particularly Indigenous victims and victims of color, and instead exacerbated the labor disparity between workers of different races, political statuses, and positions.

An advocate "on the spectrum" who regularly works many shifts chastised her rape crisis center for allowing college students to bypass the number of shadow advocacy shifts that they were required to complete. She said,

> I understand if someone's just gonna be there for a semester and they're trying to like teach people accountability. 'Cause the group that you're working with is like younger adults. And maybe they wanna be like, holding people accountable. [But] like no you can't just skip being on call because you have class in the morning, like people are doing this who have work in the morning, you know, that kinda thing. I get that, but at the same time, I had wished that there had been like some kind of permission built in, or talked about that there was some kind of structure for like . . . (exhales) asking for a break and not being made to feel like you're letting everyone down, you know?

In trying to expand their advocacy workforce, the agency inadvertently prioritized college students, who are largely made up of white, middle-class, and wealthy students who have little experience with full-time jobs and working outside of business hours, as required of victim advocacy. The advocate also points out that their excusing of college students pressured advocates who were not in school to avoid asking for a break, creating an ableist, neurotypical norm in advocate labor.

Nevertheless, expectations about advocacy as a professional social service continue to encourage prospective advocates into earning systems-based credentials. An advocate with dual bachelor's degrees commented,

> [Advocacy's] kind of the same thing in our book [as counseling]. We're not licensed counselors, by any means, but we do the same thing that

individual counseling, personal advocacy, um it's all combined in there together if that makes sense? [...] Our therapists of course are licensed therapists, [they have] master's degree[s], and then the advocates have to have their bachelor's degree, you know, to, to have those qualification[s] and then of course all of the training that goes with it, so ... My degree was actually in, majoring in human services. And nonprofit management so it's actually, kind of went in there perfectly.

Echoing white social work's therapeutic approach to victims, the advocate presents advocacy and counseling as one and the same, stating that "it's all combined together." She further notes that "we're not licensed counselors" and distinguishes direct services workers ("advocates") who have bachelor's degrees from "therapists" who have master's degrees and licenses. She elevates those with advanced credentials, implying that "of course" therapists can support survivors, and support them as well as or better than the "advocates" who "have to have their bachelor's degree."

The new norm of an advocate is professional. While formal schooling *can* complement in-house advocacy training, for instance, helping advocates to understand the background of helping work or learn about systems-based resources, expectations of formally credentialed workers preemptively dismiss prospective advocates with lived epistemologies from becoming advocates and privileges the voices of people with vested interests in state sponsorships. The privilege to attend college becomes the marker of success. But formal education cannot be a requisite or an expectation to becoming an advocate because it dismisses the political core of advocacy, which is to learn how to provide the help survivors need. An Asian advocate summarized, "I—I think one time we had a speaker for one of our conferences who was pointing out we need to emphasize people who don't have credentials. ... We can learn all of these terminologies and like [research] and stuff but, it's not reflective of survivors, the general community, society in general ... 'Cause I can point out like a whole twenty-page document that sounds like a research paper but it's like, this means nothing, to some people."

Double Binds

There is no extensive study examining the composite structure of the US advocacy workforce. However, a clear wage gap has emerged between paid administrative advocates and volunteer staff and entry-level direct services advocates. Many direct services advocates are paid meager wages, if paid at all, while administrative advocates are paid more handsomely according to their contributions to nonprofit (read: state) operations. This wage gap is substantive. As of 2024, the direct services advocate is paid nothing, paid $18.57 an hour without benefits, or salaried at $38,628 annually.[62] Comparatively, as of a 2023 US Bureau of Labor report, administrative advocates, which include community healthcare workers, case managers, therapists, and grant writers, are paid $25.03 per hour or salaried at $52,050 annually with benefits.[63] Compensation for nonprofit anti-violence executive directors is notoriously difficult to pinpoint; however, one source from 2018 estimates that they earn approximately $123,462.[64] These numbers illustrate that advocacy in a neoliberal rape crisis center is now hierarchical, with significant differences in compensation based on the advocate's position and designated tasks.

The advocacy wage hierarchy is sustained by colonial-capitalist logics. In a capitalist workplace, workers who professionalize, taking on the norms of the institution or field, can advance their careers more quickly, earning promotions, better wages, and better working conditions.[65] The idea of climbing up the ladder is a capitalist ideology, one that pushes *individuals* to "succeed" in their careers by moving up in ranks but one that also creates competition and splinters *collective* labor within an agency. Unlike grassroots mutual aid, where the collective goal is shared by individual members, the hierarchization of the neoliberal rape crisis center suggests, to advocates, that direct services advocates are simply "entry-level" workers who merely hold basic skills for supporting survivors whereas administrative advocates are extolled as authorities with an expansive skill set in budgeting, management, and state cooperation. This division of advocacy is further entrenched by the fact that administrators often navigate complex, multiyear governmental contracts and form longer-term relationships with community partners compared to direct services workers, who burn out at much faster rates and therefore cannot sustain long-term commitments.[66]

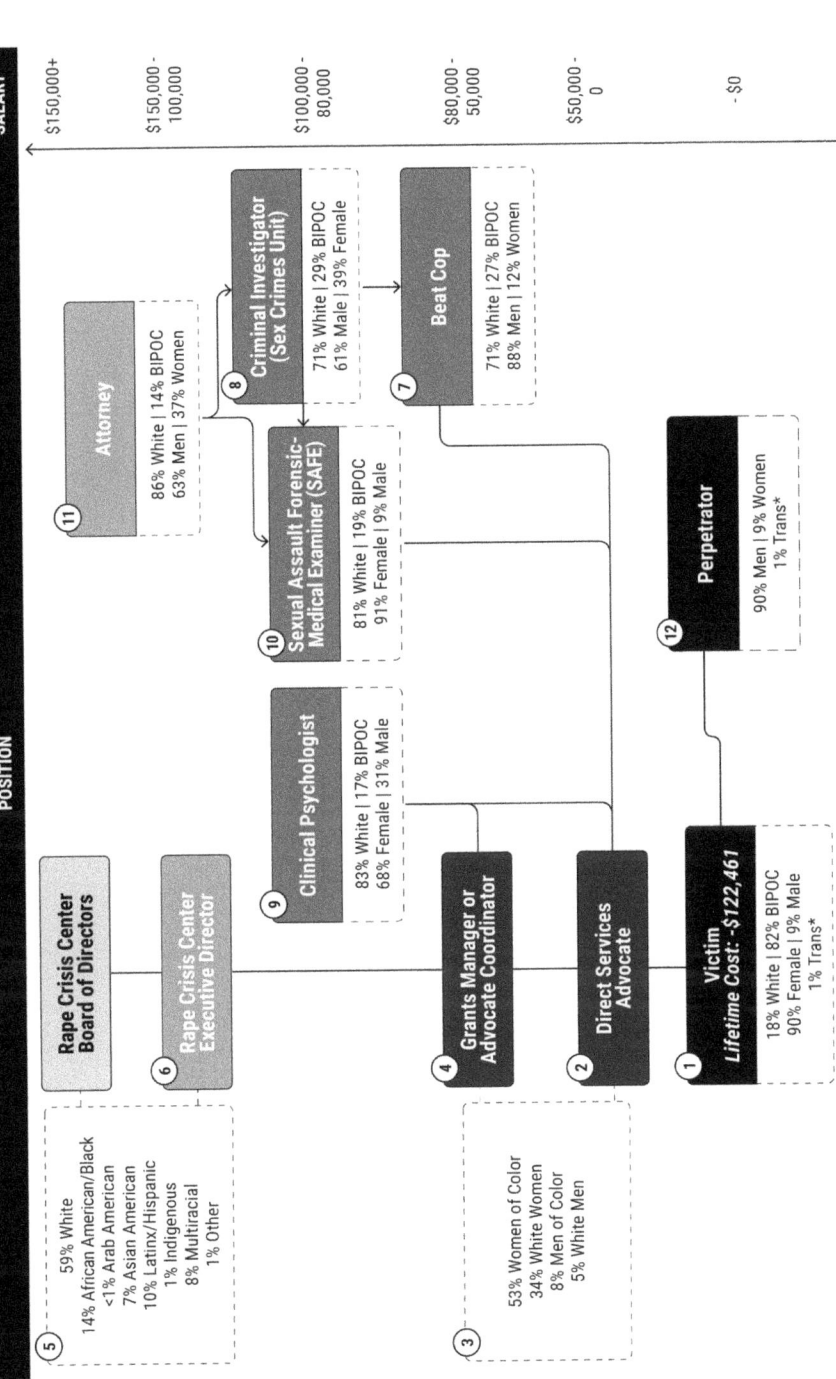

Figure 3.1 Rape Crisis Center Hierarchy with Salary, Race, and Gender. Image courtesy of the author, with design support from Jackie Chen. See page 130 for source information regarding the numbered items in Figure 3.1.

Competition in advocacy labor fosters a corporate work culture in which advocates make decisions on how to act in such a way as to advance in their agencies. Many direct services advocates, particularly those in precarious financial situations, cannot or refuse to labor on behalf of an organization without fair pay, resulting in a recent, and concerning, drain in direct victim support.[67] Simultaneously, there is a real monetary value attached to administration that is not given to direct services advocates. Administrators do not work directly with survivors and therefore can work on a nine-to-five, five-days-a-week business schedule. They are also typically provided healthcare benefits and vacation days much as in any other corporate job. These differences, coupled with higher financial compensation for administrators, persuade advocates of all ranks (but especially direct services advocates) to act in accordance with administration *and the state funders with whom administrators collaborate* to compete successfully for a higher-ranking position at the neoliberal rape crisis center. An advocate trainer with a graduate degree noted, "Once they have a degree, they're then in the administration part. They don't go out. You know? (laughs) They do not. Or, and they don't have any experiences, they just have a desire to help or in that field, or they have a degree so this job is hiring, this organization is hiring and they apply and they get it."

The financial incentives to administrate survivors persuade many advocates to abandon their radical values. Some more privileged advocates explained that their clinical training or professional demeanor helped survivors of color to feel more comfortable speaking with them, which thereby helped them to complete advocacy tasks more easily without supervisor interference. For example, a white advocate who worked at a Native-specific agency explained that her whiteness made her appear to be a legitimate "professional" who could do the work. She said,

> [The rape crisis center] had went through two previous directors that were both [tribally affiliated] prior to me. And they, neither one of them lasted long, um, and from my understanding it's because they couldn't keep their mouth shut about confidentiality and things like that. Um, so I think, as far as being an advantage, I think that actually plays to the strengths of me working with survivors, and survivors trusting me,

because I'm not someone's auntie or I'm not someone's um niece or I'm not someone's mother or I'm not someone's grandmother, and um . . . I think they look at me in a little more of a professional, um, role, because I do have that education.

The advocate implies that the former directors, who identified as Native, could not present professionally; they "couldn't keep their mouth shut about confidentiality." By comparison, she was a "professional" with extensive experience in the advocacy field who could educate Native advocates about supporting Native survivors. She explained that she is "not someone's auntie or . . . niece . . . mother . . . or grandmother" and was not beholden to tribal norms; therefore, she could step outside of personal conflicts. While a third party may have helped Native survivors feel more comfortable with accessing services, the advocate's racial identity, whiteness, is *how* she is made to appear professional to survivors and colleagues.

In comparison, BIPOC advocates explained that they frequently encountered challenges in gaining acceptance by survivors, who read these advocates as "unprofessional" because of their radical advocacy. White or white-acting professional advocates do not have to consistently fight for the right to work on behalf of victims because they act in ways similar to the norms of a helping professional.[68] However, nonnormative workers, especially BIPOC direct services advocates, are caught in a "double bind."[69] They must consistently weigh whether they can fight against professional norms and support marginalized survivors or align with the ways of white service providers' responses to rape and avoid "professional" (racial) conflicts.[70] These decisions compel survivors to read BIPOC advocates who experience heightened challenges to their work as "unprofessional" or otherwise ineffective at their jobs.

A direct services advocate described a scenario involving a white survivor who did not want a Black advocate and the subsequent pressures that she encountered to support her.

> I've had [a client] that said I—I'm just getting a bad vibe from you. I was like oh! Why is that? Okay. And really, and it was really not that she was getting a bad vibe, she just felt uncomfortable. And, it—with a mask on, you can't see my face for reals so I don't know what you're getting off of

that maybe my eyebrows are doin' it for you? But I don't know! And I usually have a hat on at night so, okay lady.

I've had clients say things that are rude to you. I've had clients who tell me that, she didn't like Black people. I'm sorry, but guess what, I'm the only one you got, 'cause I—I, that was the week that I was on backup. And I had no coverage whatsoever. Well I'm all you got! And, your officer is Black too. So, it's gonna be okay. I didn't take offense to it simply because when my nurse came in, she told my nurse that that could be her night . . . So you have to assess the situation and not take it personal. Um. And, and say—'cause it's not you. You know they're just in a moment of, of trauma. And I don't know how to handle none of this, and, and I'm just on edge about everything. And um, in reality for her she was actually she was coming off of drugs.

The advocate shares that the survivor "just felt uncomfortable." Though she does not expressly say that it is implicit racism that contributes to these feelings of discomfort, the survivor comments that "she didn't like Black people," indicating that it is anti-Blackness that compels the survivor to refuse the Black advocate. Yet the advocate does not refuse to support the white survivor, and she even apologizes for her Blackness by saying, "I'm all you got!" This case study illuminates the ways that she, as a Black advocate, was expected to endure abuse by survivors *and* execute additional labor to present as a legitimate and helpful advocate.

A Latina advocate similarly commented,

In every single conference that I have gone, the Latinas' conferences, [we] have this same conference. They have this same conversation but they're not getting paid as the same amount as a non-[Spanish]-speaking, uh [person]. It's just, and it's one of the many reasons why Latinas or Latinos quit nonprofits because they're not getting paid more, and they're doing twice the workload. Or they're doing jobs they're not supposed to be doing. [. . .] People don't understand is (sighs) we do a lot for this agency. We go out, we put out our necks into our community for y'all. And then for y'all not to pay us the same amount—to pay us a little bit higher than a non-[Spanish]-speaking Latino, Spanish people? Kind of makes us feel like we're being taken advantage [of], and that's why many Latinos quit by their first or second year.

Despite providing the agency with desired "diversity," Latina advocates are "not getting paid more" despite "doing twice the workload."

Direct services advocates are underpaid and exploited, especially BIPOC, who must draw from their specialized cultural skill sets for little to no compensation. This abuse causes them to either burn out and leave the field or concede to white professionalism.[71] By advocates' estimates, radical coworkers left within one to three years of beginning advocacy, many of them having been unable to make serious long-term connections with systems or cultural community partners. Many direct services advocates explained that they felt high compassion fatigue because of a lack of institutional supports.[72] Their personal advocacy, such as outreach to their ethnic networks, did not meet the same standards of professional social services, and their agencies therefore only compensated them with "moral wages," emotional satisfaction from executing morally altruistic labor.[73] The lack of financial compensation led advocates to express that they did not feel valued by their supervisors.

Concerningly, the double bind encourages non-Black advocates of color who remain in the profession to participate in the capitalist production of an "ideal" advocate. Neoliberal professionalism fosters "fungibility," the socioeconomic and legal term for one thing being replaced by another.[74] In the context of diversity, fungibility is the replacement of a person of one racialized identity, usually Black, for another person of any other racialized identity but in a way that ignores the historical context in which anti-Black racism occurred.[75] At rape crisis centers, fungibility expands the workloads of non-Black people of color and forces these individuals to choose between white professionalism or Black radicalism, in another form of the double bind, to preserve their own safety and presence in the workforce. For example, a Brown multilingual advocate explained that even though there are four direct services advocates at her agency, she is assigned the cases of *all* marginalized survivors, including survivors of color, non–English-speaking survivors, immigrant survivors, and incarcerated survivors. Her racial identity and multilingualism were made to be interchangeable with all other "oppressed" identities, as though her Brownness could be conflated with Blackness, or her Spanish-Portuguese-French abilities with Somali or Arabic. The advocate explained, "I'm not the one who assigns [the cases] to myself, the manager does. So I guess they, they just, I dunno, they try to take in[to] consideration (shifts tone into a more questioning voice) the person's background and maybe see what's the stronger identity of them? (resumes regular voice, rushed) I don't know I don't wanna say that." The advocate points out that she is assigned all marginalized survivors' cases because the advocate supervisor "tr[ies] to take in[to] consideration the person's background." She acknowledges the attempt by the supervisor to reconcile survivors' backgrounds by pairing them with an advocate who represents marginalized identities. However, this attempt at culturally relevant care erases both specifically Black care *and* the cultures of the non-Black advocate of color. The advocate quickly shifts between tones as well, attempting to dismiss the harm she has experienced in order to avoid retaliation. This shift in tone indicates that she is aware of the possible consequences if she takes "nonprofessional" actions to raise this issue to her supervisor. In an interview with another advocate at the same agency, I discovered that the advocate had resigned.

Even more problematic, advocates of color who choose to remain in the field, despite the constant labor inequities, sometimes place their anger onto victims themselves. A white advocate described a direct services shelter advocate of color who abused her power in the face of constant violence by both normative survivors and administrators.

> I answered the phones and got supplies for the women and so it was more of like a crisis—I—I would consider it more of like a crisis support person. I answered the hotline, that kind of thing. They treated us very differently than they did like the people who actually went to court, who were the victim advocates or the people who were the counselors, and, there was so much hierarchy, and I think it really threw me off that I, like I wasn't expecting that, and, I also felt like they didn't treat their clients very well. Like there was this very, like we are professionals, and you are here to receive services . . . There was very much a divide. [. . .]
>
> White clients will sometimes make racialized remarks about [the shelter advocate]. Like they were, like they were really frustrated. . . . They called her a bitch a lot. Sometimes they qualified that with heh! you know uh . . . I don't wanna say it but like a, a racial slur for a Hispanic person. And, she was also overweight so they would call her you know fat, that kinda thing.

Later, the advocate explained that the agency hierarchy ruptured relationships between the agency and survivors, who were "smart people" who immediately noticed hierarchical dynamics between frontline and managerial advocates.

> I—I really thought it was going to be all about—'cause they throw around words like empowerment and building people up and the word "empowerment" just kind of makes me kind of sick to my stomach now because we would throw that around all the time but it's like, how empowered are you if you have to like check in and out in a log to go to the grocery store? [. . .] [Survivors are] gonna know the person who's working at the front desk, who's making $12.50 an hour, and who is now going to, you know, power trip all over them because (laughs) that's the only, that's the only part of their job that, that they get to you know experience that hierarchy.

As the advocate suggests, the professionalization of advocacy ignores the racialized violence against marginalized advocates. In turn, marginalized advocates bearing the weight of incessant intersectional violence may eventually enforce a hierarchy in lieu of peer-to-peer advocacy, exerting another kind of power and control over those with no alternative recourse.

The double bind sustains white power at the rape crisis center and capitulates white advocates into higher-paid positions overseeing the work of BIPOC. The simultaneous privileging of white elite ways of conducting advocacy and disadvantaging of nonnormative BIPOC strategies does not happen because one group is more skilled or has more relevant experiences. Instead, in contrast to fair and democratic working relationships, advocates of all backgrounds are encouraged to compete with one another for a meager chance at better working conditions and higher wages, feeding the destructive capitalist NPIC.

White Ascendancy

Professionalism encourages all advocates to jump past direct services at faster rates, creating an invisible racialized hierarchy of advocacy. For example, a white advocate with a degree in criminology explained how her agency subliminally enforced that only formally educated (white) people could administrate direct services advocacy (of color). "We are receiving a practicum student . . . but this practicum student is . . . primarily going to be focused on how to review and how to [increase] diversity [at the rape crisis center]. This practicum student's white. Female. (laughs in disbelief) Of status. I mean, so. Okay? (laughs) Like w[hat]?" The practicum student is white and "of status," with no relevant working experience. However, she is hired over advocates without formal degrees. Her degree—or whiteness and wealth—serves as a proxy for the experiences that other advocates, primarily those of color, typically gain on the job. As the advocate criticizes, through expectations about credentialed professionals, white administrators without relevant experience come to supervise BIPOC who remain relegated to entry-level, underpaid, direct services positions.

Nevertheless, while we understand the racial hierarchy as a binary between white people with power at the top and Black people without power at the bottom, a racial hierarchy is not just about a categorical privileging of one group over another.[76] In her study of three differently racialized Third World leftist organizations, Laura Pulido defined a racial hierarchy as "a specific configuration of power relations in a given place and time based on racial ideology."[77] In other words, power relations are ideologically dialectical, meaning that they are always in dialogue with one another. This relationality suggests that power hierarchies are not based on assigned racial categories but are instead constantly changing depending on how we interact with one another.[78] Therefore, a racial hierarchy is not a simple vertically inclined top-down structure with clearly defined power roles but a hierarchy built upon continuous racialized and generational socialization of a profession. Rape crisis centers that expect advocates to hold college degrees or perform systems-based social services without understanding the social context in which survivors relate to their community and the state reify that only white people or *BIPOC acting as white people* can administrate over direct services.

In the neoliberal rape crisis center racialized hierarchy, *in most cases* white people are at the top, though not all, and *in most cases* BIPOC are at the bottom, though again, not all; few might be "exceptions" to the social rules attributed to their racial group. The hierarchy also differently compensates people *within* each racial rank based on gender, sexuality, nationality, dis/ability, and related social identities.[79] Thus, a BIPOC advocate can nevertheless participate in the capitalist exploitation of BIPOC communities, even if they racially identify as a part of the subjugated class. For example, a multiracial advocate explained how administrators, who were mostly racially BIPOC, disregarded the safety of direct services workers during the COVID-19 pandemic and thereby reinforced racialized hierarchies.

> There [were] consistent fights about, um, getting paid to get COVID testing, like if you're gonna have me go into a hospital then you're gonna pay for fucking test[ing] for COVID. Um, and then eventually, on the line we ended up getting hazard pay right before they stopped us going back in, in person. But, um, there were, um, paid time off. There are changes to like paid time off, um, like regulation or whatever, that only affected those staff that were providing in-person service. Such that you couldn't travel, like you wouldn't ... your time off would not be approved if it meant that you had to leave the state. Which like from a public health perspective like you can't fucking leave the state but like your employer shouldn't be the one, you can't leave the state or risk your, you know, your job. Um, or rather like because you did take it, then like great, you know. Um, but it only affected [the direct services] advocates, it didn't affect anybody else on staff. It didn't affect the development staff, right?

The advocate noted that though many advocate coordinators and trainers who oversaw direct services identified as racially BIPOC, these middle managers "acted white," creating a racialized hierarchy. (White) administrators refused to give direct services advocates (of color) protective gear or hazard pay for entering hospitals during crisis moments but gave (white) administrative staff paid time off and the option to work from home. These decisions exacerbated the racialized disparity in advocacy not by directly refusing to support racially BIPOC advocates or privileging racially white advocates. Instead, the agency *indirectly*, through professionalism, refused to support the labor *usually* carried out by BIPOC (direct services) and provided advantages to white-collar labor *usually* carried out by white people (administration).

Professionalism allows whiteness to ascend to the top of the neoliberal rape crisis center hierarchy.[80] White ascendancy occurs when the condition of being or acting white "is made to seem neutral and inviting or inclusive of racial, sexual, and other minorities."[81] As advocates shared, many of the tensions between themselves and administrators were cast as "professional" conflicts having to do with training, workloads, or relationships with community partners instead of what they are: colonial acts of white supremacy. The rhetoric of professionalism imposed an expectation that only those who exude a professional demeanor, that is, work as a "neutral" social services worker without raising racial tensions, can advance in their agencies. Consequently, as the vast majority of advocates in this study shared, direct services advocates are increasingly not reflective of the service area within which they worked. According to one white lesbian advocate, "[Our staff] is the most like cis-het gaggle of girls ever," in contrast to the community's demographics of predominantly Hispanic and 2SLGBTQIA+ survivors.

This professionalism is a structural, institutional problem that recreates the same racist hierarchy of the overall US cultural economy in the neoliberal rape crisis center. Nine victim advocates expressly informed me that their agency's or state coalition's boards of directors were comprised of predominantly white cisgender people, including some men from policing, legal, or healthcare industries. One multiracial advocate observed, "As a sector, we're still very much led by, right, like white people and white women with the very second wave feminist-like ideology." Another advocate of color said, "I think the coalitions, they hold a lot of power they don't even recognize sometimes? And they have the power to change those things. But also [the people who] are sitting in their chairs are also mostly white. So you know, there's that too that they're not aware of the problem."

The issues with diversity derive, thus, not from a lack of interest by marginalized communities in anti-rape work. Instead, administrators' "color-blind" approach to advocacy pushes marginalized BIPOC advocates out of the field while padding white normative advocates' pockets. According to a white advocate with a master's degree, "So the understanding of like how, um, how policies ... well frankly can be kind of racist and, and unequal and you know it doesn't really show up because [administrators are] not seeing the on the ground work in the same way [. . .] What we're seeing, the admin is always like ten steps behind, right? And that goes all the way up the chain to like policy level." On the ascendancy of whiteness in the neoliberal rape crisis center, another advocate summarized,

> In my experience, Black and Brown staff who tend to be Black and Brown women or Black and Brown queer people, right? Like queer folks, gender queer folks. There's just more burnout. But then also like if you look at like more broadly socioeconomically who has less bargaining power, who has less social mobility, who has less occupational mobility, it's those same people. And so you can't necessarily leave . . . Rape crisis centers, like any other fucking workplace, is still like built on capitalism and like white supremacy, and like therefore rests on the exploitation of frontline workers.

Hyperinstitutionalizing Advocacy

Certainly, it is vital [that] all organisations and those working to end gender-based violence should have a widely diverse staff, of various ages, genders, ethnic origins and—most difficult for what are almost entirely middle class professional organisations—classes. Yet that alone will make only a small difference. The US government and its agencies have embraced racial and gender diversity, yet far too often those hired in senior roles merely perpetuate the traditional practices of their predecessors. Sadly, if an organisation is funded by government, by wealthy philanthropists or by corporations, its values will soon change to merge with those of its donors. And that is never good for the people those organisations aim to help or, as is seen here, certain members of staff.
—Comment by Airlan1979 on "How the Mainstream Movement Against Gender-Based Violence Fails Black Workers and Survivors"

Callouts such as this one regarding the racism of the anti-rape movement (e.g., WCSAP,[82] the Rape, Abuse, and Incest National Network [RAINN],[83] and Crisis Text Line,[84] to name a few widely known examples) have encouraged rape crisis centers to diversify their workforce. Numerous anti-rape agencies have actively hired people of color and other marginalized advocates, showing an early challenge to the white majority. The hiring of diverse advocates is sorely needed to fill in a gap in victim services, and the change in advocate representation at these agencies can show survivors that the anti-rape movement cares about its marginalized members.[85] Still, while hiring diverse advocates signals a shift in direction by the mainstream anti-rape movement, BIPOC advocates in this study argued that it was not enough to simply hire them. Advocates who cannot or do not access formal education and act in white ways, mainly advocates of color, are prevented from moving past the glass ceiling of anti-violence work and can only ascend to middle management, if they reach that level at all.[86] Even if they do reach some sort of authoritative position, they encounter more and more instances of the double bind, leading to higher feelings of compassion fatigue and, eventually, burnout. Indeed, the Women of Color Network conducted a study in 2014 assessing the diversity of the advocacy managerial workforce. They found that 81 percent of executive directors of the sampled anti-violence agencies identified as white non-Hispanic, and only thirteen out of ninety programs surveyed had at least one racial or ethnic minority program director.[87] Similarly, the Building Movement Project examined the "race to lead" rates at nonprofits, finding that although BIPOC are increasingly entering managerial and executive positions at nonprofits, many experience a "glass cliff,"[88] the sharp decline of an organization when BIPOC workers are given impossible tasks yet are nevertheless expected by the institution to accomplish them.[89]

Hiring diverse people does not address the political-advocacy wage gap, nor does it solve the "double bind." It is not simply the absence of diverse people that harms advocates of color, although that forms a critical part of the problem. It is the white ascent of professionalism that produces hostile workspaces for marginalized advocates. Emerging research shows that changes to the organizational structure of rape crisis centers is needed to enhance diversity.[90] For example, Kulkarni et al. suggest that organizations must address workload imbalances, develop supervisor and peer support mechanisms, and provide spaces for direct services advocates to process compassion fatigue in order to avoid high turnover rates.[91] Çayır et al. demonstrated that advocates of color reported feeling tokenized by their supervisors, often being assigned higher caseloads because of the perceived ability to support survivors who looked like them; thus, the authors suggest dividing work evenly across all advocates, socializing labor.[92] Voth Schrag et al. also reported that workers of color (Latinx in their study) often felt isolated from white workers, and thus frequently congregated with advocates from their own cultures to collectively share work to avoid compassion fatigue.[93] Finally, Wachter et al. described helpful coping behaviors of a racially and sexually diverse sample of 623 advocates, such as stress management, participation in system change, and political action, that could alleviate occupational stress and promote compassion satisfaction at work.[94]

These are excellent avenues for exploration. But it is also necessary to address the bigger picture of colonial-capitalist white supremacy. Neoliberalism makes whiteness central to anti-rape advocacy such that even when scholars note the importance of cultural communities within anti-rape activism, these solutions remain divorced from their historic roots in radicalism.[95] BIPOC advocates pointed out that many marginalized advocates are *already* connected with one another through conferences and informal networking. One Latinx advocate shared, for example, that her white supervisor had directly connected her to the only other Latinx advocate at a mainstream rape crisis center in her state, which, while helpful, did not redress the enormous racialized labor disparity between Latinx and white advocates. Remedies to resolve white supremacy do not work when they only address one part of the larger issue of racism at rape crisis centers—the prioritization of white professionalism over generations of radical community protest.

Professional advocacy was never designed to facilitate workplace interactions; it has only served to elevate the powers of the state in anti-rape work. Further, the norms around advocacy as a profession have limited the scope of what advocates *could* do. Advocates must desist from the professionalization of advocacy to adequately counteract neoliberal normativity in the anti-rape workplace. However, we must also be cautious about how we go about making change. There are very real, material consequences for advocates who push against the dominant narrative, as we saw with Valériana at the start of this chapter and with many advocates in their stories. Therefore, at the same time that we desist from white professionalism, we must create our own professionalism, one that speaks to the radical core of victim advocacy.

In light of the abuses within the anti-violence movement, transfeminist activist emi koyama proposed the hyperinstitutionalization of advocacy, a transformative process in which expansive advocate norms are created but are premised on radical ideas about work, advocacy, and survivorship.[96] Since professionalization comes from normative state apparatuses, investing in those same norms about education and work will not help advocates better support survivors. As Audre Lorde famously put it, "The master's tools will never dismantle the master's house."[97] Thus, koyama suggests, advocates must begin to develop their own set of standards around helping survivors. This radical version of professionalism counters the racializing tendencies of mainstream professional advocacy by transforming the colonial logics inherent to capitalist nonprofit work.[98]

This transformation of advocacy can take the form of mutual aid organizing: by pooling sick and vacation days for those who need it; by caretaking advocates' dependents when they are on call; by sharing office spaces with survivors and community partners to bridge connections; by simply paying direct services advocates better, living wages with full benefits so that credentialed people are incentivized to do the "ground work" of victim advocacy.[99] It means working with systems only when survivors demand their use, and never acquiescing to systems professionals who seek to coopt advocacy.[100] One advocate offered her perspective of hyperinstitutionalizing an unprofessional advocacy, beginning by hiring and empowering people without credentials but with relevant lived experiences: "These Latinos *are* professionals. They have PhDs and MDs. They have more training and everything. You know? But at the same time, if you give a Latina who, who graduated college or who graduated high school, give them a chance, and they don't have a license or anything, give those people a chance. Because those people, they're trying to make a movement within the community." Changing how we recruit advocates and how we help survivors remakes us into abolitionists. Instead of refusing to acknowledge our own identities and biases, advocates generate our own lived experiences in a "two-way street" between survivors and helpers; we become activists who "think a lot about [our] style and what [we're] saying and listening." Collectively, this type of work refuses normative interpretations of rape responses and opens space for the establishment of critical "affinity groups"—not "employee resource groups" financed by white administrators—who may guide rape responses with culturally humble knowledge. An African American advocate ruminated positively on her experiences serving on a "minority board" of directors and the subsequent increase in specifically Hispanic and Haitian survivors feeling comfortable to reach out for support.

> *Our* approach has been to um, get volunteers from those communities. And our uh minority board has been a big part of that because we have, um, people from each one of those on the board. And I feel like um, it helps when you have someone that is a member of that community to go into that community on your behalf or with you. [. . .] It instantly lowers that guard, 'cause it's almost like oh wait a minute! You know she's with you—okay. He's with you? Okay well maybe I can trust you. And they'll [let] you in just a little bit more.

In contrast to a group of normative systems professionals who pay to be on a board, a minority board directs rape crisis centers to address the local community's needs—because it *is* the community.

Advocates with dominant identities must be willing to engage in radical work as well, actively participating in the construction of a mutual aid collective. In particular, white advocates should be prepared to address their own implicit biases. Instead of believing that white people should not advocate for survivors of color in fear of "white saviorism," or that white people cannot train other white people about racism because it's "not appropriate," *any* advocate with any dominant identity should leverage their unique life skills to support peers and advance the end of rape. A white Christian advocate described her engagements with a lesbian survivor. With surprise, she explained that transparent conversations and reflections on her heteronormative biases led her to deliver better care: "I have to be aware of my own biases, and usually, if I mess up, it's nothing to do with them. It has everything to do with me. Either I'm not understanding what's going on, or something's going on with me. I believe that every advocate does have a bias. And we all have things to improve and work on." BIPOC advocates are already learning about dominant social lives, anyway.[101] As one Black advocate joked, "I specialize in Caucasian."

Anti-rape leadership must also actively dismantle racialized hierarchies in our work. However, such leadership does not mean that a state coalition reifies a hierarchical education system inside rape crisis centers. In one example of recycling institutionalized violence, two BIPOC advocates bemoaned the coalition's "certification" of individual advocates as "Domestic Sexual Violence Response Professionals." Instead of this organizational approach, an advocate with prior administrative experience who returned to direct services explained how administrators can leverage their networks to form more meaningful relationships with diverse communities.

> At this point it's not like advocating for you know women of color on staff. It's not advocating to have a man on staff. It's how do we present ourselves in the community? [...] It needs to start with leadership. We have to have leadership on board, leadership buy-in and clearly there's support throughout processes because they're gonna be the connectors to the board. I think we talk to the board but it's more meaningful coming from [the executive director], from our director. I'm just gonna say that again. Um, in terms of community there's no reason why we aren't already doing this. Honestly.

* * *

Valériana and I met again one year later to chat about her newfound experiences with anti-violence organizing, outside the restraints of mainstream white professional anti-rape work. Like many of the advocates in this study, Valériana had initially reflected white professional norms of nonprofit work, earning qualifications like the Einstein pass and holding a master's degree relevant for recruiting immigrant and Black communities into the anti-rape movement. These professional credentials made her immediately likeable to the white and white-acting WCSAP board. Yet, as WCSAP's staff quickly found out, Valériana's insistence on radicalism in both identity (Black Immigrant) and approaches distinguished her from the white supremacist professional advocacy now pervasive at the coalition. Valériana told me that she refused to back down, which resulted in her expulsion from WCSAP, but she also told me that despite this outcome, she is proud to have served the survivors of Washington state.

Since her departure from WCSAP, Valériana has created her own racial equity consulting business called Necessary Interruptions, an organization that stresses the importance of Black liberation, change management, internal equity audits, and repair work. She has also served as the executive director of the Social Justice Fund NW, a chapter that has allowed her to focus on serving Black, Native, Brown, and marginalized communities who are impacted by social issues from a Black liberation–based perspective. Following in koyama's footsteps, and contrary to WCSAP's expectations of working with so-called systems-based community partners like the police and hospitals, Valériana repurposes white philanthropy into grassroots social justice organizing. She can speak audaciously about transformative justice without the constant threat of white supremacy. Ironically, Valériana shares, WCSAP no longer serves as the main technical provider for the state of Washington. With Valériana's interruption of their anti-Black practices, WCSAP lost considerable funding from OCVA and is now operating at half its staff capacity. In the process of sustaining white supremacist logics, WCSAP became another lesson in the making: advocacy *can* act politically without losing its soul; we can advocate with survivors through other mediums than in the NPIC.

Valériana freely pursues radical work now that she is no longer saddled with the constraints of neoliberal anti-rape organizing. Her advocacy is grounded fully in an evolving abolitionist framework. She actively invites white and white-acting folks with historical cultural wealth to examine their role in interrupting anti-Blackness and supporting BIPOC communities; she counterargues online and in person at meetings when peers say that the movement began with 1970s (white) feminisms; she writes and speaks about the connections among abolition, enslavement, and victim advocacy; and she surrounds herself with BIPOC advocates in a strong coalitional community who root themselves in traditions of resistance and revolution. She has also introduced new labor norms at her agency. Resources are regularly moved from administration to the front lines, and staff members enjoy a thirty-two-hour work week and a minimum two-week bereavement leave, which supports diverse advocates with families across the globe. This new advocacy that she has created is inspired by many Black femmes who have spoken out about interrupting unrealistic exploitative labor ideologies that seek to extract instead of to create. Valériana tells us that it is vital to build a hyperinstitutionalized, radically defiant advocacy to give breath for people—advocates, survivors, BIPOC—to find justice, freedom, and liberation from all forms of violence.

As of March 27, 2024, Valériana Chikoti-Bandua Estes officially became a US citizen. She mused, "In 2020, the month of March was once a traumatic month for me. Now it is a month where I will get to commemorate a new chapter. Despite the concerted efforts to silence me, I am reminded of a sea of my ancestors who came before my time and a sea of descendants who will follow after my time, who will continue to raise our voices to support Black liberation."

REFERENCES FOR FIGURE 3.1 on page 113

Figure statistics have been collected from a variety of sources to collate a portrait of the current rape responder workforce. However, some data are not available. To account for these gaps, this figure has amalgamated sources based on related information, for instance, estimating the racial and gender demographics of sexual assault medical-forensic examiners based on registered nurse racial and gender demographics, given that certified sexual assault examiners must hold at least a registered nursing credential. Due to data limitations, the figure may not accurately represent the rape responder workforce.

1 Cora Peterson, Sarah DeGue, Curtis Florence, and Globy N. Lokey, "Lifetime Economic Burden of Rape Among U.S. Adults," *American Journal of Preventive Medicine* 52, no. 6 (2017): 691–701, https://doi.org/10.1016/j.amepre.2016.11.014; Maria Hardeberg Bach, Nina Beck Hansen, Courtney Ahrens, Cecilie Reendal Nielsen, Catherine Walshe, and Maj Hansen, "Underserved Survivors of Sexual Assault: A Systematic Scoping Review," *European Journal of Psychotraumatology* 12, no. 1 (2021): 1895516, https://doi.org/10.1080/20008198.2021.189551 6; "Victims of Sexual Violence: Statistics," RAINN, accessed May 29, 2024, https://www.rainn.org.
2 "Social and Human Service Assistants," O*Net OnLine, accessed March 20, 2024, https://www.onetonline.org; "Victim Advocate Salary," Zippia, March 14, 2024, https://www.zippia.com.
3 Stephen McCall and Kezia Scales, "Direct Care Worker Disparities: Key Trends and Challenges," Issue Brief (New York: PHI, February 2022), https://www.phinational.org.
4 "Social and Community Service Managers," O*Net OnLine, accessed May 29, 2024, https://www.onetonline.org.
5 Building Movement Project, "Race to Lead Revisited: Obstacles and Opportunities in Addressing the Nonprofit Racial Leadership Gap" (Building Movement Project, 2020), https://buildingmovement.org.
6 Angela Ogunjimi, "Is the Salary of an Executive Director of a Non-Profit a Percentage of the Budget?," CHRON., October 26, 2018, https://smallbusiness.chron.com.
7 "Police and Sheriff's Patrol Officers," O*Net OnLine, accessed March 21, 2024, https://www.onetonline.org; Rich Morin, Kim Parker, Renee Stepler, and Andrew Mercer, "Inside America's Police Departments" (Pew Research Center, January 11, 2017), https://www.pewresearch.org.
8 "Detectives and Criminal Investigators," O*Net OnLine, 2024, https://www.onetonline.org; "Sex Crimes Detective Demographics and Statistics in the US," Zippia, accessed May 29, 2024, https://www.zippia.com.
9 Luona Lin and Alexandra Ginsberg, "American Psychological Association Uses ACS Data to Identify Need for Mental Health Services, Education, and Training" (United States Census Bureau, May 11, 2011), https://www.census.gov; "Clinical and Counseling Psychologists," O*Net OnLine, accessed May 29, 2024, https://www.onetonline.org.
10 Lisa Bowleg, "We're Not All in This Together: On COVID-19, Intersectionality, and Structural Inequality," *American Journal of Public Health* 110, no. 7 (July 2020): 917–917, https://doi.org/10.2105/AJPH.2020.305766; "Registered Nurses," O*Net OnLine, accessed March 21, 2024, https://www.onetonline.org; "Nursing Workforce Fact Sheet" (American Association of Colleges of Nursing, April 2024), https://www.aacnnursing.org.
11 "Lawyers," O*Net OnLine, accessed March 21, 2024, https://www.onetonline.org; "ABA Profile of the Legal Profession 2020" (American Bar Association, 2020), https://www.americanbar.org, 32.
12 "Sexual Violence and Transgender/Non-Binary Communities," National Sexual Violence Resource Center (NSVRC), 2019, https://www.nsvrc.org; "Perpetrators of Sexual Violence: Statistics," RAINN, accessed March 22, 2024, https://www.rainn.org.

4

Our Carceral Creep

Panoptic Policing of the Anti-Rape Community

> In the vocabulary of the prison nation, being "in the community" simply means not being in prison and occupying the same physical space as others. But community has a deeper meaning—a common bond, a sense of mutual care and responsibility—and it is this meaning that disintegrates in the face of constant surveillance and restrictions.
> —Maya Schenwar and Victoria Law, *Prison by Any Other Name*

"Community" is a fickle term. We advocates sling the word around as though there is a universal "community" that we serve (survivors) and an assumed "community" out there to whom we are responsible (the multicultural people in town). A cursory glance at our communities, however, will show that community is complex, and difficult to identify. Mia Mingus from the Bay Area Transformative Justice Collective pointed out that "many people do not feel connected to a 'community' and, even more so, most people did not know what 'community' meant or had wildly different definitions and understandings of 'community.'"[1] This obfuscation of what we mean by "community" has led many survivors in immediate need to turn to the people whom advocates frequently call "community partners."

The problem is, the people whom we call "community partners" are not, in fact, our radical community. Across the archipelago of formal rape response agencies are rape crisis centers, police stations, sexual assault forensic-medical examiner (SAFE) facilities, and courthouses. The professionals represented in these industries, including police and correctional officers, investigators, SAFEs,[2] attorneys, and judges, entered the anti-rape movement only in recent decades, yet today are considered some of the most critical members of sexual assault response teams (SARTs). Formalized through neoliberal welfare policies, particularly the Violence Against Women Act (VAWA), SARTs are multidisciplinary teams, sometimes abbreviated as "MDT," in which systems-based rape response professionals have a two-pronged agenda to prosecute the offender and to support individual victims, typically as they navigate the complex criminal legal system. Though not all rape crisis centers are a part of or lead SARTs, a significant number formally work with carceral sectors, and those who do not work in official SARTs nevertheless operate using memorandums of understanding (MOUs) between carceral agents and advocates.[3] For example, spaces like One Place or Family Justice Center usually operate in one building with advocates, police officers, SAFEs, and attorneys working as colleagues, and survivors merely need to cross a hallway to undergo a forensic exam or a police interrogation.[4]

While advocates who work in a SART and/or closely with carceral agents can support victims who wish to see justice through the criminal legal system, advocacy's present reliance on the carceral state for funding encourages advocates to prioritize carceral pathways after rape. The pressures that we place on maintaining these "community" relationships translates into managing or excusing systems-based violence against the survivors who have asked us to support them in their communities. Gradually, our routine acquiescence to carceral professionals makes us believe that our jobs are not to protest any system of surveillance or control, such as that of the prison industrial complex, and advocates begin to police survivors *for* the US settler-carceral state—all without us realizing that we have turned carceral.

This rise of carceralism in anti-rape work has been inconspicuous, to be sure.[5] I believe that anti-rape advocates likely would not have bowed to carceralism had it not been for its "stealth revolution."[6] Nonetheless, I also believe that many present-day advocates have accepted carceralism as a core component of advocacy through our relationships to systems. Though many advocates may desire an anticarceral approach to victim advocacy, many of us also admit that we are unfamiliar with restorative or transformative justice, and/or feel that we cannot practice alternative advocacy other than the carceral one as prescribed by our agencies.[7] In contrast to abolitionism of all forms of violence, anti-rape advocates have taken up a carceral liberalism that acknowledges the harms of carceralism without taking steps to address the violence endemic to it.[8]

By remaining silent about our complicity in the surveillance and punishment of survivors, advocates become carceral agents, in our bodies fermenting the very carceral disease we protest. The anti-rape movement, then, must fundamentally change. Alongside efforts to remap our advocacy strategies for both survivors and each other, we need to identify our community, which I understand as the people who will stand in solidarity with us as we advocate for the end of rape. This chapter explores the ways that advocates unknowingly perform as carceral agents and the effects of their carceral performances on marginalized victims in the neoliberal rape crisis center. I extend the arguments made by anti-carceral feminists by arguing not just that advocates *collaborate* with carceral agents, which thereby emboldens carceralism, but that advocacy itself—the way that we conduct advocacy today—*is* carceral. This carceral advocacy, manifested through state privatization of anti-rape work, mutates the rape crisis center from an independent, survivor-centered space into a kind of prison cell, displacing radicalism from its own home in anti-rape collectives.

The Carceral Creep

Carceralism is defined as the regulation of people, typically but not always through the criminal legal system. It is not a new phenomenon. But it *is* new to anti-rape advocacy. As explored in chapter 1, many scholars attribute the rise in carceralism in anti-rape work to the neoliberal turn of the 1990s.[9] However, using a feminist of color approach, a few scholars have questioned this narrative. This latter group of scholars sees carceralism as a weapon long utilized by white normative policing professionals to exploit and oppress marginalized peoples.[10] From enslavement and colonial captivity to the earliest invention of the penitentiary in the late 1700s, white settlers constructed an Anglo-American legal system to bring marginalized populations under their control.[11] However, such control is often invisible to the mainstream public today. Mimi E. Kim calls this hidden carceral intrusion into advocacy the "carceral creep": "the incremental and often imperceptible advance of carceral forces that led to the eventual domination of crime control within a feminist social movement field that was once almost devoid of its presence."[12]

State surveillance is sustained through the literal confinement of criminalized people in prisons, as well as exceptions and gaps in the law. For example, following the Civil War, white settlers who were former slave owners exploited a loophole in the Thirteenth Amendment that exempted those convicted of a crime from enslavement or indentured servitude laws.[13] They created the concept of convict leasing, in which incarcerated persons legally labor(ed) for free or under minimum wage on behalf of the state.[14] Despite having achieved emancipation, men of color, especially Black men, were accused of sexual violence and lynched, first through extrajudicial murders and then through the US criminal legal system.[15] This imprisonment has consequences for Black women and children, as well as other women and children of color, by altering family dynamics and divorcing communities from their generational knowledges and cultures.[16] Though we might think about carceralism as only about prison confinement, carceralism encompasses a broad range of activities designed to control marginalized populations through sociolegal means.

While carceralism has long been at play in US governance, the 1960s neoconservative turn jumpstarted the use of carceralism in feminist causes.[17] At the time, the Black Power, Red Power, Gay Liberation, Civil Rights, and related racial and gender justice movements had seen some success through desegregation and the passage of the Civil Rights Act. Many queer/ed communities of color had built their own responses to social woes outside the constraints of white colonial systems; they created innovative food programs, collective housing, and fair wage employment opportunities to alleviate social burdens placed on them by white colonizers.[18] The successes of local programs provoked concern from the US government, which saw mutual aid as a danger to the existing legal system. In 1961, building on Franklin D. Roosevelt's New Deal, John F. Kennedy helped to pass a series of antidelinquency programs in sixteen cities that offered education, counseling, and job training to low-income Americans. These programs were then expanded by Lyndon B. Johnson's "Great Society" programs starting in 1964 to generate public support for the federal government.[19] Johnson's program expanded the reach of the welfare state by offering more inclusive subsidies for medi-

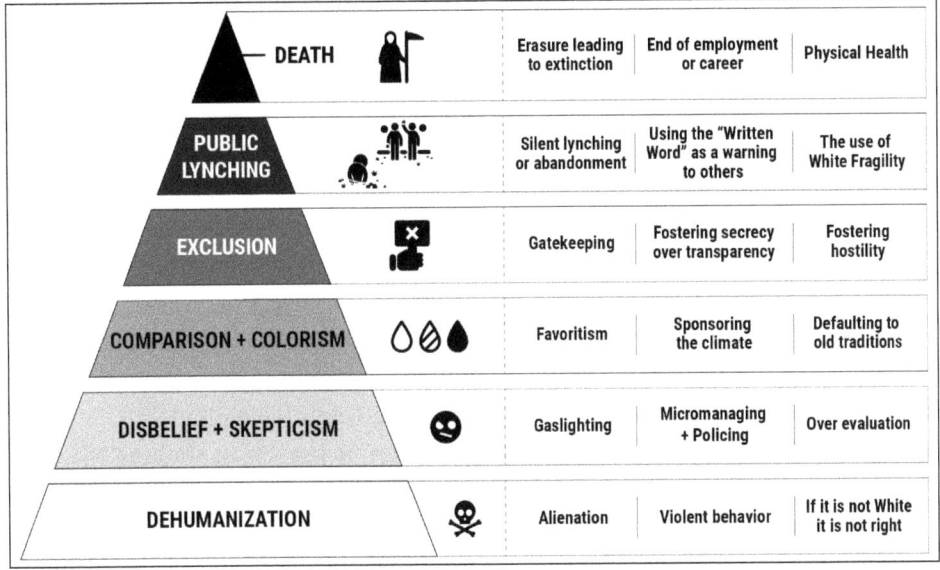

Figure 4.1. Anti-Blackness/Oppression Pyramid. Courtesy of Valériana Chikoti-Bandua Estes, with design support from Jackie Chen.

cal care, conservation, family planning, and cash assistance. Survivors, including women of color, could find temporary respite in the programs to address the violence that they had experienced.[20]

Though the Great Society programs aided some US citizens, the Johnson administration quickly shifted to a new rhetoric by the mid-1960s that would come to harm many marginalized people, called the "War on Poverty."[21] The social justice movements of the 1960s had stripped white elite Americans of some of their wealth, and faced with the prospect of losing their power, white settlers began to employ an anticrime rhetoric to oppress marginalized populations. Instead of explicitly mutilating and killing marginalized people through enslavement and racial codes, white settlers claimed that crime was a result of poor people. They labeled radical activists as "terrorists" and "criminals" who were taking away job and family opportunities from the more "worthy" and "innocent" "poor" people, namely, white cisgender and heterosexual families and normative-acting people of color.[22] This ideology, rooted in racism and sexism, entangled hard-line carceral approaches with antipoverty projects. Johnson's War on Poverty included the passage of the

Law Enforcement Assistance Act (1965), which militarized local law enforcement, and the Omnibus Crime Control and Safe Streets Act (1968), which established the federal agency, the Law Enforcement Assistance Administration (LEAA), that administrates police funding.[23] The newfound police bureaucracies amplified white settler beliefs that reducing crime would alleviate poverty while disguising normative interventions in poor and racial minority communities as "help." Michelle Alexander explains it simply: "In the era of colorblindness, it is no longer socially permissible to use race, explicitly, as a justification for discrimination, exclusion, and social contempt. So we don't. Rather than rely on race, we use our criminal justice system to label people of color 'criminals' and then engage in all the practices we supposedly left behind."[24]

Rape, and rape myths, played a significant role in shaping the War on Poverty. Criminologist Menachim Amir's widely read 1968 study on incarcerated sexual offenders falsely reported that most rapists are Black men, which exaggerated the already-existing myth that Black men frequently sexually assault (white) women.[25] In the same year, Black Panther member Eldridge Cleaver's *Soul on Ice* actively called for the rape of white women to assert Black male dominance. Both texts formed a crucial part of white anti-rape journalist Susan Brownmiller's influential book, *Against Our Will*, in 1975.[26] *Against Our Will* encouraged the American public to address sexual violence but preyed on white fears about Black masculine violence to cultivate legal anti-rape activism.[27] Resultingly, late-stage "second wave" anti-rape advocates came to form their activism not around abolitionist principles, as they had once done, but around "crime and control" policies.[28] For example, in 1972, the DC Rape Crisis Center originally cautioned against the presence of police officers in anti-rape responses, noting, "It was immediately decided when the Center first met that we did not wish to work directly with the police. . . . We do not waste much energy in having to engage in meaningless games with the police bureaucracy."[29] However, one year later, DC advocates admitted that they were having difficulty in reaching survivors before they contacted the police, and by 1977, DC advocates wrote, "It is the responsibility of the Rape Crisis Center to develop and maintain working relationships with other public institutions with which rape victims have contact, in order to facilitate our work as victim advocates."[30] In lieu of working with racial and sexual non-systems communities in a peer-to-peer network, rape response coordinators began to train their staff members to work closely with "community partners," now defined as police officers, doctors, and lawyers.[31] DC was not alone. Fueled by growing calls for the professionalization of anti-violence work, numerous anti-rape agencies opted to collaborate with LEAA to develop what they termed a "comprehensive" response to victims of crime.[32]

The War on Poverty gradually devolved into a "War on Drugs" agenda that accelerated the use of prison systems to address rape. Prior to the 1970s, drugs like marijuana were not heavily regulated by law enforcement, nor commonly used by communities of color. However, Richard Nixon spearheaded a campaign to challenge drug usage, which he and similar neoconservative politicians claimed was responsible for impoverishing American neighborhoods.[33] Under the guise that he was "helping" those communities out of poverty, Nixon increased law enforcement presence in poor Black communities.[34] Petty crimes like possession of personal marijuana were met with mandatory convictions and minimum sentencing guidelines. Many of those incarcerated were, and are, not incarcerated because of felony crimes; instead, many of those convicted were incarcerated for personal drug possession.[35] Racist myths about incarcerated persons persisted. Black men were considered the primary culprits in the war against drugs, and by extension, rape.[36] Consequently, as neoconservatives called for liberty and freedom, the United States began to incarcerate more people per capita than any other country in the world, sparking what we call today "mass incarceration."[37] Of the 1.9 million people incarcerated in the "1,566 state prisons, 98 federal prisons, 3,116 local jails, 1,323 juvenile correctional facilities, 142 immigration detention facilities, and 80 Indian country jails, as well as in military prisons, civil commitment centers, state psychiatric hospitals, and prisons in the U.S. territories," 35 percent of them identify as Black Americans and 20 percent of them identify as Latinos, despite the fact that Black Americans only make up 14 percent and Latinos make up 19 percent of the US population, respectively.[38] The War on Drugs, in short, led to higher rates of arrest, conviction, and sentencing rates of Black people and non-Black people of color, who were incorrectly presumed to make up the majority of violent criminals like rapists.

The "tough on crime" rhetoric metastasized into the neoconservative belief that poor people needed to "help" themselves out of poverty to avoid a life of crime. Just a decade after Nixon, Ronald Reagan purported that crime, including rape, would not happen if poor people simply "pulled themselves up by the bootstraps," or pulled themselves out of poverty and away from sexual violence supposedly rampant in poor neighborhoods. Reagan reduced welfare spending to "incentivize" people in need to work, making substantial cuts to programs that had previously helped marginalized people under the Johnson administration.[39] Queer Black femmes and femmes of color, particularly unpartnered mothers, were accused of using drugs that depreciated the value of their communities, and rape victim–blaming escalated. White settlers derogatorily labeled many of these women, a majority of whom had experienced intimate partner or stranger sexual violence, as being "welfare queens" who depended too heavily on the welfare state system instead of the victims of rape and the state that they were and are.[40] This racialization of poverty and drugs cast women of color as nonvictims who were deserving of punishment while the image of the ideal white woman rape victim took center stage. The rate of women's incarceration, and especially of women of color, accelerated to nearly twice that of men's rate of incarceration.[41]

Bill Clinton reshaped liberal welfare policies that explicitly used the state to alleviate social burdens into *new*-liberal policies that assumed that private markets could suitably replace public welfare.[42] Clinton eradicated social benefits that had come with earlier state welfare programs, including cash assistance, and placed substantial conditions on the uses of public funding, which mainly targeted people on food stamps and public housing assistance—many of whom were and are, again, rape victims.[43] The privatization of welfare pressured anti-rape advocates to change directions. As public welfare funding was cut, local communities became overly burdened with supporting the growing masses of people in need, and many anti-rape collectives found themselves unable to continue financing rape victim support from their local donors. Advocates looked to possible funding streams from grant agencies like LEAA and other carceral entities.[44] Instead of operating as independent mutual aid collectives with the authority to support survivors throughout the long postrape process, advocates conceded to the myth that they needed carceral systems to carry out effective rape victim services. Many advocates began to support the passage of anti-sexual harassment policies in workplaces, schools, and government offices to persuade the public to fund their work and legitimize victims.[45] They also threw support behind major anticrime legislation, including the Violent Crime Control and Law Enforcement Act, of which VAWA is a part.[46]

In 1994, Clinton signed VAWA into law, establishing rape crisis centers and thus formally sedimenting carceral presence in rape responses. VAWA fostered a climate of aggressive policing of domestic violence and sex trafficking incidents, and set aside $9.7 billion for prisons and $6.1 billion for prevention programs, primarily for the hiring of new law enforcement officers.[47] It authorized police presence in anti-violence situations, such as implementing mandatory arrest policies and expanded funding for officer anti-rape trainings.[48] VAWA also enhanced advocates' collaboration with state representatives, approving substantial funds to expand policing, including rape investigations, and streamlining victim services to increase the prosecution of sex offenders.[49] The deployment of state representatives to address sexual violence signaled a significant shift away from the state's dismissal of rape to an active acknowledgment that the harms of rape are real.[50] But it also had the effect of making advocacy into a job that only "professionals" could execute. Advocates at independent feminist collectives were funneled into formalized nonprofit rape crisis centers and, to be paid through carceral grants for their work, were expected to collaborate with carceral agents.[51] Further, VAWA reauthorizations in 2005 and 2013 expanded carceral authority over rape responses involving certain marginalized populations, including immigrants, college students, and tribal citizens. These organizational impositions over anti-rape work ensured what Benjamin Weiss termed rape crisis centers' "path dependence" toward a "carceral lock-in," a state in which anti-rape organizations cannot divine alternatives to carceralism due to procedural eminence.[52]

Undeniably, carceralism has "crept" into anti-rape advocacy. Instead of a sudden fusion between advocacy and prison systems, carceral agents slowly criminalized vulnerable populations that are more likely to be abused by perpetrators in power—poor, queer, and nonnormative families—at the same time that they extinguished comprehensive welfare supports for those same survivors. This routinized rhetoric about normative rape and carceral agents' saviorism eliminates advocates' awareness of the carceral creep, recycling and reinforcing myths about our "community" partners.[53] Gradually, we set aside our responsibility to victims, bargaining their bodies to make rape into a legitimate, state-recognized crime.

Carceral Collusions

The harms against rape victims by the carceral state are not unknown. Echoing generations of activist approaches to rape work, advocates are generally aware that police officers often revictimize survivors by refusing to investigate their cases, interrogating them, and sometimes raping them as they seek help.[54] They are aware that SAFEs can revictimize survivors by forcing them to undergo a medical-forensic exam ("rape kit") even when they do not want to report their assaults or engage with the medical industrial complex,[55] and they are aware that less than 1 percent of cases make it to jury trial.[56] In the unlikely event that a survivor's case is brought to court, advocates are familiar with how attorneys can force victims to relive their experiences while on the stand.[57]

Most advocates described at least one incident involving a systems professional harming a survivor. In one vivid narrative, an advocate with a bachelor's degree in criminology described an incident in which police officers pressured a victim into withdrawing her statement and then charged the victim with false reporting for withdrawing from the criminal legal system. She said,

> They took [the victim's] statement and then the next day she contacted me and she said, "I just can't go through with this. Like, I can't, I don't want to deal with this. I don't want to deal with this for the next couple of years. Like, I just want it over and done with." So she contacted the police department and they said pretty much under false pretenses, had her come, um, to collect her things that they had taken as evidence. Um, they put her back in a room and started questioning her and then said, "Well, we're going to be filing . . . I talked to the perpetrator and we feel like this was a, um, consensual sexual act and that you filed a false police report." And she, she just got sentenced. She had to write him an apology letter. And it's like, I can't, she's on probation now for

at least nine months. She has to have a mental health evaluation. She has to have a drug and alcohol evaluation. She has to write him an apology letter, all because she decided that because of the way she was being treated in the, at the police station, she just couldn't keep doing that. And I remember being on the call and our [district attorney] went on, and then whenever she went to say the charges against this girl, she said, "Well, this is one of the most disturbing things I've ever seen." And I'm like, are you kidding me? Like, she, she does not in her mind, see that there should ever be a call for someone not wanting to press charges. Literally, what is that telling every other survivor out there? Like, hey, if you call the police or you go forward, like this is very possible, this is what's gonna happen to you too. And her, her name was in the newspaper along with her charges.

Incidents of interpersonal carceral violence are imbricated with racialized, sexed, and interrelated oppressions. A Brown Latina advocate who supported an underage Black female victim angrily remarked on the ways that an officer treated her:

> I've had a client, for example that um, the, the prosecutor said that their case was because they tried to hurt themselves, and it was like a [domestic violence and sexual assault] case. And then, the end of the case was, oh this young Black girl of thirteen years old tried to hurt herself because she wanted to. And then I was like, what, what's going on here? [...] What's going on here? If it was, if it was a white thirteen-year-old girl that wouldn't have happened. You have the arrest and this would not have happened.

In these accounts, advocates show that they are acutely aware of how common it is for systems professionals to be violent toward victims, especially those who are marginalized.

Nevertheless, although advocates showed keen awareness of how their carceral colleagues often secondarily victimize survivors, advocates also implicitly endorsed carceral feminism. Carceral feminism is the "reliance on policing, prosecution, and imprisonment to resolve gendered or sexual violence."[58] Proponents of carceral feminism believe that rape law has "failed" to adequately punish offenders and therefore seek to reform the criminal legal system. One of the most significant justifications for reform is that few rapists face any consequences for their actions. Thus, carceral feminists have expanded rape statutes to cover a wide range of rape forms, such as intimate partner rape or more recently, stealthing, and lobbied for harsher perpetrator punishments, like minimum sentencing guidelines.[59] They also advocate for changes to the ways that rape victims are processed through the criminal legal system, for instance, lowering evidentiary standards for rape, enhancing the diversity of jury selection, and permitting the use of victim impact statements during rape trials.[60]

The ways that advocates support carceral feminism departed from reformist efforts. Instead of openly endorsing rape law reforms, which they believed too strongly reflected the values of 1970s white radical feminists, some advocates presented systems professionals as "failing" at their duties to support victims. They rationalized that SART colleagues simply need more culturally informative training; they said that systems professionals are "doing their job" and that the prosecution of the offender is inherently "uncomfortable" but will lead to positive justice outcomes if only survivors comply. Emphasizing differences in individual personality, one described her relationships with systems professionals as a "dichotomy," noting how there are "some officers who're just like nice . . . And some that I've wanted to punch in the face." Another advocate felt that systems professionals and advocates were working toward the same goal, to end rape, but sometimes systems professionals were not adequately prepared to collaborate with advocates.

> We [systems professionals and advocates] don't have fundamental differences, but we have different ways that we understand the world. And so, I spend a lotta time educating about things that I learned about in college my freshman year, right, about, you know, history is written by the oppressor, right? But I don't say that. I talk about, well, you know, you wanna—like, if we get into a political conversation about, say, food stamps or something like that. Um, then I'll bring them to talking—you know, to thinking about houses we have gone to where clearly that person is on food stamps and are they rollin' in the big money? And like, misconceptions, right?

Defending carceral feminism, if implicitly, the advocate insists that systems professionals "don't have fundamental differences"; "we," the SART, have a common cause. This perspective leads the advocate to change her advocacy behaviors, such as switching out how "history is written by the oppressor" for SNAP-eligible people who are not "rollin' in the big money." She describes, "I've been able to switch language. I've been able to get, um, a relationship that allows for people to actually be heard, because I have made that adjustment, versus the other folks who burned themselves out, are no longer doing the work in this capacity, um, and don't have access. [. . .] It's been really effective with the team I work with, to the point that they want an advocate for all of their interactions, um, because they've seen how effective it is. And I watch their language shift when they see how effective my language is." Contrary to the advocates who "burned themselves out" from resisting carceral authority, the advocate draws on carceral language to sustain her presence in rape responses. The change in language further allowed SART members to "see how effective my language is" and thus "want an advocate for all of their interactions."

Such minor adaptations to one's language may not appear to have significant impact on advocacy overall. In fact, they might even appear beneficial for survivors seeking carceral justice. However, carceral collusions are presented as individual, not structural, disagreements between advocates and systems professionals. Instead of seeing how the prison industrial complex actively criminalizes BIPOC and marginalized people, advocates buy into the myth that only a handful of individuals are responsible for systems-based secondary harm; thus, they believe that their role is also only limited to the interpersonal level. For example, an advocate shared how she had previously taken a more visibly radical feminist approach to law enforcement but then changed tactics.

> So, it—it's not uncommon, right, for there to be some tension between law enforcement and, uh, advocates, especially nonprofit advocates, uh, because of the role that nonprofit advocates play, you know? So I was in the hospitals, providing support . . . And what I found is like, what [radicalism] did is it punished the survivor, right? It was like, "Here, I'm gonna—I'm toeing this line and this like, very hard line of how advocacy should be done." But what ended up happening is that the survivor ended up getting punished because advocates created a negative relation-

ship [with law enforcement] that said there's times you have to fight and you have to, you know, have the d[ifficult], tough conversations. But what I found was that the tension wasn't necessary because law enforcement doesn't respond well to, you know, little ladies, um, comin' at them with, like, their, you know, feminist facts, right? [. . .] When you come at people that way, um, it's a turnoff, right?

Positioning herself as an ardent feminist, the advocate illustrates that law enforcement feels dissuaded from engaging with advocates when they are outwardly "feminist," such as by "comin' at them with, like, their . . . feminist facts." Thus, even though she vocalized her awareness of police brutality against BIPOC, the advocate decided to swallow her identity as an advocate and present herself as a like-minded systems professional. These changes are individualized; they are not efforts to abolish systematic intersectional violence. Further, they imply that there is, as seen in chapter 3, a "normative" advocate who can agreeably work with violent systems.

A Community Problem

Carceral logics and their intersectional implications for marginalized survivors get "baked into" the organizational structures of a SART.[61] Justified on the knowledge that carceral agents frequently perpetuate harm against survivors, advocate positions like "police victim advocates," "court advocates," "medical advocates," and so forth were created to ensure that survivors' rights are adequately represented in carceral spaces. Many of us work as "medical" or "legal" advocates whose sole function is to support victims as they testify about their rape to carceral systems. Still others work as Prison Rape Elimination Act (PREA) coordinators whose role is to report sexual assault to the state and whose salaries come from LEAA and similar carceral grants.[62] Even those who do not operate within the confinements of prison systems, such as hotline counselors, find themselves having to collaborate closely with carceral actors to respond to victims, indirectly underscoring carceral authority in anti-rape responses.[63] In one report, 78 percent of domestic violence and sexual assault coalitions reported that they collaborated with their state's Department of Corrections (DOC), with just over half

(54 percent) reporting that they received funding through VAWA or Victims of Crime Act (VOCA) to carry out DOC tasks.[64]

The financial hierarchy of SARTs reflects the state's judgment of rape response roles. On average, as of 2022, patrol officers ("beat cops") who most often engage with victims during acute rape situations earn $31.63 hourly or $65,790 annually; criminal investigators earn $43.80 hourly or $91,100 annually; and lawyers earn $65.26 hourly or $135,740 annually, irrespective of whether the perpetrator is convicted and sentenced to victims' needs.[65] SAFEs, who often work at a non-rape-specific job and conduct rape exams on a case-by-case basis, earn $39.05 hourly or $81,220 annually at their regular jobs and are incentivized to participate in anti-rape work through one-time stipends per case, such as $200 per victim examined irrespective of whether the case makes it to trial and requires SAFE testimony.[66] Advocates, on the other hand, earn paltry wages in comparison (see Figure 3.1).

Not only are advocates compensated less than systems professionals, but there is also an external *racialized* and *gendered* hierarchy between systems professionals and victim advocates in SARTs. Like the rape crisis center internalized hierarchy between administration and direct services, the majority of police officers identify as white men, over 78 percent of accredited legal professionals identify as white and 58 percent identify as men, and 81.7 percent of accredited nurses, including SAFEs, are white cisgender heterosexual women.[67] Most of these professionals are trained in white cultural ideology. For example, even if an officer does not identify as racially white, law enforcement officers work in a carceral system premised on racist "slavecatching" narratives; they must capture a presumed "bad guy" without addressing the roots of a "criminal's" deviant behaviors.[68] This approach to crime is deeply intertwined with daily interactions between police officers. Many racial minority and female police officers have reported experiencing workplace discrimination when compared to white male officers, such as an absence of supervisor support or lower rates of promotion, despite the fact that they are generally more likely to deescalate violent situations.[69] In contrast, as advocates empirically observed, many direct services advocates who coordinate with beat cops and nurses are more often BIPOC, former victims, and marginalized themselves, some with intimate experiences in grassroots feminist movements.[70] They are also more likely to serve in nonroutine work shifts without benefits and to be more recently hired, creating a division between the systems "professional" who has worked in anti-rape spaces for years compared to the "unprofessional" amateur advocate.

Combined with the institutional directives for systems collaboration, the uneven socioeconomic compensation of SART members weakens direct services advocates' power to advocate with the survivor relative to their SART colleagues. Some advocates explained that they felt "uncomfortable" with challenging systems authorities because they were either more inexperienced than they or believed that they were not allowed to interrupt systems professionals who were in the process of carrying out their work. Describing her discomfort with supporting disabled survivors, an advocate with a graduate degree elevated the SAFE's capacity to support a victim in place of herself: "The nurses are way better at memorizing stuff than I am (laughs). [. . .] I really think the nurse—there're some things I just kind of feel like the nurses kind of [have a] handle on and I think in this situation, where like, disability being relevant, um, that's something that they're probably more equipped to handle. I feel like, the nurses have a way of—I mean they have to ask the medical history. So if someone does have a disability I feel like that's the time that it comes up." An advocate who worked with an incarcerated survivor similarly ceded authority to correctional officers during resource distribution. Though she does not extol the officers in the same way that the aforementioned advocate does with SAFEs, she nevertheless hesitates to advocate for the incarcerated survivor in fear of carceral professionals.

> INTERVIEWEE: The people that are like in prisons or incarcerated or stuff like that, I'm always asking whoever transported [them] the police people (terse, hard voice) are they allowed to have this? Are you letting them take this on the [police van]? (resumes regular voice) Sometimes they're jerks and sometimes they're like totally cool and so I'll like, load them up with four Gatorades (laughs).
> INTERVIEWER: I usually just do it and then ask for permission later, like, once you give it to them what are they gonna do, take it away?
> INTERVIEWEE: Well that's the thing, I don't want them to be mean to them or like assume—this is only my train of thought. I don't want them to be mean to them, take it away, 'cause I feel like that would

hurt even worse like, there would be like, not having it and then having it like it's so close and it gets taken away from you. Or alternatively they think that they stole it, you know?

The advocate exposes the ways that carceral authorities often undercut the mission to abolish all violence, in this case, by flexing their power to manage victim capital over incarcerated survivors. She, like many other advocates, is acutely aware that policing agents often revictimize survivors in the process of "helping" them. Nevertheless, she implicitly uplifts systems professionals' authority by asking for permission to carry out her role as an advocate from the correctional officers, in doing so reducing her authority in the SART.

Through the negation of advocacy in SART contexts, advocates come to see their work as it interfaces with systems, not around survivors' worlds. One advocate shared this view of her work: "We provide like direct crisis counseling um, which is kind of responding to the immediate needs of the victim, like in the ER. And then on top of that, there's both like legal and medical advocacy. [. . .] What it really is is knowing how to answer questions about the medical and legal systems and where you become an advocate is like, actually interfacing with those systems." Another advocate described her role as a "court victim advocate." Although she was adamant about her allegiance to survivors, she explained how she saw other "court advocates" perceive their work.

> Technically you're responsible to the prosecutors, not position, not to the client, not to the survivor . . . But I think fundamentally that [advocacy] role is still very much centered around the criminal legal process. Like it, it revolves around that process. . . . That technical assistance really rests on both having a very, I think deep understanding of not only the way that things are supposed to work, but how things work in practice and then where you can . . . where is there room to move from how it works to where it's—how it's supposed to work. And I mean like those, those, um, entry points to make things less shitty for your client or for your survivor. Um, having a deeper understanding of those. [. . .] Well, you have to know the law, right? Like the legislation and its implementation. You have to have an understanding of what it looks like in practice. And then you have to have relationships with the pla—the people involved in all of that system in or-

der to push towards not just what the law says or what should be happening or what . . . but also what your client or survivor is, is most interested in seeing. What healing, what accountability means to that person.

The advocate points out that because anti-rape work is tied to the criminal legal system, advocates are expected to hold a "deeper understanding" of the carceral process. This "need" to know about carceral systems, despite that they are there to listen to "what healing, what accountability means to that person," compels advocates to work more closely with the "people in all of that system." With time, these relationships to systems bring advocates closer to the agendas of the carceral state rather than the inverse, bringing systems professionals closer to the agenda of abolishing intersectional rape.

Although carceral knowledge can help advocates navigate systems better, advocates have become devalued in the SART relative to systems professionals because of their routine relationships with the state. In a study of three SARTs involving seventy-nine professionals, police officers and SAFEs reported seeing themselves as having greater value in SARTs than advocates, even though advocates have been shown to be most respectful, clear, and culturally sensitive to survivors compared to their team members.[71] In part, advocates implied, the closer one reflects carceral professionalism, or white cultural ideology, the more likely it is that one is seen as a legitimate authority, gains promotions, is paid better wages, and thus remains in the field for longer periods of time. Despite the fact that they created rape responses, victim advocates are gradually pushed to the margins of their own SART communities.

An advocate who serves as the SART liaison for her agency described the gradual shift in her position from that of a mainstay responder to that of an "assistant" to SART colleagues.

> Now it's required that there's a SANE nurse always available to each hospital, um, so it feels like in a lot of ways, my responsibil[ity]—(laughs)—the like, oh good someone who knows what they're doing is here has lightened, um. 'Cause I've definitely had, you know, kind of had to like, help walk nurses through calls and be like—you know, we need to do the evidence collection like this, not like that, oh we don't have to do it in order. And seeing nurses and medical staff open it for the first time

and be like, hm! What's all this now? Um. And that's, that's lightened a lot [of the advocacy work] so now it's more, um, sometimes it feels more assist-y? Kind of like assistant-y? Like you know it's it feels more like backup than like a guide.

Changes to SART dynamics have real implications for advocates' capacity to support marginalized victims. Unlike previous mutual aid arrangements in which peers worked with and for peers, advocates elevate the power of systems professionals in another version of the normative anti-rape work hierarchy, suggesting to victims that they should be grateful for *any* rape response.[72] One white advocate admitted that she was "conditioned" to trust police: "I have been conditioned and taught from a young age that like, police are good, police are friends you know?" And while she resisted parroting the narrative of "good" police with a "few bad apples," the advocate nonetheless asserted the expertise of her SART colleagues.

> I think um, my sort of number one thing is (slows pace) to recognize . . . the person who I'm working with, whether it's law enforcement or um, attorneys, nurses, recognize their knowledge and their expertise um. And try and make sure that I'm approaching the conversation in a way is going to honor that, um. (laughs, resumes regular pace) And making sure that they know that I know that they care, um, about what they're doing 'cause I think that's the biggest, the biggest thing that gets in the way is that oftentimes, I'm thinking law enforcement in particular, um, doesn't feel seen by us, they often feel attacked by advocates, they often feel like we're out to get them in some way, um, and so I think that starting the conversation by even if it's like even if it's like I have to lay it on a little bit thick like, "Thank you for being here, thank you for doing what you're doing," um I respect you, I'm not here to step here to step on your toes . . . So that way I've already sort of prepped that like, sometimes things aren't going to go perfectly but like please know that I'm like here to, to, to respect your expertise, um, and work with you and then, it just makes it a little bit easier when uncomfortable conversations, um, come up with a client.

The advocate comments that police officers "[don't] feel seen by us" and therefore sometimes preemptively engage with advocates in negative ways. To respond to the potential abuse, the advocate explains that she merely needs to "lay it on a little bit thick" to cooperate effectively with victims and avoid "uncomfortable conversations." Yet as another white advocate pointed out, "I'm quite pale (smiles) and so, like, that, may make a white woman from the suburbs more comfortable, that may make a Black person—or you [Asian American]—more leery that I'm less likely to be able to understand them, or if the police are being racist or the nurse is making comments about a survivor's hair. [. . .] Then the survivor's probably wondering, what side of the table am I on?" As the latter advocate explicates, subtle changes in advocacy behaviors suggest to marginalized victims that they are allies of the police and SAFEs. Survivors who are wary of systems professionals may perceive such actions as antithetical to their needs and withdraw from help-seeking services. Indeed, the advocate who "[laid] it on a little bit thick" later commented that she felt unsuccessful when attempting to support a survivor of color with limited English proficiency through the court system: "Really limited, sort of the connection that I was able to build with her and the rapport that I was able to build and and then of course, I mean I would make the assumption that for her trying, you know trusting somebody who doesn't speak her language, someone who doesn't look like her, um, someone who basically shares none of her identities, um, also made her not want to connect with me, more than what was necessary to get her protection order."

Third Party Policing

Advocates' implied support of carceral feminism through small shifts in language and behaviors has made rape and victims legible to the state and its representatives. But our efforts have not had the effects we intended. Advocates shared that they spend *most* of their time managing the responses of carceral agents to victims instead of identifying victims' needs in their social worlds. One advocate justified the high frequency with which she engaged with law enforcement: "We spend a lot of time doing trainings for law enforcement, um, and keeping that relationship with them, because when they get called out to a domestic violence or a sexual assault you know things have gotten bad to the point that somebody's finally decided to, to reach out to law enforcement and um, continuing that relationships so they continue to, to get victims to our services."

Though well-intentioned, advocates' constant negotiations with carceral professionals become a large part of advocacy and, with time, *become carceral advocacy*. This slow creep of carceral intrusions opens the gateway for advocates to take up the labor of their systems colleagues, moving from carceral leanings to carceral surveillance itself. Carceral theorists have illustrated that people who do not actively resist hegemonic discourses are most likely to be used to manifest carceralism in nonprison spaces.[73] In particular, Michel Foucault suggested that carceral agents often force docile bodies into motion to sustain carceral logics.[74] Motivated by good intentions to facilitate victims' experiences through criminal legal proceedings, advocates explained that they carried out additional labor to fill in for carceral actors when they failed or refused to carry out victim services in the ways that survivors needed.

In several accounts, advocates shared that they were asked by investigators how to conduct their work. An advocate with a medical background explained that she had to intervene when an officer did not understand the difference between anonymous and identified rape reporting: "Here in [this US state], they have an option to do the kit, but it's not identified with their information, um. Police never know (waves hand in defeat), God bless 'em but—(laughs) but they don't understand this third option, 'That's not a thing!' and like I've been accused by them of having a fake, like, instructions from the chief of pol[ice]—I don't know they're just like so, *heh*." An advocate with degrees in psychology and nursing similarly complained, "Some of these investigators are not even trained in sexual violence. They don't even know—ha, one of the investigators [. . .] He literally called me up and asked me, What do I do with these kits, with these rape kits? Who do I send it to, what am I supposed to do with it? Literally asking me for what to do on the case." The extension of advocates' duties into carceral territory moves advocacy from *independent* to *conditional* support premised on working with carceral actors. However well-intentioned, their actions form what is known as "third party policing," the "police recruitment of nonstate actors into the functions of crime control."[75] Due to learned incompetence by systems professionals, advocates become third party police when they carry out the work of monitoring and regulating victims on behalf of SART colleagues. This regulatory process is not an explicit defense of criminal legal actors or the carceral state. Instead, rather than support victims as the leading rape response authority in a SART, advocates pick up the labor of the police, inseminating carceralism into advocacy practices.

An advocate explained how he inadvertently policed the boundaries of a survivor's linguistic capabilities during a case:

> [The survivor] was really proud about developing [her] English abilities 'cause it really opened the doors for her, to her opportunities, which it shouldn't be her working so hard to get to those doors open, but that's another discussion on its own. But when it came to doing advocacy work with her, her English wasn't good enough [and] the first thing that I was trying to communicate to fully register with her—and [as] advocates we're always taught to, you know, don't do anything that the client doesn't wish. And I know for a while I'd ask, "Do you want a translator" and she would say no. And then after a while, when it came to communication issues, especially with the legal system, that was something I didn't want to roll the dice on. And we talked with our director about it. This is a case where you can say, "I'm sorry, but we have to use a translator." Um, especially when you think of like legal repercussions that come from it. Um, it's like, yeah, the advocate in me was like screaming. Like my client doesn't want this, but this is also making things worse if we don't.

Despite the fact that "the advocate in me was like screaming" at his overruling of survivor consent, the advocate shared that he "didn't want to roll the dice on" "communication issues" and therefore informed the survivor that "this is also making things worse if we don't" use legal translators during a rape trial.

Third party policing has, Mimi Kim warns, "contributed to a heightened understanding of the coercive mechanisms driving carceral expansion into civil society."[76] That is, though rape victims may not always wish for justice through the criminal legal system, advocates unintentionally sustain carceralism in noncarceral spaces. We displace radicalism by remaking what is supposed to be survivor-centered advocacy into a mechanism of state control and containment. This shift in the role of nonprofits is a common outcome of neoliberal welfarism. Using Foucault's theory of discipline and punishment in his analysis of neoliberal housing organizations, Korey Tillman showed that housing authorities frequently pressured unhoused people into complying with standards set forth by shelters in a form of "coercive benevolence." To avoid disrupting their relationship with the police, housing workers often relayed to unhoused people that they could not do anything about carceral policies, and over time, despite the fact that they verbalized their denouncement of the police, housing workers came to enforce the same carceral principles as the police, to organize unhoused people in a confined location.[77] Advocates' behaviors are no different in this respect. They insisted on a kind of carceral coercive benevolence, arguing that carceral agents are merely there to do their job. A Latina advocate explained, "I bite my tongue, for my victims. And um, I try to do as much as I can, but um, it's it's always—the ball is always in their court. And I'm kind of like the ball handler (laughs)."

As a byproduct of inserting carceralism into advocacy, advocates have even begun to apologize for carceral violence instead of stopping it from happening. These apologies are made with deep empathy for survivors, but they also imply that survivors should, or at least should *expect*, to endure secondary abuse, offsetting advocates' responsibility to fight institutionalized violence for victims onto victims themselves. For example, one advocate, frustrated with the countless incidents of secondary violence, exclaimed, "I understand [prosecutors] completely because they wanna win a case where there's solid evidence. Everyone knows that sexual violence, or sexual assault [needs] concrete evidence, it's a he-said she-said thing. Kind of thing. And there's no point in going to court with something like that because they will tear down the victim.... I tell my victims, you know if you go to court prepare for this. Prepare for them to victim-blame you." The advocate shows that she understands the violence of testifying in court without "solid" evidence. However, rather than protest the criminal legal system for requiring "solid evidence," she inadvertently endorses the idea that carceral violence against rape victims is inevitable, telling victims to "prepare for them to victim-blame you."

Similarly, an advocate shared that she understood the problems of carceralism but, instead of actively challenging the police, she encouraged survivors to work around carceral violence. She explained,

Because you don't wanna just automatically like have that mistrust and not, and then tell them, well I don't trust cops either, it's like I'm never gonna tell them that but you know, but it's just like, trust yourself. Like, do you trust law enforcement that's handling your case? Okay maybe you don't, okay, well these are the things that you can do to help that situation. Get that officer's name. Get their badge number, write it down or that . . . case worker or whatever agency you're working with, make sure that you're getting at least people's names down, so then that way, if in the future you needed to file some kind of complaint or file some kind of grievance or, like, you know you're writing this to say something, then you know at least who was there to help you or not help you.

Although the advocate seeks to prepare victims for carceral violence, her suggestions imply to the survivor that she will not intervene directly with the police. Her inaction tells survivors that they need to manage the secondary violence themselves, even though her position as an advocate is to defend the victim from harm. Moreover, her good intentions are overshadowed by the fact that the police officer can still harm the victim. A grievance is only an option *after* an officer has harmed the victim; there is no preempting the violence when the advocate does not actively denounce policing at the onset.

A multilingual advocate admitted, with resignation,

I (sighs), I try to use the extent of my politeness in you know, you know tried—like the language changes, depending on which part of a person you're talking about. So if I'm talking to law enforcement [it's] gonna [be] different than when I'm talking to [the district attorney]. And then it's different when I'm talking to another advocate and it's different, if I'm talking to the survivor, so. It's almost I'm a chameleon and sometimes, it's, it's good that I don't speak English as my first language because I can get away with some things, or being direct. [. . .] (laughs) You know like, I'm sorry like I didn't have another way to say that.

The advocate explains that "I'm a chameleon" and changes her language to match carceral agents' language. Even though she understands that she should not have to acquiesce to carceral agents as an advocate, commenting that "I'm sorry like I didn't have another way to say that," she apologizes for her behaviors to law enforcement and, importantly, to herself and the survivor. She presents her advocacy as though she is playing by the rules of carceralism and simply broke decorum this one time. These performances are not unapologetically open about abolitionism; they suggest that the advocate *would have otherwise* performed carceralism if not for her inability to speak English. Ultimately, her actions force the survivor to look elsewhere to find unconditional advocacy support.

By serving as third party police, advocates eventually turn the space of the rape crisis center into a panopticon. The panopticon is, according to Foucault, "a machine for dissociating the see/being seen dyad: in the peripheric ring, one is totally seen, without ever seeing; in the central tower, one sees everything without ever being seen."[78] It is an architectural spatial dimension in which the imprisoned monitor themselves in a self-regulatory confinement. Especially in SARTs, advocates might take actions to defend their relationships with carceral professionals, even when others might disagree, because they believe that they are doing the right thing *for victims*. Yet what they are doing is in fact expanding the carceral state. To the victims who seek advocacy independent of the criminal legal system, advocates who change their actions to accommodate carceral actors are the same as said carceral authorities. An Indigenous advocate explained, with repulsed anger, "It's been this difficult road of, in our movement, for linking arms with systems, because we become eloquent in their language. . . . At the same time, we gotta separate [from systems]. We gotta, we gotta do somethin' different and look different because, clerks' offices and police departments and hospitals think we are an arm of them. They think that we're beholden to them and we are not!"

The Cost of Crime

Advocates are not ill equipped to support victims through the aftermath of rape, nor do they seek to harm survivors. Instead, advocates' responses to neoliberal carceralism cause secondary violence because they deepen the myth that carceralism could be helpful for survivors if systems were modified for survivors. But this perspective refuses to recognize that the US legal system *by design* harms some people rather than others. In his examination of carceralism, Andrew Dilts argued that carceralism produces affective enjoyment, those "parasitic forms of social life, 'purchased' through the racialized social death of others, effected in our contemporary moment by the practice of incarceration."[79] Advocates' apologies, for instance, are predicated on the belief that we are doing "good" for survivors, to prepare them for violence. Unintentionally, however, by hanging onto the happy belief that we are rerouting systems harms, by arguing that the legal system has simply failed and requires reform, or by implying to victims that carceral agents are merely "doing their job" and simply need more training, we create carceralism in a space that should not be carceral. We forget that the criminal legal system was never made to be about some omnipotent, objective "justice," but about controlling some people for the benefit of others.

Advocates' behaviors follow larger social trends in the anti-rape movement toward carceral feminism. Much as in the decades prior, few rapists are held accountable, whether through prosecution or through nonlegal measures.[80] Many sexual offenses are routinely pled down from higher charges to lower charges unattached to sexual violence, such as turning a kidnapping and rape charge into a kidnapping-only charge, to avoid sexual offender registration.[81] These outcomes, which have not reduced violence nor prevented violence by deterrence, have made victims even more vulnerable to lethal retributive attacks by perpetrators, especially those in intimate partner violence arrangements.[82] They have also only fueled public drives toward mass incarceration. Fears about "superpredators" enhanced racialized stereotypes about rape, and many anti-rape advocates in the (post)#MeToo era have endorsed carceral feminism as the only way to monitor the actions of abusers.[83]

Whether by visibly endorsing criminal legal measures to respond to rape or by excusing its existence, carceral feminism merely recycles carceral violence. For example, the Sexual Offender Registry and Notification Act (SORNA) requires that people convicted of sex offenses register with federal and state governments and notify employers, housing authorities, and many others about their sex offense status.[84] Registered persons are also banned from visiting areas densely populated with children and other "vulnerable" populations. This act is typically welcomed by neoliberals, who see the criminal punishment of offenders as morally righteous.[85] However, SORNA assumes that these post-imprisonment punishments are "just desserts" for sex offenders, despite the fact that offenders have already served their sentence. SORNA restrictions can make life difficult for sexual assault offenders, especially BIPOC convicted persons, by forcing them to disclose their sexual offender status to potential employers and landlords. They essentially create a lifelong punishment, even if the imprisonment sentence has been completed, leading to recidivism of typically nonsexual crimes.[86] As Michelle Alexander rightly pointed out, the criminal legal system is a "*gateway* into a much larger system of racial stigmatization and permanent marginalization."[87]

Carceral feminism victimizes the people who have already been victimized. About 25–50 percent of incarcerated women and 6–24 percent of incarcerated men reported experiencing childhood sexual abuse.[88] Over half of all trans and gender-diverse people have experienced sexual assault at least once in their lifetimes, and many of them have been incarcerated at least once in their lifetimes as well for nonviolent reasons.[89] The high rate of people who are incarcerated and experienced sexual abuse suggests that rape victims are being punished for being victims. It also artificially divides victims and perpetrators, splintering communities apart on the basis of normative ideas about victimhood, deviance, and criminality. For instance, queerphobic people frequently portray 2SLGBTQIA+ people who experience rape as sexual predators, which incorrectly scripts 2SLGBTQIA+ victims of rape into sex offenders deserving of carceral punishment.[90] Similarly, an estimated 30 percent of the people in federal prisons and 40 percent of those in jails are disabled, with a majority of those imprisoned having cognitive disabilities such as autism, Down syndrome, and learning disorders.[91] The high rates of incarcerated disabled individuals are due to the ways that the criminal legal system continuously mediates disability such that disabled people are more likely to be found suspicious, arrested, and jailed than nondisabled people.[92]

The division between victims and perpetrators as a result of carceral measures divorces advocacy from seeing communities as complex social ecosystems and imposes only normative interpretations of rape victims and perpetrators of all backgrounds.[93] Rape crisis centers continue to operate under the auspices that their role is to support primarily survivors and not perpetrators, and they often refuse to respond to persons with criminal records.[94] But Black men are 3.5 times more likely than white men to be convicted of sexual assault and are more likely to be arrested for nonviolent offenses than white people, with Black people incarcerated for felonies at greater rates than white offenders. They are also more likely to be exonerated than any other racial group.[95] These trends of arrest, conviction, and sentencing track for non-Black racialized and gendered groups, albeit to different degrees.[96] Collectively, the focus on criminalizing marginalized populations and ignoring normative histories of the prison industrial complex leads advocates at "victim-centered" agencies to renew rape unto themselves.

The incarceration of specifically marginalized survivors is no accident, either. In the decades leading up to the mass incarceration of the poor, BIPOC, and women, private companies introduced privatization practices within prisons, seeking to profit from the marginalized masses. They argued that they needed to generate funds to manage the rapidly increasing number of incarcerated persons. Though federal private *prisons* were briefly outlawed,[97] private *corporations* and their governmental backers continue to control markets—including the anti-rape market—within and outside of prison walls.[98] For example, corporations can and often do price gouge communication devices incarcerated persons use to communicate with loved ones, privatize and thereby increase healthcare expenses for people in prison, and rely on prison labor to manufacture many consumer goods.[99] Like cancerous growths, these privatized systems diminish the voices of marginalized incarcerated victims and their communities to ensure long-term dominance of carceral authorities in critical governmental and rape response decisions.

Our advocacy replaces a formerly radical peer consciousness-raising collective with a carceral feminist neoliberal "community." Unlike (neo)conservatives who openly express support for the punishment of marginalized people, (neo)liberals rely on professional care logics to claim that they are "helping" marginalized people—rape victims, and marginalized rape victims especially—at the same time that they are perpetuating violence against the people whom they purport to help. Advocates claim that they seek to prevent victims from experiencing systems-based harms when we change our actions; however, the result is that advocates, not carceral agents, have changed. Indeed, a 2020 study reported that just 10 percent of DOC leaders identified anti-violence coalitions as a "community partner," showing how little the carceral state thinks of us as advocates.[100]

By refusing to resist carceralism in all forms, advocates become responsible for the serious socioeconomic secondary victimization faced by victims. There are many lifetime costs experienced by rape victims in and out of prisons, costs that *should* be paid for by the state or the rape crisis center that professes to abolish rape. Despite attempts to reimburse victims for the violence that they have experienced through programs like VOCA and VAWA (and noticeably, these are not costs paid in advance; they are *reimbursements* of thousands of dollars that many victims cannot afford up front), the average lifetime cost of rape is $122,461, and the economic burden for the overall US population is $3.1 trillion.[101] These numbers are calculated by examining the out-of-pocket and insured payments of rape victims for medical and therapeutic treatment by the current US neoliberal privatized healthcare system, as well as the costs associated with travel and time to commute to police and attorneys' offices during trials, if the case even makes it to trial.[102] Given the high costs of healthcare, the victims most impacted by our carceral advocacy are most likely to be poor people, BIPOC, disabled people, immigrants and undocumented people, and Others marginalized by the US healthcare system, who may or may not have health insurance due to larger socioeconomic issues with late-stage capitalism.[103] Moreover, while victims who are raped while in prison may not financially pay for healthcare expenses, as the violation of rape is considered a state problem under PREA, the very fact that people are extremely vulnerable to rape while in prison should be concern enough. Even still, however, they "pay": the dangers of reporting rape often outweigh the violence of acute assault, leaving many victims to repeatedly endure abuse in a form of trafficking to exchange resources while incarcerated to survive.[104]

The costs of making rape into a crime are too high. Carceral feminist neoliberalism is violent, and any attempt to use the criminal legal system that levies violence to meet violence expunges the potential for us to eliminate violence in its intersectional forms. Black feminist Kimberlé Crenshaw even said as much while speaking about legal reform for intimate partner violence: "Modest attempts to respond to certain problems can be ineffective when the intersectional location of women of color is not considered in fashioning the remedy."[105] Our refusal to actively dismantle the carceral complex forces survivors to endure a prolonged second rape, one that repeats the violence of acute sexual assault through repetitive interrogation and testimony. It also positions us as the direct frontline actors who enforce the boundaries of justice, traitors to the advocacy role we espouse.[106] As a result of our refusal to assert abolitionism in the face of carceral violence, rape victims, but especially rape victims already marginalized by the neoliberal state, become the payment for legitimizing rape as a crime.

"Do They Know You Are a Radical Feminist?"

Advocates' unwillingness to practice transparent abolitionist advocacy transforms the rape crisis center into another prison. Our presence in SARTs has diverted advocate attention away from institutional protest by tightening our focus onto only the "community partners" with whom we are mandated to work. We need to remember that we have not "failed" to reform the system; rather, the system never intended to adopt advocacy. And if the system cannot be reformed, at least not by individual advocates, then we need to rethink with whom we coconspire for abolition.[107]

The recalibration of advocacy from carceral to abolitionist involves thinking critically about for whom we advocate, "killjoying" carceral enjoyments.[108] As Dilts illustrated, we need to disrupt the happy affect of thinking that we are still doing good, that remaining silent in the face of systems-based violence can support current and future victims. An advocate put it simply: "If you can't listen to the person, it doesn't matter how much systems-based knowledge you have." We need to reflect on our larger mission to end all rapes, ending systematic injustice of many names. These feelings of abolitionist resistance do not feel "good," but they are critical to holding ourselves accountable as advocates.

Many advocates are victims, of some kind. Most of us have experienced rape personally, and those of us who have not usually know a loved one who has experienced rape.[109] Even if one is not familiar with survivor circles, we are still members of this US prison nation, whether citizens or not, and therefore engage regularly with violent policing, healthcare, and welfare systems. Our connections to each other and the prison we reside in give us knowledge about how we want to approach responses to sexual assault. An advocate shared, for example, "We work in the same building as [special victims unit] detectives and . . . I try to do trainings on like best practices for serving immigrant victims but also like I try to leverage rapport I have with law enforcement . . . But it, it's hard because like I can't, I don't feel that I can be honest because if I was honest, it would hur—, it would end up hurting my clients because then that law enforcement might not feel comfortable coming to me." Illuminating the desire to safeguard good "rapport" with law enforcement for future victims, the advocate illustrates that "it's hard" to conduct effective advocacy because she "do[esn't] feel that I can be honest." This absence of honesty and the feelings of guilt and fear remind us why we must advocate for survivors against systems violence. Rather than protecting systems professionals, we should make decisions that empower victims and their people.

Contemplating our feelings, however, is not enough. Likely the biggest challenge to advocating for institutional justice is the present state of anti-rape communities. The socioeconomic framework of SARTs and legalized systems collaboration ensure that systems professionals will remain in the anti-rape field for the next several decades, until public opinion perhaps changes tides. But such a presence is not necessarily evil, I argue, *if* survivors wish to seek legal recourse, including increasing their physical safety, or as the law continues to be radically reformed. Anti-rape lawyer Susan Caringella suggested, after all, "The law holds the uniquely influential power to change conceptualizations about what we hold to be decent, acceptable, and good as opposed to bad, unacceptable, and criminal. Hence the law stands as the moral posture for a culture."[110] Similarly, I believe that the carceral system and its outposts, like SARTs, are reflections of the larger kaleidoscopic US culture. Subsequently, our work within these rape response arrangements also carries the potentiality to transform our cultures toward more radically inclined ends.

This inside-out transformation, however, is not a matter of apologizing for who we are as advocates. Instead, the mainstay nature of contemporary neoliberal carceralism requires that we think in a multilevel way, moving from the ground up.[111] Currently, much like an intimate abuser who surveilles their victim's every movement, the carceral core of SARTs forces advocates to, as one advocate put it, "walk on eggshells" with their "community partners," demanding that we ask permission or stay out of carceral agents' way.[112] But as another advocate explained, advocacy is a "collaborative... dance if you will and it's really an honor to, to be there *for* survivors and to be *with* survivors." We are not there to support systems professionals; *they* are here to help *us*. An advocate explained how she asserted her role:

> The police officer who was there... was (exhales)... It really made me angry (laughs bitterly). Made me so angry the way that he was acting. Like he stood... And I have, I had dealt with this officer before in other situations, um, with other survivors who were white. And it was really coming across to me that he was not seeing this [multiracial Indigenous] girl as [human]... He was standing right in front of her with his crotch like basically in her face 'cause she was sitting and and I was trying to like get him, "Can you step back, please? 'Cause you're really close."

Advocacy plays *throughout* the long game of life, not just in the crisis of a rape moment. Thus, unlike a police officer or SAFE who only responds to a crisis moment, advocates stake claim as leaders in intervention, prevention, and outreach anti-rape responses, whether in SARTs or in nonlegal transformative avenues. An advocate explained that she needs people like police officers and SAFEs but explains that they cannot control rape responses: "You cannot, nobody can do this by themselves. It's too hard and if you, if you ever think you can do it all by yourself then you need to find a new job but, you have to have partners, you have to have, you gotta, you gotta build relationships, um, so that everybody can have ownership in, you know, what, what's transpiring through the system." With frustration, she then emphasized the need for advocates to affirm themselves as powerful actors in rape responses, refusing carceral cooptation.

> (sighs) Well I think that you need, um (sighs, frustratedly). I think, um (clears throat), your powers that be have to be there to kind of make it mandatory. And to say this is what's gonna happen we're gonna have these commu—these multidisciplinary team meetings, and this is what's gonna happen and you're gonna go. [...] We're all playing by the same rules 'cause we all have the same laws to go by, um, you know whatever

system we're working in. So I think we all have to have some accountability and ownership and here judges are immune from liability, and prosecutors and district attorneys think that they're god, um, and they don't have to do anything, um. I think until we can take them down a notch, so they can be [. . .] part of the team and part of the solution, um, and again go into the academy, I think if you had that, that training at the academy level so that your officers understand what your judges and prosecutors want, um, understand how things work, I think that would probably divert a lot of the um, the stuff, the negative stuff that happens along the way.

Holding systems professionals accountable, the advocate demands that systems professionals be "take[n] down a notch." Rather than center carceral agents, she believes advocates can put systems professionals in their (limited) place in SART dialogues.

An advocate with a medical background also explained how she held SAFEs accountable when they assumed that legitimacy in anti-rape work was based on likeness to systems professionalism.

> INTERVIEWEE: I personally have found that survivors who go to [the hospital] tend, if they're admitted they tend not to come here [to the rape crisis center] afterwards and I don't know why that is, um. I have also found that, when I go to the hospital and I'm in my scrubs, I get better attention, I get what I need, and I'm more respected.
> INTERVIEWER: By who?
> INTERVIEWEE: By the workers. That actually really ticked me off to the point that I spoke (laughs) with some of the residents there, um. Because I was really appalled by that.

More than holding systems professionals accountable, advocates should reaffirm the strength of advocacy to support rape victims and end rape. An advocate who serves as her agency's SART liaison explained how this process happens.

> INTERVIEWEE: I asked other staff the other day in a meeting. I was like, we go to a quadzillion meetings for child boards and food assistance boards and all these other meetings. I said when you walk into

> those meetings, did they know you are an anti-racist, anti-oppression worker? Do they know that? Do they know that you are a radical feminist? Do they know that? And I think we've gotten by many years with, like, well I don't know 'cause we're friends and like, I want them to like me—yeah!
>
> INTERVIEWER: But they should also like you for doing anti-racist, anti-oppressive work.
>
> INTERVIEWEE: Correct. And there's this fear, especially because we're in a red—now crazy red state, and, very conservative beliefs it was founded upon and Christian beliefs and all these other things thrown at us and we're women, most of us. So be quiet girls, be pleasant, be whatever, but like not only breaking that but also . . . Yeah, I just need everyone to know that we support Black Lives Matter. Just say that in a meeting. I mean, why don't we? Why don't we? And food assistance board, you know? But they need to know us in a way and then we can invite them to know them in that way and not be quiet and share niceties.

Still, some advocates expressed concern at the prospect of openly endorsing radicalism to SART colleagues. Like the advocates at Embrace who found their legitimacy and funding slashed, some advocates shared that they or their survivors would face or have already faced material consequences if they spoke out. For example, an advocate who protested the abusive actions taken by a correctional officer against a victim undergoing a rape examination was accused of "staff splitting" and reprimanded by an administrator for troubling relations between the agency and the prison. Another advocate underscored their abolitionist values but could not foresee how advocates could be abolitionists in the nonprofit industrial complex, leading them to resign.

> I stand [with] defund the police, a hundred percent. It's hard 'cause that's been working in this work. It's one of the reasons I left my job. Um, I don't think I practice it every day. [But] I believe in it. It's how I want my community to move towards and also I have to be very transparent that like, there aren't enough safety mechanisms that I think we're putting enough time and energy into. [. . .] I'm trying to move towards a more abolitionist defund the police, well life slash practice slash work. And it's difficult

when you're living in those systems, and also against them. Yeah, as a white person it's hard for me to be like, a hundred percent defund the police, let's do it and also I don't always put my—like my actions where my mouth is. Like look where I was working.

These concerns with workplace hostility, burnout, and carceral affiliations are valid. Unfortunately, they also persuade us to continue narrowing our lenses to short-term, individualized solutions, such as amending existing rape law, enhancing cultural competency trainings for systems professionals, or changing our individual behaviors.[113] These proposals, made in fear of what *could* happen if we were to be transparent, only prolong the death of radicalism by cloaking our eyes to the bigger agenda of abolitionism. As an advocate with policing background remarked of the tendency to rely on just one person, "You can give [police departments] all the training in the world, [and] you can have the best-trained officer in the world but if you're expecting one officer to do all of this work, the vicarious trauma, and the PTSD that the officer's going to encounter, they're only human." In essence, even nonexplicitly violent measures will cause us to harm victims because we have not yet invested in a collective care community.[114]

With imagination, advocates must envision an integrated, holistic approach that uplifts marginalized communities out of poverty and reduces overall vulnerability to rape. The criminalization of marginalized survivors shattered our community relationships and weakened our agenda to abolish generational rape, making us think that we cannot make any substantive change. But cultivating a transformative justice community that sees each other for who we are, we should invite conversations with abolitionist partners, beginning with the "people who actually wanna be there" like survivors, bystanders, and assailants. This work is already being done by radical organizations like BYP100, Project NIA, and Interrupting Criminalization. Following their guidance, we can put faith into our people—friends, families, and neighbors—and trust that they will step up and fulfill the role originally given to SARTs: to support survivors and hold perpetrators accountable, irrespective of criminal legal intervention.

These complex relations are rooted in honesty. One advocate explained, "It's more than just like hiring the right people, it's putting the resources into the spaces that are already doing the work and they're doing it in a way where, they're sharing skills, they're building their community and they're building trust. And it should start, you know, in the community, and build out from there, and, and network together rather than someone just popping in. [. . .] We don't need to network with cops!" This deliberate outreach to noncarceral actors encourages anti-rape agency leaders, including boards of directors, hospital and police administrators, and many powerful people, to join the anti-rape movement not because of the profit they can make off survivors but because they are vested in the end of all violence. An administrative advocate explained this approach: "We send out letters constantly to the hospitals, to law enforcement. There's always been a little racism goin' on occasionally. [. . .] I usually try to nip it in the bud when I walk in and somebody says something." She turned to her experiences working with survivors seeking support from her tribal agency. Resisting the pull to present like a normative systems professional, she actively chooses to participate in the anti-rape movement as herself, a Native feminist advocate.

> It totally looks Native in the office and you know. That's what we have to keep in mind that they [survivors] can relate to because they know that you're Native and you understand them more than anybody else will. And well we come to the office in a casual kind of dress. You know I'm not wearing heels and a skirt, never do that because I want them to feel comfortable and we don't have any, you know the office is open and we have chairs sittin' in the middle of it to where, we don't have any kind of barriers between us and them, ever. Our desks are against the wall so we're always facing them, full body facing and, there's just a lot of things that we've incorporated to help these people feel comfortable.

For us to begin dismantling the prison nation we have inadvertently built, we must begin communing differently, in solidarity and in liberation with one another. We should be proud radical feminists, leading our teams down the path to abolitionism. In trust, and with time, our advocacy crafts another kind of community, restored, transformed, and liberated from our self-made panopticons.

5

Who Counts?

Quantifying Victims in Grant Applications

> We relied upon process that created networked relationship. Our intelligence system is a series of interconnected and overlapping algorithms—stories, ceremonies, and the land itself are procedures for solving the problems of life.... Governance was *made* every day.... Daily life involved making politics, education, health care, food systems, and economy on micro- and macro-scales. I didn't need to look for catastrophe or crisis-based stories to learn how to rebuild.
> —Leanne Betasamosake Simpson (Mississauga Nishnaabeg),
>   As We Have Always Done

"You're defining me based on the way I look," said a victim to a pair of advocates. The victim, a light-skinned young woman with brown hair, had come to seek postrape services at her local tribal agency. There the victim had requested access to counseling, as was her right as a Native survivor of sexual violence. The advocates at the agency, however, were not certain that this young woman was indeed Native, a qualification that was necessary for them to disburse resources from a federally funded tribal agency. She certainly didn't *look* like a Native woman with her hair and skin color, and she didn't have her tribal identification card with her to prove what she was saying. She also didn't *act* like a "real rape" victim when she demanded services in a self-important kind of way.[1] Was she simply exploiting the resources available for only Native women? the advocates wondered. Was this some white woman who could not tell that these services are meant only for Native people? The risk that this survivor was merely draining the already stretched resources from the agency was "too high." Other "more Native" survivors needed the help. After a few brief moments of deliberation, the advocates decided to deny the young woman's request for services.

A few months later, the young woman killed herself.

The narrative presented here is an excerpt from an Indigenous advocate's experiences, and it illustrates the quandaries of quantification when imposed on anti-rape advocacy.[2] Quantification is the measurement of prevalence and incidence rates or, more simply, the ways that we count and categorize sexual victimization.[3] Advocates quantify by counting the number of rape victims that they see at their rape crisis center. They also calculate the amount of work that they conduct per victim, counting the hours spent on each case and the number of material supplies provided to the survivor. Altogether, the numbers produce a taxonomy, or a list of categories with an associated numerical value. When advocates count, they are also categorizing people. Advocates may count the number of victims served, but who constitutes a victim—someone who reports sexual assault to the police, someone who discloses sexual assault, or someone who has experienced any type of harm that is sexual in nature—determines the act of counting. In other words, the framework of counting is always undergirded by a structured taxonomy; if there are numbers, then there are also categories that guide us in our counting schema. Taxonomies illustrate the composite numbers and the calculation of them, neatly representing violence in consumable ways.[4]

For many, quantification is considered an objective, "neutral" act for its reliance on numbers and classifications. Numbers convey a sense of impartiality unsullied by human errors, and taxonomies parse unruly phenomena into neatly defined boxes.[5] Through quantification, a survivor who reports becomes clearly distinguished from a survivor who does not report. However, though quantification is often thought of as objective, it is actually highly subjective.[6] When advocates apply quantification to sexual violence, they precast their interpretations of categories into the taxonomy.[7] For example, the survivor in this narrative was quantified: She was "counted" as one survivor whom the agency *could* be responsible for supporting. But she was not simply counted as a possible survivor. Advocates classified her as an "ineligible" victim (the category) based on her "non-Native" appearance and presentation. Their quantitative production of "eligible" or "ineligible" victimhood relied on subjective interpretations of socially constructed identities like race, gender, sexuality, and more.[8] Far from building objective taxonomies, advocates impose their own stereotypes and biases about those categories onto their quantitative records.

The use of quantification in sexual violence normalizes rape, with very real consequences for survivors. As explained in the introduction, normativity is the normalization of a given social identity by only acknowledging one identity and forgoing the recognition of intersectional and fluid identities.[9] Advocates who quantify usually only understand the given numbers and categories present but do not view the overall effects of their taxonomies that legitimize some victims over others. As a result, when they count and categorize, they also portray survivors within statistical data in ways that embolden normative (including racialized, gendered, and able-bodied) myths about survivors. This classification method is a form of biopower in which the advocate chooses, sometimes literally, the life or death of the survivor.[10] A victim who is classified as a specific race, gender, and dis/ability may be read as "ineligible" for support and rejected from help-seeking services. And just like the aforementioned Native survivor, they may then be killed shortly thereafter from an abuser and/or structural systemic violence.[11] Quantification in anti-violence work is not a "neutral" method of understanding violence but a political weapon defining the limits of a "normal victim."

At contemporary rape crisis centers, advocates are expected to quantify survivors. Despite the problematic nature of quantification, neoliberal funders regulating advocacy routinely argue that quantitative data that produce victim taxonomies help them decide where to best spend their money.[12] As capitalism dictates, there are limited funds; therefore, funders seek to stretch their dollars as far as possible to reach the largest number of survivors. In grant applications, advocates who work at state-funded nonprofits must record survivors' identities to inform their funders how many and which survivors they support to demonstrate the validity of their work.[13] This mandate to quantify, however, makes advocates central to the normalization of survivors *but without their knowledge* in another form of carceral control. If funders present quantification as a useful tool for understanding violence, then advocates who receive these implied messages from funders also begin to limit the scope of their work to simply the most effective use of money, creating taxonomies that sustain normativity. Quantification is uniquely problematic precisely because it is justified as an objective, "helpful" act at the same time that it makes advocates responsible for perpetrating normative violence on victims.

This chapter explores the ways that advocates normalize survivors through quantification. I begin by examining why advocates use quantification in their work, showing how the quantification of victims gradually transformed from a subjective political act into a measurement of the state. I then reflect on advocates' experiences with quantification at the front lines. Advocates frequently feel pressured to quantify survivors, and many wield normative classification methods in their day-to-day work. Our actions inadvertently override survivors' interpretations of their own identities by "speaking for" them on grant forms. This exact(ing) count of survivors pushes advocates into sustaining neoliberal normativity. Through this chapter, I argue that it is the grant-required quantification of survivors that maintains normativity at the neoliberal anti-violence agency and results in the death of radical advocacy.

In this chapter, I am not interested in the number of victims who are white or BIPOC, women or men, and so on and so forth. That literature has been made well known to many anti-violence scholars who acknowledge that survivors who identify as marginalized are indeed disproportionately affected by sexual violence.[14] I am instead making a more nuanced argument about the way we approach victim support. The act of quantification is harmful and misguided; it demands that advocates speak for victims about the way that victims themselves identify. Our capacity to respectfully acknowledge and represent survivors in the postrape process disappears when we are forced to configure victims on state documents. In addition, I suggest that taxonomies produced by advocates for the state serve no purpose. While quantification has the potential to benefit *survivors* by recognizing the disparities in rape, quantification diminishes the potential for *advocates* to understand the fluidity of identities and thus the possibilities of intersectional advocacy. Instead of recording survivors' identities to bolster financial support from the state, we should rethink the way that we collect victim services data and the methods we use to fund survivor advocacy. This chapter expands our understanding of neoliberal normativity beyond the use of quantification to measure state violence and guides us toward a more critical look at our roles in surveilling normativity in helping work.

The Rise of Rape Victim Statistics

The use of statistics in anti-rape work can be traced to Ida B. Wells's anti-lynching campaign. In the late nineteenth century, southern whites used racist imagery of Black men as rapists to lynch activists who challenged the Reconstruction period's racialized socioeconomic status quo.[15] Indigenous people had long wielded counting schemas as a method of transferring knowledges and constructing realities, and Wells adopted their strategies to counter white supremacist depictions of Black communities.[16] In an 1893 speech entitled "Lynch Law in All Its Phases," Wells showed that between 1882 and 1891, white men lynched 728 Black men, 269 of whom were charged with rape. Of the ones accused of rape, Wells illustrated that most of them were likely falsely charged by white men and women who wanted to preserve their socioeconomic power in the neighborhood.[17]

Wells's quantification of lynching allowed the growing literate public, white and Black, to see the prejudices inherent to lynching rhetoric and stand against extralegal murders. But it also sparked interest in the quantification of crime. Quickly coopting Wells's statistical methods, the Federal Bureau of Investigation (FBI) in 1927 developed the Uniform Crime Reports (UCRs) (now called the National Incident-Based Reporting System, or NIBRS), which are reports detailing the number of violent crimes in the United States annually. The reports originally covered seven major crimes, including rape. Creators of the UCRs aimed to consolidate information across jurisdictions and demonstrate the average prevalence of crime in the country.[18] They also sought to reduce the ambiguity between reported crimes and recorded crimes, which they hoped would simultaneously dissuade law enforcement administrators from falsifying crime data.[19] The UCRs were put into motion by 1930, and, by the 1950s, surveying rape became a staple strategy of government officials, criminal justice researchers, and the media in their efforts to understand crime prevalence.[20]

Unsurprisingly, the use of rape statistics by the FBI centered on deviancy, causing a racial normalization of victims in the numbers. The period from 1920 to 1940 involved a series of spree gang activities in which white gangsters actively stole from and murdered civilians. It was also the same period in which numerous white mobs racially terrorized and lynched

Black and Brown communities at significant rates. To maintain racial hierarchy and legitimize federal white law enforcement as viable state authorities, the FBI—many of whose members identified as white men with ancestral ties to "slave catchers"—took an interest in rape, calling it a felony worthy of imprisonment and capital punishment.[21] J. Edgar Hoover was especially interested in distinguishing between white defendants and Black defendants accused of rape and framed rape as a product of BIPOC cultures. Under the guise of objective counting, the federal and state designation of a felony charge for rape made it possible for Black defendants to be rendered visible within crime reporting statistics but only through the amplification of the Black male rapist myth, all while such prominence erased white domestic terrorism from the public eye.[22]

The National Association for the Advancement of Colored People (NAACP) attempted to counteract state crime rhetoric by also wielding statistical reporting. Throughout the first half of the twentieth century, the NAACP published an annual report on the number of lynchings occurring in the US South, noting the names of Black people who had been lynched, their locations, and the reason that white mobs used to lynch them without legal repercussions.[23] These efforts to combat the erasure of lynching violence told a very different story than the one presented by the FBI, and they helped to provide evidence of bias and discrimination in several anti-rape cases, such as the cases of *Coker v. Georgia* and the Scottsboro Boys, though often with limited effects.[24] In 1965, the NAACP Legal Defense & Educational Fund (LDF) hired the sociologist Marvin Wolfgang to conduct a study examining the racial differences between white and Black defendants accused of rape. Wolfgang found that Black defendants were more likely to be convicted for rape and sentenced to capital punishment than white defendants, with "only 2.1 percent of those [white defendants] convicted ... similarly sentenced."[25] Contra UCR reporting, Wolfgang's study showed, like Wells's study, that the designation of rape as crime was in fact a way to justify state-sponsored murder of Black men. Such results further exposed the reality that public-spectacle lynchings had indeed transformed by the mid-twentieth century into legal lynchings—a crime of violence interwoven in the very fabric of the US sociolegal system.[26]

Still, there were unintended consequences to Wolfgang's study. Though intended to counteract white racial terrorism and stop the excessive use of the death penalty against Black people, Wolfgang's study pressured academic researchers, including the criminologist Menachem Amir, to examine the racial differences in crime convictions and sentencing without necessarily employing feminist methodologies rooted in social justice to report results. Tutored by Wolfgang, Amir had previously studied state crime reporting measurements primarily through governmental documentation, such as the UCRs. In 1968, drawing on FBI reporting numbers, Amir argued in a now-discredited article, "Victim Precipitated Forcible Rape," that the vast majority of "forcible" (i.e., physically injurious) rapes were committed by Black men against Black women.[27] However, he neglected to account for the overrepresentation of Black men accused of rape in arrest rates. Nevertheless, while Amir was quickly dismissed by many grassroots feminists because, among many reasons, his study was premised on the wrongful assumption that victims "precipitate" rape, the white journalist Susan Brownmiller used Amir's study in her bestseller *Against Our Will* to claim that Black men were indeed the primary perpetrators of sexual assault, calling attention to the "typical American rapist" as a nineteen-year-old "boy next door" in the "ghettos."[28]

Against Our Will had serious implications for academic investigations on rape. Global acclaim and the dominance of governmental statistical reporting of crime allowed Brownmiller's misrepresentations of Black people in crime reporting to spread to multiple anti-rape spaces, including the University of Alabama's anti-violence research conference in 1975.[29] Researchers interested in the increasingly popular crime of rape premised their work on the same racist assumptions of rape perpetrators, such as the sociologist Diana E. H. Russell. While Russell's seminal anti-rape book, *The Politics of Rape from the Victim's Perspective*, included sections related to Black women victims and was published three years prior to Brownmiller's book, Russell noted in an exchange of letters between herself and Brownmiller that she began to use Brownmiller's reporting of rape while speaking at academic conferences, recycling discriminatory portrayals of rapists and innocent people and erasing women of color survivors in so-called professional anti-rape research.[30]

These studies collectively persuaded direct services advocates in the mainstream feminist anti-rape movement to take up rape quantification. In New York, the UCRs helped to increase interest in the numbers of rape victims and proliferated the idea that quantification could justify rape responses. In the 1970s, for example, the Women's Anti-Rape Coalition doubled down on the idea that rape was one of the "fastest growing crimes" in the United States, a call that was replicated many times by other rape crisis organizations in the United States and globally.[31] While activists were intimately familiar with the reality that rape had been widespread prior to these statistics, many of them participated in the trend of rape reporting to spread awareness of rape as a crime. This shift changed rape from a "passion" gone wrong into a crime of violence necessitating legal action. Many national and state anti-rape organizations, including the National Organization for Women (NOW)'s National Task Force on Rape, adopted UCR statistics to advocate for more funding to be directed toward victim services.[32]

With high publicity and subsequent political pressures to understand rape prevalence, psychologists jumped on the rape-study bandwagon, seeking to develop valid statistical measurements for rape—but also introducing notions of objectivity to a clearly subjective rape counting schema. One of the most influential psychological studies that emerged by the mid-1980s was Mary P. Koss's study on rape prevalence, which sought to determine the extent of the problem of rape on college campuses.[33] Koss was not the first white researcher nor the first psychologist to study rape; rather, Ann W. Burgess and Lynn L. Holmstrom were among the first psychologists to study behaviors of rape victims in the postassault period, diagnosing victims' actions as "rape trauma syndrome."[34] However, Koss was catapulted into academic and public fame well beyond that of Burgess and Holmstrom through her "one in four" statistic.[35] From a study on young women experiencing violence on college campuses, the number "one in four" proclaimed that one in every four women is a victim of sexual assault. It was immediately met with skepticism. Critics pointed out that Koss's definition of rape was overly broad and that Koss sampled from a majority-white heterosexual women population.[36] Less than 9 percent of the participants identified as nonwhite, with a mean age of 21.3.[37] Nonetheless, the "one in four" statistic animated conversations around the need for systemic responses to violence, including measurable studies with large sample sizes that defined the scale of rape.[38] Koss's study was especially effective at persuading the state to take an interest in sexual violence. Maria Bevacqua shared that Koss's study "[uncovered] the actual numbers behind this social problem and . . . [described] the reality behind the numbers. The studies of rape have, in turn, led to further organizing and policy refinements."[39] The uses of Koss's study in normative state bureaucracies, alongside the rise of neoliberal capitalism within rape crisis centers, inseminated ideas of neutrality in the quantification of rape victims for state purposes.[40]

Women of color sought to challenge the racialized (racist) reporting of rape victim statistics. In 1980, at the Third World Women and Violence conference, anti-violence activists of color acknowledged that "little documentation exists detailing the extent of sexual abuse that Third World women suffer" and attributed the lack of statistical research to "the low priority given this problem by society in general, and research funding agencies in particular."[41] They also called out the repeated abuses by academics to mislead public interpretations of sexual violence, including Brownmiller's and Amir's anti-Black studies. But though BIPOC women and gender-diverse people had initiated the charge for statistical measurements for marginalized populations, academic communities only took an interest when white feminist consciousness raising emerged. Studies led by white psychologists and criminologists bolstered attention to "expert" academic scholarship that could legitimize anti-rape advocacy, which was then circulated among white-directed rape crisis centers across the country.[42]

By the 1990s, no white academic nor white grassroots advocate listened to queer and femme people of color and their insistence on the subjectivity of quantification. Instead, neoconservative politicians suggested that social scientists and anti-rape feminists were merely making up the numbers of rape prevalence to divert attention away from "real rape," a claim that collapsed more nuanced dialogues about how quantification *can* lead to radical change by unpacking the binary between "real" and "false" rapes.[43] Studying rape surveys, Alexandra Rutherford explains that with the neoliberal push, rape "went from a topic 'hitherto as well known to conventional scholars as the dark side of the moon' to a phenomenon that feminist social scientists, through their surveys, were implicated in actually creating."[44] In response to conservative outcries, feminists chose to reinforce, not abandon, quantification as a method of legitimacy. Advocates turned to academic reporting methods like generalizable social science surveys and biological brain scans to defend their work. But, in lieu of emphasizing the *political* roots of quantification, anti-violence advocates neutralized any notion that they were biased to represent themselves as legitimate and "professional" authorities on equal footing with the state.[45] The strategy worked: Government officials, most notably then-senator Joe Biden, leveraged feminist quantifiable data to facilitate the passage of the Violence Against Women Act (VAWA).[46]

Since the merger between feminist and state surveillance measures, anti-rape activists have wielded quantification to justify their work. VAWA helped to spawn numerous federal anti-violence agencies, such as the Office on Violence against Women (OVW), as well as the introduction of several key anti-rape task forces within existing federal agencies, including at the Office of Justice Programs (OJP), Department of Justice (DOJ), and the Centers for Disease Control and Prevention (CDC), that evaluate rape as a public health or legal problem.[47] OVW provides a majority of the VAWA-sanctioned funding through programs like the Sexual Assault Services Program (SASP) and the Services, Training, Officers, and Prosecutors program (STOP). SASP assists states and territories "in supporting rape crisis centers and other nonprofit, nongovernmental organizations or tribal programs that provide services, direct intervention, and related assistance to victims of sexual assault and their families" and "is the first federal funding stream solely dedicated to the provision of direct intervention and related assistance for victims of sexual assault." In 2023, OVW disbursed "56 awards totaling $51.86 million" to each of the parent agencies overseeing local rape crisis centers as a part of SASP.[48] STOP formula grants are intended to enhance "the capacity of local communities to develop and strengthen effective law enforcement and prosecution strategies to combat violent crimes against women and to develop and strengthen victim services in cases involving violent crimes against women."[49] It specifies that "each state and territory must allocate 25 percent for law enforcement, 25 percent for prosecutors, 30 percent for victim services (of which at least 10 percent must be distributed to culturally specific community-based organizations), 5 percent to state and local courts, and 15 percent for discretionary distribution," and, in 2024, OVW disbursed "56 awards totaling $172.93 million" for the STOP program.[50]

As of 2020, it is estimated that at least two-thirds of an anti-violence agency's funding comes from a complex assemblage of federal and state grants like SASP or STOP. Only a fraction of most agencies' funding comes from foundation and individual donor contributions, making advocates highly reliant upon state grants and their quantitative approach to violence.[51] Yet these grant programs often ask advocates to report the numbers of victims served as well as the distribution of an advocate's time, money, and effort to a calculable number of victims served. In effect, grant reporting mandates to use systems-based quantification measures in advocacy extinguish the politics of statistics from visibility.

Over the last decade, grant opportunities for "underserved" victims have emerged, directing advocates to not only quantify survivors generally but quantify survivors' specific social identities like race, gender, dis/ability, and immigrant status.[52] Each presidential administration greatly influences the direction of rape responses, and the Biden administration made equity a top priority. In Biden's 2022 Executive Equity Action Plan, released through the DOJ and Executive Order 13985, state, tribal, and US territory anti-violence coalitions were asked to develop programming for cultural and linguistic minorities who have historically been excluded from anti-rape prevention and response research and services.[53] "Minorities" as defined by the plan include LGBT people, racial minorities, D/deaf or hard of hearing people, immigrants, refugees and asylum seekers, and people of a minority faith or religion. Applications for minority grant opportunities ask advocates to record the percentage of their work that supports marginalized victims as well as the number of underserved survivors they see at their centers. In 2024, the DOJ updated the plan to include measures that strengthened law enforcement responses in the "equity" plan.[54]

Federal and state agencies justify quantification as a way to fairly distribute limited resources to survivors. Administrators argue that numbers destigmatize rape victimization, support survivors, and inform the public about the prevalence of rape. For example, the Bureau of Justice Statistics (BJS), which reports violent crime (including rape) rates annually, states, "The mission of BJS is to collect, analyze, publish, and disseminate information on crime, criminal offenders, victims of crime, and the operation of justice systems at all levels of government . . . to improve both [state and local government] statistical capabilities and the quality and utility of their criminal history records."[55] The justification extends to marginalized survivors. In their 2024 grant solicitation, OVW wrote that they support "the maintenance and replication of existing successful services in domestic violence, dating violence, sexual assault, and stalking community-based programs providing culturally specific services, as well as the development of innovative culturally specific strategies and projects to enhance access to services and resources for victims who face obstacles to using more traditional services and resources."[56] However, they also demanded that agencies "present a clear link between the specific project activities and the proposed budget items," which necessitates the financialization of anti-rape advocacy, and thus quantification.[57]

Today, advocates feel compelled to quantify victims in their work because of the high stakes of grant writing. Successful applications to funding opportunities enable rape crisis centers to hire and retain frontline crisis response staff, conduct programming that directly supports victims and funds prevention and outreach education, and research new ways of eliminating sexual violence.[58] These are desirable outcomes for a rape crisis center because grants sustain victim services, expanding resources in the anti-rape market. But unsuccessful applications, usually those applications that use qualitative or humanistic methods, lead to little to no external support. This is the case because their client samples are seen to have a much "smaller" impact based on rigidly defined units of measurement—the bodies of rape victims.[59] Anti-violence advocates feel immense pressure therefore to quantify survivors.

The pressures to support *marginalized* survivors are especially intense. Though culturally responsive grant solicitations frequently ask applicants to use approaches appropriate for each population, minority grant opportunities are few and far between, only funding a handful of agencies that can demonstrate they have supported high numbers of minority survivors.[60] Moreover, as explored in chapter 2, the idea that some survivors can be distinguished as "cultural" and require additional services feeds the myth of the "perfect victim" who needs fewer resources and is therefore more deserving of support. Though grants are not at all a "safe" option to generate money, they are nevertheless a familiar way to generate financial support.

In 2025, Donald Trump's administration temporarily froze minority grant funding while it examined whether programs were pursuing a "woke" agenda. While it remains to be seen whether Donald Trump's executive orders pertaining to diversity, equity, and inclusion (DEI) will eliminate specific questions about victims' social identities on grants, direct services advocates continue to fill out forms during victim intake and processing to comply with current grant expectations.[61] On service forms are questions such as "What is the victim's race?" and "What is the victim's gender?" as well as a list of possible predetermined answers in checkboxes such as African American, Asian, White, and so forth. Once completed, these forms are sent to a grants officer who aggregates the data in the agency's grant applications.[62] The data transform from a stack of messy paperwork into a clean, taxonomic table to show funders the number of survivors served and the distribution of advocacy labor at the agency. In contrast to the past radical uses of quantification, today's advocates no longer perceive quantification in the same spirit, simply using numbers in rote formation for the all-consuming neoliberal state.

Speaking for Survivors

At the direct services level, advocates do not directly write grants. Instead, advocates are responsible for drafting a summary report, sometimes referred to as an intake form. This document usually asks advocates to answer questions related to a case, such as the type of sexual assault experienced (e.g., partner rape, stranger sexual assault), resources utilized (e.g., shower, clothing, food), safety planning (e.g., follow-up counseling, STI testing), and the victim's social identities (e.g., race, gender, dis/ability). The degree to which these forms are completed largely depends on the individual advocate as well as the location of the advocate, as some states may subpoena advocates' records for rape trials. One advocate admitted, for example, "I kept the sparsest records I could because I was already like I feel like we're documenting too much." Typically, this report is the last remaining task to be completed after a survivor leaves a rape crisis center for the first time, sometimes occurring late in the evening into the early morning. Because of the timing of the report, some advocates shared that they did not spend considerable time completing the forms in their entirety or with as much care as they devoted to other parts to their work.

That advocates fill out summary forms as the last part of their on-call duties might be an issue of interest in examinations of the labor of advocates and how questions are phrased on the forms themselves to encourage careful completion.[63] Here, however, I want to turn to the ways that the *writing* of forms, which thereby gets translated onto agency grants, is a form of biopower. "Biopower" is a term coined by Michel Foucault, who argued that administrative institutions, such as schools or public health systems, confer power onto the administrator over the subjects being administrated.[64] This administrative power is often used to regulate the social life of administrated subjects, usually in ways that have corporeal effects on oppressed populations.[65]

At rape crisis centers, administration occurs through intake forms. Sharing anecdotal stories of the neoliberalization of domestic violence advocacy, Mehrotra et al. reported that "accountability to funders . . . requires organizations to document and provide endless financial records, case notes, and program evaluation results."[66] Closer associations with state funding entities, who are invested in showing that they have supported high numbers of (particularly identified) victims, has compelled administrative advocates to collect victim demographics en masse. These grant managers and advocate coordinators often add questions to intake forms pertaining to victims' social identities that are then completed by direct services advocates.[67] For example, an Indigenous advocate with administrative experience pointed out that systems professionals frequently dismiss Native survivors because they do not make up a significant percentage of the survivors who report rape. She insisted, "I have trained everybody that I know, people at the hospital or . . . police officer[s] [that they should] make sure they put in, make sure they put your race in because those statistics are how we get funding. We need those statistics. . . . When the police say they've only had contact this month with twenty-three American Indians we're goin' that's not right, you know, you're just making an assumption." The advocate seeks to justify the funding of Indigenous support services to rape responders by showing the high numbers of Indigenous survivors who report sexual assault.

However, the ways that advocates record information about victims' identities are often incongruent with how victims themselves identify.

In her study about the limitations of state funding, Shana L. Maier explained that "when programs compete for funding, they adapt to the preferences of the funding source . . . or avoid action that alienates them from financial supporters."[68] These adaptations to reflect funders' (or advocate administrators') interests involve the presentation of data in easily consumable, quantified ways. Most administrative advocacy forms about gender, for example, ask for the number of people who identify as man and woman, and may offer a third option of "nonbinary" or "other." While this last category may expand the taxonomic data set, it provides no option for queered (dis)identification.[69] The quantification of gender into rigidly defined classifications misrepresents, misrecognizes, and "others" more fluid queered identities and negates antisettler being (such as "Two-Spirit") by collapsing the identity into one recognizable to the state.[70]

The reliance on funders' perspectives leads to a list of social identities, indexed by race, gender, sexual orientation, and so forth, that have little salience to the people assigned to those categories. In the aforementioned advocate's example, "American Indians" is a category premised on the assumption that Indigeneity is a racial identity that can be equated to others such as "Asian" (another contested category) in the American taxonomic racial hierarchy.[71] However, Indigeneity has been forcibly classified as "nonwhite" and added to "people of color" in the neoliberal settler-colonial discourse, even though it is (also) a political and legal identity.[72] Particularly when it comes to enrollment and blood quantum, this insistence on reporting victims as "American Indian" may disempower victims who do not subscribe to "American Indian" but rather to their tribal affiliation or another term. Another Native advocate provided an example that illuminates how data collection via intake forms can be limiting for Native American victims, in ways that counter the earlier advocate's justification for quantification: "I had a woman come in and said like I'm one-thirty-second Native American and I said well where is that in your big toe? I mean I'm kidding but I try to make light of things but um. So it's, a lot of times when they don't look Native it's like well, how does a Native look? You know." Using humor, the advocate points out that the survivor believed she had to report as one-thirty-second Native to receive support from a tribal agency. She notes to us and the survivor that Native cultures are much more complex than a person's looks or quantity of Native blood, through this explanation illustrating that the documentation of a survivor's social identity can reinforce the boundaries around survivors' sense of being.

Importantly, the problem of mischaracterizing victims on forms is not only about the ways that form questions restrict identity representations. It is also the ways that *advocates subscribe to the form's identities* through the stroke of a check mark. Rape theorist Linda Martín Alcoff explained that "a speaker's location (which I take here to refer to their *social* location, or social identity) has an epistemically significant impact on that speaker's claims and can serve either to authorize or disauthorize one's speech."[73] All people, including every individual advocate, has a standpoint that shapes how we see the world.[74] At rape crisis centers, advocates serve as the people who seek to support survivors; they are *the* designated professionals managing survivors' cases. Though they might justify quantification to gain legitimacy, advocates who fill out forms as they are implicitly accept the identities as the state sees them. This act subverts the role of the advocate from one who is independent of funders and administrators into one who polices the boundaries around victim services. In other words, *the administration of intake forms* makes advocates into administrative biopower technologies dictating the life of survivors, "speaking for" them. A bilingual advocate summed it up when she pointedly asked, "Who gets to translate [the survivor's] story?"[75]

Intentionally or not, administrating survivors through quantification has serious material ramifications for survivors. An Indigenous advocate explained,

> I'll use for example, an intake form. And it can be anything from registering for school, becoming a client at a nonprofit, uh. Being sent to prison. Each of those systems has some sort of form that they can say okay okay you're this, you're that, dahdahdahdahdah uh, you've worked here, you've lived there, you have eight children, you're heterosexual, you're not, and so people think with that form, uh, and whatever that looks like, is somehow, they not only tend to find you but who you are and what you need. And, obviously [with] any of those things there's huge gaping holes. . . . They didn't [ask about]

medications ... [or] the services they were already getting, services they needed.

As the advocate shows, the taxonomies of identities on intake forms often subsume the needs of the survivor, such as their medications, in favor of clean counting. Accordingly, the advocacy services that are offered are considered in isolation from the survivor's identities, normalizing the survivor on paper while ensconcing the voice of the designer of the intake form over the survivor's own ways of seeing their needs. This "speaking for" the survivor, the advocate later argued, leads systems to "decid[e] who you are."

Another advocate explained the intersectional challenges with the form: "I think the checklist's kinda messed up. I hate that! The thing is, a lot of people come in and they have needs and we're not able to meet their needs *because* [the survivor] might mark in one area but they don't mark in another area, so we didn't have this person but we can't help that person and it just gets very, um, that's, that's where the advocate burnout happens." Reports also have significant ramifications for victims during engagements with nonadvocate rape responders. A queer advocate recounted a scenario in which a sexual assault forensic examiner (SAFE) insisted on the "legal" deadname of a trans survivor. While the advocate was quick to rectify the error, she was unable to intervene quickly *enough* because of the dominance of the form. The rigidity of the intake form directly created a situation in which an anti-rape worker deadnamed a survivor in an emergency room.

> [The hospital] is extraordinarily Catholic ... And they, they've got so much work to do. Calling people out by deadname in the waiting room? Which is horrifically scary and terrifying for someone who is—presents primarily, I mean, calling out a male name in front of all the people in the waiting room, very unsafe, and then not being mindful, or at that point not caring, what that person's name is because insurance doesn't match right? So, if [Jane] walks in and says blee-bloo-blah blah blah but in the system [Jane] is [John], what does that look like? And then, to go through the processes of being checked out in the [emergency department], to get to forensics I mean, literally there was

a person that was in stirrups and was experiencing such dysmorphia, the forensic nurses didn't know that she had a penis, until they removed the, the sheet."[76]

The consequences of intake forms have serious long-term effects as well. One advocate explained how reporting disability on an intake form could affect how disabled survivors engaged with welfare institutions: "Depending on the context like how relevant is it if you know [the survivor has] a disability? You know if you ask them that . . . then I feel like they would think, well, does this count against me you know? You know if I don't have a visible disability but you know then it's reported, does that mean that, this is going to get reported to DHR [the Department of Human Resources] or something like that. Um, and like fearing institutions which people with disability have every right to." The advocate illustrates that even though advocates have a responsibility to the survivor, summary reports also encouraged them to disclose survivors' identities to institutions outside of the rape crisis center, like DHR. Through checking the disability box, advocates inadvertently make disabled survivors vulnerable to ableist systems outside of the rape crisis center or foreclose their opportunity to receive disability-specific anti-rape care.

Advocates' examples show that normalization via quantification is not explicit. The rote Q&A of predetermined quantitative forms encourages direct services advocates, particularly those without the knowledge about why these questions are included, to subliminally interrogate victims instead of asking for victims' stories in their own language. Several advocates told me that they had to remind themselves to pause before engaging with victims; for one, "After a while you almost become robotic. I have to like pull myself back because I just go in this checklist order." The form of the form transforms advocacy into a weapon of state funding agencies because we do not question their purpose. Examining the taxonomy of queer(ed) identities, Kadji Amin explains the pervasiveness of such rigid normalized quantification: "Taxonomy's biological inheritance brings with it the conceit that taxonomical categories and divisions are objective and innate, the hidden laws that govern what manifests in the natural world. . . . It is *taxonomy's implicit bid for universal validity* that serves as the carrier of the method's racist and colonialist histories."[77] Simply put, whoever writes the forms controls victims' lives, at least as they navigate the postrape terrain, because forms escape political scrutiny.

Advocates are imbricated in the creation of normative victims when we do not question the purpose of quantification. Despite good intentions, the problem of writing summary reports is that they are written *by advocates* for carceral or otherwise neoliberal ends. Though it can be argued that advocates are designated representatives of survivors and that victims may have "consented" to advocates' assistance, victims often do not consent to have their information shared with funders or anyone outside of the rape crisis centers, and they rarely, if ever, consent to have their information represented *in that way*. Advocates "speak for" them when they do not request explicit permission to use their information in their grant applications (or any other agency operation). As one white advocate warned, on the subject of racial tensions between herself as a white advocate and a survivor of color, "Being an advocate, we're still in a position of power." Indeed, Alcoff similarly concluded, "The problem with speaking for others exists in the very structure of discursive practice, no matter its content, and therefore it is this structure itself that needs alteration."[78] Though survivors may share their identities with advocates throughout the advocacy process, victims themselves do not fill out the forms; they do not and cannot speak in the neoliberal rape crisis center.[79]

Who Counts?

Who "counts" at a rape crisis center? The answer is complex. Advocates *get to count* but only in ways that are amenable to systems professionals and funding agencies. Often, that means *who is counted* is premised on dominant norms of the neoliberal funders. Systems authorities and advocates, not survivors, represent victims, and only those survivors who fit into rigid and singular boxes of identities, usually white, cisgender, heterosexual, able-bodied, and neurotypical survivors, are counted and thereby supported. All Others are checkmarked into deviancy.

The extent of neoliberal normativity in advocacy quantification is vast. Quantification touches any anti-violence agency that seeks funding from government entities. Accordingly, given that culturally specific organizations also quantify, they are not immune to the problems of normativity. Despite that their nature is to support historically underserved populations, tribal organizations and agencies that operate for specific racial, sexual, immigrant, and disability groups also normalize identities when they quantify victims. The survivor referred to at the beginning of this chapter, for example, was quantified by a tribal agency, upholding norms about Native and woman identities. Quantification normalizes, and it persuades advocates from all kinds of neoliberal agencies to do the same. In Shannon Winnubst's astute characterization of fungible quantification, "We are, living in these strained neoliberal times, thereby losing hesitation about expanding the reach of this calculative rationality beyond particular kinds of objects, phenomena, and relations. . . . Social values begin to be determined through the single barometer of this calculative rationality abstracted from and extracted out of any historico-social context."[80]

Like salt in a wound, feminist acquiescence to quantification has not led to any improvement in victim services. In fact, the overall amount distributed to victim services has decreased since VAWA's inception. Upon initial authorization in 1994, VAWA programs provided $1.6 billion over the course of six years for domestic violence and sexual assault services.[81] Each year, that is approximately $266,666,667. Calculating for inflation, the amount provided in 1994 would be worth $459,944,754 in 2019.[82] In comparison, in 2019, "$559 million was appropriated for VAWA-authorized programs administered by OVW, OJP, and CDC."[83] While the amount for 2019 appears to be about the same as or slightly higher than it was in 1994, the number obscures three key facts: first, government block grants for social services generally, such as housing, food, or childcare assistance, have largely held at the same level *or decreased*; second, the overall amount disbursed for victim services—notably including domestic violence *and* sexual assault, though domestic violence oftentimes gets the lion's share of the money—has not changed, meaning that the numbers *have not accounted for expansion of advocacy services and victims' daily living costs*; and third, there were *fewer* rape crisis centers in 1994 than in 2019.[84] Rape crisis centers today experience much more significant pressures to apply for funding contracts because there is much more competition. To break the numbers down, if in 1994 there were three hundred agencies, each agency would receive the equivalent of approximately $1.5 million, assuming equal payouts, but in 2019, if there was an estimate of twelve hundred agencies, as the National Sexual Violence Resource Center estimates,[85] each agency would only receive about $465,833.[86] Thus, while the overall number provided for victim services appears to have risen over the years, the amount provided to each anti-violence agency for victim services is substantially lower today than at the start of quantification in anti-violence work in 1994. Moreover, as one advocate summarized, "You start these grants and then, they run out, and you don't get another grant to keep it going."

Minority grants have likewise decreased in funding over time. In 2023, OVW reported that the Culturally Specific Services Program disbursed "53 awards totaling over $25 million."[87] These numbers divert attention from the reality that the number of culturally specific organizations that are eligible for federal grants has drastically *risen* over the last decade with the recognition that minorities may need culturally specific services.[88] This rise means that even though OVW granted $25 million to fifty-three agencies, culturally specific organizations as a whole receive less funding for their work. Their status as culturally specific organizations also makes them inherently less likely to receive federal and state funding from "open," non–culturally specific grants because they cannot demonstrate an overall high number of diverse survivors served. Simultaneously, the vast majority of mainstream anti-violence agencies do not receive financial support from the federal government to provide "special" services for underrepresented survivors. As one advocate at a mainstream agency noted, "The big grants are in the cities." Thus, she was unable to finance mobile advocacy for rural survivors, who made up most potential help-seeking victims in the service area. The bifurcation of ideal versus marginalized victims and organizations with the competitive nature of grants leads to decreased funding for marginalized survivors at *both* culturally specific and mainstream organizations.

A corollary issue to wielding quantification to finance victim services is the distribution of advocacy labor. As described in chapter 3, direct services advocates, many of whom identify as queer people and people of color, more likely encounter heightened labor expectations compared to their white, cisgender, and heterosexual colleagues. Paperwork is no different; the majority of service forms are filed by marginalized advocates, some of whom do not speak directly to grants officers about the data they collect.[89] As the advocates in this study bemoaned, the quantification framework reveals that the disproportionate burden of normalizing survivors through quantification falls on the shoulders of those who are most impacted by said normalization. It is a mechanism that keeps marginalized people oppressed by our own hands.

These consequences expose the larger, looming problem within antirape work. If quantification does not lead to more money, then what purpose does quantification serve for advocates? One advocate articulated, "Survivors' experiences again while unique to that individual do have their commonalities but, the needs for the healing journey if that's in fact what that advocate's end goal is, is to . . . understand them as a whole. I think what, what's really interesting when I think of checklist-y all I'm thinking of is getting paid by the government, you know under VAWA or VOCA [Victims of Crime Act]. Like oh we gotta check these boxes so we make sure we get our funding. Well then you have a messed-up mission statement, you know? (laughs)." The advocate's perspective highlights the urgency of subverting normative quantification now. Quantification à la Wells and Wolfgang was used in the past to identify and acknowledge *humans*; as of late, however, such quantification is carried out by professionals who seek to normalize survivors and therefore change what we advocates do. Not only do professionals now determine the value of individual victims, as explored in chapter 2, but they also now control the *mechanisms* by which victims become valued, further cementing the carceral panopticon within advocacy, just as we saw in chapter 4. By counting survivors, we have lost our ability to conceptualize the purpose of advocacy to abolish intersectional violence, feeding the prison nation. To be sure, it is important for advocates to understand survivors' identities and how they influence sexual victimization experiences to support them better. But the state ropes in advocates to do the dirty work of counting, extinguishing our ability to represent ourselves. Quantification is not just a way to forcibly impose extra labor on advocates; it is a way of speaking for us.[90]

We cannot quantify using state means. Taxonomies are, according to Mel Y. Chen, a "crude . . . device to keep my columns neatly divided and my rows suggestively linked,"[91] and, according to Kadji Amin, a way "to contain and safely domesticate the unruly and disruptive potential of the terms that might otherwise deconstruct the basis of the entire category in which they are housed."⁹² Quantification is not a "neutral" process that can be carried out by anyone; rather, it is an acutely subjective process that suppresses our instinct to search for another nonnormative way of knowing each other. In thinking about the purpose of advocacy, we must ask ourselves, For what reasons do we need a "magic number" of victims harmed and deserving of support?⁹³ Do we really need to count to help survivors? For whom do we count?⁹⁴ *Who counts?*

The Resurrection of Zombie Taxonomies

Why do we quantify if the cost of funding is secondary violence? Reflecting on her case forms, a heteronormative-presenting bisexual advocate mused,

> One thing that's always bothered me about like the paperwork we fill out is that our funding agency, for some reason, wants us to notate someone's sexual orientation on the sheet, after the fact you know, we do the pages after so, um, the case is over. And I never ask anybody what sexual orientation they are. Because, that just seems like a triggering question in the like context of what they have come to us for. But, at the same time I feel bad every time I check heterosexual or someone who looks like me. Because anyone, you know, could identify as bi and be invisible. [. . .] But, I don't know. I just feel like I know that [the rape crisis center] is kind of beholden to you know keep up with documentation because it's part of like I guess the funding and contract agreement and so I don't want that to like interfere with you know, us keeping the lights on. (Laughs) [. . .] Yeah and honestly I don't, I mean I don't really even know if I've even asked like the director how important is it that we do this, if we do not know.

Although advocates have, generally speaking, yet to rally against quantifying victims using state forms, quantification has been historically privileged to prevent marginalized people from remedying violence on our own terms.⁹⁵ Western and patriarchal researchers consciously labeled their work as "objective" and therefore academically rigorous to suppress "subjective" women's and marginalized histories.⁹⁶ Speaking to the suppression of Black feminist thought by both white and male studies, Patricia Hill Collins comments, "Suppressing the knowledge produced by any oppressed group makes it easier for dominant groups to rule because the seeming absence of dissent suggests that subordinate groups willingly collaborate in their own victimization."[97] Naming quantification a "fair" method renders the biases inherent to quantification invisible. It then presents subordinate groups as making their own oppression by resisting quantification. This decision was deliberate. As Kamden Strunk explains, "The creation of categories . . . is an exercise of power and cannot be separated from the sociohistorical contexts that give rise to different categorization schemes."[98] Though advocates may quantify victims with the intent to better support them, quantification subjects advocates to executing normativity quietly, against our intentions to eliminate intersectional violence.

As this book is sent to the press, federal grant agencies have implemented the specific identification of race and ethnicity of victims on grant forms.[99] While such an initiative comes forty-five years after the Third World Women and Violence conference called for inclusive statistical reporting on rape, it is perhaps coming at a time that no longer requires these data. Today, we are well aware of the racial and ethnic disparities between victims, and the documentation of these identities—even if they are open ended—will almost certainly result in some misrepresentation on the ground. To think about this issue simply, the drive to quantify comes from administration, which filters down onto grassroots advocates without clear guidelines on *how* to collect these data. Consequently, it may be that we see an increase in racial and ethnic minorities represented in rape victim statistics, expanding our power to negotiate with funders, but it may also be the case that due to a lack of specialized guidance on queering and decolonizing methodologies *and* the emboldened institution of the neoliberal rape crisis center to consolidate data for grants, advocates will end up re-creating the violence of state-based quantification onto victims through a different medium, forcibly imposing representation onto victims whose identities need no further pathologization.

Ultimately, grants pressure advocates to quantify and resurrect what queer methodologists have called "zombie" taxonomies. Like a zombie, the taxonomies produced by grant quantification continue to exist despite the fact that they no longer accomplish what they originally intended to do.[100] The first quantitative feminists sought to make the issue of rape prevalence known to the public, who at that time did not understand the scale of rape. But in today's world, few but far-right conservatives argue that rape is not a social problem.[101] By rehashing quantification and justifying it as a way to equalize anti-violence work, advocates contribute to the beleaguered lifeblood of normativity.

Solutions to advocates writing forms and normalizing survivors are not simple. Transforming a singular intake form will not stop the greed for numbers by the neoliberal capitalist state, nor will it change the pressures experienced by advocates to quantify and "speak for" survivors. Structural remedies are necessary. But even in this endeavor, we must be cautious. Anti-capitalist theorist Lucia Hulsether reminds us, "Every document occasions a future document."[102] Changes to the system of processing victim data, including the ways that we collect information about victims' social identities, are charged with the possibility of resurrecting yet another form. For example, having victims fill out their own summary reports to eliminate advocates' overruling altogether should not be our answer. By the time they conclude their first interaction at a rape crisis center, victims have already endured substantial trauma and likely filled out multiple forms demanded from other rape responders. Hospitals or SAFE facilities may require "consent" from the victim to conduct a bodily examination, and police officers often require that survivors detail their experiences and sign their statements.[103] These interviews and subsequent form filings usually immediately follow an acute rape attack and can be lengthy in duration, spanning in most cases over several hours at each location. One advocate exclaimed in reference to the stacks of paperwork required of victims before they exit the agency, for example, "What the fuck is all this paperwork?!" Requiring victims to detail yet another summary of the violence they experienced and the services that they utilized is not a viable option.

Additionally, creating yet another form in which victims "give consent" for advocates to explicitly "speak for" them in the rape crisis center will also not address this problem of normalization. For one, while advocates are trained to address survivors' concerns, advocates' attention to survivors is still premised on the vantage point of the advocate, not the survivor. Therefore, consent forms do not capture one's fully informed consent. Biopower held by the neoliberal institution only makes visible *legally* binding consent, not consent as survivors understand it.[104] For example, a Puerto Rican advocate gave an example of how *consent forms* could not be equated with *consent* at her white-centric English-speaking agency. In an interview recorded through fieldnotes,

> The interviewee said that she translated all the information statements, consent forms, and [other] documents into Spanish by herself. Once complete, she presented these documents to an administrator and asked her to sign them. The white monolingual administrator responded by giggling and saying that "Oh, I can't sign that; I don't understand what it says." The interviewee proceeded to raise her tone in frustration and exclaim: "That's exactly my point! How can you expect someone who has gone through a traumatic event to sign something they don't understand!?" When asked about what other advocates do when faced with a non-English-speaker survivor, the interviewee explained that these other advocates will "refer" the survivor to other services or the language line, without offering additional linguistic support. For example, advocates will proceed to do all advocacy in English and refer them to Planned Parenthood or similar agencies. The interviewee, again with a frustrated tone, said, "That's not advocating; that's just giving [survivors] a piece of paper."

Similarly, a white woman advocate recounted the difficulties with obtaining informed consent from a Black disabled youth survivor.

> It was a case where the client was like . . . a seventeen—yeah, I was pretty sure he was seventeen but a seventeen-year-old um, Black boy. And, he was at . . . one of the local hospitals. [. . .] I walk up in there, I meet with his auntie, and like I'm talking to her um and they said that you know he had um, he had special needs but they didn't like, like in the dispatch whenever they called they like didn't really know what was, like what what the issues were. I was like okay. And she was like he is um, like, severely autistic um. He has no ability to vocalize, um, and uh he is also incredibly violent. And I was like, okay well I'm not really sure, like, if we're gonna be able to get consent to do this.

To be clear, having a disability or being disabled or speaking a language other than English does not signal nonconsent; humans can engage in sexual relations.[105] Instead, I want us to reflect on the purpose of consent when it is attached to state form(s). What is "consent" when routed through itineraries of victim assessment?[106] I wager that consent as invoked by advocate "vampires" is not empowerment but necromancy cloaked as radical life.[107] Advocacy as quantification resurrects a lifeless taxonomy that does nothing to support victims, a "zombie" relic of past feminist anti-violence activism.

(Re)Animating Who We Are

Our ill-placed faith in grants continues to chip away our power to support survivors.[108] We have chosen to submit ourselves and victims to the very taxonomic schemes that reinforce more violence, despite the fact that they do little for us now. As we move into an actively anti-DEI presidential administration, our agenda cannot be to double down on such a problematic method much as we did in the past when faced with conservative rewriting of measurements. As Hulsether in *Capitalist Humanitarianism* shrewdly remarked, "Capitalists are already historicizing capitalism, and numbers are really not the name of that game."[109]

Our next question, then, must be why advocates need to gather numerical data about survivors at all. In light of recent critiques of quantification, some scholars have argued against quantitative studies altogether. Muscogee (Creek) scholar Sarah Deer, for example, suggests that while some quantitative studies call attention to the urgent problem of missing and murdered Indigenous women, the numbers have not done anything to change our responses to the rape of Indigenous people. She comments, "The data we currently have [on the prevalence of Native victimization] do little more than 'prove' that Native women experience extremely high rates of rape. But do we need more data in order to move forward?"[110] Deer raises an important point: The purpose of quantification is often justified as raising awareness about rape, but our task as advocates does not end with awareness.

Critical Indigenous and queer quantitative scholars have started the work of designing research protocols that attune to communities' way of knowing. Maggie Walter (palawa, Tasmania) and Michele Suina (Cochiti Pueblo) argue that statistical narratives about Indigenous people are often centered on difference from white settlers, such that they build a "raced reality" devoid of Indigenous methodologies.[111] In other words, quantitative avoidance makes us forget how the state has already been playing the game of statistics over the years and dispossessed people from their own houses of knowledge. Advocacy is displaced from the rape crisis center when we refuse to look back on past politicized ways that we have come to know rape and anti-rape work. But instead of shunning quantification, Walter and Suina suggest that data sovereignty is a "methodological imperative" that helps scholars to "disrupt deficit narratives" and "reflect the embodied social, political, historical, and cultural realities of Indigenous people's lives."[112] Making radical advocacy *through* decolonial quantitative method/ologies helps us to reclaim stolen land, bodies, and numbers.

I turn to "animacies" to envision this alternative advocacy. Animacies is an approach that breathes politics and humanity into deceased subjects of study, enabling them to make and remake worlds of their own. Animacies reconceptualizes the traditional taxonomy, eschewing the "final superiority of either word or image" by subverting lines across social identities.[113] Chen calls animacies "an invitation to play, to take up alternative means of apprehending the offerings of a text," and illustrates that the act of refusing a normative taxonomic device allows us to reimagine identities other than the "life" or "death" presupposed by normative institutions.[114] Animacies "put the key axes—gender, sexual, romantic, and relational orientation—*into motion* in order to capacitate a nearly infinite range of combinations, and thereby, forms of personhood."[115] Rather than taking each identity as holding an innate or essentialist definition, animacies sees social identities as endlessly shifting forms.

Understanding advocacy as a *growing* animated practice helps advocates to accept victims as they are, refusing the cultural capitalist production of survivors. Presently, our anxieties about form filing pressure us to interject the state's voice in justice- and help-seeking responses, what one advocate explained is "a huge lack in the Western system, because we've divided time and tasks." However, as an Indigenous advocate explained of the intake process,

My most important role as an advocate [is to] understand that you don't have to get the whole story right now, you know get the particulars and understand the neurobiology of trauma and how the story is going to change. And also to help the victims coordinate the story with them, the prosecutor's office, so that they, so that everybody could just kinda be on the same page but also be trauma-informed to understand, and kinda walk through the trauma with the victim. [. . .] Because there's so much ego there, and frustration [but] if you can figure out a way to take them away from that focus and kind of walk in that victim's shoes . . . it gives the victim some autonomy to what happens in the process which, in sexual assault cases, is extremely tricky to navigate.

Animacies are, importantly, attentive to race, gender, sexuality, and interrelated social identities because they trace our lineages back to our communities. Two-Spirit scholar Alex Wilson (Opaskwayak Cree Nation) points out that Cree language is "gendered" through animacies; categories and words shift depending on their liveliness. In a similar way, though Cree language is sacred to Cree people, we must think about advocacy not as a rigidly defined procedure but as a flexible, constantly shifting form of forms that allows us to remember who we are. Studying the case of #SurvivedAndPunished, a volunteer grassroots organization dedicated to freeing criminalized survivors of domestic violence, trans theorist Vox Jo Hsu illustrated an early vision of the ways that animacies can operate in anti-rape work.[116] They analyzed #SurvivedAndPunished during the #MeToo movement as a case study to show that "bottom-up" trans networked responses to sexual violence can disrupt the violence of systems, including the carceral state. Though Hsu does not explicitly use the term "animacies," Hsu points out that "social taxonomies" endanger and engender the lives of trans people by separating social hierarchies of power around survivors, like housing, employment, and health care.[117] Therefore, Hsu describes how the advocates at #SurvivedAndPunished considered what "freedom" from violence means for survivors and used their definitions to design their activist practices. This deep consideration of community-designed action plans "forg[ed] connections—among individuals, organizations, institutions, movements, and histories."[118] Data about survivors are not solely the product of one actor (the advocate or the state) but are produced and continuously revised in movement to reflect how communities of survivors see themselves.

This critical quantification is early in the making; however, a small group of advocates pondered on the remaking—re-aliving, as it were—of victim quantification. Illustrating the importance of community-driven quantification, a white advocate surmised, "You know our, our demographics show—of clients, show that we're pretty reflective of the community. Which if we're—you know, so I've spent a lot of time thinking lately like okay well that's, that's a start I guess but um, if we're also saying that some people are disproportionately affected by domestic and sexual violence or [are] more vulnerable to it than maybe some of those like, like historically, and presently heh um marginalized groups maybe we should be seeing higher numbers of those folks instead of just the same number of those folks." As she articulates, if survivors who are already made vulnerable by state institutions are more likely to experience violence, then "we should be seeing higher numbers of those folks."

Another advocate, identifying as Black, joined the chorus: "I don't think the majority of the rapists are white. I think the other populations we don't report. So you won't know who uh sexually assaulted us? Do[es] that make sense? (laughs) So, I can't get past that question [about racialized rape] because I'm like I don't think they're majority white. People that look like me [Black] sexually assault as well, people that look like you [Asian] sexually assault as well but we don't report. So then you won't *know*, um, the demographics of the offender." The advocates point to a different way of conceptualizing quantification's use. Instead of calculating the bodies of victims for predetermined dollars, they suggest that we turn our attention onto the ways we come to know knowledge about rape, such as the knowledge of rape vulnerability and personal engagements of our communities with the state. This alternative quantification is not "data-driven policing" because our drive is not to regulate, punish, and incarcerate, nor is it coming from places of administrative confinement. Rather, we seek a medium for victims to *speak with* perpetrators on equitable footing in a mutually understanding and complex community, moving toward a transformative calculated justice.[119]

An advocate at a tribal agency offered a tangible example of how animated quantification can deconstruct capitalist logics at the rape crisis center.

> We just have this rule of like, no paperwork in the office. You just sit there and you listen to them, and you listen to them until they're done talking. And then, when we get to that point, then we can start doing the paperwork. Then we can start filling in some of the details, and if we can't fill 'em all in that one, um, that one session, we just go back and bring the paperwork back or we send it to 'em in an email or we do it some other way, we get creative about how we're gonna do it. And um, it's really been working really well and it is, it's such a simple change. But I—I, but letting those relationships develop organically in that first meeting is really really important. Because we're never going to have, we're never gonna have that opportunity to have that first connection again. [. . .] We can always edit.

The advocate then turned to her responsibility as an administrator. Arguing against the capitalist motive to count survivors' bodies, she said,

> The primary concern for our advocates is to support the victims, and the primary concern of me as the administrator is to make sure that we have the data. And we work together to get that, but I don't want them, I don't want them feeling like if they didn't check a box or um, fill something in right or something like that that that needs to be the focus of their experience. [. . .] I think that ag[encies]—I think that grants, need to stop being competitive. I don't think that grants should be, um competitive in any way because what this creates is it creates, and we run into this all the time, where it's like, you don't, I don't wanna work with you because then that lowers our numbers, when in reality we can just both count the numbers like we're two separate agencies, we can both count 'em (laughs). And um, but, it so I think that that is like one of the huge ways we could close the gap, is if we increase funding and then made the funding formula, formalized.

Here, "formalized" does not refer to the state's methodological quantification schema but to the connections with other advocates in a hyperprofessionalized network. The advocate points out that some agencies feel as though they "don't wanna work with you because then that lowers our numbers," a kind of foreclosure of collaboration that may prevent the marginalized rape victim from accessing the services that they need. However, by increasing funding and pooling resources in a mutual aid network, advocates animate strong solidarity relationships.

Indeed, calling attention to the power of advocates to negotiate their role in the larger US prison nation, the advocate described how her advocacy at the agency level transformed the financing of anti-rape work itself. Moving away from the belief that funding relationships cannot change, she advocated making financial relationships helpful for survivors.

> [The state coalition grant program manager] had approved all the grants, he approved every grant . . . I was like I don't understand, I was like I literally said to him I don't understand why you're here. I was just like I just don't. I flat out was like well you need to talk with our, with OVW who funds our grant because according to our grant, according to our program I'm doing exactly what I need to do . . . Oh man, it really pissed me off, I was mad for days. [. . .]
>
> Talk to the funders . . . because that's really how we were able to make this model kind of come alive, is that we were given flexibility under our state VOCA funding.

Like advocates who reclaimed their power from systems professionals, the advocate retains her radical core by protesting the normativity of funding. Undaunted by the power of the state, she speaks *out* with survivors to erase culpability in speaking *for* survivors.

To "reanimate" identities is to give life to victims by pushing ourselves into motion when the normative taxonomy tells us to stop for a form. This movement is *kinetic*, what Mississauga Nishnaabeg feminist Leanne Betasamosake Simpson writes "isn't just praxis; it also generates and animates theory within Indigenous contexts, and it is the crucial intellectual mode for generating knowledge."[120] Our animacies empower victims to choose their own representations but not in ways that separate them from critical advocacy care. Under the animacies framework, the Native survivor who sought services as described in the beginning of this chapter would not have been denied help. Advocates can center the meaning of "Native" on the basis of the survivor's interpretations, reshaping the social parameters of "Native," and they can reach out to other organizations that can alleviate financial hardships in a mutual aid framework. There is no taxonomy, no hierarchy of "Native" identity, but a fluid collective acceptance that "Native" is a mutable concept determined by the people who embody it. Through community-based counting, advocates can call back to what we have always done as advocates, to support survivors in whatever form that they need. In lieu of acquiescing to neoliberal funder demands for quantification, advocates (re)animate quantification, reanimating *advocacy* as abolitionist mutual aid, to envision a world without neoliberalism's incessant drive to normalize.

Conclusion

An Open Letter to the Anti-Rape Movement

January 10, 2025

Dear Advocates:

I was inspired to write this final, and first, letter to you by two groups of people. First, community organizers in Oklahoma sat with me after I had organized a cultural competency training where systems professionals had belittled advocates. With transparency, they told me that while they did not blame me for my efforts, I needed to do better—be more open, more radical, more attentive to the challenges of survivors in this region. My emotions of embarrassment and guilt spurred me to huddle up on the third floor of the university student activities center, teary-eyed and humbled into doing something different, and I took up a pen to draft this letter.

Second, this book's participants who are also survivors encouraged me to be honest with myself and with them. I was specifically inspired by the story of this advocate-survivor, who told me about her introduction into advocacy in 2016:

> Trump got elected and that honestly had a huge impact of um me being of like, aware, sort of the identity that I had tried to fit into was harmful, um, that I was . . . associating myself with people that maybe voted for Trump, um, and that I was like trying to not [be] a feminist and trying to be this certain image. . . . There was a lot of cognitive dissonance with like, who I had tried to be and who I actually was. (laughs). [. . .] Trump getting elected . . . had a big impact in snapping me out of whatever it was I had been trying to do.

The advocate went on to say, "The day [Trump was elected,] I was in shock, and I wrote like this, I dunno like this five-page essay about my feelings. . . . That was the first time I shared with anyone that I had been sexually assaulted." Well, I am a survivor-advocate-scholar, and don't I have complex feelings about the presidential administration, too?

Later, I finished writing this conclusion in the solitude of my home, a place where I can be with myself. This letter is a self-reflection of why I wrote this book, composing into form the feelings I've long evaded. It is also a tribute to everyone who has brought me here. Though I am physically alone, I am spiritually and theoretically connected with every Other in the long anti-rape movement. This is my story.

* * *

Every now and again, I am reminded that advocates live in a constant state of crisis. Many of us have become so accustomed to violence that we expect to feel it around every corner. We draft every email as though we are about to step in a minefield of corporate HR violations; we take the long way to a police station or hospital to give us time to shake off fear before we walk into a case; we toss a Narcan or stuff an extra set of clothes in our go-bag for the "just in case" scenarios. These behaviors, we say, are justified. Just last week, or just last month, or just last year, we had to deescalate a situation, talk someone down from hanging themselves, call an ambulance for an OD, a friend we remember had been chased into addiction by their abusive ex-partner. We have lived so long with these fears of what might happen that we don't remember what it is like to do advocacy freely. Jasbir Puar has described this way of living as existing in a "paranoid temporality," a time and space "embedded in a risk economy that attempts to ensure against future catastrophe. This is a temporality of negative exuberance—for we are never safe enough never healthy enough never prepared enough—driven by imitation (repetition of the same or in the service of maintaining the same) rather than innovation (openness to disruption of the same calling out to the new)."[1] Fearful of what might happen next, we wrap ourselves with the idea that we only need to take a few protective measures to stop violence, keeping it moving just to stay still.

The thing is, the crisis of every person who becomes a victim-survivor is still a crisis, and one that deserves all our feelings. But because of the gargantuan size of the state and its problems, we advocates have stopped breathing through our challenges. As I write this conclusion, I am facing yet another crisis, this time in the academy instead of the day-to-day of a rape crisis center. At my institution, diversity, equity, and inclusion (DEI) initiatives are under attack by neoconservatives who believe that DEI is divisive. They leverage the astronomical prices of college and mountains of student debt for which we faculty are somehow responsible (and as though we are cut checks from the coffers of student exploitation), and they criticize the low enrollment of students in our classes to justify slashing funding for anything they read as wasting taxpayers' money. Of course, their targets are the queers, the nonnormative, the rejects who do not produce any "good" for normative institutions. University administrators have overly complied with the demands of neoconservatives. I have watched, body hot with emotions, as they scrubbed our websites of any inciteful language, renamed our centers and courses with benign labels like "education" and "assistance," called officers to peaceful protests on the greens to tear down encampments. These administrators, and now some of my peer colleagues, argue that these measures were taken "for our safety."

I can't help but feel disgusted at their excuses. As a junior scholar but longtime radical feminist, I am furious, confused, and disappointed at the ways some colleagues and friends have turned away from their values of equity and justice in favor of what they call "peace" and "conflict avoidance." I frown, clench my fists, and gnash my teeth when they say we would rather comply with a few small-scale changes than to take transformative change, which they don't believe is possible anyway. For me, though DEI should not be equated with radicalism, the neoliberal cooptation of DEI is a means of white institutional powers speaking for those of us who see DEI's value. Still, I am thankful that this academic DEI "crisis" reminded me of the rage, fear, and frustration necessary to do good crisis work. The secret—and what an open secret it is!—is that DEI, like any crisis, *is* divisive as the neoconservatives say. Crises are not meant to unify; they're meant to collectivize and incite different actions. According to the Fireweed Collective, a transformative disability and healing justice grassroots organization, "A crisis is a moment of great tension and a moment of meeting the unknown. It's a turning point when things can't go on the way they have, and the situation isn't going to hold."[2] I turn to this definition because it's exactly what we have forgotten. A crisis doesn't mean austerity or precarity, or some other neoliberal bullshit. It just signals that we are at a moment of change.

Anti-violence advocacy has been running toward its demise since we began thinking about our work "in crisis" rather than as "a crisis." We understand crisis as change, but we have been told to quell our anger, talk it out, communicate with the state, perpetrators, and bystanders who can help us end violence for all in a bipartisan or otherwise "equalizing" alliance. The arguments go something like this: Any nonlegal action is "better" than legal action; cultural advocacy that listens to minority survivors is "better" than mainstream advocacy; having colleges that train incoming advocates in helping professionalism is "better" than no training by individual rape crisis centers; remaining silent to stay in a police interrogation room with a survivor is "better" than not being present; and quantifying identities is "better" than not funding minority support services. These "better" choices, however, don't actually move us any closer to the end of rape. And this is the case largely because they are still tempered by fears and apathy. Restorative justice and carceral justice are two sides of the same coin; cultural advocacy that is "separate but equal" is not equality at all; education without civics is just another name for class-fucking-privilege; advocates who apologize for systems are just police allies; and calculating justice isn't justice if we abuse in the process of counting. These problems converge, multiply, and aggrandize to make the anti-rape nonprofit industrial complex in a neoliberal prison nation. As abolitionist Ruth Wilson Gilmore warned, "Crises are territorial and multiscalar; they overlap and sometimes interlock."[3] By thinking along the binary because we are "in crisis," by forgetting that we can choose our own stories and how we show up, we inch our actions closer to a "normal" and "neutral" advocacy devoid of politically valent radicalism.

One of the most ironic parts of the neoliberalization of advocacy is that most advocates probably agree with the points raised in this book. Hungrily, our eyes have pored over this book's pages, realizing that we are not alone in this quest to end violence for everyone. An advocate burst aloud, for instance,

> One of the things that's frustrating is in advocacy work, the way that [my agency] does it, the way that we have done it, um. There's only that one pathway and a *looot* of folks in the LGBTQ+ community, a lot of folks

in these marginalized communities, don't want to go that path and so it's almost like yes the caseload and then also then running as fast as you can to try to build, heh, new pathways, support those pathways and find ways to help people access them in a way that's gonna feel safe for them. I think as someone who's part of the LGBTQ+ community, realizing that pathway that I was working in wasn't safe for most of my community is heartbreaking so it's like the burnout and also, what the hell am I doing for my community right now?

Though I feel the same emotions, I surmise that many of the proposals suggested at the end of each chapter will not be executed so easily. As an advocate, I'm aware of how little we think of ourselves. We are often too humble about our work, preferring to divert attention away from ourselves and onto victims who we believe are the strength of the movement. (This, too, is ironic itself; many of us are survivor-advocates.)[4] We also think that, to some degree, professionals like therapists or lawyers have better chances of shaping change than we poor advocates do. As one advocate said during the 2020 social justice reckoning, "A lot of us have PTSD, a lot of us have ADHD, a lot of us have mental disorders and anxiety disorders. . . . How do we manage this because we can't dial in."

This inability to be selfish for a moment and accept ourselves *as advocates* has pushed us toward our end. Dispossession of a tribe, Joanne Barker (Lenape, Delaware Tribe of Indians) informs us, arrives not through explicit warfare between two nations but through the insemination of corporate values into one tribe by another.[5] In the case of anti-rape work, systems professionals have constantly belittled us into thinking that normative unification is good and the multiplicity of ways we do advocacy are bad. Sheriff Chris Fitzgerald, for example, spat at Embrace advocates, attempting to frighten them into complicity when he wrote in his resignation, "I believe we have lost focus on what we are supposed to be doing, serving victims of domestic abuse and sexual assault. Embrace is trying to take a stand on many of the social issues in the nation and while I think it can be good, the focus these are getting is overshadowing our true mission. We also have to remember where we live and some of these issues do not exist to the extent they do elsewhere. We have to pick the battles we want to fight and cannot pick everyone of them that happens across the nation."[6] This gaslighting—that intersectional issues of racial and gendered justice are too big for us advocates to handle—has made us easy prey for the neoliberal state that divides, conquers, and kills. Advocates have displaced ourselves from our own homes in anti-rape collectives, banished to the margins of social justice work, because we feel pressured into conceptualizing advocacy not as the abolition of all forms of violence but as interpersonal victim services.

For many of us, rage continues to bubble underneath our skins. At least I am enraged. Just as bell hooks felt the rage of complicity, so too do I feel the rage when advocates side with the powerful and abandon our loyalties to abolition. I believe, as radical social workers Jennifer Zelnick and colleagues put it, "It would be foolish to pretend that our jobs aren't political."[7] Nevertheless, I admit that I am not *the* perfect advocate, either. This messiness is no more striking than my current choices to serve as an academic at a public university, credentialed to the brim with a PhD and under the thumb of conservative administrators. I myself have been prone to neoliberal tendencies, in my brief time as an academic already delivering subliminally oppressive cultural competency trainings, writing grants, and reinforcing professionalism in my classroom, sustaining the carceral-capitalist state at the same time I denounce their outcomes. I have been called out precisely for the same things that I critique, by advocates or academics or others in and out of my circles. I am aware, as the new presidential administration threatens our grants and positions, that my research might just be the undoing of radical advocacy.

Still, as a fellow academic-advocate put it, "When you write a book, part of the process of why you're doing it is to raise awareness and sometimes that means you piss people off." This echoes the perspective of Gilmore, who admitted for all us feminist scholars that "plenty of bad research (engaged or not) is produced for all kinds of reasons, and plenty of fruitless organizing is undertaken with the best intentions."[8] She advises us to reorient our mission: "Activist scholarship attempts to intervene in a particular historical-geographical moment by changing not only what people do but also how all of us think about ourselves and our time and place, by opening the world we make."[9] In other words, activist scholarship—like this very book—seeks not just to expose social disparities but also to reimagine how we can live without violence, opening our minds and bodies for otherworldly possibilities. Thus, even though I may not be the "perfect" advocate (and shouldn't strive to be one), and even though I continue to make mistakes (and will continue to do so, though hopefully less often), we can change our worlds if only we inspire and spark change in our communities.

The opening of the end (of rape) starts with us. I believe, just as this advocate believes,

> Even in the darkest, bleakest moments of your life where you can't do much, you still are offering something to the community and we still have a responsibility to care, to care for you. We have a responsibility of working together to make sure we all have the tools we need because we're all gonna be funded at different levels, we're gonna have different capacities, we're all gonna have all of those things. But . . . it doesn't mean somebody should suffer if they're one single person in the community trying to do all this work, when I have myself and several advocates over here in my group, who can help kind of take on whatever [the advocate's] doing so she can be successful 'cause ultimately, we're all here for the same reason. Well, if we're all here for the same reason, we should be able to help each other. Like it's not a contest—there's certainly more than enough work to go around for everyone.

I am called to Brittney Cooper's "eloquent rage." Departing from hooks, who stressed that rage can be "consuming" if not tempered correctly,[10] Cooper sees rage as a helpful weapon in its messiness. Arguing that rage need not be "focused with precision," Cooper writes that rage is "Clear. Expressive. To the point."[11] Genealogies of violence have long erased our narratives of radical resistance, and small attempts to rectify such complex stories—a timeline, a diploma, or a checklist, for instance—should not dilute our anger. Our feelings of eloquent rage and other ugly emotions empower us to envision an alternative future, to make choices presented to us by affective disagreements. They give us permission to advocate for ourselves as ourselves. They tell us that we may loosen the grip of fear and loss for the potentiality for something else. Through our emotions, we can begin to ask, as one advocate implores, "What can I do or what can I get to heal myself?" If we are at a moment of change, then we may "slow down and reevaluate how we're spending our time," to advocate differently for our communities.

What would it look like to release our feelings? Thinking about the possibility of a radical future for the first time, an advocate spoke slowly, as though fatigued. Gradually, they picked up speed, and their voice became stronger, angrier, wistful, louder, and defiant.

> If I had the power in any, um, anti-violence organization, uh, or I would change (slows down) [the] structure of them to be, um, nonhierarchical. No boards. Um. And, I don't even know the language but like a flat decision-making team. Flatten it right out . . . And I wanna say I would, survivor-led orgs. It's a complicated conversation. Because of harm and paying people and all the things that come into that so I wouldn't even go that far into it, but the other thing I would say is um . . . (exhales) Figure out restorative justice. It's there, it's doable. Put a lot of money into it. There are so many people in this country and in this world who have been practicing [it] and figuring it out. Um. I would ask the state to just, (laughs) get their shit together and a little faster and put money into restorative justice and paying folks who are good at it, who are practicing it and know how hard it is. Um. And yeah, build some, build some spaces for folks to not invest their time into law enforcement, they do not want to invest their time into the restorative practice to lend to transformative justice um. And it doesn't have to be transformative justice right off the bat. People are always so scared of it, especially in, um . . . especially in like survivor orgs and (laughs) sexual assault, sexual violence um and um, but fear is, you know intertwined into everything you're trying to do—trying to call our helpline and also the folks who work at these places, it's just this big fear cloud. Um, we don't have to do it perfectly because law enforcement definitely isn't, um. So yes, money into restorative justice. Would be my other thing. And training.

These ideas *are* possible. We need to stop being "in crisis" and start thinking about the benefits of "a crisis." We are survivors of neoliberalism, and this is our moment of change. We *can* stumble towards healing and justice, if only we let ourselves fall into all our emotions again.[12] Freeing us from the constraints of neoliberal normativity, an advocate asks us,

What are you afraid of? This is what it means to take care of your culture, your community, your family and do this work at once. This is what it looks like! We've [chosen] to look away, or to choose something different or follow these silly rules, but there are people out there who are being actively oppressed actively in their own lives, and still choosing to do advocacy work. Those are the folks we need to look [for], those are the champions, those are the heroines. Those are the people we need to be more like. And I think that until we start respecting what knowledge looks like and what advocacy looks like in all its different ways, then . . . we have to have something to look to.

Our fellow advocates have already started dreaming, holding ourselves accountable as we empower the movement once more.

There has to be another future that we imagine together. And I think that really has shaped the work I do with clients.

Black Lives Matter gives me hope that there is room for a better future. And I look forward to matching that future.

#MeToo.

In killing rage,
Melinda

ACKNOWLEDGMENTS

This book is a product of many years of love, relationship building, and trust. I am forever grateful to Sarah Deer, who responded to my cold email in 2017. You had no idea who I was or why I was interested in the subject of rape victim advocacy, but I am thankful that you saw something in that email and communed with me. Your solidarity, kindness, and sheer will power to do this kind of work has made me a better person, teaching me things that are fundamental to both academic life and "real"—well, as "real" as it will ever be—life. We have gone through so much together.

In addition to Sarah, my circles at the University of Kansas (KU) guided me through some tumultuous years. Endless gratitude to my academic mentors Kim C. Warren, Alesha Doan, Akiko Takeyama, Xiao (Faye) Hui 肖慧, and Meg Paceley, who sharpened my theories, methodologies, and commitment to anti-violence work. I must also thank Hannah Britton, Nick Syrett, and Megan Wilson, who supported me in their own ways. Huge thank you to my research assistants, who helped me to transcribe and analyze interviews: Cassiopeia Porter, Rachael A. Lawler, and Naomi Mendoza. Friends and brilliant interlocutors include Marcy Quiason, Abigail Barefoot, Agnes Phoebe Muyanga, Shawna Shipley-Gates, Elise Higgins, Pere DeRoy, Rachel Trusty, Kelsey Carls, Sameen, Jessina Emmert, Jo Kipgen, and Mie Takikawa.

At the University of Oklahoma (OU), I share gratitude with Traci Brynne Voyles, Chie Noyori-Corbett, Susy Jorgenson, Rodney Bates, Meg Sibbett, David Song, Jenny Sperling, Quan Phan, Brittney Morrissey, Zeynep Aydogdu, and Mike Sladek. Thank you as well to the faculty and staff at the OU Center for Faculty Excellence and Arts & Humanities Forum. To the students in my Sex, Race & Violence (Spring 2023 and Spring 2025) and Feminist Research Methods (Fall 2023) courses, I can't wait to see where we'll go. Our classroom discussions truly helped me to think critically about sexual violence, empowerment, and justice.

A small but mighty group of individuals reviewed an early manuscript of this book and encouraged me to fall freely into abolitionist and transformative justice literature: Wendy Mallette, Corinne Schwarz, Michelle Velasquez-Potts, and Cat Jacquet. Michele Eodice and Ron Martinez provided excellent feedback on this book's organization and writing style. I am also thankful for my editor, Ilene Kalish, and the anonymous reviewers from the press for validating this project and offering insightful feedback about my theories and methodologies.

I have been supported through conversations with fellow scholar-activists, whom I want to thank for generating ideas with me: Val Kalei Kanuha, Beth Whalley, Rachel Voth Schrag, Leila G. Wood, Benjamin R. Weiss, and Fran S. Danis. Shoutout to my NCFDD cohort for being there through the rough patch: Natalia Duong, Zi Ye, Amy Chin, and Jo Huh. To my NWSA colleagues and friends, you have been my "home" feminist studies community: Ionah Scully, Ying-Chao Kao 高穎超, Moya Bailey, Ana Bernal, Lisa Covington, Hsiao-Lan Hu, Valerie Taylor, and the Women of Color Leadership Project. Thank you to the Abolitionist Pedagogy reading group at the Carceral Studies Consortium (OU) for showing me how to talk about abolitionist feminism. To my activist co-conspirators, you continue to amaze me with your strength and compassion: Phil Garcia, Rhiannon Reese, Rebecca Henderson, Kellie Melloun, Theodore Longlois, Shai Khanam, Jaya Kolisetty, Sarah Colomé, everyone at OU Advocates and/but especially Amber May, Ann Schafer, and Erin Simpson, and the Women's Resource Center (Norman, Oklahoma) advocates. Special thanks to Valériana Chikoti-Bandua Estes, Brittny Olson, and Katie Bement for allowing me to reshare your stories.

I am grateful for the support of the anti–sexual assault coalitions who shared my study with prospective interviewees (listed in alphabetical order): Alabama, Arizona, Arkansas, District of Columbia, Florida, Hawai'i, Illinois, Iowa, Kansas, Maine, Massachusetts, Minnesota, New Hampshire, New Mexico, New York, North Carolina, Oklahoma, Oregon, Pennsylvania, South Carolina, South Dakota Coalition, South Dakota Network, Vermont, Washington, and West Virginia. Thank you as well to the National Sexual Violence Resource Center, National Indigenous Women's Resource Center, Nisaa African Family Services, Iowa Social Change, the Sexual Assault Advocacy Network, and Crisis Center, Inc. (Birmingham, Alabama).

This project was financially supported in part through awards from the following: the University of Kansas College of Liberal Arts & Sciences Research Excellence Initiative; the University of Kansas Office of Graduate Studies Summer Research Scholarship; the University of Kansas Hall Center for the Humanities Supplemental Funding; the University of Kansas Center for East Asian Studies; the Arts & Humanities Forum Faculty Fellowship at the University of Oklahoma; the Research Council of the University of Oklahoma Norman Campus Office of the Vice President for Research and Partnerships Junior Faculty Fellowship; and the University Libraries Subvention Funding from the Office of the Vice President for Research and Partnerships and the Office of the Provost, University of Oklahoma. I am aware of the irony of drawing upon institutional grants to write a book against neoliberal grant funding. However, as I share at the end of chapter 5, nonconditional funding that amplifies otherwise quiet voices can also prove useful in our quest to end violence if we are mindful about their presence. Thus, I am grateful for their financial support, without which I could not have completed this project. Any opinions, findings, conclusions, or recommendations expressed in this material are my own and do not necessarily reflect the views of the funding agencies or acknowledged persons.

My friends and family have supported this project in so many ways. To Melanie and Jackie, thank you for giving me the space to complete this project. Both of you consistently pushed me to play games or deal with family events instead of writing, but somehow this book turned out all the same. To Will, we have made a home for ourselves. Our daily adventures, from quiet coffee mornings to treks in the desert, mountains, and seas, will always remain in my heart. Love you.

Finally, but no less important, thank you to the victim advocates and survivors who took time out of their demanding schedules to participate in my study. I am grateful for your thoughts, and I stand with you in your vision for a radical future.

APPENDIX A

Study Design

This book draws on research conducted at the University of Kansas from 2019 to 2022 and continued dialogues thereafter with colleagues and friends who also serve as victim advocates and/or study sexual violence. My interest in the subject of sexual violence began, as with most, with my own experiences. I wielded my feelings of anger and confusion of that period in my life to identify spaces where I could end rape. Eventually, I landed at a suicide hotline and then, finally, rape crisis centers, where I learned to support survivors. While at these organizations, I observed numerous BIPOC advocates resign from their positions or move to independent collectives because of racialized and intersectional violence by white cis-het normative colleagues. After a particular series of incidents involving a group of racially white rape responders who verbally abused and denied support to several BIPOC survivors (survivors who were "my" cases or otherwise under "my" care), I came to realize that, one, advocates are not immune from causing harm, and, two, the ways that advocates cause harm are not readily apparent as violence. On the basis of these incidents, I decided to critically examine intersectional oppressions within victim advocacy.

Guided by my lived experiences, I began with a literature review of anti-violence scholarship. Charlene Carruthers's *Unapologetic* (2018) was particularly formative to my understanding of how interlocking violence may still occur even in the places with the best intentions at heart. Nevertheless, my academic search most often led me to studies that tended to privilege administrators or other executive-level staff members at rape crisis centers (e.g., Rose Corrigan's *Up Against a Wall*), which implicitly privileged racially white, formally educated, and middle- or upper-class individuals. The elevation of formal academic studies and their samples violates a key principle of intersectionality. Kimberlé Crenshaw reminds us, "This focus on otherwise-privileged group members creates a distorted analysis of racism and sexism because the operative conceptions of race and sex become grounded in experiences that actually represent only a subset of a much more complex phenomenon."[1] Indeed, I found that existing academic knowledge showed a very different reality than the one I was experiencing on the ground. By premising our stories on the privileged norm, we forgot to question whether we too can inflict intersectional harm on survivors and on each other.

This book seeks to amplify the voices of grassroots feminist activists. In the victim advocacy field, this aim means speaking with direct services anti-rape workers who operate hotlines and accompany survivors, usually to systems spaces like police stations or hospitals. I took guidance from welfare analyst Michael Lipsky, who explained, "Too often social analysts offer generalizations about organizational and governmental actions without concretely explaining how individual citizens and workers are affected by the actions."[2] To address this gap, Lipsky advocated for a methodology that captures the perspectives of frontline bureaucrats, the people at the front lines of a social movement who enforce or subvert institutional norms. As described in the introduction, victim advocates are best suited to expressing how neoliberalism manifests at rape crisis centers because they are often designated by state granting agencies to perform services that conform to or subvert norms about rape.[3] Between 2020 and 2022, I interviewed sixty-three advocates who conducted direct services within the previous five years of the interview (2016–2021), inclusive of both volunteer and paid staff direct services advocates. After listening to their perspectives, I realized that additional information about the legacies of victim advocacy was necessary to situate advocates' stories in the complex timelines of the anti-rape movement and therefore conducted archival research between 2023 and 2024, targeting the abolitionist strategies of past anti-rape advocates that could be used in the present.

My choice to study direct services advocates may exclude key parts of the anti-rape movement. Advocate careers are routinely cut short with the termination of a grant, stopping and starting with federal funding cycles. The precarity of advocates' work suggests that the participants' experiences shared in this book may be eclipsed by rapid changes in the anti-rape movement overall. Furthermore, the study of street-level direct services advocates excludes the voices of prevention educators and minimizes the contributions of administrators who more regularly engage directly with neoliberal funders. While I recognize this limitation, this book redirects attention onto grassroots queer of color activism, following what Carrie N. Baker and Maria Bevacqua argued make up the core (and oft-neglected part) of the anti-rape movement.[4] There are also no clean lines between administration and direct services; 61.9 percent of the sample also carried out managerial labor in addition to grassroots organizing. Finally, a significant portion of advocacy is carried out on hotlines, where advocates may not easily ascertain the identities of survivors. Yet even hotlines engage with neoliberal normativity in that advocates are still making decisions about victim care on the basis of their judgments of victims and agency expectations of victim services. Chapter 2, for example, describes how an advocate over a hotline restricts the scale of her work despite not knowing the specific racial identity of the victim, showing the *process* by which victims are marginalized. Therefore, although a study specifically examining hotline advocacy is needed, this book blends hotline advocacy with in-person advocacy to speak across advocacy's mutable forms. Most staff advocates and some but not all volunteer advocates in this study are trained in and respond to crisis calls in addition to engaging in in-person advocacy.

QUALITATIVE STUDY DESIGN

The bulk of this book relies on qualitative interview data collected from sixty-three victim advocates who work at rape crisis centers in the United States, Indian Country, DC, and Puerto Rico. I obtained IRB approval from the University of Kansas in November 2020 and, when I transferred institutions, from the University of Oklahoma in July 2022. I chose to recruit from across the United States because, while rape laws may vary by state, neoliberalism is a practice widespread across the United States.[5] Almost all anti-rape agencies in the United States draw most of their funding from government entities. Therefore, sampling from multiple locations could illustrate just how far neoliberalism has encroached on the anti-rape movement. Moreover, this study wanted to show the similarity of themes across vastly different anti-violence agencies.[6] I analyzed the political context (i.e., whether the agency was in a liberal or conservative area), geography (e.g., rural, urban), and size of advocates' agencies, as well as the viewpoints of individual advocates at the same agency or different agencies in the same region. This cross-sectional analysis enabled me to develop a more comprehensive portrait of the connections between different types of oppressions in the anti-rape field. All advocate-participants shared stories about the ways that normativity impacted their work, affecting diverse survivors.

To recruit participants, I emailed the executive directors or marketing managers of all state and tribal coalitions against sexual violence that had their contact information publicly available. I included mainstream agencies, or those agencies that support all victims irrespective of their identities and backgrounds, as well as culturally specific and tribal agencies, to recognize that rape victims can seek out services from multiple types of advocacy organizations. Because of the wide variation in agencies, a small minority of agencies represented in this project do not hold a 501(c)(3) nonprofit status; a handful of sampled advocates work or have previously worked at for-profit or public organizations, though in these cases, I made sure to ask about the agency's financial situations. (Nearly all advocates, however, had experience working at a "typical" nonprofit rape crisis center.) I employed a targeted sample of convenience because of the difficulties in recruiting direct services advocates without the support of anti-violence coalitions. Twenty-five parent agencies responded. Of the ones who responded, I requested that they disseminate study information to agencies within their jurisdiction, following snowball sampling. In most cases, once one advocate had participated in the study, they often felt compelled to encourage the participation of their fellow advocates at their agency, leading to clustered samples.

Recruitment at the coalitional level had its drawbacks. I learned after several interviews that many advocates who work at culturally specific agencies, mainly people of color and immigrants, are not in the networks of state coalitions because state coalitions sometimes do not consider culturally specific organizations to be legitimate rape crisis centers. Consequently, while the demographic composite of participants was somewhat even across social identities, including between white advocates and advocates of color (see appendix B), recruiting through coalitions likely prevented many otherwise eligible advocates from sharing their stories. Moreover, it is very likely that the explicitly "cultural" element to this study persuaded advocates who are already invested in radicalism (rather than those who should read this book) to share their experiences, leading to sampling bias.

Interested participants first completed a survey about their demographics and basic work information, such as whether they were a direct services or administrative advocate, and the sector of anti-rape work in which they worked, such as prevention or intervention. This survey was used to filter participant eligibility. I removed participants from eligibility if they did not interact directly with survivors at some point during their regular workdays. Two hundred and ten prospective interviewees began filling out the survey, and 115 completed the survey in its entirety. Upon confirmation of eligibility, I asked participants to sign up for an interview time slot and complete a sixty-minute interview. Seventy-five rape responders completed an interview, though only sixty-three advocates made it into this book due to eligibility, incomplete data, active abuse, or withdrawal.

I selected in-depth, semistructured interviewing as my method. This kind of interview generates insight into a participant's worldview without preemptively qualifying their voice.[7] That is, by framing the interview more as a guided conversation than a question-and-answer, as in the cases of structured interviewing, the researcher can capture insight into participants' beliefs as they see them *and* understand predetermined themes of interest, in my case, neoliberalism and oppressions within the helping professions.[8] For a study examining the ways that advocates and survivors may experience violence, it was critical to employ a method that would allow participants to flexibly express their perspective on violence without interjecting strong researcher bias.[9] This method was also helpful for evaluating the extent to which ethnic relations and rape laws factored into the production of secondary violence by allowing me to hear participants contextualize their geopolitical position in their own words.

Interviews took place over Zoom or phone, for three reasons. First, I did not have funds to compensate participants, and I did not want participants to feel as though they had to expend more resources, such as travel, to partake in a study meant to support them. Second, I collected data during the COVID-19 pandemic during lockdown orders, and I could not travel to meet with advocates in person. Collecting data during the pandemic likely solicited stories that would have not been shared otherwise.[10] Third, remote interviewing has been shown to feel more anonymous, making it an easier medium in which to discuss sensitive topics such as rape and racism.[11] While remote interviewing facilitated communication, the distance between myself and participants created by a screen or phone made it somewhat more difficult for me to establish rapport initially, likely contributing to the unusually long duration of the interviews. Furthermore, only having the option for remote interviewing made it likely that advocates who did not have technological access, usually low-income people, and advocates uncomfortable with using technology chose not to participate. Interviews were recorded via Zoom or handheld recorder and then transcribed, or else they were not recorded and I took notes during and immediately following an interview, then converted the "field note" into a research memo. On average, recorded interviews were 82 minutes in duration, ranging from 40 minutes to 232 minutes.[12] Five interviewees declined to be recorded, and I do not include the length of their interviews in the average recorded time.

Before every interview began, I re-requested consent verbally and informed participants how their information would be used. The interview protocol was divided into two parts. The first part solicited stories about participants' experiences supporting survivors of diverse backgrounds. I asked them to describe themselves and a time when they supported a marginalized "cultural minority" survivor, evaluating the differences in advocates' responses to victims and SART collaborators based on their social identities like ethnicity/race, sex/gender, disability, immigration status, faith, and housing and incarceration status. The second part focused on the policies and expectations set forth by the advocate's agency. I asked participants to describe their training around marginalized victim support and how they currently supported survivors of diverse backgrounds. The bifurcation of the interview was necessary to evaluate how advocates first conceptualized advocacy *outside* explicit neoliberal boundaries and then compare these notions to how they worked *under* neoliberalism. The two-part nature of the interview sometimes resulted in repetition, which was commented upon by several interviewees. On occasion, I prompted participants to think about different forms of social identity–based oppressions to generate a more intersectional portrait of their advocacy. For example, I asked participants about what they would do to support a racial minority victim or a disabled victim given their agency guidelines if they had not raised race or disability yet during their interview. After every interview, I followed up with a thank you email and resources on conducting and receiving culturally specific advocacy.

All participants directly engaged with diverse victims of normative and marginalized cultural identities, with most providing examples of the ways they navigated their and victims' racial-ethnic relations. The automatic association between "cultural minority" and "race" is not surprising given the historic link between rape definitions and race.[13] Yet advocates' assumed connection between "race" and "Blackness" reflects embedded social assumptions of deviancy, whereby the normative (whiteness) is unseen at the same time the most marginalized (Blackness) is rendered acute such that it is surveilled.[14] Throughout this book, therefore, I draw heavily on advocates' examples of navigating race/ethnicity and its intersections with sex/uality, gender, and interrelated identities; chapter 3 especially highlights *anti-Black* racism. I seek to underscore the often invisible, uncomfortable assumptions we hold about intersecting social movements. While some readers might believe that I should "balance" discussions about social identities by giving attention equally across race/ethnicity, sexual orientation, disability, and so on, I believe those divisions would merely reinforce biological essentialist myths about race and identity and minimize the violence experienced by BIPOC by and in the anti-rape field.[15] If we are to topple the hegemonic structures that sustain rape culture, the most politically divisive and affectively troubling identity, race, remains our litmus test for the survival of radicalism.

I completed forty-eight transcriptions using a transcription pedal and Express Scribe software. I outsourced thirteen interviews to a HIPAA-compliant transcription service, Rev, using funding from the University of Kansas. Two transcripts were completed by an undergraduate research assistant. I verified all transcriptions that were completed by another person by listening to the interview and reviewing the transcript or by creating my own transcript and comparing it with the one produced by another person. If there were discrepancies between my transcript and the transcript produced by another person, I marked those differences in the file.

I used two consecutive data analysis strategies: grounded theory and discourse analysis. Grounded theory is a method of categorizing themes on the basis of the participant's own words. It is typically employed by researchers who seek to develop a theory "grounded" within the participants' worldviews, building codes alongside study questions as a coparticipant as opposed to predetermining codes.[16] Given that I was interested in conceptualizing how each advocate ascribes meaning to their work, grounded theory was an appropriate choice. I analyzed as I interviewed. As Kathy Charmaz writes, coupling interviewing with grounded theory allows the researcher to "add new pieces to the research puzzle or conjure entire new puzzles—*while we gather data*."[17] This iterative process allowed me to continuously refine the interview instrument to better communicate with interviewees. To code, I employed open pattern and *in vivo* coding (coding that uses the same language as participants), which helped me to stay close to the story language and build themes. Units of analysis were parsed into narrative ebbs and flows rather than predetermined paragraphs, sentences, or words to remain as close to the style of the interview as possible. I repeated open pattern coding until theoretical saturation at around interview sixty.

Upon grounded theory analysis completion, I moved onto discourse analysis. Discourse analysis is "the analysis of language as it is used to enact activities, perspectives, and identities."[18] While grounded theory could capture participants' perspectives at face value, many participants spoke about neoliberalism without referencing it explicitly. Therefore, asking whether they restricted the scale of their work directly because of funding would not have elicited the responses that I was looking for. I had to rely primarily on *what* information the participant relayed about their work and its impact on survivors and *how* the participant relayed that information—i.e., discourse—to understand their navigation of neoliberal normativity. I used a combination of process and values coding: *Process coding* captures the actions that take place, and *values coding* captures the values, attitudes, and beliefs of participants.[19] Together, these two kinds of coding made it possible for me to get a sense of what advocates did to support survivors and how their support affected survivors. While I looked at narrative portions of data earlier in the analysis process, in this part, I reduced my unit of analysis to a singular or a handful of sentence(s) because participants would frequently contradict themselves within a single story of supporting a survivor, and I needed to separate their two beliefs for clarity. In addition to process and values coding, I also tagged information like identities (e.g., race, gender, sexuality) and evaluated whether differences in identities changed what advocates did and why. To code, I did not use conventional transcription or coding symbols, instead relying on explanatory descriptions for ease of understanding. Ellipses (. . .) marked pauses or removed incomprehensible stutters that were three seconds or shorter in length; bracketed ellipses ([. . .]) were used to mark pauses that were substantial in duration or if I had elided a portion of an interview for ease of reading.

I conducted discourse analysis with critical and queer methodologies in mind. Critical methodologies assume that systematic oppression (usually racism) is maintained by institutional powers (like state funding agencies), which inhibits free-flowing communication across differently positioned social groups.[20] Queer methodologies understand that marginalized people, particularly 2SLGBTQIA+ individuals, are frequently read through cisheteronormative lenses, and they demand that we listen carefully for the dissonances and silences within interviews.[21] The two methodologies collectively emphasize that participants may have different ways of communicating than we assume of the general population. Because I was interested in hearing marginalized perspectives, I intentionally took the identities of participants and applied their social statuses to their language, excavating both spoken word and dissonances, like "ums" or pauses, that explained how they navigated neoliberalism as a *particularly identified* (racialized, sexualized, heteronormatively femme/masculine performing, etc.) advocate.

To ascertain the validity of my analysis, I employed the help of a research assistant, Cassiopeia Porter, to collaboratively review the codebook with me. We reviewed each code and an example of where the codes were used to consider whether the codes made sense. After this review, I went back and recoded, over and over, until I had established a codebook that did not change significantly with time or more interviews. While Cassi was enormously helpful in clarifying code definitions, I conducted all coding by myself due to budget constraints. The single-person coding process may have limited study results, missing key insights or misconstruing data. However, whenever the data were unclear, I solicited advice from a faculty mentor. I also engaged in limited member checking. I followed up with my participants over time through emails and text messages to verify information and simply stay in touch. Several have sent follow-up information about themselves, such as when they moved locations or positions, some of which I added to the analysis. I did not return transcripts to participants because, to my surprise, many did not want to verify them, seeing such verification as a "reminder" of the problems of advocacy or their experiences with violence, or they entrusted their stories to me as a fellow advocate-scholar. In July 2022, because of ethics concerns pertaining to my institutional move, I emailed participants on how to contact me at my new university and destroyed participants' contact information.

File types for this project involved electronic and physical data. Within forty-eight hours of every interview, I uploaded all audiovisual files, field notes, and memos to an encrypted research file storage (RSF) accessible only to the research team and destroyed any interview metadata. Notes that I took by hand during the interview were immediately scanned, uploaded, then shredded. A hard copy with participants' personally identifiable information, such as name and email address, was preserved in a locked safe in my home office during active participant research. (Due to COVID-19 and personal reasons, I did not complete this study on site at the University of Kansas.) All interview transcripts were formatted to Microsoft Word. I employed the qualitative data analysis software Atlas.ti to assist with memo-ing, coding, and data visualization. I used Microsoft Excel to build my codebooks and conduct simple analyses. For the duration of active data collection, analysis, and writing, I kept electronic files on the secured RSF. For the duration of deidentified analysis, writing, and revisions at the University of Oklahoma, I kept the files on an encrypted OneDrive folder.

All advocate participants were assigned a randomly generated numeric code. This code followed all documents pertaining to them throughout the study and no names or contact information appeared on any analysis or published documents. However, I needed to keep some potentially identifying information to conduct my analysis. Specifically, advocates' work is influenced by their identities. For example, an advocate of color who works at a small agency in a rural, predominantly white area engages with neoliberal advocacy differently than a white advocate at a large, urban, and racially diverse agency. For this reason, I kept a file that contained participants' individual code and their social identities. This file was separated from the other files to ensure that no one with just one of the documents could easily identify the participant.

When writing about participants' identities, I made sure to use the language that they used to refer to themselves. For example, I used "African American" and not "Black" when a participant described their racial identity as African American. The exceptions are with Asian/Pacific Islander and Indigenous people, whom I could not adequately protect given how few Asian/Americans and Pacific Islanders are advocates in the United States and participated in my study, and the small population size of Indigenous Americans, especially when considering tribal affiliation. On pronouns, although most participants are cisgender females who use "she/her" pronouns, I decided to retain the pronouns used by non-cis-female advocates to preserve their voices.

While research examining the overlap between advocate and survivor populations remains too tentative to make conclusions, it is estimated that about 60 percent of advocates have also experienced some form of sexual violence.[22] In this study, I found that 57 percent of the sample have personally experienced sexual assault ($n=36$), with many pointing out that their personal experiences were the direct reason for their entry into anti-violence work. Compared to an estimated quarter of the population, this rate of victim status is remarkably high. The percentage, 57 percent of sixty-three advocates, is qualified by the fact that within my IRB protocol, advocates had to disclose their sexual assault without my directly asking about it. Twenty-eight and a half percent of advocates did not share whether they had personally experienced sexual violence ($n=18$), and 20 percent of advocates openly disclosed that they were not survivors ($n=9$). I am also sad to report that three prospective interviewees were actively experiencing abuse. Their voices expose how few resources exist for advocates and the stigma of reporting abuse while serving as an advocate. Although I recognize the importance of seeing advocates as survivors, I removed information pertaining to the three from this project to maintain their safety.

This study does not use data from a sample of the general victim population. Although I had conducted interviews with nonadvocate survivors about their postrape experiences, that stage of the project led to an extremely skewed racially white sample. This racial bias probably occurred because I sampled victims through anti-violence agencies. Normative victims are more likely to be supported by neoliberal agencies, and the more one feels one was helped by the agency, the more likely it is that one would be willing to participate in a study about those experiences. However, of the advocates who actively reported victim status, I interviewed eight of them about their victimization experiences and their influences on their current careers in advocacy. This book uses some excerpts from these follow-up interviews, which generally show a strong connection between social justice orientations and advocate-victims' lived experiences.

As discussed in the introduction, I have chosen not to name specific victim advocates by either name or pseudonym throughout this book, though I have retained advocate-participants' social identities. There are two major reasons for this anonymity. First, advocates were rightly cautious about participation in this study. Seventy-eight percent of participants ($n=49$) worked as full- or part-time staff members and were concerned about the possibility of making their perspectives public, particularly negative viewpoints, and losing a source of income or access to anti-violence organizing. Several advocates were also concerned about disclosing to the public that they are *survivors*, even if they were open to the possibility of their name as an *advocate* being known. The high variability of confidentiality requests was coupled with the fact that all advocate-participants shared their specific identities such as ethnicity, gender, and so forth, that make it easy for readers to ascertain specific individuals if all identities were presented. For example, if I were to state that participant X is a "queer East Asian American cisgender woman in her twenties with a graduate degree and approximately four to five years of advocacy experience as of 2022" and adjoin this description with a direct quotation about my institution, it would be easy for readers to identify me and how I feel about colleagues and my work while at work. These reasons persuaded me to refrain from referencing any individual advocate consistently in the same way (i.e., by name, correlating identities, and perspective).

Second, and more attentive to the theoretical underpinnings of this project, advocates shared many stories that echoed one another. Even if advocates' attitudes toward subjects like capitalism or incarceration diverged from one another, the case studies of victims and perpetrators adopted similar characteristics, often framed as either normative (for most, a white, cisgender, female victim against an older male perpetrator) or "othered" (a trans* or male victim or assigned female victim of color against a male perpetrator or a same-sex abuser). Notably, normative cases were not unusual; all advocates were able to describe at least one case in which they encountered the "perfect" victim, demonstrating that the "myth" of the perfect victim is not, in fact, mere fantasy. It did not make a significant difference to distinguish *whose* case specifically was discussed; most of the distinctions in scenarios were based on the advocates' social identities, some of which were shared by other participants. It made more sense therefore to describe scenarios through the lens of advocates' social identities and to do so in a way that offers one or two of the *most* salient identities (not all) held by the advocate in that given case study for both theoretical and participant-safety reasons.

Some readers might disagree with my approach, believing that we should use participants' chosen names or separate advocates' social identities entirely from their interview excerpt(s). However, I believe that describing advocates in this way best honors participants' identities and how they showed up in their work while maintaining privacy, to the extent of my ability. I also believe that we need to call in some participants, particularly the ones who identified with dominant communities, to strengthen our coalitional commitment to end rape together. Excluding advocates' names avoids victim blaming and instead allows us to have hard, honest dialogues about our work.

I have endeavored to protect participants, but not in ways that limit their voices. In every interaction with the advocate-participant, I made it explicit that participants could talk to me "offline" about their experiences, as a means of giving participants space to process their experiences outside of their (sometimes oppressive) workplace contexts, where they may not have had the chance to speak as themselves.[23] I also asked open-ended questions and affirmed the participant. I prepared a resource document prior to each interview and emailed or texted it to the participants following their interview. This document included not only well-known, generalizable resources such as the National Suicide Hotline but also agencies and collectives that deliberately focus on intersectional oppressions within anti-rape work, such as the Women of Color Network, autobiographical or fictional stories such as Chanel

Miller's *Know My Name* (2019), and emerging intra-advocate networks, such as the Sexual Assault Advocacy Network on Facebook (Meta). At the beginning of each interview, I also informed each participant that they could pause or reschedule an interview for a later date if they were called to a case or felt discomfort to a point where they did not wish to continue with the interview.

I want to leave with one final reminder: The advocates in this study are not those who deserve malevolent criticism. They are extraordinarily brave for sharing their stories with me and exposing the problems within rape victim supports. They are also amazing people who participated in this study without remuneration. As one advocate told me, "It feels bad. But I would rather know [the problems] than let it go." I affirm her perspective, and I hope that the advocates in this study feel likewise. It is only by identifying and then remedying the problems, with transparency that allows for empathetic accountability, that we can rethink what it means to be anti-rape activists today.

ARCHIVAL RESEARCH

The remaining data in this book come from the archives. Chapter 1 draws most heavily on this research, though pockets of such research may be found in the other chapters. I initially began this project with the intent to study contemporary advocacy. However, as I reviewed interviews, it became clear that few advocates knew about the histories of advocacy in civil liberties activism. Their ignorance—by no means a fault of theirs but a fault of the neoliberal rape crisis center—affected how they behaved toward survivors. Although some advocates had been trained by more radical grassroots activists, many assumed that current advocacy was and has been synonymous with (white) social services, in ways that ran counter to their beliefs of how advocacy should be. I wrote chapter 1 to lay the groundwork for the remainder of this book, showcasing the decline of radicalism and not advocacy itself. I also wanted to show advocates how to excavate their own histories, empowering us to take charge of our own work.

Initially, I chose to visit the Sophia Smith Collections at Smith College and Schlesinger Library at Harvard University for two reasons. First, due to budget constraints, I could only visit a handful of places. While I was awarded a faculty fellowship from the Arts & Humanities Forum at OU to conduct archival research, the fellowship covered a semester of teaching and service release, and I turned to my start-up budget instead to pay for this trip. This constraint was a mundane reason for choosing to only visit a handful of places, but an important one to note. Just as advocacy is imbricated in neoliberal normativity, so too is academic research through normative research grants and similarly constrained funding streams. Second, to identify advocacy histories, I reviewed secondary texts pertaining to rape histories, including Sharon Block's *Rape and Sexual Power in Early America*, Estelle Freedman's *Redefining Rape*, and Catherine Jacquet's *Injustices of Rape*. I referred to their methods section and bibliography and found that common sources of information came primarily from these two archives.

As I pulled data from the two databases, I realized that anti-violence archives are not organized in the same way as I understand advocacy. For the most part, Smith College and Harvard University categorized rape materials based on "sex" and "gender," which excluded or misconstrued pivotal information about the racial politics of anti-violence activism. For example, while Smith College preserved information about the University of Alabama conference in 1975, it assumed that "research" could only be conducted by credentialed academics. This qualification invalidated research conducted by BIPOC activists by obscuring the fact that all academic "researchers" at that conference identified as racially white. I sought out the guidance of two university archivists, who helped me to filter documents based on my research interests. I replaced my searches of "sexual violence" with words such as "ravishment," "rape," and "sodomy," and I narrowed my scope to extra- or nonlegal organizing around issues of sexual violence. This second filtering process helped to exclude materials from rape trials and other criminal legal proceedings that make up most anti-violence documents, creating a more manageable archive of mainly advocacy materials.

I also decided to trace key historical racial minority figures whom I knew from secondary sources were pivotal for the anti-violence movement, like Ella Baker and Dorothy Height. This tracing of advocate lineages led me to the Schomburg Center for Research in Black Culture at the New York Public Libraries. With the support of a Schomburg archivist, I located materials that were possibly connected to the anti-rape movement and reviewed files that connected 1970s radical feminists to earlier generations of the 1950s and 1960s Civil Rights Movement, including Rosa Parks and Alfreda Duster, as well as 1880–1920 activists like Ida B. Wells. Using Atlas.ti's data-visualization function, I mapped out a network of historic advocacy figures, and, from this map, I traced how different advocacy tactics, like marooning, changed over time. This tracing process, specifically the connections between activists across generations, became the basis for chapter 1.

I accessed several online archives as well to fill in the gaps left by visits to the three archives. Online archives included the Library of Congress, Digital Transgender Archive, the Catt Center at Iowa State University's Archives of Women's Political Communication, the Digital Public Library of America, the University of Chicago Library (specifically, the Ida B. Wells Papers), Project Guttmacher, BlackPast, and Equal Justice Initiative, among others. Several of these archives are not considered "academic"; however, given that advocacy is also "nonacademic," I found that some archives provided tangible evidence of grassroots organizing that would have not been made visible in a more formal archive.[24] Undoubtedly, the genealogies that I have recreated in this book are partial. Future scholarship may wish to investigate other archives not reviewed in this book to uncover the "other" genealogies of sexual violence advocacy.

My approach to analyzing archival documents relied on critical queering and decolonial methodologies. Much as with my interviewing methodologies, I sought to listen to voices often missing or fragmented in the archives.[25] When examining a primary source, I sought to identify who else was or would have been in conversation aside from the owner of the document and connect Others to the document. For example, despite her significant contributions to anti-rape organizing, Angela Davis's name does not appear in materials in the Loretta J. Ross Collection until the late 1980s. This delay in identifying Davis in the Ross collection suggests that Davis was not seen as a major player in anti-rape advocacy until after Davis reviewed Brownmiller's work in 1976 and spent considerable time in Black feminist networks. Nevertheless, the specter of Davis's work appears in the Ross collection as the protests for Assata Shakur, which then transferred to activism for justice for Yulanda Ward and finally Davis herself, who references Ross in later writings.

While at the archives, I photographed materials that could be reprinted and took notes; upon returning home, I labeled all documents with the date of creation and filed them under type of advocacy, not type of rape. For example, I. Nkenge Touré's speech from the Third World Women and Violence Conference was dated as 1981 and classified under "gatherings." This process of cataloguing by advocacy strategy and date, as opposed to person or the subject of "sexual violence" broadly, helped me to identify documents relevant to historic advocacy while retaining the item's origins and purpose to contemporary advocacy.

Below are lists of documents that I reviewed for this book, in alphabetical order. While many of these files are not explicitly included in this book, analyzing them was pivotal for conceptualizing advocacy throughout its multiple, intersecting histories.

Sophia Smith Collections, Smith College
- Anti-Violence Collection
- Deb Friedman Collection of Feminist Anti-Violence Records
- I. Nkenge Touré Papers
- Loretta J. Ross Papers
- Ms. Magazine Records
- National Asian Pacific American Women's Forum Records
- Safe Passage Records

Schlesinger Library, Harvard University
- Alma Lutz collection of documents by and about abolitionists and women's rights activists
- Papers from the Berkshire Conference on the History of Women
- Papers of Angela Y. Davis
- Papers of Dorothy I. Height
- Papers of Florence Luscomb
- Papers of Gerda Lerner
- Papers of June Jordan
- Papers of Susan Brownmiller
- Papers of Susan Schechter (restricted file; written permission granted for publication in this book)
- Papers of Yolanda Bako
- Quest: A Feminist Quarterly

- Records of the Boston Women's Fund
- Women's newsletter and periodical collection

Schomburg Center for Research in Black Culture
- Black Economic Research Center records
- Black Women's Oral History Project
- Cheryl Clarke papers
- Ella Baker papers
- Lorraine Hansberry papers
- Olivia Pleasants Frost papers

FOLLOW-UP RESEARCH

Conditions pertaining to the anti-violence political landscape changed between my first draft and publication of this book. Therefore, I expanded my interlocutors to include advocates at Embrace and Valériana Chikoti-Bandua Estes. These advocates were not interviewed as "participants" in this study for two reasons. First, their names are already well known in the anti-violence field, and they requested that they be named in this study to educate advocates with full contextual information. Second, the circumstances surrounding both agencies (Embrace and WCSAP) occurred during or after active data collection. Katie Bement and Brittny Olson at Embrace have been kind to share with me an archive of Embrace's email exchanges and related nonconfidential legal information. Valériana Chikoti-Bandua Estes was wonderful for graciously providing an oral history of her experiences at WCSAP, as well as for covering the fees for one of her consultation presentations in February 2023, which I attended with much appreciation. I submitted an online request for information from WCSAP via their website in June 2023 and then again in October 2024 but heard no response. Materials were shared from Embrace and Chikoti-Bandua Estes with written permission for publication in this book.

APPENDIX B

Voices of a Movement

Referencing any individual advocate by name and corresponding identities may breach confidentiality without advancing research knowledge. However, I also want to make known who participated in this project to give thanks to them and respond to researcher inquiries about the demographic validity of this project. Typically, such information is presented in a table. But as noted in chapter 5, a table can reproduce violence by privileging the designer's voice. Here, I present the identities as advocates self-reported. This appendix allows advocate-participants to see themselves in this book but does not allow someone who does not know the participant personally to recognize them. It also allows for the participants to speak as themselves without attaching them to their perspectives, removing any potentially negative consequences from speaking out. Each of the advocate descriptions may include sex/gender, race/ethnicity, sexual orientation, educational background, and duration in anti-rape advocacy, though not all contain the same information. Several extremely specific demographics have been removed or altered (e.g., "electrician training" to "trade school") to protect the advocate unless the advocate explicitly elaborated on how that identity is critical to their work. All identities are written in the order in which participants reported them, thus making the self-identifications unique to that person. I have reorganized advocates' self-identification in alphabetical order to further anonymize participants and assist readers in identifying shared demographics.

AFAB (assigned female at birth) Genderqueer Trans Man, White, Some Medical and Divinity School, on/off 5 years
African American Female Heterosexual, MA, 10+ years
African American Heterosexual Female with a Master's, 13 years

Bi White Female with Trade Apprenticeship, 7–8 years

Bi White Woman with MA in Social Justice and 200 hours of continuing education, 2 years

Bilingual English-Spanish Puerto Rican, 4 years domestic violence/sexual assault advocate and 3 years sexual assault–only advocate

Biracial Hispanic and White Straight Woman, Bachelor's Degree, 1 year

Bisexual White Assigned Female with Interdisciplinary PhD, 3 years

Bisexual White Cisgendered Female, 4 years

Bisexual White Female, 1L (first year) law student, 3 years

Bisexual White Female, MA, LPC (licensed professional counselor), NCC (national certified counselor), 15 years

Caucasian Bisexual Female Woman with an "incomplete" BSW (bachelor of social work), 1 year and 6 months

Caucasian Heterosexual Female, Associate's Degree in-progress, 4 years

Caucasian International Polyglot Heterosexual Female, Medical Student, less than 1 year

Caucasian Straight Multilingual Woman, 1L (first year) law student, 1 year advocate, 5 years immigration/asylum interpreter

Caucasian/White Cis Woman, BSW (bachelor of social work), 1 year internship, 1 year staff

Chippewa Cree Native American PhD Heterosexual Female, 24 years

Choctaw Nation of Oklahoma MA, in process of obtaining license, Heterosexual Female, 3 years

Cis Bisexual Female, MSW (master of social work), 9 months volunteer, 1.5 months staff

Cisgender Black Female with a Bachelor of Science, 1 year hotline and medical advocate

Cisgendered White Woman with Unknown Sexuality, English-Spanish-ASL (American Sign Language), JD, 1.5 years

Female Hetero White LMSW (licensed master of social work), 2 years rape response, 4 years domestic violence response

Filipino Pacific Islander Heterosexual Male, BA, 9 years

First Nations Cree American Indian BA Social Worker Female, 6–7 police officer, 20 years victim services officer, 30 years of advocacy

Gay Lesbian White Female, BA, 1 year

Genderqueer White BA, 3 years staff, 10 months coalition

Hawaiian Bilingual Female with GED, 3 years

Hispanic Latina Brown Brazilian Cisgender Heterosexual Female Multilingual Portuguese-English-Spanish with Some Graduate Courses, 1 year

Jordanian (Middle Eastern) Multilingual, 2 Associate Degrees, 2 months

Lesbian Cisgender Female/Woman Bilingual MA, 2 years

Maeqtekuahkihkiw Metaemohsak Female with Bachelor's in Behavioral Health, 20 years

Mexican (Hispanic) Female attracted to "he/him," Proud High School Diploma and Community College "drop out," 2.5 years

Mexican American (Latina) Bi Female, MA, 16 years advocate, 18.5 years police officer

Native American Heterosexual Female, MA, 11 years

Native and White, Enrolled Muscogee Creek Nation citizen, Female, Straight, MA with thousands of training hours, 6 years tribal advocate, 5 years federal victim specialist, 4 years rape crisis center executive director, 5 years law enforcement officer

Non-Hispanic/Latino White Straight Woman, Bachelor's Degree, 3 years

Northern Arapaho (enrolled), Meskwaki Descent Multilingual Female Heterosexual PhD student, 6 years

Pansexual White Female with a Bachelor's, 5 years rape response, 3 years child abuse response

Peruvian Indigenous Female with Associate's Degree and Certification in Substance Abuse Counseling, 24 years rape advocacy, 3 years substance abuse counseling

PhD with military and civilian advocate training, Black Straight Woman, 10 years

Queer assigned female at birth, API and Latinx mixed woman with MA, 6 years staff, 4 years volunteer

Queer Bisexual Chinese Malaysian Cisgender Female, Bachelor's Degree, 6 years

Queer Pansexual Female, Dual Bachelor's Degrees, 6 years suicide hotline, 1 year mobile sexual assault crisis dispatch, 4 years substance abuse

Queer White Female with Dual Bachelor's Degrees, 1 year volunteer, 8 years staff advocate, 1 year at the Department of Corrections

Straight African American Female with a Bachelor's and 1,000+ hours of advocate training, 2 years

Straight White Bilingual Female, Bachelor's Degree, less than 1 year

Straight White Female, BA, 5 years police officer, 1 year advocate

Straight White Female, BA, 5 years sexual violence advocate, 5 years child investigator
Straight White Woman, BA, 3 years
Suquamish Heterosexual Female, MA, 11 years
White Bisexual Female, Korean-English lingual abilities, BS, 4 years
White, Caucasian, Bisexual Female, 1.5 years (staff for 5 months)
White Heterosexual English-ASL (American Sign Language) Female, MA, 21 years
White Heterosexual Female Monolingual but formerly fluent in Spanish, MA, 11 years
White Heterosexual Female with Degrees in African American Studies and Women's Studies, 2 years staff, 1 year volunteer
White Heterosexual Female, MA, BSW, Accredited SafeStar, National Tribal College Certification, 7 years domestic violence/sexual assault, 2.5 years child protective services, 5 years Department of Homeland Security, 5 years probation officer
"White passing" with Native ancestry, Heterosexual Female, Associate's Degree with Drug/Alcohol Counseling License
"White passing" with Native and Black ancestry Cisgender Queer Woman "on the spectrum" with English-Spanish medical-translation skills, on/off 4 years
White Straight Female with English-German fluency, Bachelor's Degree, 5 years
White Polish Straight Female, Graduate Degrees in African American Studies & Women's Studies, 1.5 years
White Straight Female, 1 semester short of a bachelor's, 16 years
Woman-identified and married to a man but probably somewhere in between, White, BA, 20 years
Woman-identified Heterosexual German MSW, 3 years

APPENDIX C

Terminology

Term	Definition
2SLGBTQIA+	Two-Spirit, lesbian, gay, bisexual, trans, queer, intersex, asexual, nonbinary, and sexual and gender-expansive people[1]
Abolition	the eradication of all forms of violence, including rape, racism, sexism, transphobia, classism, nativism, ableism, and more, and the imagination that this world is possible[2]
Acute Rape	the act of rape itself[3]
Advocate	the grassroots community and neighborhood organizers, social workers, psychologists, legal aids, and volunteers who provide support to rape victims and seek the abolishment of all interlocking violence[4]
Affect	a subjectively experienced emotion or feeling[5]
Biopower	an administrative power that dictates the life or death of the administrated subject[6]
Carceral Feminism	the "reliance on policing, prosecution, and imprisonment to resolve gendered or sexual violence"[7]
Carceralism	the regulation of people, often through the criminal legal system[8]
Compassion Fatigue	the feeling of exhaustion and hopelessness that comes with care labor[9]
Consciousness Raising	an advocacy tactic in which survivors come together to raise consciousness or awareness of the widespread prevalence of sexual violence and do something about it[10]
(Cultural) Capitalism	the conglomerate of theories around the sociality and culture of and around capitalism[11]
Double Bind	the simultaneous expectation to perform as white and BIPOC[12]
Everywoman Analysis	the belief that sexual violence affects everyone, including middle-class and wealthy able-bodied cisgender white women, and the subsequent equation of sexual violence experiences between elite women with that experienced by nonelite, marginalized people[13]
Feminist Killjoy	the feminist who kills the joy of others by raising consciousness about existing social discomfort and subverting the expectation to be joyous[14]
Fungibility	the replacement of a person of one racialized identity, usually Black, for another person of any other racialized identity but in a way that ignores the historical context in which (anti-Black) racism occurred[15]
Glass Ceiling	the invisible barrier in which a group of people can only rise to a given point in an organizational hierarchy on the basis of their identities[16]

Intersectionality	a sociolegal framework that addresses the ways in which multiple interlocking identities such as race and gender compound to create aggrandized violence[17]
LGBT	See "2SLGBTQIA+"
Liberalism	the deployment of equality initiatives to counteract dominant control over capital assets, oftentimes with the consequence of producing new carceral norms about race and culture[18]
Marginalized Survivors	sometimes termed "minoritized," "underserved," or "underrepresented," the primary targets of rape victimization and the vast group of people who do not receive adequate and culturally appropriate rape-victim services[19]
Medical Industrial Complex	the web of privatized medical systems, such as hospitals, primary care, school nurses, and more, that seek to profit from instead of care for patients in need of medical support[20]
Moral Wages	emotional satisfaction from executing morally altruistic labor[21]
Multiculturalism	a framework that recognizes the centrality of culture in interpersonal support work but fails to address the social institutions that contribute to cultural violence[22]
Mutual Aid	"a form of political participation in which people take responsibility for caring for one another and changing political conditions, not just through symbolic acts or putting pressure on their representatives in government but by actually building new social relations that are more survivable"[23]
Neoliberalism	a sociopolitical and economic framework in which federal and state agencies control the funding available for nonprofit human services like anti-violence advocacy[24]
Nonprofit Industrial Complex	the web of nonprofit systems, including nonprofit rape crisis centers, that seek to process and profit from people in need instead of empowering them[25]
Normativity	the production of a "norm" such that all differences are erased from recognition[26]
Panopticon	"a machine for dissociating the see/being seen dyad: in the peripheric ring, one is totally seen, without ever seeing; in the central tower, one sees everything without ever being seen"[27]
Pathology	the categorization of individuals such that their complex social lives are neglected or dismissed[28]
Perfect Victim	sometimes called "ideal victim," a weak, young, or elderly female who has been harmed by a "big and bad" stranger, often coded as racially Black[29]
Positionality	See "Standpoint"
Precarity Crisis	the fear that there is a shortage of capital to provide to victims[30]
Predominantly White Institutions (PWIs)	those spaces in which white people and/or white norms dominate and are valued by the organization[31]
Prison Industrial Complex	the web of privatized prison systems both within and external to incarceration institutions that seek to profit from its incarcerated members[32]
Prison Nation	"those dimensions of civil society that use the power of law, public policy, and institutional practices in strategic ways to advance hegemonic values and to overpower efforts by individuals and groups that challenge the status quo"[33]
Quantification	the measurement of prevalence and incident rates[34]

Queer/ed or Queer/ing	the actions, beliefs, or people who are in the process of becoming or unbecoming queer[35]
Racial Capitalism	the pursuit of a racial social ordering through the "development, organization, and expansion of capitalist society"[36]
Racial Hierarchy	"a specific configuration of power relations in a given place and time based on racial ideology"[37]
Radicalism	the personal and political, messy and affective activism of feminist antiviolence advocates who strive to create a world free from violence and welcoming of multiple, diverse, and intersecting identities
Rape	the corporeal violation of the body and mind, transgressing one's sexual autonomy through the touching or feeling of sexual organs, inclusive of sexual assault, domestic violence, intimate partner violence, and more[38]
Restorative Justice	justice that seeks to remedy violence by using noncarceral strategies, such as mediation or restitution[39]
Second Rape	the abuse by rape responders of the people they mean to help[40]
Secondary Traumatic Stress (STS)	the stress as a result of listening to stories of traumatic events[41]
Sexual Assault Forensic-Medical Examiner	sometimes called "sexual assault nurse examiner" (SANE) or "sexual assault medical-forensic examiner" (SAMFE), the medical professionals, typically nurses, who perform sexual assault forensic-medical exams ("rape kits") that collect evidence of a sexual assault from a victim's body, and medically examine any physical or emotional injuries from rape[42]
Sexual Assault Response Teams (SARTs)	teams comprised of police officers, SAFEs, prosecutors, and victim advocates that are usually supported by government funding and contracts[43]
Socialization	the process by which one learns behaviors and values[44]
Standpoint	a positionality linked to one's intersectional social identities, such as race, gender, and class, that influences how one engages with their worlds[45]
Survivor Discourse (Empowerment Model)	a discourse of empowerment in which a victim becomes a survivor[46]
System(s) Professional	a professional who works within carceral, medical, or nonprofit systems[47]
Taxonomy	a subjectively produced list of categories with an associated numerical value[48]
Technical Assistance	the skilled support to victims, often provided in the form of community partner connections, provisions of survivor equipment, and negotiations with systems professionals[49]
Third-Party Police	non–police officers who serve as carceral agents enforcing the law[50]
Transformative Justice	the hard and messy grassroots advocacy actions that create abolition[51]
White Ascendancy	the state in which an institution is rooted in whiteness such that whiteness is made to seem inviting or neutral[52]
White Cultural Ideology	the sociopolitical values of people with lighter skin and/or European ancestry[53]

APPENDIX D

Abbreviations

2SLGBTQIA+ Two-Spirit, Lesbian, Gay, Bisexual, Trans, Queer, Intersex, Asexual, and Plus Gender and Sexually Expansive
ACLU American Civil Liberties Union
BIPOC Black, Indigenous, and People of Color
BJS Bureau of Justice Statistics
BPP Black Panther Party
BWLC Black Women's Liberation Committee (SNCC)
CCT Cultural Competency Training, sometimes called "cultural sensitivity training"
CDC Centers for Disease Control and Prevention
DEI Diversity, Equity, and Inclusion
DHR Department of Human Resources
DOC Department of Corrections
DOJ Department of Justice
FAAR Feminist Alliance Against Rape
FBI Federal Bureau of Investigation
GED Graduate Equivalency Degree or General Educational Diploma
HIPAA Health Insurance Portability and Accountability Act
KU University of Kansas
LDF Legal Defense and Educational Fund (NAACP)
LEAA Law Enforcement Administration Assistance [Act] or Law Enforcement Assistance Administration
MDT Multidisciplinary Team (see SART)
MECASA Maine Coalition Against Sexual Assault
MWTFR Michigan Women's Task Force on Rape
NAACP National Association for the Advancement of Colored People

NABSW National Association of Black Social Workers
NASW   National Association of Social Workers
NCN   National Communication Network
NIBRS National Incident-Based Reporting System
NOW   National Organization for Women
NPIC   Nonprofit Industrial Complex
NYRF   New York Radical Feminists
NYT   *The New York Times*
OCVA   Office of Crime Victims Advocacy
OJP   Office of Justice Programs
OU   University of Oklahoma
OVW   Office on Violence against Women
PREA   Prison Rape Elimination Act
PREP   Pre-exposure Prophylaxis
RSF   Research File Storage
SAFE   Sexual Assault Forensic Examiner (includes certified sexual assault nurse examiners, SANEs, as well as uncertified examiners)
SANE   Sexual Assault Nurse Examiner (certified only)
SART   Sexual Assault Response Team, sometimes called Multidisciplinary Team (MDT)
SASP   Sexual Assault Services Program
SCWAR Santa Cruz Women Against Rape
SNCC   Student Nonviolence Coordinating Committee
SORNA Sexual Offender Registry and Notification Act
STOP   Services, Training, Officers, and Prosecutors (program)
SVU   Special Victims Unit
TWWA   Third World Women's Alliance
UCR   Uniform Crime Reports
VAT   Victim Assistance Training
VAWA   Violence Against Women Act
VOCA   Victims of Crime Act
WCSAP Washington Coalition of Sexual Assault Programs
WRP   Women's Rights Project (ACLU)
YWCA   Young Women's Christian Association

NOTES

INTRODUCTION

Epigraph: Charlene A. Carruthers, *Unapologetic: A Black, Queer, and Feminist Mandate for Radical Movements* (Beacon Press, 2018), 7.

1 The email exchange between the sheriff of Barron County, Chris Fitzgerald, and the advocates at Embrace, Brittny Olson and Katie Bement, occurred between September 2, 2020, and September 14, 2020. Email records were preserved by Embrace and shared confidentially with me. Embrace advocates have granted verbal and written permission for me to use their story, including excerpts from documents, without anonymity, for this book.

2 While I recognize the need to name whiteness with capital letters, I do not capitalize "white" in references to race because whiteness continues to dominate conversations around race. I do not believe that it should be given more space than it already takes in a book about and for marginalized people of color.

3 Accurate statistical data on the racial identities of perpetrators are not available through government sources. See www.ojjdp.gov. However, the Rape, Abuse & Incest National Network (RAINN) estimates that approximately 57 percent of all US perpetrators identify as white. Primary data aggregated by RAINN are not available to the public. "Perpetrators of Sexual Violence: Statistics," RAINN, accessed March 22, 2024, www.rainn.org.

4 Maria Hardeberg Bach, Nina Beck Hansen, Courtney Ahrens, Cecilie Reendal Nielsen, Catherine Walshe, and Maj Hansen, "Underserved Survivors of Sexual Assault: A Systematic Scoping Review," *European Journal of Psychotraumatology* 12, no. 1 (2021): 1895516, https://doi.org/10.1080/20008198.2021.1895516.

5 Kimberlé Crenshaw, "Demarginalizing the Intersection of Race and Sex: A Black Feminist Critique of Antidiscrimination Doctrine, Feminist Theory, and Antiracist Politics," *University of Chicago Legal Forum* 1989, no. 1 (1989): 139–67; Kimberlé Crenshaw, "Mapping the Margins: Intersectionality, Identity Politics, and Violence Against Women of Color," *Stanford Law Review* 43, no. 6 (1991): 1241–99.

6 Katie Bement, "Legal Advice Regarding Embrace Barron County Office Lease" (email, September 8, 2020), Embrace Email Records.

7 Rich Kremer, "Barron County Cuts $25K from Domestic Violence Shelter over Support of Black Lives Matter," *Wisconsin Public Radio*, October 14, 2020, www.wpr.org.

8 Gail M. Harmon, Jessica A. Ladd, and Eleanor A. Evans, "Being a Player: A Guide to the IRS Lobbying Regulations for Advocacy Charities" (Harmon, Curran, Spielberg & Eisenberg, LLP and Alliance for Justice, 2011), 3.
9 Kremer, "Barron County Cuts $25K from Domestic Violence Shelter."
10 Critical Resistance and Incite! Women of Color Against Violence, "Statement on Gender Violence and the Prison Industrial Complex (2001)" (INCITE!, 2001), https://incite-national.org; Kristin Bumiller, *In an Abusive State: How Neoliberalism Appropriated the Feminist Movement Against Sexual Violence* (Duke University Press, 2008); INCITE!, ed., *The Revolution Will Not Be Funded: Beyond the Non-Profit Industrial Complex* (Duke University Press, 2017).
11 Shana L. Maier, "'We Belong to Them': The Costs of Funding for Rape Crisis Centers," *Violence Against Women* 17, no. 11 (2011): 1383–1408, https://doi.org/10.1177/1077801211428599.
12 Ruth Wilson Gilmore, "In the Shadow of the Shadow State," in *Abolition Geography: Essays Towards Liberation* (Verso, 2022), 224–41.
13 Gita R. Mehrotra, Ericka Kimball, and Stéphanie Wahab, "The Braid That Binds Us: The Impact of Neoliberalism, Criminalization, and Professionalization on Domestic Violence Work," *Affilia* 31, no. 2 (2016): 153–63, https://doi.org/10.1177/0886109916643871; Winnie Gunther, "What Are Rape Crisis Centers and How Have They Changed over the Years?," National Sexual Violence Resource Center, September 15, 2021, www.nsvrc.org.
14 Lester M. Salamon, *The State of Nonprofit America*, 2nd ed. (Brookings Institution Press, 2012), 12.
15 Bumiller, *In an Abusive State*.
16 Rose Corrigan, *Up Against a Wall: Rape Reform and the Failure of Success* (NYU Press, 2013).
17 Rebecca Campbell, Sharon M. Wasco, and Holly E. Barnes, "Preventing the 'Second Rape': Rape Survivors' Experiences with Community Service Providers," *Journal of Interpersonal Violence* 16, no. 12 (December 2001): 1239–59, https://doi.org/10.1177/088626001016012002.
18 Andrew E. Taslitz, *Rape and the Culture of the Courtroom* (NYU Press, 1999); Sameena Mulla, *The Violence of Care: Rape Victims, Forensic Nurses, and Sexual Assault Intervention* (NYU Press, 2014); Leah A. Jacobs et al., "Defund the Police: Moving Towards an Anti-Carceral Social Work," *Journal of Progressive Human Services* 32, no. 1 (2021): 37–62, https://doi.org/10.1080/10428232.2020.1852865.
19 I've chosen to use "marginalized survivors" rather than the more common term "underserved survivors" for most of this book because some survivors are not *under*resourced but are instead *hyper*resourced such that their actions are heavily surveilled and restricted.
20 Beth E. Richie, "Reimagining the Movement to End Gender Violence: Anti-Racism, Prison Abolition, Women of Color Feminisms, and Other Radical Visions of Justice (Transcript)," in *Converge! Reimagining the Movement to End*

Gender Violence Symposium (University of Miami Race & Social Justice Law Review, 2015), http://repository.law.miami.edu.
21 Shannon M. Peters, "Medical Neoliberalism in Rape Crisis Center Counseling: An Interpretative Phenomenological Analysis of Clinicians' Understandings of Survivor Distress," *Journal of Social Issues* 75, no. 1 (2019): 238–66, https://doi.org/10.1111/josi.12316; Paige L. Sweet, *The Politics of Surviving: How Women Navigate Domestic Violence and Its Aftermath* (University of California Press, 2021).
22 Dean Spade, *Normal Life: Administrative Violence, Critical Trans Politics, and the Limits of Law* (Duke University Press, 2015).
23 Beth E. Richie, *Arrested Justice: Black Women, Violence, and America's Prison Nation* (NYU Press, 2012).
24 bell hooks, *Killing Rage: Ending Racism*, 1st paperback ed. (Henry Holt, 1996), 11.
25 Sara Ahmed, *The Feminist Killjoy Handbook: The Radical Potential of Getting in the Way* (Seal Press, 2023).
26 Lolita Buckner Inniss and Bridget J. Crawford, eds., *Social Movements and the Law: Talking About Black Lives Matter and #MeToo* (University of California Press, 2024), 10.
27 Sianne Ngai, *Ugly Feelings* (Harvard University Press, 2007).
28 Brittney C. Cooper, *Eloquent Rage: A Black Feminist Discovers Her Superpower* (Picador, 2019), 122.
29 Becky Thompson, "Multiracial Feminism: Recasting the Chronology of Second Wave Feminism," *Feminist Studies* 28, no. 2 (2002): 336, https://doi.org/10.2307/3178747.
30 Alice Echols, *Daring to Be Bad: Radical Feminism in America, 1967–1975* (University of Minnesota Press, 2019), 6.
31 Echols, *Daring to Be Bad*, 9.
32 "Trans" and "gender-diverse" people include people who identify as transgender, nonbinary, or another gender identity other than cisgender.
33 Rosemarie Tong and Tina Fernandes Botts, *Feminist Thought: A More Comprehensive Introduction*, 5th ed. (Routledge, 2018), 2–3.
34 Thompson, "Multiracial Feminism."
35 Thompson, "Multiracial Feminism," 347.
36 Thompson, "Multiracial Feminism," 345–46.
37 Jodi Melamed, "The Spirit of Neoliberalism," *Social Text* 24, no. 4 (2006): 1–24, https://doi.org/10.1215/01642472-2006-009.
38 Spade, *Normal Life*.
39 Ejeris Dixon and Leah Lakshmi Piepzna-Samarasinha, eds., *Beyond Survival: Strategies and Stories from the Transformative Justice Movement* (AK Press, 2020).
40 José Esteban Muñoz, *Cruising Utopia: The Then and There of Queer Futurity* (NYU Press, 2009).
41 Bumiller, *In an Abusive State*.
42 Corrigan, *Up Against a Wall*.

43 Carrie N. Baker and Maria Bevacqua, "Challenging Narratives of the Anti-Rape Movement's Decline," *Violence Against Women* 24, no. 3 (2018): 350–76, https://doi.org/10.1177/1077801216689164.
44 Baker and Bevacqua, "Challenging Narratives of the Anti-Rape Movement's Decline," 353–54.
45 Mimi Kim and V. Kalei Kanuha, "Restorative Justice and the Dance with the Devil," *Affilia* 37, no. 2 (2022): 189–93, https://doi.org/10.1177/08861099221084830.
46 Clare McGlynn, Nicole Westmarland, and Nikki Godden, "'I Just Wanted Him to Hear Me': Sexual Violence and the Possibilities of Restorative Justice," *Journal of Law and Society* 39, no. 2 (2012): 213–40, https://doi.org/10.1111/j.1467-6478.2012.00579.x.
47 Kim and Kanuha specifically link carceralism to restorative justice. I apply their analysis to neoliberalism because carceralism is correlative with and a part of neoliberalism.
48 Kim and Kanuha, "Restorative Justice and the Dance with the Devil," 4.
49 Mary Hawkesworth, "The Semiotics of Premature Burial: Feminism in a Postfeminist Age," *Signs* 29, no. 4 (2004): 961–85, https://doi.org/10.1086/383492.
50 Rebecca Campbell, Charlene K. Baker, and Terri L. Mazurek, "Remaining Radical? Organizational Predictors of Rape Crisis Centers' Social Change Initiatives," *American Journal of Community Psychology* 26, no. 3 (1998): 457–83, https://doi.org/10.1023/A:1022115322289.
51 Campbell, Baker, and Mazurek, "Remaining Radical?," 477.
52 Baker and Bevacqua, "Challenging Narratives of the Anti-Rape Movement's Decline."
53 Lee Edelman, *No Future: Queer Theory and the Death Drive* (Duke University Press, 2004).
54 Crenshaw, "Mapping the Margins," 1265.
55 Corrigan, *Up Against a Wall*, 61.
56 Steven Rathgeb Smith and Michael Lipsky, *Nonprofits for Hire: The Welfare State in the Age of Contracting*, 3rd ed. (Harvard University Press, 1998).
57 Michael Lipsky, *Street-Level Bureaucracy: Dilemmas of the Individual in Public Services* (Russell Sage Foundation, 2010), xi.
58 Estelle B. Freedman, *Redefining Rape: Sexual Violence in the Era of Suffrage and Segregation* (Harvard University Press, 2013).
59 Adela C. Licona and Karma R. Chávez, "Relational Literacies and Their Coalitional Possibilities," *Peitho: Journal of the Coalition of Feminist Scholars in the History of Rhetoric & Composition* 18, no. 1 (2015): 102.
60 Roderick A. Ferguson, "Queer of Color Critique," in *Oxford Research Encyclopedia of Literature* (Oxford University Press, 2018), https://doi.org/10.1093/acrefore/9780190201098.013.33.
61 Kath Browne and Catherine Jean Nash, *Queer Methods and Methodologies: Intersecting Queer Theories and Social Science Research* (Ashgate, 2010); Amin Ghaziani and Matt Brim, *Imagining Queer Methods* (NYU Press, 2019).

62 Spade, *Normal Life*; Wendy Brown, *Undoing the Demos: Neoliberalism's Stealth Revolution* (Zone Books, 2017).
63 Stephen J. Schulhofer, *Unwanted Sex: The Culture of Intimidation and the Failure of the Law* (Harvard University Press, 2000).
64 Freedman, *Redefining Rape*.
65 Judith Butler, "Critically Queer," *GLQ: A Journal of Lesbian and Gay Studies* 1, no. 1 (November 1, 1993): 17–32, https://doi.org/10.1215/10642684-1-1-17.
66 Maria Bevacqua, *Rape on the Public Agenda: Feminism and the Politics of Sexual Assault* (Northeastern University Press, 2000), 9, italics in original.
67 Jennifer Patterson, ed., *Queering Sexual Violence: Radical Voices from Within the Anti-Violence Movement* (Riverdale Avenue Books, 2016).

CHAPTER 1. WEAVING OUR STORIES

Epigraph: Lucia Hulsether, *Capitalist Humanitarianism* (Duke University Press, 2023), 45.

1 Benjamin R. Weiss, "'When You're Here, You're Not a Militant Feminist': Volunteer Professionalization in a Rape Crisis Center," *Theory and Society* 50, no. 2 (2021): 231–54, https://doi.org/10.1007/s11186-020-09420-2.
2 Mimi E. Kim, "From Carceral Feminism to Transformative Justice: Women-of-Color Feminism and Alternatives to Incarceration," *Journal of Ethnic & Cultural Diversity in Social Work* 27, no. 3 (July 3, 2018): 219–33, https://doi.org/10.1080/15313204.2018.1474827; Baker and Bevacqua, "Challenging Narratives of the Anti-Rape Movement's Decline"; Angela Y. Davis, Gina Dent, Erica R. Meiners, and Beth E. Richie, *Abolition. Feminism. Now.* (Haymarket Books, 2022), 96–100.
3 Jacquelyn Dowd Hall, "The Long Civil Rights Movement and the Political Uses of the Past," *Journal of American History* 91, no. 4 (2005): 1233, https://doi.org/10.2307/3660172; Danielle L. McGuire, *At the Dark End of the Street: Black Women, Rape, and Resistance* (Vintage Books, 2010).
4 Paulo Freire, *Pedagogy of the Oppressed*, 30th anniversary ed. (Continuum, 2000); Patricia Hill Collins, *Black Feminist Thought: Knowledge, Consciousness, and the Politics of Empowerment*, 2nd ed. (Routledge, 2009).
5 Rebecca Campbell, *Emotionally Involved: The Impact of Researching Rape* (Routledge, 2002); Eve Tuck, "Suspending Damage: A Letter to Communities," *Harvard Educational Review* 79, no. 3 (2009): 409–27.
6 Campbell, *Emotionally Involved*.
7 Sunil Bhatia, Wahbie Long, Wade Pickren, and Alexandra Rutherford, "Engaging with Decoloniality, Decolonization, and Histories of Psychology Otherwise," in *Decolonial Psychology: Toward Anticolonial Theories, Research, Training, and Practice*, ed. Lillian Comas-Díaz, Hector Y. Adames, and Nayeli Y. Chavez-Dueñas (American Psychological Association, 2024), 61–85, https://doi.org/10.1037/0000376-004.
8 Emma Pérez, *The Decolonial Imaginary: Writing Chicanas into History* (Indiana University Press, 1999); Linda Tuhiwai Smith, *Decolonizing Methodologies: Research and Indigenous Peoples*, 3rd ed. (Bloomsbury, 2022).

9 Darlene Clark Hine, "Rape and the Inner Lives of Black Women in the Middle West," *Signs* 14, no. 4 (1989): 912–20.
10 Shani D'Cruze, "Approaching the History of Rape and Sexual Violence: Notes Towards Research," *Women's History Review* 1, no. 3 (September 1992): 379, https://doi.org/10.1080/09612029300200016.
11 Gayatri Chakravorty Spivak, "Can the Subaltern Speak?," in *Marxism and the Interpretation of Culture*, ed. Cary Nelson and Lawrence Grossberg (Macmillan, 1988).
12 Saidiya Hartman, "Venus in Two Acts," *Small Axe* 26, vol. 12, no. 2 (June 2008): 12.
13 Marisa Joanna Fuentes, *Dispossessed Lives: Enslaved Women, Violence, and the Archive* (University of Pennsylvania Press, 2016).
14 Fuentes, *Dispossessed Lives*, 7.
15 Susan Ghanbarpour and Ada Palotai, "Survivor-Centered Advocacy in Culturally Specific Communities: A Community-Based Participatory Research Project" (Asian Pacific Institute on Gender-Based Violence, 2019), https://api-gbv.org, 9, italics in original.
16 Baker and Bevacqua, "Challenging Narratives of the Anti-Rape Movement's Decline."
17 Ruth Wilson Gilmore, "Race, Prisons, and War: Scenes from the History of US Violence," in *Abolition Geography: Essays Towards Liberation* (Verso, 2022), 176.
18 Linda Nicholson, "Feminism in 'Waves': Useful Metaphor or Not?," *New Politics* 7, no. 4 (2010), http://newpol.org.
19 M. Jacqui Alexander and Chandra Talpade Mohanty, eds., *Feminist Genealogies, Colonial Legacies, Democratic Futures* (Routledge, 1997).
20 Nancy Whittier, *Frenemies: Feminists, Conservatives, and Sexual Violence* (Oxford University Press, 2018), 31–32.
21 Susan Griffin, "Rape: The All-American Crime," *Ramparts*, September 1971, accessed March 20, 2024, https://nyheritage.contentdm.oclc.org; Whittier, *Frenemies*, 43–45.
22 Emily L. Thuma, *All Our Trials: Prisons, Policing, and the Feminist Fight to End Violence* (University of Illinois Press, 2019), 4–7.
23 Sharon Block, "Lines of Color, Sex, and Service: Comparative Sexual Coercion in Early America," in *Sex, Love, Race: Crossing Boundaries in North American History* (NYU Press, 1999), 141–63.
24 Catherine Jacquet, *The Injustices of Rape: How Activists Responded to Sexual Violence, 1950–1980* (University of North Carolina Press, 2019), 162.
25 Maria Bevacqua, *Rape on the Public Agenda: Feminism and the Politics of Sexual Assault* (Northeastern University Press, 2000), 97–101.
26 Corrigan, *Up Against a Wall*, 34–35.
27 Susan Caringella, *Addressing Rape Reform in Law and Practice* (Columbia University Press, 2008), 28, https://doi.org/10.7312/cari13424.

28 Susan Schechter, *Women and Male Violence: The Visions and Struggles of the Battered Women's Movement* (South End Press, 1982), 34–41.
29 Jacquet, *The Injustices of Rape*, 166.
30 Sweet, *Politics of Surviving*, 34–36.
31 Jacqueline Delahunt, "National YWCA Racial Justice Group Opposes Video 'Game' as Racist/Sexist," 1982, LaDonna Harris Native American Collection, The University of New Mexico Digital Repository, https://digitalrepository.unm.edu.
32 Andrea Dworkin, "Against the Male Flood: Censorship, Pornography, and Equality," in *Letters for a War Zone* (Martin Secker & Warburg, 1997).
33 Robin Morgan, "Theory and Practice: Pornography and Rape," in *Take Back the Night: Women on Pornography*, ed. Laura Lederer (William Morrow, 1980), 139.
34 Bevacqua, *Rape on the Public Agenda*, 178–83; Whittier, *Frenemies*, 48–60.
35 "50 Years of Building Solutions, Supporting Communities, and Advancing Justice," US Department of Justice, Office of Justice Programs, February 14, 2020, www.ojp.gov; Bumiller, *In an Abusive State*, 40.
36 Bumiller, *In an Abusive State*, 140–46.
37 Whittier, *Frenemies*, 93–104.
38 Hawkesworth, "Semiotics of Premature Burial"; Bumiller, *In an Abusive State*, 11, 148.
39 Jacquet, *The Injustices of Rape*, 166–83.
40 Andrea Dworkin, "Prostitution and Male Supremacy," *Michigan Journal of Gender & Law* 1, no. 1 (1993): 1–12.
41 Lisa Duggan and Nan D. Hunter, *Sex Wars: Sexual Dissent and Political Culture* (Routledge, 2006).
42 Phyllis Schlafly, "Women's Responsibility for Sexual Harassment (1981)," in "The Triumph of the Right," *The American Yawp Reader*, www.americanyawp.com, accessed May 14, 2025; Germaine Greer, *The Female Eunuch* (HarperCollins, 2008).
43 "50 Years of Building Solutions, Supporting Communities, and Advancing Justice."
44 Catherine O. Jacquet, "Fighting Back, Claiming Power," *Radical History Review* 2016, no. 126 (2016): 71–83, https://doi.org/10.1215/01636545-3594421.
45 Baker and Bevacqua, "Challenging Narratives of the Anti-Rape Movement's Decline."
46 Kimberly Springer, *Living for the Revolution: Black Feminist Organizations, 1968–1980* (Duke University Press, 2005), 9.
47 Frances M. Beal, "Double Jeopardy: To Be Black and Female," *Meridians* 8, no. 2 (2008): 173.
48 Dorothy E. Roberts, *Killing the Black Body: Race, Reproduction, and the Meaning of Liberty*, 2nd ed. (Vintage Books, 2017); Thuma, *All Our Trials*, 55–87.
49 Adriane Vani Kannan, "The Third World Women's Alliance: History, Geopolitics, and Form" (PhD diss., Syracuse University, 2018), 46–47, 50, https://surface.syr.

edu; Tiana U. Wilson, "The Making of Triple Jeopardy," *WSQ* 51, no. 1–2 (2023): 201–7, https://doi.org/10.1353/wsq.2023.0014.
50 Boston Women's Health Collective, *Our Bodies, Ourselves* (New England Free Press, 1971).
51 Jacquet, *The Injustices of Rape*, 78–79.
52 Jasmin A. Young, "Strapped: A Historical Analysis of Black Women and Armed Resistance, 1959–1979" (Dissertation, Rutgers University, 2018), 218, https://rucore.libraries.rutgers.edu.
53 Jacquet, *The Injustices of Rape*, 93.
54 Thuma, *All Our Trials*, 41.
55 Jacquet, *The Injustices of Rape*, 81.
56 New York Radical Feminists, *Rape: The First Sourcebook for Women*, ed. Noreen Connell and Cassandra Wilson, 1st ed. (New American Library, 1974).
57 Bevacqua, *Rape on the Public Agenda*, 95–96.
58 Thuma, *All Our Trials*, 36–37.
59 "How to Start a Rape Crisis Center" (DC Rape Crisis Center, 1972), Smith College, Sophia Smith Collection of Women's History, Deb Friedman collection of feminist anti-violence records (SSC-MS-00795), Box 1, 15.
60 "How to Start a Rape Crisis Center," 24.
61 "How to Start a Rape Crisis Center," 24.
62 Bevacqua, *Rape on the Public Agenda*, 81.
63 Jacquet, *The Injustices of Rape*, 89.
64 Deb Friedman, "Rape, Racism—and Reality," *Aegis* (July/August 1978): 25, 17, I. Nkenge Touré Papers (SSC MS 00563), Box 8, Folder 5, Smith College Collection of Women's History.
65 Jacquet, *The Injustices of Rape*, 149–53.
66 Bevacqua, *Rape on the Public Agenda*, 30.
67 robin mc'duff, deanne pernell, and karen saunders, "Letter to the Anti-Rape Movement" (Project NIA, 1977), 4, https://issuu.com/projectnia.
68 I. Nkenge Touré, "An Overview of Third World Women and Violence: Report from the First National Conference on Third World Women and Violence," Rape Crisis Center, Washington, DC (August 1980), Smith College, Sophia Smith Collection of Women's History, Violence Against Women Collection (SSC-MS-00410), Box 3, 2; "Research on Service Delivery to Battered Women and Crime Victims, 1980," Smith College, Sophia Smith Collection of Women's History, Violence Against Women Collection (SSC-MS-00410), Box 3.
69 Sweet, *Politics of Surviving*.
70 mc'duff, pernell, and saunders, "Letter to the Anti-Rape Movement," 11.
71 Bevacqua, *Rape on the Public Agenda*, 78.
72 Cheryl Clarke, "Weekend One: Keynotes and Women of Color Gathering, Friday, June 7th" (New York Women Against Rape, Adam Clayton Powell, Jr. State Office Bldg., Art Gallery, 163 W. 125 St., at Seventh Avenue, New York, 1983), Schomburg Center for Research in Black Culture, Cheryl Clarke Papers (MG 642), Box 9.

73 Loretta J. Ross, "Third World Women and Rape" (D.C. Rape Crisis Center, 1980), Box 34, folder 10, Smith College Archives, Loretta J. Ross papers, Series IV Organization Files (SSC-MS-00504).
74 Thuma, *All Our Trials*, 145.
75 Richie, *Arrested Justice*, 149–50; Thuma, *All Our Trials*, 150.
76 Thuma, *All Our Trials*, 147–50.
77 Melamed, "The Spirit of Neoliberalism."
78 Touré, "Third World Women and Violence," 16.
79 Ross, "Third World Women and Rape," 47.
80 Thuma, *All Our Trials*, 150–56.
81 Corrigan, *Up Against a Wall*, 8–10.
82 Kim, "From Carceral Feminism to Transformative Justice," 224; Richie 2012.
83 Bumiller, *In an Abusive State*, 11.
84 Corrigan, *Up Against a Wall*, 7.
85 Clare Hemmings, *Why Stories Matter: The Political Grammar of Feminist Theory* (Duke University Press, 2011).
86 Hall, "The Long Civil Rights Movement," 1233.
87 Dixon and Piepzna-Samarasinha, *Beyond Survival*.
88 Davis et al., *Abolition. Feminism. Now.*, 96–100.
89 "The History of Movements to End Sexual Violence" (Maine Coalition Against Sexual Assault [MECASA]), accessed March 22, 2024, www.mecasatoolkit.org.
90 Pérez, *The Decolonial Imaginary*.
91 "The History of Movements to End Sexual Violence," 1.
92 Val Kalei Kanuha, "Colonization and Violence Against Women" (Asian Pacific Institute on Gender-Based Violence, 2002), 2, https://api-gbv.org.
93 Davis et al., *Abolition. Feminism. Now.*, 160.
94 Merril D. Smith, ed., *Sex Without Consent: Rape and Sexual Coercion in America* (NYU Press, 2001); Sharon Block, *Rape and Sexual Power in Early America* (University of North Carolina Press, 2006); Freedman, *Redefining Rape*.
95 G. Geis, "Lord Hale, Witches, and Rape," *British Journal of Law and Society* 5, no. 1 (1978): 26, https://doi.org/10.2307/1409846.
96 Smith, *Sex Without Consent*; Freedman, *Redefining Rape*.
97 Miroslava Chávez-García, *Negotiating Conquest: Gender and Power in California, 1770s to 1880s* (University of Arizona Press, 2004), 6–20.
98 Antonia I. Castañeda, "Sexual Violence in the Politics and Policies of Conquest: Amerindian Women and the Spanish Conquest of Alta California," in *Building with Our Hands: New Directions in Chicana Studies*, ed. Adela de la Torre and Beatriz M. Pesquera (University of California Press, 1993), 21.
99 Castañeda, "Sexual Violence in the Politics and Policies of Conquest."
100 Ramón A. Gutiérrez, "Honor, Ideology, Marriage Negotiation, and Class-Gender Domination in New Mexico, 1690–1846," in *Sexual Borderlands: Constructing an American Sexual Past*, ed. Kathleen Kennedy and Sharon Ullman (The Ohio State University Press, 2003), 155–56.

101 Albert L. Hurtado, *Intimate Frontiers: Sex, Gender, and Culture in Old California* (University of New Mexico Press, 1999); Richard Godbeer, "Eroticizing the Middle Ground: Anglo-Indian Sexual Relations Along the Eighteenth-Century Frontier," in *Sex, Love, Race: Crossing Boundaries in North American History*, ed. Martha Hodes (NYU Press, 1999), 91–111.

102 Gutiérrez, "Honor, Ideology, Marriage Negotiation, and Class-Gender Domination in New Mexico, 1690–1846," 155–56.

103 Patricia Hill Collins, "The Tie That Binds: Race, Gender, and US Violence," *Ethnic and Racial Studies* 21, no. 5 (1998): 917–38, https://doi.org/10.1080/014198798329720.

104 Sylviane A. Diouf, *Slavery's Exiles: The Story of the American Maroons* (NYU Press, 2014); Julia Sudbury, "Maroon Abolitionists: Black Gender-Oppressed Activists in the Anti-Prison Movement in the U.S. and Canada," *Meridians* 9, no. 1 (2009): 11.

105 Angela Davis, "Reflections on the Black Woman's Role in the Community of Slaves," *Massachusetts Review* 13, no. 1/2 (1972): 81–100.

106 Young, "Strapped," 56–57.

107 Deborah G. Gray, *Ar'n't I a Woman? Female Slaves in the Plantation South* (Norton, 1985), 85; Randolph Roth, "Twin Evils? Slavery and Homicide in Early America," in *The Problem of Evil: Slavery, Freedom, and the Ambiguities of American Reform*, ed. Steven Mintz and John Stauffer (University of Massachusetts Press, 2007); Roberts, *Killing the Black Body*, 22–23.

108 Gray, *Ar'n't I a Woman?*, 89; Roth, "Twin Evils?," 76; Lauren Berlant, "Slow Death (Sovereignty, Obesity, Lateral Agency)," *Critical Inquiry* 33, no. 4 (2007): 754–80, https://doi.org/10.1086/521568.

109 Gerda Lerner (ed.), *Black Women in White America: A Documentary History* (Vintage Books, 1992), 61.

110 Jeffrey Ansloos and Shanna Peltier, "A Question of Justice: Critically Researching Suicide with Indigenous Studies of Affect, Biosociality, and Land-Based Relations," *Health: An Interdisciplinary Journal for the Social Study of Health, Illness, and Medicine* 26, no. 1 (2022): 100–119, https://doi.org/10.1177/13634593211046845.

111 Sharon Patricia Holland, *The Erotic Life of Racism* (Duke University Press, 2012), 79, italics in original.

112 Elizabeth Bernstein, "Militarized Humanitarianism Meets Carceral Feminism: The Politics of Sex, Rights, and Freedom in Contemporary Antitrafficking Campaigns," *Signs* 36, no. 1 (2010): 45–71, https://doi.org/10.1086/652918.

113 Evelyn Brooks Higginbotham, *Righteous Discontent: The Women's Movement in the Black Baptist Church, 1880–1920* (Harvard University Press, 2003), 7.

114 Margaret Hope Bacon, "By Moral Force Alone: The Antislavery Women and Nonresistance," in *The Abolitionist Sisterhood: Women's Political Culture in Antebellum America*, ed. Jean Fagan Yellin and John C. Van Horne (Cornell University Press, 1994), 275–97; Ruth Bogin and Jean Fagan Yellin, "Introduction,"

in *The Abolitionist Sisterhood: Women's Political Culture in Antebellum America*, ed. Jean Fagan Yellin and John C. Van Horne (Cornell University Press, 1994), 1–19; Louise Michele Newman, *White Women's Rights: The Racial Origins of Feminism in the United States* (Oxford University Press, 1999); Beth A. Salerno, *Sister Societies: Women's Antislavery Organizations in Antebellum America* (Northern Illinois University Press, 2005).

115 Paula Giddings, *When and Where I Enter: The Impact of Black Women on Race and Sex in America* (W. Morrow, 1984); Elisabeth Lasch-Quinn, *Black Neighbors: Race and the Limits of Reform in the American Settlement House Movement, 1890–1945* (University of North Carolina Press, 1993).

116 Michelle Alexander, *The New Jim Crow: Mass Incarceration in the Age of Colorblindness* (New Press, 2020), 36–44.

117 Kerry Abrams, "Polygamy, Prostitution, and the Federalization of Immigration Law," *Columbia Law Review*, 2005; Helen H. Jun, "Black Orientalism: Nineteenth-Century Narratives of Race and U.S. Citizenship," *American Quarterly* 58, no. 4 (2006): 1047–66.

118 "YWCA Through the Years," YWCA, accessed March 22, 2024, www.ywca.org.

119 Giddings, *When and Where I Enter*, 155.

120 Margaret E. Berry, "Settlement Movement: 1886–1986," Social Welfare History Project, Virginia Commonwealth University Libraries, 1986, https://socialwelfare.library.vcu.edu.

121 Judith Weisenfeld, *African American Women and Christian Activism: New York's Black YWCA, 1905–1945* (Harvard University Press, 1997), 35.

122 Bettina Aptheker, *Lynching and Rape: An Exchange of Views* (American Institute for Marxist Studies, 1977).

123 Elizabeth Ammons, "Black Anxiety About Immigration and Jessie Fauset's 'The Sleeper Wakes,'" *African American Review* 42, no. 3/4 (2008): 461–76; Jessica Toft, "History Matters: Racialized Motherhoods and Neoliberalism," *Social Work* 65, no. 3 (2020): 225–34, https://doi.org/10.1093/sw/swaa021.

124 Lasch-Quinn, *Black Neighbors*.

125 Evelyn Nakano Glenn, "The Dialectics of Wage Work: Japanese-American Women and Domestic Service, 1905–1940," *Feminist Studies* 6, no. 3 (1980): 428, https://doi.org/10.2307/3177475; Lois Rita Helmbold, "Beyond the Family Economy: Black and White Working-Class Women During the Great Depression," *Feminist Studies* 13, no. 3 (1987): 629, https://doi.org/10.2307/3177885.

126 Olivia Pleasants Frosts, "A Study of Some of the Characteristics of 150 Multi-Problem Families," 1957, Box 6 Folder 2, The New York Public Library Archives & Manuscripts, Schomburg Center for Research in Black Culture, Olivia Pleasants Frost papers (Sc MG 430).

127 Glenn, "Dialectics of Wage Work."

128 Aptheker, *Lynching and Rape: An Exchange of Views*, 2.

129 Kay Pranis, Barry Stuart, and Mark Wedge, *Peacemaking Circles: From Crime to Community* (Living Justice Press, 2003).

130 Young, "Strapped."
131 Edward J. Gumz and Cynthia L. Grant, "Restorative Justice: A Systematic Review of the Social Work Literature," *Families in Society* 90, no. 1 (2009): 119–26, https://doi.org/10.1606/1044-3894.3853; Weisenfeld, *African American Women and Christian Activism*.
132 Yolanda Bako, "Essay by Bako Re: Domestic Violence; Autobiographical Letter, 1983–1985; Clipping Re: Bako, 1978," 1983–1985, Box 1, Harvard Schlesinger Library, Radcliffe Institute, Papers of Yolanda Bako, 1970–1995 (MC 943: Vt-105); Jayme Sokolow and Mary Ann Lamanna, "Women and Utopia: The Woman's Commonwealth of Belton, Texas," *Southwestern Historical Quarterly* 87, no. 4 (1984): 371–92.
133 Elizabeth Freeman, *Time Binds: Queer Temporalities, Queer Histories* (Duke University Press, 2010).
134 Kadji Amin, *Disturbing Attachments: Genet, Modern Pederasty, and Queer History* (Duke University Press, 2017).
135 Sara Ahmed, *The Cultural Politics of Emotion* (Edinburgh University Press, 2014).

CHAPTER 2. CAPITALIZING EMPOWERMENT

Epigraph: Angela Y. Davis, "Rape, Racism and the Capitalist Setting," *Black Scholar* 9, no. 7 (1978): 30, https://doi.org/10.1080/00064246.1978.11414005.
1 Davis, "Rape, Racism and the Capitalist Setting," 24.
2 Saidiya V. Hartman, *Scenes of Subjection: Terror, Slavery, and Self-Making in Nineteenth-Century America* (Norton, 1997).
3 INCITE!, *The Revolution Will Not Be Funded*.
4 Bumiller, *In an Abusive State*; Corrigan, *Up Against a Wall*.
5 Mehrotra, Kimball, and Wahab, "The Braid That Binds Us"; Shana L. Maier, "Rape Crisis Centers and Programs: 'Doing Amazing, Wonderful Things on Peanuts,'" *Women & Criminal Justice* 21, no. 2 (2011): 141–69, https://doi.org/10.1080/08974454.2011.558802; Maier, "'We Belong to Them.'"
6 Shana L. Maier, "Rape Victim Advocates' Perception of the Influence of Race and Ethnicity on Victims' Responses to Rape," *Journal of Ethnicity in Criminal Justice* 6, no. 4 (2008): 303–34, https://doi.org/10.1080/15377930802533530.
7 Nils Christie, "The Ideal Victim," in *From Crime Policy to Victim Policy: Reorienting the Justice System*, ed. Ezzat A. Fattah (Macmillan, 1986), 17–30.
8 INCITE!, *The Revolution Will Not Be Funded*.
9 Crenshaw, "Mapping the Margins."
10 Lisa Duggan, "Queering the State," *Social Text*, no. 39 (1994): 1, https://doi.org/10.2307/466361; Spade, *Normal Life*.
11 Brown, *Undoing the Demos*.
12 Karl Marx, *The German Ideology*, 1845, www.marxists.org.
13 Pierre Bourdieu, "Cultural Reproduction and Social Reproduction," in *Knowledge, Education, and Cultural Change: Papers in the Sociology of Education*, ed. Richard Brown (Routledge, 1973), 42, https://doi.org/10.4324/9781351018142.
14 Pierre Bourdieu defines three types of capital: economic, cultural, and social. Economic capital is financial wealth. Cultural capital is the knowledge and commodi-

ties of a given culture. Social capital is the networks and communities that affect the degree of profiteering. I use the term "cultural capitalism" to encompass both cultural and social capital, as I believe that cultural and social capitalism share substantive features. I also see cultural capital as having an inextricable link with economic capital. The value of knowledge comes from one's networks and communities, which then influence one's material belongings; therefore, inherently, social capitalism is a part of cultural capitalism and cultural capitalism is a part of economic capitalism.

15 Discourses around "culture," including cultural capitalism, have frequently eliminated race, often in oppressive ways (Melamed, "The Spirit of Neoliberalism"). While I understand the argument to use racial capitalism more explicitly, I use the term "culture" here to recognize the interconnected nature of multiple forms of oppression. Nevertheless, I acknowledge that racial/ethnic capitalism theorists as well as anticapitalist feminists stand at the forefront of our understanding of cultural capitalism, and I have emphasized race, ethnicity, gender, and sex/uality in this chapter.

16 Tara J. Yosso, "Whose Culture Has Capital? A Critical Race Theory Discussion of Community Cultural Wealth," *Race Ethnicity and Education* 8, no. 1 (2005): 69–91, https://doi.org/10.1080/1361332052000341006; Jodi Melamed, "Racial Capitalism," *Critical Ethnic Studies* 1, no. 1 (2015): 76, https://doi.org/10.5749/jcritethnstud.1.1.0076; Susan Koshy, Lisa Marie Cacho, Jodi A. Byrd, and Brian Jordan Jefferson, eds., *Colonial Racial Capitalism* (Duke University Press, 2022).

17 Racial capitalism diverges, in part, from ethnic capitalism, which focuses on the ways that ethnicity as constructed by ethnic communities, not "race" as constructed by white Global North hegemonies, interfaces with the economy. Given this definition of ethnic capitalism, it may be more accurate to use the term "ethnic capitalism" than "racial capitalism." Still, both racial and ethnic capitalism make similar arguments: that legacies of racial and ethnic violence through economic and financial systems are commonplace and ongoing, and that capitalism organizes cultural and social groups in racist and oppressive ways. I use "racial capitalism" because it is more known than "ethnic capitalism," but I recognize the utility of ethnic capitalism in anti-oppressive work. Min Zhou and Mingang Lin, "Community Transformation and the Formation of Ethnic Capital: Immigrant Chinese Communities in the United States," *Journal of Chinese Overseas* 1, no. 2 (2005): 260–84, https://doi.org/10.1353/jco.2007.0027.

18 Cedric J. Robinson, *Black Marxism: The Making of the Black Radical Tradition* (University of North Carolina Press, 1983), 2.

19 Robinson, *Black Marxism*.

20 Hartman, *Scenes of Subjection*.

21 Todd L. Savitt, "Slave Life Insurance in Virginia and North Carolina," *Journal of Southern History* 43, no. 4 (1977): 583, https://doi.org/10.2307/2207007.

22 Alexander, *The New Jim Crow*.

23 Mary Church Terrell, "Lynching from the Negro's Point of View," *North American Review* 178 (1904): 853–68; Gilmore, "Race, Prisons, and War"; Ruth Wilson Gilmore and Craig Gilmore, "Restating the Obvious," in *Abolition Geography: Essays Towards Liberation* (Verso, 2022), 259–87.
24 Bourdieu, "Cultural Reproduction and Social Reproduction."
25 Bourdieu, "Cultural Reproduction and Social Reproduction"; Yosso, "Whose Culture Has Capital?"
26 Melvin Delgado, *Social Work with Latinos: A Cultural Assets Paradigm* (Oxford University Press, 2013).
27 Otava Piha, "My Body Is My Temple? Comparing Sexual Crimes and Property Crimes in a Human Rights Tradition," *German Law Journal*, 2024, 1–16, https://doi.org/10.1017/glj.2023.97.
28 Dorothy E. Roberts, "Rape, Violence, and Women's Autonomy," *Penn Carey Law: Legal Scholarship Repository*, 1991, 359–88; Donald A. Dripps, "Beyond Rape: An Essay on the Difference Between the Presence of Force and the Absence of Consent," *Columbia Law Review* 92, no. 7 (1992): 1780, https://doi.org/10.2307/1123045; Rebecca Stringer, *Knowing Victims: Feminism, Agency, and Victim Politics in Neoliberal Times* (Routledge, 2014).
29 Dripps, "Beyond Rape," 1786.
30 Stringer, *Knowing Victims*, 19, 41–42.
31 Dripps, "Beyond Rape."
32 Susan Estrich, *Real Rape* (Harvard University Press, 1987); Bennett Capers, "Real Rape, Too," *California Law Review* 99 (2011): 1259–1308.
33 Joseph J. Fischel, *Screw Consent: A Better Politics of Sexual Justice* (University of California Press, 2019).
34 Christie, "The Ideal Victim," 12.
35 Estrich, *Real Rape*.
36 Corey Rayburn Yung, "Rape Law Fundamentals," *SSRN Electronic Journal*, 2013, https://doi.org/10.2139/ssrn.2337621; Piha, "My Body Is My Temple?"
37 Lucia Hulsether, *Capitalist Humanitarianism* (Duke University Press, 2023), 58.
38 Schulhofer, *Unwanted Sex*; Fischel, *Screw Consent*.
39 Hartman, *Scenes of Subjection*.
40 Hartman, *Scenes of Subjection*, 195.
41 Hartman, *Scenes of Subjection*, 197.
42 Robin West, "Legitimating the Illegitimate: A Comment on 'Beyond Rape,'" *Columbia Law Review* 1459 (1993): 1442–59.
43 Nada DeCat and Zahra Stardust, "Against Inclusion: Sex Work Research, Racial Capitalism, and the Knowledge Industrial Complex," in *Handbook of Social Inclusion*, ed. Pranee Liamputtong (Springer International Publishing, 2021), 1–26, https://doi.org/10.1007/978-3-030-48277-0_28-1.
44 Cathy J. Cohen, "Punks, Bulldaggers, and Welfare Queens: The Radical Potential of Queer Politics?," *GLQ* 3, no. 4 (1997): 437–65, https://doi.org/10.1215/10642684-

3-4-437; Ange-Marie Hancock, *The Politics of Disgust: The Public Identity of the Welfare Queen* (NYU Press, 2004).
45   Ann J. Cahill, *Rethinking Rape* (Cornell University Press, 2001); Linda Alcoff, *Rape and Resistance: Understanding the Complexities of Sexual Violation* (Polity Press, 2018); Fischel, *Screw Consent*; Piha, "My Body Is My Temple?"
46   Collins, "The Tie That Binds."
47   Orlando Patterson, *Slavery and Social Death: A Comparative Study* (Harvard University Press, 1982); Robinson, *Black Marxism*; Hartman, *Scenes of Subjection*.
48   "How to Start a Rape Crisis Center," 3.
49   Maier, "Rape Crisis Centers and Programs"; Maier, "'We Belong to Them.'"
50   Sweet, *Politics of Surviving*.
51   Joe Soss, Richard C. Fording, and Sanford Schram, eds., *Disciplining the Poor: Neoliberal Paternalism and the Persistent Power of Race* (University of Chicago Press, 2011); Sanford F. Schram and Basha Silverman, "The End of Social Work: Neoliberalizing Social Policy Implementation," *Critical Policy Studies* 6, no. 2 (2012): 128–45, https://doi.org/10.1080/19460171.2012.689734; Mulla, *Violence of Care*.
52   David Harvey, *A Brief History of Neoliberalism* (Oxford University Press, 2005); Salamon, *The State of Nonprofit America*; Brown, *Undoing the Demos*, 17.
53   Mehrotra, Kimball, and Wahab, "The Braid That Binds Us."
54   Linda Alcoff and Laura Gray, "Survivor Discourse: Transgression or Recuperation?," *Signs* 18, no. 2 (1993): 260–90, https://doi.org/10.1086/494793; Sweet, *Politics of Surviving*.
55   Alcoff, *Rape and Resistance*, 9.
56   Stringer, *Knowing Victims*.
57   Sweet, *The Politics of Surviving*, 37, italics in original.
58   Alcoff and Gray, "Survivor Discourse."
59   Jasbir Puar, ed., "Precarity Talk: A Virtual Roundtable with Lauren Berlant, Judith Butler, Bojana Cvejić, Isabell Lorey, Jasbir Puar, and Ana Vujanović," *TDR: The Drama Review* 56, no. 4 (2012): 163–77.
60   Donileen R. Loseke, *The Battered Woman and Shelters: The Social Construction of Wife Abuse* (State University of New York Press, 1992).
61   Mary V. Wrenn, "The Social Ontology of Fear and Neoliberalism," *Review of Social Economy* 72, no. 3 (2014): 337–53, https://doi.org/10.1080/00346764.2014.927726.
62   Maier, "Rape Crisis Centers and Programs," 144.
63   Elizabeth Whalley, "The 'Bait and Switch' of Sexual Assault Response: Expanded Carceral Power at a Rape Crisis Center," *Affilia* 35, no. 2 (2020): 200–217, https://doi.org/10.1177/0886109919890706.
64   Bumiller, *In an Abusive State*, 84–85.
65   Terry L. Cross, Barbara J. Bazron, Karl W. Dennis, and Mareasa R. Isaacs, "Towards a Culturally Competent System of Care: A Monograph on Effective

Services for Minority Children Who Are Severely Emotionally Disturbed" (Georgetown University Child Development Center, CASSP Technical Assistance Center, 1989), https://eric.ed.gov/?id=ED330171; David Nylund, "Critical Multiculturalism, Whiteness, and Social Work: Towards a More Radical View of Cultural Competence," *Journal of Progressive Human Services* 17, no. 2 (2006): 27–42, https://doi.org/10.1300/J059v17n02_03; Cindy Brach and Irene Fraser, "Can Cultural Competency Reduce Racial and Ethnic Health Disparities? A Review and Conceptual Model," *Medical Care Research and Review* 57, no. 1 (2000): 181–217, https://doi.org/10.1177/1077558700057001S09.

66 Lettie L. Lockhart and Fran S. Danis, eds., *Domestic Violence: Intersectionality and Culturally Competent Practice* (Columbia University Press, 2010).

67 Ghanbarpour and Palotai, "Survivor-Centered Advocacy in Culturally Specific Communities."

68 Autumn M. Bermea, Brad Van Eeden-Moorefield, and Lyndal Khaw, "Serving Queer Survivors of Intimate Partner Violence Through Diversity, Inclusion, and Social Justice," *Journal of Gay & Lesbian Social Services* 31, no. 4 (2019): 521–45, https://doi.org/10.1080/10538720.2019.1653805; Sid P. Jordan, Gita R. Mehrotra, and Kiyomi A. Fujikawa, "Mandating Inclusion: Critical Trans Perspectives on Domestic and Sexual Violence Advocacy," *Violence Against Women* 26, no. 6–7 (2020): 531–54, https://doi.org/10.1177/1077801219836728; Melinda Chen, "'Are You—?' 'Are You?' Queer Advocacy at Contemporary Neoliberal Rape Crisis Centers," *Violence Against Women* 29, no. 15–16 (2023): 3072–3100, https://doi.org/10.1177/10778012231192606.

69 Cross et al., "Towards a Culturally Competent System of Care."

70 Annie Wegrzyn, Peggy Tull, Megan R. Greeson, Catherine Pierre-Louis, Emily Patton, and Jessica Shaw, "Rape Crisis Victim Advocacy: A Systematic Review," *Trauma, Violence, & Abuse* 24, no. 3 (2023): 13, https://doi.org/10.1177/15248380221082089.

71 Ebru Çayır, Mindi Spencer, Deborah Billings, DeAnne Hilfinger Messias, and Alyssa Robillard, "Working Against Gender-Based Violence in the American South: An Analysis of Race, Ethnicity, Gender, and Sexuality in Advocacy," *Qualitative Health Research* 31, no. 13 (2021): 2454–69, https://doi.org/10.1177/10497323211041327.

72 National Sexual Violence Resource Center (NSVRC), "Podcasts," accessed May 17, 2025, www.nsvrc.org; "Cultural Responsiveness" (Pennsylvania Coalition to Advance Respect [PCAR], 2019), accessed May 17, 2025, https://pcar.org.

73 Davis, "Rape, Racism and the Capitalist Setting."

74 Chen, "Are You—?'"

75 Lisa Lowe, "Heterogeneity, Hybridity, Multiplicity: Marking Asian American Differences," *Diaspora* 1, no. 1 (March 1991): 24–44, https://doi.org/10.1353/dsp.1991.0014.

76 Melamed, "The Spirit of Neoliberalism."

77 Harriet Bromley, Sarah K. Davis, Blaire Morgan, and Holly Taylor-Dunn, "The Professional Quality of Life of Domestic and Sexual Violence Advocates: A Systematic Review of Possible Risk and Protective Factors," *Trauma, Violence, & Abuse* 25, no. 2 (April 2024): 1113–28, https://doi.org/10.1177/15248380231171187.

78 Jody Agius Vallejo and Stephanie L. Canizales, "Ethnoracial Capitalism and the Limits of Ethnic Solidarity," *Social Problems* 70, no. 4 (2023): 975, https://doi.org/10.1093/socpro/spab067.

79 Nancy Fraser, "Rethinking Recognition," *New Left Review* 3 (2000), https://newleftreview.org. Paige L. Sweet in *The Politics of Surviving* argues against Nancy Fraser's argument that the redistribution of resources can be read as the recognition of resources. Sweet suggests that feminists advocated for redistribution, not recognition at all, and that it was merely a difference in the kinds of redistribution of resources that produced discord. Feminists and state funders alike wanted to redistribute toward services, but feminists' other redistribution aims, like marriage reforms, went unmet while state stakeholders successfully redistributed toward criminal and therapeutic services. In this author's opinion, redistribution was still designated for some sort of visible feminist end (i.e., legal reform) as opposed to more radical efforts (i.e., protest, coalition building); thus, Fraser's argument appears to hold. In Sweet, *The Politics of Surviving*, 257, chapter 1, note 41.

80 Elizabeth A. Grosz, *Space, Time, and Perversion: Essays on the Politics of Bodies* (Routledge, 1995); Iyko Day, *Alien Capital: Asian Racialization and the Logic of Settler Colonial Capitalism* (Duke University Press, 2016).

81 Wrenn, "The Social Ontology of Fear and Neoliberalism," 343.

82 Kim and Kanuha, "Restorative Justice and the Dance with the Devil."

83 Shannon M. Peters, "Demedicalizing the Aftermath of Sexual Assault: Toward a Radical Humanistic Approach," *Journal of Humanistic Psychology* 61, no. 6 (2021): 939–61, https://doi.org/10.1177/0022167819831526; Sweet, *Politics of Surviving*.

84 Mariame Kaba and Shira Hassan, *Fumbling Towards Repair: A Workbook for Community Accountability Facilitators* (Project NIA, 2019).

85 Lisa Marie Cacho and Jodi Melamed, "'Don't Arrest Me, Arrest the Police': Policing as the Street Administration of Colonial Racial Capitalist Orders," in *Colonial Racial Capitalism*, ed. Susan Koshy et al. (Duke University Press, 2022), 159–205, https://doi.org/10.2307/j.ctv2vr9ckn.

86 Davis, "Rape, Racism and the Capitalist Setting," 24.

87 Bevacqua, *Rape on the Public Agenda*.

88 Kathi Weeks, *The Problem with Work: Feminism, Marxism, Antiwork Politics, and Postwork Imaginaries* (Duke University Press, 2011).

89 Dean Spade, *Mutual Aid: Building Solidarity During This Crisis (and the Next)* (Verso, 2020).

90 Barbara J. Love, "Developing a Liberatory Consciousness," in *Readings for Diversity and Social Justice*, ed. Maurianne Adams et al., 4th ed. (Routledge, Taylor & Francis Group, 2018), 610–15.

91 New York Radical Feminists, *Rape: The First Sourcebook for Women*.
92 Benjamin R Weiss, "Carceral Lock-in: How Organizational Conditions Stymie the Development of Justice Alternatives in a Rape Crisis Center," *Theoretical Criminology* 26, no. 1 (February 2022): 91–111, https://doi.org/10.1177/1362480620971784.
93 LaShawn Faith Washington, Rachelle Winkle-Wagner, and Khadejah Ray, "Closer to My Dreams: Exploring Black Women's Graduate School Aspirations and Community Uplift Through a Community Cultural Wealth and Black Feminist Approach," *Journal of Higher Education*, November 19, 2024, 1–27, https://doi.org/10.1080/00221546.2024.2429977.

CHAPTER 3. A HIERARCHY OF ADVOCACY

Epigraph: Madison Pauly, "How the Mainstream Movement Against Gender-Based Violence Fails Black Workers and Survivors," *Mother Jones*, March 1, 2022, www.motherjones.com.

1 Pauly, "The Mainstream Movement."
2 WCSAP's practices were exposed in March 2022 in an article written by white journalist Madison Pauly, which was heartily endorsed by Black advocates across Washington state who had been wronged by the coalition. Pauly, "The Mainstream Movement."
3 This excerpt is a condensed account of Valériana's experiences at WCSAP. Her story thankfully did not end with her unlawful termination at WCSAP in 2020. It led her to open up her own racial equity consulting firm called Necessary Interruptions LLC, for which she has provided consulting services to over twenty organizations since 2020. She has also served as the executive director of the Social Justice Fund NW, a Black liberation–based intermediary that radically moves resources to uplift Black, Native American, Brown, and historically exploited communities. Moreover, she and her organization actively encourage advocates to interrupt anti-Blackness and challenge the ways that traditional philanthropy historically has operated. If you wish to contact Valériana and learn more about her story, please visit https://necessaryinterruptionsllc.com and fill out the "Contact Us" page.
4 I have permission from Valériana Chikoti-Bandua Estes to share her story without anonymity in this book. In addition, the lifetime NDA that WCSAP forced her to sign is not legal. Although Washington state is an "at-will employment" state, meaning that employers can terminate employees at any point for any reason, the Whistleblower Act protects employees who file complaints from employer retaliation. Valériana has shared that upon amendments to the Whistleblower Act, WCSAP did not take any measures to lift the NDA; the responsibility to change the situation fell upon her—an act that echoes many of the situations experienced by advocates of color in this study to remedy their own racist encounters. Only after significant pushback by Valériana and the community did WCSAP declare, on September 29, 2021, that it would not enforce NDAs.

5 Devon W. Carbado and Mitu Gulati, *Acting White? Rethinking Race in "Post-Racial" America* (Oxford University Press, 2013).
6 Philip R. Popple and Leslie Leighninger, *Social Work, Social Welfare, and American Society*, 5th ed. (Allyn and Bacon, 2002).
7 Pascale Joassart-Marcelli, "For Whom and for What? Investigating the Role of Nonprofits as Providers to the Neediest," in *The State of Nonprofit America*, ed. Lester M. Salamon, 2nd ed. (Brookings Institution Press, 2012), 658, www.jstor.org/stable/10.7864/j.ctt1xx6fn.22; Shane Brady, Jason M. Sawyer, and Nathan H. Perkins, "Debunking the Myth of the 'Radical Profession': Analysing and Overcoming Our Professional History to Create New Pathways and Opportunities for Social Work," *Critical and Radical Social Work* 7, no. 3 (November 2019): 315–32, https://doi.org/10.1332/204986019X15668424193408.
8 Roxanne Dunbar-Ortiz, *An Indigenous Peoples' History of the United States* (Beacon Press, 2014).
9 Amanda Gebhard, Sheelah McLean, and Verna St. Denis, eds., *White Benevolence: Racism and Colonial Violence in the Helping Professions* (Fernwood Publishing, 2022).
10 David Wallace Adams, *Education for Extinction: American Indians and the Boarding School Experience, 1875–1928* (University Press of Kansas, 1995).
11 Richard Henry Pratt, "'Kill the Indian in Him, and Save the Man': R. H. Pratt on the Education of Native Americans" (Speech, Conference of Charities and Correction, Denver, Colorado, 1892), Carlisle Indian School Digital Resource Center, https://carlisleindian.dickinson.edu.
12 Popple and Leighninger, *Social Work, Social Welfare, and American Society*, 4.
13 Gary R. Lowe and P. Nelson Reid, eds., *The Professionalization of Poverty: Social Work and the Poor in the Twentieth Century* (Aldine de Gruyter, 1999).
14 Brady, Sawyer, and Perkins, "Debunking the Myth of the 'Radical Profession'"; Toft, "History Matters."
15 I. Carlton-LaNey, "African American Social Work Pioneers' Response to Need," *Social Work* 44, no. 4 (1999): 311–21, https://doi.org/10.1093/sw/44.4.311; Joyce Marie Bell, *The Black Power Movement and American Social Work* (Columbia University Press, 2014).
16 Forrester B. Washington, "The Need and Education of Negro Social Workers," *Journal of Negro Education* 4, no. 1 (1935): 79, https://doi.org/10.2307/2292089.
17 Diane Lynn Gusa, "White Institutional Presence: The Impact of Whiteness on Campus Climate," *Harvard Educational Review* 80, no. 4 (2010): 464–89.
18 Polly Cowan and Dorothy Height, November 11, 1974, The New York Public Library Archives & Manuscripts Division, Schomburg Center for Research in Black Culture, Black Women Oral History Project transcripts, volume 30, https://archives.nypl.org.
19 Bell, *The Black Power Movement and American Social Work*.
20 "Our Roots: Position Statement of the National Association of Black Social Workers" (National Association of Black Social Workers, 1968).

21 "NASW Apologizes for Racist Practices in American Social Work," *National Association of Social Workers News Releases* (blog), June 17, 2021, www.socialworkers.org.
22 Carlton-LaNey, "African American Social Work Pioneers' Response to Need."
23 Mimi E. Kim, "The Carceral Creep: Gender-Based Violence, Race, and the Expansion of the Punitive State, 1973–1983," *Social Problems* 67, no. 2 (2020): 251–69, https://doi.org/10.1093/socpro/spz013.
24 Lester M. Salamon, "The Nonprofit Sector at a Crossroads: The Case of America," *Voluntas: International Journal of Voluntary and Nonprofit Organizations* 10, no. 1 (1999): 5–23.
25 Thuma, *All Our Trials*; Sweet, *Politics of Surviving*.
26 Peters, "Demedicalizing the Aftermath of Sexual Assault."
27 INCITE!, *The Revolution Will Not Be Funded*.
28 Bumiller, *In an Abusive State*.
29 Gilmore, "Shadow State."
30 Jennifer Wies, "Professionalizing Human Services: A Case of Domestic Violence Shelter Advocates," *Human Organization* 67, no. 2 (June 2008): 221–33, https://doi.org/10.17730/humo.67.2.l43m2v542217ll3; Sonia E. Alvarez, "Beyond NGO-ization? Reflections from Latin America," *Development* 52, no. 2 (June 2009): 175–84, https://doi.org/10.1057/dev.2009.23.
31 Gilmore, "Shadow State."
32 Wies, "Professionalizing Human Services."
33 Janine Zweig, Lauren Farrell, Kelly Walsh, and Lilly Yu, "Community Approaches to Sexual Assault: VAWA's Role and Survivors' Experiences," *Violence Against Women* 27, no. 1 (2021): 30–51, https://doi.org/10.1177/1077801220949696.
34 Sweet, *The Politics of Surviving*, 37.
35 While the STOP program did support some anti-rape efforts insofar as they intersected with intimate partner violence, SASP formalized the use of government funds for specifically anti-rape work.
36 Zweig et al., "Community Approaches to Sexual Assault."
37 "OVW Fiscal Year 2014 Sexual Assault Services Formula Grant Program Solicitation" (Office on Violence Against Women [OVW], US Department of Justice, 2014), www.justice.gov.
38 Maier, "'We Belong to Them.'"
39 Deb Friedman, "Professionalism." *Feminist Alliance Against Rape (FAAR) Newsletter*, Fall 1975, 2.
40 Campbell, Baker, and Mazurek, "Remaining Radical?"; Maier, "Rape Crisis Centers and Programs"; Mehrotra, Kimball, and Wahab, "The Braid That Binds Us."
41 INCITE!, *The Revolution Will Not Be Funded*.
42 Shana L. Maier, "Are Rape Crisis Centers Feminist Organizations?," *Feminist Criminology* 3, no. 2 (2008): 82–100, https://doi.org/10.1177/1557085107310623; Maier, "'We Belong to Them'"; Mehrotra, Kimball, and Wahab, "The Braid That Binds Us."

43 Femida Handy, Laurie Mook, and Jack Quarter, "The Interchangeability of Paid Staff and Volunteers in Nonprofit Organizations," *Nonprofit and Voluntary Sector Quarterly* 37, no. 1 (2008): 76–92, https://doi.org/10.1177/0899764007303528.

44 INCITE!, *The Revolution Will Not Be Funded*; Jennifer Cole, "Structural, Organizational, and Interpersonal Factors Influencing Interprofessional Collaboration on Sexual Assault Response Teams," *Journal of Interpersonal Violence* 33, no. 17 (2018): 2682–2703, https://doi.org/10.1177/0886260516628809.

45 Bumiller, *In an Abusive State*; Maier, "'We Belong to Them.'"

46 Friedman, "Professionalism," 3.

47 Koshy et al., *Colonial Racial Capitalism*, 14.

48 Wies, "Professionalizing Human Services," 222.

49 Carbado and Gulati, *Acting White?*

50 David B. Wilkins, "Identities and Roles: Race, Recognition, and Professional Responsibility," *Maryland Law Review* 57, no. 4 (1998): 1502–94; "ABA Profile of the Legal Profession 2020" (American Bar Association, 2020), 34, www.americanbar.org.

51 Most US state coalitions require that advocates undergo at least forty hours of advocacy training prior to working with victims but leave the responsibility for ensuring compliance up to individual rape crisis centers. In some states, advocates who work with both sexual assault and domestic violence victims are required to undergo at least eighty hours of training: forty hours of sexual assault training and forty hours of domestic violence training.

52 Thuma, *All Our Trials*; Peters, "Demedicalizing the Aftermath of Sexual Assault"; Sweet, *Politics of Surviving*.

53 Chen, "'Are You—?'"

54 Friedman, "Professionalism," 3.

55 Melanie Hanson, "Average Cost of College & Tuition" (Education Data Initiative, November 18, 2023), https://educationdata.org.

56 Hanson, "Average Cost of College & Tuition."

57 Laura T. Hamilton and Kelly Nielsen, *Broke: The Racial Consequences of Underfunding Public Universities* (University of Chicago Press, 2021).

58 The numbers of Asian people with associate's degrees or higher conflates the vast diversity of Asian people in the United States. East and South Asians, including Asian Indian, Taiwanese, Chinese, Korean, and Japanese, make up the majority of Asian people in the United States with collegiate degrees; Southeast Asians, including Cambodian, Laotian, and Hmong, are disproportionately represented in the class of people in the United States without collegiate degrees, and are often ignored in education statistics—a phenomenon explored further in chapter 5. National Center for Education Statistics, "Indicator 27 Snapshot: Attainment of a Bachelor's or Higher Degree for Racial/Ethnic Subgroups," Status and Trends in the Education of Racial and Ethnic

Groups (National Center for Education Statistics, February 2019), https://nces.ed.gov.

59 "2020 Statistics on Social Work Education in the United States: Summary of the CSWE Annual Survey of Social Work Programs" (Council on Social Work Education [CSWE], 2020), 3, www.cswe.org.

60 Hamilton and Nielsen, *Broke*.

61 Davis et al., *Abolition. Feminism. Now.*, 162.

62 O*Net, which is the standard database for occupational wages, education, and openings information, classifies "advocate" under "21-1093.00 Social and Human Service Assistants" and reports wages at $38,520 annually or $18.52 hourly. "Social and Human Service Assistants," O*Net OnLine, accessed March 20, 2024, www.onetonline.org. These rates are on par with reports from Zippia regarding the wage fluctuations and wage gap over the years. In the absence of national data on advocates, I use Zippia's wage here because Zippia offers a detailed description of an advocate's job functions and is therefore more credible than other sources. "Victim Advocate Salary," Zippia, March 14, 2024, www.zippia.com.

63 The salary per hour and annually for administrative advocates is based on the category, "Community and Social Service Specialists, All Other," then "Social Advocacy Organizations" in the report by the US Bureau of Labor Statistics that uses 2022 data. "Occupational Employment and Wages, May 2022, 21-1099 Community and Social Service Specialists, All Other" (US Bureau of Labor Statistics, 2022), www.bls.gov.

64 Data on the average wages for advocates of different statuses, ranks, and educational background are not available. Many nonprofit organizations choose to compensate directors on the basis of local standards. Given the lack of data, I have chosen to source from Angela Ogunjimi, "Is the Salary of an Executive Director of a Non-Profit a Percentage of the Budget?," *CHRON*, October 26, 2018, https://smallbusiness.chron.com. However, I recognize that this salary may not be accurate to victim advocacy, especially as anti-rape advocacy functions differently than other welfare services given more extreme gender differences than in other carceral-welfare industries. Moreover, there is a significant gender wage gap between women and men executive directors. On average, women earn 26 percent less than men (Wolfgang Keller, Teresa Molina, and William W. Olney, "The Gender Gap Among Top Business Executives," National Bureau of Economic Research Working Paper Series 28216, Cambridge, MA, 2022, www.nber.org). Given that most identity-based or social justice (like anti-violence) executive directors are women, the wages presented here may not accurately reflect the salaries of nonprofit rape crisis center executive directors. Building Movement Project, "Trading Glass Ceilings for Glass Cliffs: A Race to Lead Report on Nonprofit Executives of Color," Race to Lead (Building Movement Project, 2022), https://buildingmovement.org.

65 Lena Dominelli, "Deprofessionalizing Social Work: Anti-Oppressive Practice, Competencies, and Postmodernism," *British Journal of Social Work* 26, no. 2 (1996): 153–75, https://doi.org/10.1093/oxfordjournals.bjsw.a011077.
66 D. M. Van Slyke, "Agents or Stewards: Using Theory to Understand the Government-Nonprofit Social Service Contracting Relationship," *Journal of Public Administration Research and Theory* 17, no. 2 (June 7, 2006): 159, 164, https://doi.org/10.1093/jopart/mul012.
67 Leila Wood, Karin Wachter, Diane Rhodes, and Alex Wang, "Turnover Intention and Job Satisfaction Among the Intimate Partner Violence and Sexual Assault Workforce," *Violence and Victims* 34, no. 4 (2019): 678–700, https://doi.org/10.1891/0886-6708.VV-D-18-00134; Çayır et al., "Working Against Gender-Based Violence in the American South"; National Council of Nonprofits, "The Nonprofit Workforce Shortage Crisis" (National Council of Nonprofits, 2023), www.councilofnonprofits.org.
68 Leah Goodridge, "Professionalism as a Racial Construct," *UCLA Law Review* 69, no. 38 (2022): 38–54.
69 Beal, "Double Jeopardy."
70 As the famed feminist abolitionist Sojourner Truth noted, in one of the earliest remarks on the "double bind" (before W. E. B. Du Bois), women of color have not only different presentations but also different ways of living and moving through the world compared to white women. Consequently, they must seriously weigh the consequences of their marginalized status with their desire for accurate representation. Sojourner Truth, "Ain't I a Wummon" (Women's Rights Convention, Old Stone Church [since demolished], Akron, Ohio, 1851), www.nps.gov; Carbado and Gulati, *Acting White?*, 15.
71 Wood et al., "Turnover Intention and Job Satisfaction."
72 Michelle Bemiller and L. Susan Williams, "The Role of Adaptation in Advocate Burnout: A Case of Good Soldiering," *Violence Against Women* 17, no. 1 (January 2011): 89–110, https://doi.org/10.1177/1077801210393923; Ga-Young Choi, "Organizational Impacts on the Secondary Traumatic Stress of Social Workers Assisting Family Violence or Sexual Assault Survivors," *Administration in Social Work* 35, no. 3 (June 2011): 225–42, https://doi.org/10.1080/03643107.2011.575333; Rachel J. Voth Schrag, Sophia Fantus, Sarah Leat, Saltanat Childress, and Leila Wood, "Experiencing Moral Distress Within the Intimate Partner Violence and Sexual Assault Workforce," *Journal of Family Violence*, April 27, 2023, https://doi.org/10.1007/s10896-023-00567-x; Shana L. Maier, "Keepers of Trauma: Rape Victim Advocates' Secondary Traumatic Stress, Burnout, and Coping Techniques," *Violence Against Women*, June 22, 2023, https://doi.org/10.1177/10778012231182414.
73 Kenneth H. Kolb, *Moral Wages: The Emotional Dilemmas of Victim Advocacy and Counseling* (University of California Press, 2014).
74 Wayne Au, "Asian American Racialization, Racial Capitalism, and the Threat of the Model Minority," *Review of Education, Pedagogy, and Cultural Studies* 44, no. 3 (2022): 201, https://doi.org/10.1080/10714413.2022.2084326.

75 Shannon Winnubst, "The Many Lives of Fungibility: Anti-Blackness in Neoliberal Times," *Journal of Gender Studies* 29, no. 1 (2020): 102–12, https://doi.org/10.1080/09589236.2019.1692193.
76 Collins, *Black Feminist Thought*.
77 Laura Pulido, *Black, Brown, Yellow, and Left: Radical Activism in Los Angeles* (University of California Press, 2006), 25.
78 Michael Omi and Howard Winant, *Racial Formation in the United States: From the 1960s to the 1990s*, 2nd ed. (Routledge, 1994).
79 Lowe, "Heterogeneity, Hybridity, Multiplicity."
80 Jasbir K. Puar, *Terrorist Assemblages: Homonationalism in Queer Times*, 10th anniversary expanded ed. (Duke University Press, 2017), 24.
81 Maile Arvin, Eve Tuck, and Angie Morrill, "Decolonizing Feminism: Challenging Connections Between Settler Colonialism and Heteropatriarchy," *Feminist Formations* 25, no. 1 (2013): 10, https://doi.org/10.1353/ff.2013.0006.
82 Airlan1979 in Pauly, "How the Mainstream Movement Against Gender-Based Violence Fails Black Workers and Survivors." Quotation posted on April 27, 2023, accessed on January 2, 2025.
83 Michelle Mark and Bradford William Davis, "6 Executives Depart RAINN Following Employee Allegations of Racism and Sexism at the Organization," *Business Insider*, April 8, 2022, www.businessinsider.com.
84 Audra Heinrichs, "What Happened at Nancy Lublin's Crisis Text Line: Lublin's Departure, Internal Strife, and Where They Are Now," *Teen Vogue*, September 14, 2021, www.teenvogue.com.
85 Bach et al., "Underserved Survivors of Sexual Assault"; Wegrzyn et al., "Rape Crisis Victim Advocacy."
86 Christine L. Williams, "The Glass Escalator: Hidden Advantages for Men in the 'Female' Professions," *Social Problems* 39, no. 3 (1992): 253–67, https://doi.org/10.2307/3096961. The phenomenon of the "glass ceiling" in feminized workplaces is known as the "glass escalator," where men, even in feminized workplaces, advance more quickly and beyond women simply because the institution privileges masculinized labor. I use "glass ceiling" as a term here because it is more well known than "glass escalator."
87 C. Nicole Mason, Lisette Garcia, and Supurna Banerjee, "Gaining Ground, Breaking Through: A Report on the Leadership Experiences of Women of Color, Lesbian, Gay, Bisexual, Transgender, and Queer Individuals of Color, Individuals with Disabilities, Native Women, Aspiring Allies, Immigrant Women Working in the Anti-Violence Movement in Four States" (Women of Color Network, 2014).
88 The Building Movement Project acknowledges that the "glass cliff" "was initially coined in reference to the phenomenon of women being put into leadership roles under risky circumstance, particularly as new business executives of already struggling or failing companies" (Building Movement Project, "Trading Glass Ceilings for Glass Cliffs: A Race to Lead Report on Nonprofit Executives of Color," 22, endnote 1).

89 Building Movement Project, "Trading Glass Ceilings for Glass Cliffs: A Race to Lead Report on Nonprofit Executives of Color," 13.
90 Building Movement Project, "Meeting the Need: Building the Capacity of Community-Based Organizations," Movement Infrastructure Series (Building Movement Project, 2022), https://buildingmovement.org.
91 Shanti Kulkarni, Holly Bell, Jennifer L. Hartman, and Robert L. Herman-Smith, "Exploring Individual and Organizational Factors Contributing to Compassion Satisfaction, Secondary Traumatic Stress, and Burnout in Domestic Violence Service Providers," *Journal of the Society for Social Work and Research* 4, no. 2 (2013): 114–30, https://doi.org/10.5243/jsswr.2013.8.
92 Çayır et al., "Working Against Gender-Based Violence in the American South."
93 Voth Schrag et al., "Experiencing Moral Distress."
94 Karin Wachter, Rachel Voth Schrag, and Leila Wood, "Coping Behaviors Mediate Associations Between Occupational Factors and Compassion Satisfaction Among the Intimate Partner Violence and Sexual Assault Workforce," *Journal of Family Violence* 35, no. 2 (February 2020): 143–54, https://doi.org/10.1007/s10896-019-00072-0.
95 Maier, "Keepers of Trauma."
96 emi koyama, *Disloyal to Feminism: Abuse of Power and Control Within the Domestic Violence Shelter System* (Survivor Project, 2003), https://eminism.org.
97 Audre Lorde, *The Master's Tools Will Never Dismantle the Master's House* (Penguin Books, 2018).
98 koyama, *Disloyal to Feminism*.
99 Spade, *Mutual Aid*.
100 Davis et al., *Abolition. Feminism. Now.*
101 Freire, *Pedagogy of the Oppressed*.

CHAPTER 4. OUR CARCERAL CREEP

Epigraph: Maya Schenwar and Victoria Law, *Prison by Any Other Name: The Harmful Consequences of Popular Reforms* (The New Press, 2020), 113–14.
1 Mia Mingus, "Pods and Pod-Mapping Worksheet," in *Beyond Survival: Strategies and Stories from the Transformative Justice Movement*, ed. Ejeris Dixon and Leah Lakshmi Piepzna-Samarasinha (AK Press, 2020), 119.
2 I consider SAFEs to be carceral agents given their role as a forensic evidence collector and court witness. Though SAFEs may also execute medical functions, the primary function of a SAFE is to gather evidence for criminal proceedings. Mulla, *Violence of Care*.
3 Jennifer Zajac, "National Sexual Assault Response Team Survey Report" (NSVRC, 2009).
4 Patricia Y. Martin, *Rape Work: Victims, Gender, and Emotions in Organization and Community Context*. Perspectives on Gender (Routledge, 2005).
5 Kim, "Carceral Creep."
6 Brown, *Undoing the Demos*.

7 Maier, "Are Rape Crisis Centers Feminist Organizations?"; Whalley, "'Bait and Switch' of Sexual Assault Response"; Weiss, "Volunteer Professionalization in a Rape Crisis Center."
8 Andrew Dilts, "Carceral Enjoyments and Killjoying the Social Life of Social Death," in *Building Abolition: Decarceration and Social Justice*, ed. Chloë Taylor and Kelly Struthers Montford (Routledge, 2021), 196–223; Korey Tillman, "Carceral Liberalism: The Coloniality and Antiblackness of Coercive Benevolence," *Social Problems* 70, no. 3 (2023): 635–49, https://doi.org/10.1093/socpro/spac003.
9 Bumiller, *In an Abusive State*; Corrigan, *Up Against a Wall*.
10 Jaron Browne, "Rooted in Slavery: Prison Labor Exploitation," *Race, Poverty & the Environment* 14, no. 1 (2007): 42–44; Baker and Bevacqua, "Challenging Narratives of the Anti-Rape Movement's Decline"; Thuma, *All Our Trials*; Kim, "Carceral Creep."
11 Lisa Guenther, *Solitary Confinement: Social Death and Its Afterlives* (University of Minnesota Press, 2013), 13.
12 Kim, "Carceral Creep," 254.
13 Browne, "Rooted in Slavery."
14 "A Different Kind of Slavery," Equal Justice Initiative (EJI), July 25, 2018, https://eji.org.
15 Davis, "Reflections on the Black Woman's Role in the Community of Slaves"; Ersula J. Ore, *Lynching: Violence, Rhetoric, and American Identity* (University Press of Mississippi, 2019).
16 Patricia Hill Collins, "The Meaning of Motherhood in Black Culture and Black Mother-Daughter Relationships," *Sage Women's Educational Press, Inc.* 4, no. 2 (1987): 3.
17 Schram and Silverman, "End of Social Work"; Whittier, *Frenemies*.
18 Dean Spade, "Solidarity, Not Charity," *Social Text* 38, no. 1 (March 1, 2020): 131–51, https://doi.org/10.1215/01642472-7971139.
19 E. Hinton, "'A War Within Our Own Boundaries': Lyndon Johnson's Great Society and the Rise of the Carceral State," *Journal of American History* 102, no. 1 (2015): 100–112, https://doi.org/10.1093/jahist/jav328.
20 INCITE!, *The Revolution Will Not Be Funded*, xv.
21 Hinton, "'A War Within Our Own Boundaries.'"
22 Soss, Fording, and Schram, *Disciplining the Poor*.
23 Thuma, *All Our Trials*, 4.
24 Alexander, *The New Jim Crow*, 2.
25 Menachem Amir, "Victim Precipitated Forcible Rape," *Journal of Criminal Law and Criminology* 58, no. 4 (1968): 493–502.
26 Angela Davis, "Angela Davis's Radio Show on KPFA, Berkeley, Including Review of Against Our Will, 1976. Version 1. Side 1," accessed March 21, 2024, HOLLIS for Archival Discovery, Harvard Library, https://hollisarchives.lib.harvard.edu.
27 Susan Brownmiller, *Against Our Will: Men, Women, and Rape*, 1st ed. (Fawcett Columbine, 1993).

28 Kim, "From Carceral Feminism to Transformative Justice"; Anna Terwiel, "What Is Carceral Feminism?," *Political Theory* 48, no. 4 (2020): 421–42, https://doi.org/10.1177/0090591719889946.
29 "How to Start a Rape Crisis Center," 7.
30 "How to Start a Rape Crisis Center," "How to Start a Rape Crisis Center, Revised and Expanded Second Edition," 1, (D.C. Rape Crisis Center, 1977), Smith College, Sophia Smith Collection of Women's History, Deb Friedman collection of feminist anti-violence records (SSC-MS-00795), Box 1, 51.
31 Sharon L. McCombie, ed., *The Rape Crisis Intervention Handbook: A Guide for Victim Care* (Plenum Press, 1980).
32 Sweet, *The Politics of Surviving*, 34–36.
33 Alexander, *The New Jim Crow*.
34 Soss, Fording, and Schram, *Disciplining the Poor*; Hinton, "'A War Within Our Own Boundaries.'"
35 Wendy Sawyer and Peter Wagner, "Mass Incarceration: The Whole Pie 2024" (Prison Policy Initiative, March 14, 2024), www.prisonpolicy.org.
36 Bevacqua, *Rape on the Public Agenda*; Richie, *Arrested Justice*; Alexander, *The New Jim Crow*.
37 "Capitalizing on Mass Incarceration: U.S. Growth in Private Prisons" (The Sentencing Project, 2018), https://dataspace.princeton.edu.
38 Sawyer and Wagner, "Mass Incarceration."
39 Hinton, "'A War Within Our Own Boundaries.'"
40 Cohen, "Punks, Bulldaggers, and Welfare Queens"; Hancock, *The Politics of Disgust*; Richie, *Arrested Justice*.
41 Aleks Kajstura and Wendy Sawyer, "Women's Mass Incarceration: The Whole Pie 2024" (Prison Policy Initiative, March 5, 2024), www.prisonpolicy.org
42 Salamon, *State of Nonprofit America*; Lisa Duggan, *The Twilight of Equality? Neoliberalism, Cultural Politics, and the Attack on Democracy* (Beacon Press, 2014), 16, 44.
43 INCITE!, *The Revolution Will Not Be Funded*.
44 Kim, "From Carceral Feminism to Transformative Justice."
45 Catharine A. MacKinnon, "Feminism, Marxism, Method, and the State: Toward Feminist Jurisprudence," *Signs* 8, no. 4 (1983): 635–58.
46 Bumiller, *In an Abusive State*.
47 "50 Years of Building Solutions, Supporting Communities, and Advancing Justice."
48 Lisa N. Sacco, "The Violence Against Women Act: Overview, Legislation, and Federal Funding" (Congressional Research Service, May 26, 2015), https://sgp.fas.org; Bevacqua, *Rape on the Public Agenda*, 169–73.
49 Tara Aday, "The Effectiveness of the Violence Against Women Act (VAWA) in Creating System-Level Change," *SPNHA Review* 11, no. 1 (2015): 8–9.
50 Bevacqua, *Rape on the Public Agenda*, 173; Zweig et al., "Community Approaches to Sexual Assault."

51 Bumiller, *In an Abusive State*.
52 Weiss, "Carceral Lock-In."
53 Collins, "The Tie That Binds."
54 Doug Meyer, "'So Much for Protect and Serve': Queer Male Survivors' Perceptions of Negative Police Experiences," *Journal of Contemporary Criminal Justice* 36, no. 2 (May 2020): 228–50, https://doi.org/10.1177/1043986219894430; Alondra D. Garza and Cortney A. Franklin, "The Effect of Rape Myth Endorsement on Police Response to Sexual Assault Survivors," *Violence Against Women* 27, no. 3–4 (March 2021): 552–73, https://doi.org/10.1177/1077801220911460.
55 Mulla, *Violence of Care*.
56 Kimberly A. Lonsway and Joanne Archambault, "The 'Justice Gap' for Sexual Assault Cases: Future Directions for Research and Reform," *Violence Against Women* 18, no. 2 (2012): 145–68, https://doi.org/10.1177/1077801212440017; Bach et al., "Underserved Survivors of Sexual Assault."
57 Taslitz, *Rape and the Culture of the Courtroom*; Susan Ehrlich, *Representing Rape: Language and Sexual Consent* (Routledge, 2001).
58 Terwiel, "What Is Carceral Feminism?," 2.
59 Susan Caringella, *Addressing Rape Reform in Law and Practice* (Columbia University Press, 2008), 20, https://doi.org/10.7312/cari13424; Alexandra Brodsky, "'Rape-Adjacent': Imagining Legal Responses to Nonconsensual Condom Removal," *Columbia Journal of Gender and Law* 32, no. 2 (2017): 183–210.
60 Patricia L. N. Donat and John D'Emilio, "A Feminist Redefinition of Rape and Sexual Assault: Historical Foundations and Change," *Journal of Social Issues* 48, no. 1 (1992): 9–22, https://doi.org/10.1111/j.1540-4560.1992.tb01154.x; Taslitz, *Culture of the Courtroom*; Ehrlich, *Representing Rape*; Stephen J. Schulhofer, "Reforming the Law of Rape," *Law & Inequality* 35, no. 2 (2017): 335–52.
61 Weiss, "Carceral Lock-In," 2.
62 "Frequently Asked Questions," National PREA Resource Center, February 3, 2020, www.prearesourcecenter.org.
63 Martin, *Rape Work*.
64 Storm Ervin et al., "Addressing Trauma and Victimization in Women's Prisons" (Urban Institute, October 2020), 29, www.urban.org.
65 "Police and Sheriff's Patrol Officers," O*Net OnLine, accessed March 21, 2024, www.onetonline.org; "Detectives and Criminal Investigators," O*Net OnLine, 2024, www.onetonline.org; "Lawyers," O*Net OnLine, accessed March 21, 2024, // www.onetonline.org.
66 "Registered Nurses," O*Net OnLine, accessed March 21, 2024, www.onetonline.org.
67 Rates for specifically sex crimes detectives, patrol officers, and attorneys are not available; SANEs are, by default, specialized in sexual assault. However, the stated rates in this book are estimates based on available data. Shelley S. Hyland and Elizabeth Davis, "Local Police Departments, 2016: Personnel" (U.S. Department of Justice, Office of Justice Programs, Bureau of Justice Statistics, October 2019), NCJ 252835, https://bjs.ojp.gov, 6; Rich Morin, Kim Parker, Renee Stepler, and

Andrew Mercer, "Inside America's Police Departments" (Pew Research Center, January 11, 2017), www.pewresearch.org; "Sex Crimes Detective Demographics and Statistics in the US," *Zippia*, accessed May 29, 2024, www.zippia.com; Connor Brooks, "Federal Law Enforcement Officers, 2020—Statistical Tables," U.S. Department of Justice, Office of Justice Programs, Bureau of Justice Statistics (September 2022), bjs.ojp.gov, 8; "Demographics," ABA Profile of the Legal Profession 2024, www.americanbar.org; "Enhancing Diversity in the Nursing Workforce" (American Association of Colleges of Nursing, April 2023), www.aacnnursing.org; "Results of the Job Analysis Study: Sexual Assault Nurse Examiner-Adult/Adolescent (SANE-A) Examination" (International Association of Forensic Nurses [IAFN], November 2017), www.forensicnurses.org, 12; Gusa, "White Institutional Presence."

68 Alexander, *The New Jim Crow*.
69 Rich Morin, Kim Parker, Renee Stepler, and Andrew Mercer, "Inside America's Police Departments" (Pew Research Center, January 11, 2017), www.pewresearch.org.
70 Leila Wood, "'I Look Across from Me and I See Me': Survivors as Advocates in Intimate Partner Violence Agencies," *Violence Against Women* 23, no. 3 (2016): 309–29, https://doi.org/10.1177/1077801216641518.
71 Cole, "Structural, Organizational, and Interpersonal Factors Influencing Interprofessional Collaboration on Sexual Assault Response Teams."
72 Alcoff and Gray, "Survivor Discourse."
73 Michel Foucault, *Discipline and Punish: The Birth of the Prison* (Vintage Books, 1977). Translated from the French by Alan Sheridan, 136.
74 Foucault, *Discipline and Punish*.
75 Kim, "Carceral Creep," 252.
76 Kim, "Carceral Creep," 252.
77 Tillman, "Carceral Liberalism."
78 Foucault, *Discipline and Punish*, 201–2.
79 Dilts, "Carceral Enjoyments and Killjoying the Social Life of Social Death," 198.
80 Lonsway and Archambault, "Justice Gap."
81 Jonathan M. Golding, Kellie R. Lynch, Sarah E. Malik, and Olivia Foster-Gimbel, "Justice Served? Perceptions of Plea Bargaining Involving a Sexual Assault in Child and Adult Females," *Criminal Justice and Behavior* 45, no. 4 (2018): 503–18, https://doi.org/10.1177/0093854817743538.
82 Jacquelyn C. Campbell, Nancy Glass, Phyllis W. Sharps, Kathryn Laughon, and Tina Bloom, "Intimate Partner Homicide: Review and Implications of Research and Policy," *Trauma, Violence, & Abuse* 8, no. 3 (July 2007): 246–69, https://doi.org/10.1177/1524838007303505.
83 "The Superpredator Myth, 25 Years Later," Equal Justice Initiative (EJI), April 7, 2014, https://eji.org.
84 Alex Press, "#MeToo Must Avoid 'Carceral Feminism,'" *Vox*, February 1, 2018, www.vox.com.

85 Corrigan, *Up Against a Wall*, 231–35; Bernstein, "Militarized Humanitarianism Meets Carceral Feminism."
86 Corey Rayburn Yung, "The Emerging Criminal War on Sex Offenders," *Harvard Civil Rights: Civil Liberties Law Review (CR-CL)* 45 (2010): 435.
87 Alexander, *The New Jim Crow*, 15, italics in original.
88 Nancy Wolff, Jessica Huening, Jing Shi, and B. Christopher Frueh, "Trauma Exposure and Posttraumatic Stress Disorder Among Incarcerated Men," *Journal of Urban Health* 91, no. 4 (2014): 707–19, https://doi.org/10.1007/s11524-014-9871-x.
89 Lexie Bean, ed., *Written on the Body: Letters from Trans and Non-Binary Survivors of Sexual Assault and Domestic Violence* (Jessica Kingsley Publishers, 2018).
90 Capers, "Real Rape, Too."
91 Rebecca Vallas, "Disabled Behind Bars: The Mass Incarceration of People with Disabilities in America's Jails and Prisons" (Center for American Progress, 2016), https://cdn.americanprogress.org.
92 Sheri Lynn Johnson, John H. Blume, and Amelia Courtney Hritz, "Convictions of Innocent People with Intellectual Disability," *Albany Law Review* 82, no. 3 (2019): 101–31.
93 Aya Gruber, *The Feminist War on Crime: The Unexpected Role of Women's Liberation in Mass Incarceration* (University of California Press, 2021).
94 Whalley, "'Bait and Switch' of Sexual Assault Response"; Weiss, "Carceral Lock-In."
95 Samuel R. Gross, Maurice Possley, and Klara Stephens, "Race and Wrongful Convictions in the United States," National Registry of Exonerations, Newkirk Center for Science and Society, University of California–Irvine, March 7, 2017, https://repository.law.umich.edu.
96 Sawyer and Wagner, "Mass Incarceration."
97 "Executive Order 14006 on January 26, 2021, Executive Order on Reforming Our Incarceration System to Eliminate the Use of Privately Operated Criminal Detention Facilities," *Code of Federal Regulations* 2021(02070), www.whitehouse.gov.
98 Kyle Virgien and Nina Patel, "President Biden's Order to Ban Private Prisons Faces a Persistent Internal Challenge: The U.S. Marshals Service," *ACLU Oregon*, March 4, 2024, www.aclu-or.org.
99 Alexander, *The New Jim Crow*, 288.
100 Ervin et al., "Addressing Trauma and Victimization in Women's Prisons," 33.
101 Cora Peterson, Sarah DeGue, Curtis Florence, and Globy N. Lokey, "Lifetime Economic Burden of Rape Among U.S. Adults," *American Journal of Preventive Medicine* 52, no. 6 (2017): 691–701, https://doi.org/10.1016/j.amepre.2016.11.014.
102 Sarah Gonzalez Bocinski and Malore Dusenbery, "The Financial Cost of Rape," Institute for Women's Policy Research, June 28, 2017, https://iwpr.org.
103 Heeju Sohn, "Racial and Ethnic Disparities in Health Insurance Coverage: Dynamics of Gaining and Losing Coverage over the Life-Course," *Population Research and Policy Review* 36, no. 2 (April 2017): 181–201, https://doi.org/10.1007/s11113-016-9416-y.

104 Nicole M. Heath, Shannon M. Lynch, April M. Fritch, and Maria M. Wong, "Silent Survivors: Rape Myth Acceptance in Incarcerated Women's Narratives of Disclosure and Reporting of Rape," *Psychology of Women Quarterly* 35, no. 4 (2011): 596–610, https://doi.org/10.1177/0361684311407870; Wolff et al., "Trauma Exposure and PTSD."
105 Crenshaw, "Mapping the Margins," 1250.
106 Lipsky, *Street-Level Bureaucracy*.
107 Beth E. Richie and Kayla M. Martensen, "Resisting Carcerality, Embracing Abolition: Implications for Feminist Social Work Practice," *Affilia* 35, no. 1 (2020): 12–16, https://doi.org/10.1177/0886109919897576.
108 Dilts, "Carceral Enjoyments and Killjoying the Social Life of Social Death," 213–15.
109 Wood, "'I Look Across From Me and I See Me.'"
110 Caringella, *Addressing Rape Reform in Law and Practice*, 203.
111 Richie, *Arrested Justice*, 133.
112 Kim and Kanuha, "Restorative Justice and the Dance with the Devil."
113 Marie Gottschalk, "Razing the Carceral State," *Social Justice* 42, no. 2 (2015): 35.
114 Mingus, "Pods and Pod-Mapping Worksheet."

CHAPTER 5. WHO COUNTS?

Epigraph: Leanne Betasamosake Simpson, *As We Have Always Done: Indigenous Freedom Through Radical Resistance* (University of Minnesota Press, 2017), 23–24, italics in original.

1 Estrich, *Real Rape*.
2 The interviewee is an Indigenous advocate who had watched the scene presented in this chapter between two other Native advocates unfold before her. She does not agree with the other advocates' approaches and had raised this experience to criticize quantification. I have rendered the scene as described by the advocate as a third party would have seen it, for two reasons. First, the advocate's retelling of this story was lengthy, and I do not have the space to recount the entire story here. Second, the rewritten story is a metacritique of the ways in which advocates retell stories for the purposes of grant writing. Just as advocates "speak for" survivors, here, I have "spoken for" the advocate and survivor, though in this case, unlike the way advocates collect data from victims for grant writing without their permissions, I have the express permission of the advocate to use her stories and perspectives for the purposes of advancing knowledge about victim advocacy.
3 Sally Engle Merry, *The Seductions of Quantification: Measuring Human Rights, Gender Violence, and Sex Trafficking* (University of Chicago Press, 2016).
4 Merry, *The Seductions of Quantification*; E. C. Levine, *Rape by the Numbers: Producing and Contesting Scientific Knowledge About Sexual Violence* (Rutgers University Press, 2021).
5 Frances K. Stage, "Answering Critical Questions Using Quantitative Data," *New Directions for Institutional Research* 2007, no. 133 (2007): 5–16, https://doi.org/10.1002/ir.200.

6 Merry, *Seductions of Quantification*.
7 Levine, *Rape by the Numbers*, 17.
8 Collins, "The Tie That Binds"; Kadji Amin, "Taxonomically Queer?," *GLQ: A Journal of Lesbian and Gay Studies* 29, no. 1 (2023): 91–107, https://doi.org/10.1215/10642684-10144435.
9 Spade, *Normal Life*, 2015.
10 Michel Foucault, *The Birth of Biopolitics: Lectures at the Collège de France, 1978–79*. Lectures at the Collège de France (Picador, 2010); Michel Foucault, *The History of Sexuality*. Vol. 1, *An Introduction* (Vintage Books, 1990), 140.
11 Crenshaw, "Mapping the Margins"; Collins, "The Tie That Binds."
12 Mehrotra, Kimball, and Wahab, "The Braid That Binds Us," 155; Merry, *Seductions of Quantification*, 50; Whittier, *Frenemies*, 171–78, 190–92.
13 Maier, "'We Belong to Them.'"
14 Bach et al., "Underserved Survivors of Sexual Assault"; Wegrzyn et al., "Rape Crisis Victim Advocacy."
15 Lisa Lindquist Dorr, *White Women, Rape, and the Power of Race in Virginia, 1900–1960* (University of North Carolina Press, 2004); Freedman, *Redefining Rape*.
16 Simpson, *As We Have Always Done*, 23.
17 Ida B. Wells, "Lynch Law in All Its Phases" (Speech, Boston, February 13, 1893), www.blackpast.org.
18 Notably, the UCRs continue to be hampered by police officers falsifying data. Corey Rayburn Yung analyzed the rates of rape crime reporting in 210 police departments across the United States and found that 22 percent of the reports produced by these departments contained irregularities, most of which can be attributed to police officers undercounting the number of rape reports. The crime of rape does not need to be reported if "evidence" produced by the victim witness is determined to be "unfounded." Corey Rayburn Yung, "How to Lie with Rape Statistics: America's Hidden Rape Crisis," *Iowa Law Review* 99, no. 3 (2014): 1197–1256.
19 "About the Uniform Crime Reporting (UCR) Program," Federal Bureau of Investigation Uniform Crime Reporting Program, accessed March 21, 2024, https://ucr.fbi.gov.
20 Alexandra Rutherford, "Surveying Rape: Feminist Social Science and the Ontological Politics of Sexual Assault," *History of the Human Sciences* 30, no. 4 (2017): 100–123, https://doi.org/10.1177/0952695117722715.
21 Jeffrey S. Adler, "Less Crime, More Punishment: Violence, Race, and Criminal Justice in Early Twentieth-Century America," *Journal of American History* 102, no. 1 (2015): 34–46, https://doi.org/10.1093/jahist/jav173.
22 Marie Gottschalk, *The Prison and the Gallows: The Politics of Mass Incarceration in America* (Cambridge University Press, 2006), 42.
23 "History of Lynching in America," NAACP, accessed March 21, 2024, https://naacp.org.
24 Freedman, *Redefining Rape*, 265–69; Jacquet, *The Injustices of Rape*, 172–82.

25 Jacquet, *The Injustices of Rape*, 51–55.
26 Ersula J. Ore, *Lynching: Violence, Rhetoric, and American Identity* (University Press of Mississippi, 2019).
27 Amir, "Victim Precipitated Forcible Rape."
28 Brownmiller, *Against Our Will*, 174.
29 "Rape Research: Correspondence, 1971–1975, Undated," Harvard Schlesinger Library, Radcliffe Institute, Papers of Susan Brownmiller, 1935–2000, Series III. WRITINGS, Subseries C. Against Our Will, Box 11, accessed January 23, 2024, https://hollisarchives.lib.harvard.edu.
30 "Correspondence (Friends), 1975–1979, Undated; Correspondence (Feminists), 1975–1979, Undated; Correspondence (Critical Letters), 1975–1977," Harvard Schlesinger Library, Radcliffe Institute, Papers of Susan Brownmiller, 1935–2000, Series III. WRITINGS, Subseries C. Against Our Will, Box 7, accessed January 23, 2024, https://hollisarchives.lib.harvard.edu.
31 Yolanda Bako, "'Rape Coalition,' 1973–1979," Harvard Schlesinger Library, Radcliffe Institute, Papers of Yolanda Bako, 1970–1995 (MC 943: Vt-105), Box 1, accessed January 25, 2024; "Correspondence (Friends), 1975–1979, Undated; Correspondence (Feminists), 1975–1979, Undated; Correspondence (Critical Letters), 1975–1977," Box 3, accessed January 25, 2024, https://hollisarchives.lib.harvard.edu.
32 Mary Ann Largen, "A Report on Rape in the Suburbs: Rape Rate on the Rise in Northern Virgina, Washington" (NOW, 1973), Harvard Schlesinger Library, Radcliffe Institute, Papers of Yolanda Bako, 197–1995 (MC 943: Vt-105), Box 3, accessed January 25, 2024, https://hollisarchives.lib.harvard.edu.
33 Rutherford, "Surveying Rape," 105.
34 Ann Burgess and Lynda L. Holmstrom, "Rape Trauma Syndrome," *American Journal of Psychiatry* 131, no. 9 (1974): 981–86.
35 Mary P. Koss's study initially produced a "one in five" statistic; however, since the publication of her study, the number has shifted in many rape crisis center reporting measures to "one in four." Rutherford, "Surveying Rape." Mary P. Koss, "Hidden Rape: Incidence and Prevalence of Sexual Aggression and Victimization in a National Sample of Students in Higher Education" (National Institute of Mental Health, 1985), https://files.eric.ed.gov.
36 Rutherford, "Surveying Rape."
37 Koss, "Hidden Rape," 7.
38 Bevacqua, *Rape on the Public Agenda*, 170; Rutherford, "Surveying Rape."
39 Bevacqua, *Rape on the Public Agenda*, 190.
40 Mehrotra, Kimball, and Wahab, "The Braid That Binds Us"; Rutherford, "Surveying Rape"; Levine, *Rape by the Numbers*.
41 "Third World Women and Rape," in "Report from the First National Conference on Third World Women and Violence August 1980," 8, Smith College Archives, Loretta J. Ross papers, SSC-MS-00504, Series IV Organization Files, Box 34, folder 10: National Women's Health Network, Rape Crisis Center 1980–93, n.d.

42 Levine, *Rape by the Numbers*.
43 David Gillborn, Paul Warmington, and Sean Demack, "QuantCrit: Education, Policy, 'Big Data,' and Principles for a Critical Race Theory of Statistics," *Race, Ethnicity, and Education* 21, no. 2 (2018): 158–79, https://doi.org/10.1080/13613324.2017.1377417.
44 Rutherford, "Surveying Rape," 111.
45 Mary P. Koss, "The Under Detection of Rape: Methodological Choices Influence Incidence Estimates," *Journal of Social Issues* 48, no. 1 (April 1992): 61–75, https://doi.org/10.1111/j.1540-4560.1992.tb01157.x; Rutherford, "Surveying Rape," 114; Levine, *Rape by the Numbers*, 96–100.
46 Bevacqua, *Rape on the Public Agenda*, 170.
47 Aday, "The Effectiveness of the Violence Against Women Act (VAWA) in Creating System-Level Change," 8–9.
48 "Sexual Assault Services Formula Grant Program (SASP)," US Department of Justice, Office on Violence Against Women (OVW), 2024, www.justice.gov.
49 "STOP Violence Against Women Formula Grant Program," US Department of Justice, Office on Violence Against Women (OVW), 2024, www.justice.gov.
50 "STOP Violence Against Women Formula Grant Program."
51 There is no study that has sampled all US nonprofit rape crisis centers and assessed their finances. Faulk et al. studied just charitable nonprofits, excluding major hospitals or other corporate interests from their study, and estimated that charitable nonprofits receive around 62 percent of their funding, on average, from federal and state grants. Faulk et al.'s study is probably more accurate for rape crisis centers than other studies on nonprofit revenue because rape crisis centers do not usually seek (large) corporate (private) partnerships. Lewis Faulk et al., "Nonprofit Trends and Impacts 2021: National Findings on Donation Trends from 2015 Through 2020, Diversity and Representation, and First-Year Impacts of the COVID-19 Pandemic" (Urban Institute, 2021), www.urban.org; The NonProfit Times, "80% Of Nonprofits' Revenue Is from Government, Fee for Service," *Non-Profit Times*, September 19, 2019, https://thenonprofittimes.com.
52 Recording survivors' social identities is not new in crime reporting methods. The FBI has recorded crime victims' racial and gender identities for the UCRs since 1957. However, interest in collecting demographic data within rape prevalence studies only began in the 1990s and came to full force by the 2010s. "About the Uniform Crime Reporting (UCR) Program"; Levine, *Rape by the Numbers*, 99–100.
53 Joseph R. Biden, "Advancing Racial Equity and Support for Underserved Communities Through the Federal Government," Pub. L. No. Executive Order 13985 (2021), www.federalregister.gov.
54 "Justice Department Releases Update to Equity Action Plan" (U.S. Department of Justice, Office of Public Affairs, February 14, 2024), www.justice.gov.
55 "About BJS," Bureau of Justice Statistics, accessed March 21, 2024, https://bjs.ojp.gov.
56 "OVW Fiscal Year 2024 Grants to Enhance Culturally Specific Services for Victims of Domestic Violence, Dating Violence, Sexual Assault, and Stalking

Program—Solicitation" (US Department of Justice, Office on Violence Against Women, March 13, 2024), www.justice.gov, 5.

57 "OVW Fiscal Year 2024 Grants to Enhance Culturally Specific Services for Victims of Domestic Violence, Dating Violence, Sexual Assault, and Stalking Program—Solicitation," 19.

58 Maier, "Rape Crisis Centers and Programs"; Aday, "Effectiveness of VAWA."

59 Maier, "'We Belong to Them'"; Mehrotra, Kimball, and Wahab, "The Braid That Binds Us."

60 For example, only ten agencies in the United States received a minority grant in 2022. "Culturally Specific Services Program," US Department of Justice, Office on Violence Against Women (OVW), 2023, www.justice.gov.

61 "Executive Orders Affecting Charitable Nonprofits" (National Council of Nonprofits, January 22, 2025), www.councilofnonprofits.org.

62 One could argue that every rape crisis center has its own system to track and record survivor data. Indeed, grant agencies do not regulate the information shared among centers. However, the grants to which advocates apply are identical. As grant agencies are a federal and state funding source, grant opportunities must be the same to all applicants. Therefore, even though funding agencies do not explicitly require the same tracking system, advocates nevertheless collect the same information, acquiescing to funders' normative interpretations of identity.

63 Pamela Nilan, "'Dangerous Fieldwork' Re-Examined: The Question of Researcher Subject Position," *Qualitative Research* 2, no. 3 (December 2002): 363–86, https://doi.org/10.1177/146879410200200305.

64 Foucault, *The Birth of Biopolitics*.

65 Spade, *Normal Life*.

66 Mehrotra, Kimball, and Wahab, "The Braid That Binds Us," 155.

67 It is arguable that advocate documents are collected not for the purposes of funding alone but for the prosecution of the offender. In her examination of sexual assault forensic examiners, Sameena Mulla explained that documents by both advocates and other systems professionals "are not as disparate as they appear both in content and in purpose. In addition, though they originate and pass through different trajectories, they share overlapping trajectories. The narratives collected by the [patrol] police officer, the police detective, and the forensic nurse examiner will be reunited in the files of the state's attorney if the case moves toward prosecution." I believe that Mulla's assessment of the social life of advocacy documents does not contradict my assessment but rather complements it. As the nonprofit industrial complex is interrelated with the prison industrial complex under the prison nation, the documents serve the same purpose: to monitor and regulate victims. Mulla, *Violence of Care*, 157.

68 Maier, "'We Belong to Them,'" 1401.

69 Kath Browne, "Queer Quantification or Queer(y)Ing Quantification: Creating Lesbian, Gay, Bisexual, or Heterosexual Citizens Through Governmental Social

Research," in *Queer Methods and Methodologies*, ed. Kath Brown and Catherine J. Nash (Routledge, 2018), 231–50.

70 Scott Lauria Morgensen, *Spaces Between Us: Queer Settler Colonialism and Indigenous Decolonization* (University of Minnesota Press, 2011), 109; Alex Wilson, "Our Coming In Stories: Cree Identity, Body Sovereignty, and Gender Self-Determination," *Journal of Global Indigeneity* 1, no. 1 (2015): 1–5.

71 Au, "Asian American Racialization."

72 Morgensen, *Spaces Between Us*.

73 Linda Alcoff, "The Problem of Speaking for Others," *Cultural Critique* 20 (Winter 1991–1992): 7, italics in original, https://doi.org/10.2307/1354221.

74 Donna Haraway, "Situated Knowledges: The Science Question in Feminism and the Privilege of Partial Perspective," *Feminist Studies* 14, no. 3 (1988): 575, https://doi.org/10.2307/3178066.

75 To be sure, advocates "speak for" survivors when they serve as representatives on behalf of survivors to funders. As a key part of their work, advocates emotionally validate survivors' experiences by listening to their stories and then ensuring that victims' stories are treated with respect and care by other systems professionals. However, when advocates *record* survivors, their identities, and their experiences for the purposes of aggregating data for grants, they are altering the story.

76 It is unknown whether the advocate accidentally disclosed the names of the survivor; therefore, I have altered the names in the event of unintended disclosure.

77 Amin, "Taxonomically Queer?," italics in original.

78 Alcoff, "The Problem of Speaking for Others," 23.

79 Spivak, "Can the Subaltern Speak?"

80 Winnubst, "The Many Lives of Fungibility," 108–9.

81 David M. Heger, "The Violence Against Women Act of 1994" (National Violence Against Women Prevention Research Center, University of Missouri–St. Louis, December 7, 2000), https://mainweb-v.musc.edu.

82 I used the Inflation Counter at InflationTool (www.inflationtool.com) to calculate for inflation.

83 Lisa N. Sacco and Emily J. Hanson, "The Violence Against Women Act (VAWA): Historical Overview, Funding, and Reauthorization" (Congressional Research Service, April 23, 2019), https://crsreports.congress.gov, i.

84 Janelle A. Kerlin and Tom H. Pollak, "Nonprofit Commercial Revenue: A Replacement for Declining Government Grants and Private Contributions?," *American Review of Public Administration* 41, no. 6 (2011): 686–704, https://doi.org/10.1177/0275074010387293.

85 Gunther, "What Are Rape Crisis Centers."

86 Data on the exact number of rape crisis centers in the United States per year are unavailable, and estimates are unreliable. The National Sexual Violence Resource Center estimates that there are twelve hundred anti-violence agencies, while the National Network to End Domestic Violence, which only accounts for anti–domestic violence and dual (not anti-rape-only) agencies, estimates that there are about two

thousand community agencies. The variation may occur because some organizations do not count culturally specific agencies or for-profit or public agencies; it may also occur because many anti-violence agencies open and close quickly, or for another reason. Despite the unknown number, anti-violence scholar-activists generally presume that there are more anti-violence agencies today than in the 1990s precisely because of VAWA and the formalization of rape crisis centers. Indeed, the number of *nonprofits*—including human services nonprofits—grew exponentially between the 1990s and the 2010s, and recent data show that this trend is likely to continue into the 2020s despite the COVID-19 pandemic. This trend, correlated with the increase in the absorption of rape crisis centers into larger social services programs, suggests that there are more rape crisis centers, albeit ones that are not independent, than in the 1990s. Salamon, *State of Nonprofit America*; Faulk et al., "Nonprofit Trends and Impacts 2021"; Maier, "'We Belong to Them'"; "Domestic Violence Counts Annual Summary," National Network to End Domestic Violence, 2022, www.nnedv.org.
87   "Culturally Specific Services Program."
88   Levine, *Rape by the Numbers*.
89   Mehrotra, Kimball, and Wahab, "The Braid That Binds Us."
90   Dian Million, *Therapeutic Nations: Healing in an Age of Indigenous Human Rights* (University of Arizona Press, 2014).
91   Mel Y. Chen, *Animacies: Biopolitics, Racial Mattering, and Queer Affect* (Duke University Press, 2012), 38.
92   Amin, "Taxonomically Queer?," 94.
93   Browne, "Queer Quantification," 241.
94   Michelle Fine, Lois Weis, Susan Weseen, and Loonmun Wong, "For Whom? Qualitative Research, Representations, and Social Responsibilities," in *The Landscape of Qualitative Research*, 2nd ed. (Sage, 2003), 167–207.
95   Kamden K. Strunk, "QuantQueer: Renovating Quantitative Methods Through Queer and Critical Theoretical Traditions," *Educational Studies* 60, no. 1 (2024): 5–18, https://doi.org/10.1080/00131946.2023.2276229.
96   Smith, *Decolonizing Methodologies*.
97   Collins, *Black Feminist Thought*, 4.
98   Strunk, "QuantQueer," 6.
99   "API-GBV Applauds the Revisions to Collecting Federal Data on Race and Ethnicity Statistical Policy Directive No. 15: Standards for Maintaining, Collecting, and Presenting Federal Data on Race and Ethnicity," Asian Pacific Institute on Gender-Based Violence, April 1, 2024, www.api-gbv.org.
100 Ghaziani and Brim, *Imagining Queer Methods*, 17.
101 Some scholars contest the idea that rape is still a social problem, suggesting that rape *used to be* a social problem but, because of anti-rape organizing, it is now no longer a problem. However, while rape may not be as pressing an issue as it was in activist discourses in the 1970s, even these scholars admit that rape at least *was* a social problem. Thus, the only point of difference is the *degree* to which rape is a social problem.

102 Hulsether, *Capitalist Humanitarianism*, 143.
103 Mulla, *Violence of Care*.
104 Schulhofer, *Unwanted Sex*.
105 Fischel, *Screw Consent*.
106 Hulsether, *Capitalist Humanitarianism*, 134–35.
107 Hulsether, *Capitalist Humanitarianism*, 64, 66.
108 Lauren Berlant, *Cruel Optimism* (Duke University Press, 2011).
109 Hulsether, *Capitalist Humanitarianism*, 143.
110 Sarah Deer, *The Beginning and End of Rape: Confronting Sexual Violence in Native America* (University of Minnesota Press, 2015), 9.
111 Maggie Walter and Michele Suina, "Indigenous Data, Indigenous Methodologies, and Indigenous Data Sovereignty," *International Journal of Social Research Methodology* 22, no. 3 (May 4, 2019): 235, https://doi.org/10.1080/13645579.2018.1531228.
112 Walter and Suina, "Indigenous Data, Indigenous Methodologies, and Indigenous Data Sovereignty," 236.
113 Chen, *Animacies*, 39.
114 Chen, *Animacies*, 39.
115 Amin, "Taxonomically Queer?," 97, italics in original.
116 V. Jo Hsu, "(Trans)Forming #MeToo: Toward a Networked Response to Gender Violence," *Women's Studies in Communication* 42, no. 3 (2019): 269–86, https://doi.org/10.1080/07491409.2019.1630697.
117 Hsu, "(Trans)Forming #MeToo," 283.
118 Hsu, "(Trans)Forming #MeToo," 280.
119 Schenwar and Law, *Prison by Any Other Name*, 162.
120 Simpson, *As We Have Always Done*, 20.

CONCLUSION

1 Puar, *Terrorist Assemblages*, xxv.
2 The Fireweed Collective, "When It All Comes Crashing Down: Navigating Crisis," in *Beyond Survival: Strategies and Stories from the Transformative Justice Movement*, ed. Ejeris Dixon and Leah Lakshmi Piepzna-Samarasinha (AK Press, 2020), 128.
3 Ruth Wilson Gilmore, "Forgotten Places and the Seeds of Grassroots Planning," in *Abolition Geography: Essays Towards Liberation* (Verso, 2022), 412.
4 Wood, "'I Look Across from Me and I See Me.'"
5 Joanne Barker, "The Corporation and the Tribe," in *Colonial Racial Capitalism*, ed. Susan Koshy et al. (Duke University Press, 2022), 33–59.
6 Chris Fitzgerald, (no subject), email to Embrace Board of Directors, September 15, 2020.
7 Jennifer R. Zelnick, Sara Goodkind, and Mimi E. Kim, "'It Would Be Foolish to Pretend That Our Jobs Aren't Political': Social Workers Organizing for Power in the Nonprofit Sector," *Affilia* 37, no. 1 (February 2022): 5–12, https://doi.org/10.1177/08861099211065926.

8   Gilmore, "Forgotten Places and the Seeds of Grassroots Planning," 448, italics in original.
9   Gilmore, "Forgotten Places and the Seeds of Grassroots Planning," 448.
10 hooks, *Killing Rage*, 19.
11 Brittney C. Cooper, *Eloquent Rage: A Black Feminist Discovers Her Superpower* (Picador, 2019), 5–6.
12 Kaba and Hassan, *Fumbling Towards Repair*.

APPENDIX A
1   Crenshaw, "Demarginalizing the Intersection," 140.
2   Lipsky, *Street-Level Bureaucracy*, x.
3   Corrigan, *Up Against a Wall*, 61–62.
4   Baker and Bevacqua, "Challenging Narratives of the Anti-Rape Movement's Decline."
5   Bumiller, *In an Abusive State*, xii, xv.
6   Corrigan, *Up Against a Wall*, 55–56, italics in original.
7   Herbert Rubin and Irene Rubin, *Qualitative Interviewing: The Art of Hearing Data* (Sage, 2005).
8   Charles L. Briggs, *Learning How to Ask: A Sociolinguistic Appraisal of the Role of the Interview in Social Science Research* (Cambridge University Press, 1986), 2.
9   Sandra Harding, "'Strong Objectivity': A Response to the New Objectivity Question," *Synthese* 104, no. 3 (1995): 331–49.
10 Holly Taylor-Dunn, Lis Bates, Dominic Reed, Anna Hopkins, and Shona Morrison, "Researching Gender-Based Violence Remotely During a Pandemic: Challenges, Opportunities, and Methodological Implications," *Journal of Gender-Based Violence*, December 14, 2023, 1–17, https://doi.org/10.1332/23986808Y2023D000000009.
11 Sarah E. Ullman, "Conducting Virtual Interviews with Sexual Assault Survivors and Their Informal Supports During COVID-19 and Beyond," *Journal of Interpersonal Violence* 39, no. 7–8 (2024): 1398–1420, https://doi.org/10.1177/08862605231207619.
12 The duration of each interview was calculated by rounding up or down to the closest whole minute mark.
13 Freedman, *Redefining Rape*.
14 Frantz Fanon, *Black Skin, White Masks* (Pluto Press, 2002); Maier, "Rape Victim Advocates' Perception of the Influence of Race and Ethnicity on Victims' Responses to Rape."
15 Anna Carastathis, "The Concept of Intersectionality in Feminist Theory," *Philosophy Compass* 9, no. 5 (2014): 304–14, https://doi.org/10.1111/phc3.12129.
16 Barney G. Glaser and Anselm L. Strauss, *The Discovery of Grounded Theory: Strategies for Qualitative Research* (Routledge, 2017).
17 Kathy Charmaz, *Constructing Grounded Theory* (Sage, 2014), 14, italics in original.

18 James Paul Gee, *An Introduction to Discourse Analysis: Theory and Method* (Routledge, 1999), 4.
19 Johnny Saldaña, *The Coding Manual for Qualitative Researchers*, 2nd ed. (Sage, 2013), 96, 110.
20 Teun A. van Dijk, "Principles of Critical Discourse Analysis," *Discourse & Society* 4, no. 2 (1993): 249–83.
21 Browne and Nash, *Queer Methods and Methodologies*.
22 Wood, "'I Look Across From Me and I See Me.'"
23 Rebecca Hanson and Patricia Richards, *Harassed: Gender, Bodies, and Ethnographic Research* (University of California Press, 2019).
24 D'Cruze, "Approaching the History of Rape."
25 Gesa E. Kirsch, Romeo García, Caitlin Burns Allen, and Walker P. Smith, eds., *Unsettling Archival Research* (Southern Illinois University Press, 2023), https://doi.org/10.2307/jj.9669312.

APPENDIX C

1 Eve Kosofsky Sedgwick, *Epistemology of the Closet* (University of California Press, 1990); Wilson, "Our Coming In Stories."
2 Davis et al., *Abolition. Feminism. Now.*
3 Freedman, *Redefining Rape*.
4 Martin, *Rape Work*.
5 Ahmed, *The Cultural Politics of Emotion*.
6 Foucault, *The Birth of Biopolitics*.
7 Terwiel, "What Is Carceral Feminism?," 2.
8 Foucault, *Discipline and Punish*.
9 Wood et al., "Turnover Intention and Job Satisfaction."
10 New York Radical Feminists, *Rape: The First Sourcebook for Women*.
11 Bourdieu, "Cultural Reproduction and Social Reproduction."
12 Truth, "Ain't I a Wummon?"
13 Richie, "Reimagining the Movement to End Gender Violence."
14 Ahmed, *Feminist Killjoy Handbook*.
15 Winnubst, "The Many Lives of Fungibility."
16 Williams, "The Glass Escalator."
17 Crenshaw, "Demarginalizing the Intersection"; Anna Julia Cooper, *A Voice from the South* (Aldine, 1982). Reprinted by Project Gutenberg, April 2, 2020, www.gutenberg.org.
18 Savannah Shange, *Progressive Dystopia: Abolition, Antiblackness, and Schooling in San Francisco* (Duke University Press, 2019).
19 Bach et al., "Underserved Survivors of Sexual Assault."
20 Sweet, *The Politics of Surviving*.
21 Kolb, *Moral Wages*.
22 Melamed, "The Spirit of Neoliberalism."
23 Spade, "Solidarity, Not Charity," 136.

24 Harvey, *A Brief History*.
25 INCITE!, *The Revolution Will Not Be Funded*.
26 Spade, *Normal Life*.
27 Foucault, *Discipline and Punish*, 201–2.
28 Mulla, *The Violence of Care*.
29 Christie, "The Ideal Victim."
30 Puar, "Precarity Talk."
31 Gusa, "White Institutional Presence."
32 Critical Resistance and INCITE!, "Statement on Gender-Based Violence."
33 Richie, *Arrested Justice*, 3.
34 Merry, *Seductions of Quantification*.
35 Judith Butler, *Gender Trouble: Feminism and the Subversion of Identity* (Routledge, 1990); Roderick Ferguson, *Aberrations in Black: Toward a Queer of Color Critique* (University of Minnesota Press, 2003).
36 Robinson, *Black Marxism*, 2.
37 Pulido, *Black, Brown, Yellow, and Left*, 25.
38 INCITE!, *Color of Violence: The INCITE! Anthology* (Duke University Press, 2016).
39 Annalise Acorn, *Compulsory Compassion: A Critique of Restorative Justice* (UBC Press, 2005).
40 Campbell et al., "Preventing the 'Second Rape.'"
41 Suzanne Slattery and Lisa A. Goodman, "Secondary Traumatic Stress Among Domestic Violence Advocates," *Violence Against Women* 15, no. 11 (2009): 1358–79. https://doi.org/10.1177/1077801209347469.
42 Mulla, *The Violence of Care*.
43 Cole, "Structural, Organizational, and Interpersonal Factors Influencing Interprofessional Collaboration on Sexual Assault Response Teams."
44 Bobby Harro, "The Cycle of Socialization," in *Readings for Diversity and Social Justice*, ed. Maurianne Adams et al., 27–34 (Routledge, 2018).
45 Haraway, "Situated Knowledges."
46 Alcoff and Gray, "Survivor Discourse."
47 Martin, *Rape Work*.
48 Merry, *Seductions of Quantification*.
49 Office for Victims of Crime Training & Technical Assistance Center.
50 Kim, "Carceral Creep."
51 Dixon and Lakshmi Piepzna-Samarasinha, *Beyond Survival*.
52 Arvin et al., "Decolonizing Feminism."
53 Gusa, "White Institutional Presence."

INDEX

NOTE: The following abbreviations are used in this index: "RCC" for rape crisis center; "NPIC" for nonprofit industrial complex; and "CCTs" for cultural competency trainings. Page numbers in *italics* denote tables and other illustrative material.

2SLGBTQIA+ people: CCTs about, 70, 71–72; definition of, 237; and queer methodologies of the text, 223; radical advocacy advancements by, 9–10, 11, 12, 126; Two-Spirit people, 16, 91, 181, 237. *See also* lesbians; marginalized advocates; marginalized survivors; queer communities of color; queer people (inclusive of 2SLGBTQIA+ people and those who live outside of normative constructs); trans and gender-diverse people

abbreviations used in this text, 241–42
abolition, definition of, 50, 237
abolitionist histories: definition of abolition, 50, 237; as long history, 9, 13, 27–28, 41; no single "real" movement or "right" way of doing advocacy, 32, 40, 41, 42, 44, 50. *See also* anti-rape movement history, recovering

—DECONSTRUCTION OF PAST HISTORIES: active armed defense, 45; banishment, 44; democratic values, 49; industrialization and housing and labor justice, 46–50; maroon communities, 44–45; murder, suicide, and self-harm, 44, 45–46; mutual aid collectives and community building, 48–50; myth that rape didn't exist in Indigenous communities prior to colonization, 41–42; nonviolence as response to violence (restorative justice), 49; property law analysis elides rape of marginalized women and girls, 42–43, 59; raiding, 43–44, 45; vs. secondary victimization by dominant/hegemonic histories, 41; social protests and movements, as first to be cut from neoliberal budgets, 83; spectrum of anti-rape advocacy activities, 43–46; spiritual reclamation, 44, 73

—IMAGINED FUTURE HISTORIES: advocacy as multiplicity of actions taken, 44, 45–46; as beyond the binary between rape law reform and non- or extralegal anti-rape justice, 44; community building, 49–50; creation of transformative justice organizations armed by practices of mutual aid, 45; hyperinstitutionalization of advocacy, 126–30, 197–99; mutual aid collectives, 45, 48–50, 126–27; mutual aid principle of coalitional consciousness raising, 49; and the question: "Is this still advocacy?," 51–53; wage improvements, 126, 129. *See also* radicalism, reclaiming for advocacy; radical rape crisis advocacy (outside carceral systems)

abortion, 33; call-outs, 34
ACLU (American Civil Liberties Union), 30; Women's Rights Project (WRP), 30
activist scholarship, 206–7
acute rape, definition of, 237
Addams, Jane, Hull House and the settlement house movement, 47–48
administration: direct services advocates also working in, 217; diversity as low among top management, 124; grants manager mandated by law, 98; hiring and recruitment formalization, 99. *See also* direct services advocates; funding by government grants; professionalization of the rape crisis center
—HIERARCHY BETWEEN DIRECT SERVICES AND: overview, 98–99; authorization requests from advocates for services and, 99–100; survivors noticing and affected by, 119; upper management, lack of diversity in, 124; wage hierarchy, 112–14, 116–17, 119, 122, 264nn62,64; wage hierarchy chart with salary, race, and gender, *113*. *See also* BIPOC—administrators; professional advocacy
—ADVOCATE COORDINATORS: authorization requests from advocates for services, 85, 99–100; insufficient time allocated for training, 107; and professionalization of anti-violence work, 137; and quantification of victims, 180; trainings hosted by, 103, 105, 121
advocacy. *See* anti-rape advocacy
advocacy trainings: cultural humility training, 77, 78; difficulty of covering intersectional issues in time allotted for, 77; Sexual Assault Services Program (SASP), 98, 176–77, 262n35; should offer all possible assistance to all survivors, 82; Victim Assistance Training (VAT), 74, 75. *See also* cultural competency trainings (CCTs)
—AND PROFESSIONALIZATION: overview, 102; attrition rates of marginalized advocates, 106, 107; barriers to participation by prospective marginalized advocates, 104–7; baseline training (sample), *103*; college degrees allowed to substitute for, 107–11; hours-of-training requirements for incoming advocates, 102, 105–6, 107, 263n51; implicit biases not addressed in, 104–5; introducing social norms about who can and should conduct advocacy, 104–7; lived experience of marginalized advocates as devalued in, 104–5, 107; locations of, geographic discrimination in, 106; marginalized survivors' culturally specific needs not taught in, 102–4, 106; as only discussing identities per mandatory reporting requirements, 102; radical protest elided in, 103–4; systems responses as focus of, 102–4, 106. *See also* college education and professionalization; professional advocacy
advocates: definition of, 21–22, 237; intersectional harm done by, 215–16; radical self-image of, 7, 55; as survivors of sexual assault, 14, 160, 201–2, 205, 225, 226. *See also* advocacy trainings; direct services advocates; professional advocacy
advocates of color: and CCTs, 70, 73; expectation they will remedy their own racist encounters, 260n4; lived experience of, utilized in support, 104, 105; non-Black, fungibility and overburdening of, 117–18. *See also* BIPOC—advocates
affect, definition of, 237

affective advocacy, 8. *See also* care work; ugly emotions
affective enjoyment produced by carceralism, 155–56, 160
African Americans. *See* Black communities
African People's Socialist Party, 38
agricultural justice, 88, 104. *See also* farming communities
Ahmed, Sara, feminist killjoy, 8
Alcoff, Linda Martín, 182, 185
Alexander, Michelle, 136, 157
Amin, Kadji, 184, 188
Amir, Menachim: anti-Black rape study (discredited), 136, 173, 175. *See also* Brownmiller, Susan
anti-Blackness and anti-Black racism: advocates experiencing from survivors in workplace, 115–16; advocates experiencing in workplace, expectation they will remedy their own racist encounters, 260n4; apology by National Association of Social Workers for their contributions to racist practices, 97; arrests, convictions, sentencing, and exonerations as disproportionate, 30, 158, 172, 173; Black survivors as vulnerable in RCCs, 36; fungibility, 117–18, 237; methodology as highlighting, 221; Oppression Pyramid, 135; tensions in RCCs cast as "professional" conflicts, instead of acts of anti-Black racism, 90–94, 122, 128–29, 260nn2–4; white and white-acting folks interrupting, 129; and white settler economic dispossession as oppression, 57. *See also* lynching of Black men; racism; racist rape myths used to target Black men
anticrime rhetoric: anti-rape agencies turning to "crime and control" solutions, 136–37; Black men's existence criminalized, 134–38; entangling carceral approaches with antipoverty projects, 135–38; labeling people of color "criminals," 135–38; poor people declared to be the cause of crime, 135–36, 137–38; radical activists labeled "terrorists" and "criminals," 135; white normative families and normative-acting people of color as "worthy" and "innocent" poor, 135. *See also* mass incarceration
anti-rape advocacy: as arsenal of tools, 85–86; ethos of, to continuously reduce harm and build a safe and liberated world free from violence, 5, 27, 50; in relation, 85–89. *See also* abolitionist histories; anti-rape movement history, recovering; domestic violence movement; mainstream advocacy histories; radical rape crisis advocacy (outside carceral systems); rape crisis centers, neoliberal; rape law reform
anti-rape movement history, recovering: overview, 23–24; archival fractals and destabilization of normativity, 26, 42; conventional storytelling as insufficient for, 24; critical fabulation method, 25–26, 42–46; as discourse on and around the surviving evidences, 25; dissemblance as challenge in, 25; dominant narratives as erasing the radicalism of, 23–24, 26–27, 31–32, 39–40; dominant narratives as reworking the mechanisms by which we know history (colonial epistemicide), 24–25, 42; dominant narratives redefining past advocacy as illegitimate or unprofessional, 26–27; feeling rape is anti-rape work, 24; no single "real" movement or "right" way of doing advocacy, 32, 40, 41, 42, 44, 50; patterned or scenic storytelling, 27. *See also* abolitionist histories; radicalism, reclaiming for advocacy; radical rape crisis advocacy (outside carceral systems)

anti-violence movement: anti-pornography, 29, 31, 32; anti-sexual harassment policies, 139; child sexual abuse, 28, 103, 108–9, 157; Missing and Murdered Indigenous People/Women, Girls, and Two-Spirit People (MMIP/WG2S), 43, 91, 109, 193; stalking, 178. *See also* anti-rape movement history, recovering; domestic violence movement; mainstream advocacy histories; rape law reform

Aptheker, Bettina, 49

Arab women, and the Third World movement, 33

archival research: overview, 228–29; archival fractals and destabilization of dominant historical narrative, 26, 42; assumption in some archives that research can only be conducted by credentialed academics, 229; critical queering methodology, 230; decolonial methodology, 230; finding the voices of BIPOC activists' research, 229; Harvard University, Schlesinger Library, 228–29, 231–32; listening for missing or fragmented voices, 230; list of documents reviewed, 231–32; online archives, academic and nonacademic, 230; recording and cataloguing materials, 231; Schomburg Center for Research in Black Culture (New York Public Library), 229–30, 232; Smith College, Sophia Smith Collections, 228–29, 231; "third" reading of primary materials in conversation with secondary sources, 14–15; timeframe of, 216. *See also* methodology

Asian communities: CCTs about, 72; college degrees held by, 108, 263–64n58; immigrants, and housing and labor justice, 47, 48. *See also* Hawai'i; Pacific Islander communities

—ASIAN WOMEN: socialist-like communes during industrialization, 48; as survivors, vulnerability to racism by anti-rape advocates, 36, 72; and the Third World movement, 33

Asian rape crisis advocates: on class and disparities of care, 67; on the exclusion of noncredentialed advocates, 111

attorneys: secondary victimization by, 141; significant majority identify as white men, 145; wage hierarchy and state's judgment of rape response roles, 145, 270–71n67; wage hierarchy chart with salary, race, and gender, *113*

attrition and alienation: of BIPOC advocates who ascend to middle management, 124; of direct services advocates vs. administrators, due to the wage gap, 112, 114, 116–17, 122; of marginalized advocates, 7, 116–17, 118, 122–23, 215; of marginalized advocates, from training, 106, 107; of marginalized survivors, due to lack of culturally specific advocacy, 67–68, 74, 75, 83, 87–88, 150, 192. *See also* compassion fatigue and burnout

azithromycin, 57

Baker, Carrie N., 11, 12, 217
Baker, Charlene K., 12
Baker, Ella, 229
Bako, Yolanda, 50
Barker, Joanne, 205
Bay Area Transformative Justice Collective, 131
Beal, Frances, 33
BenDor, Jan, 28
Berkeley Women's Liberation, *It Ain't Me Babe* prints "first" major explicit story about rape, 33
Bevacqua, Maria, 11, 12, 174–75, 217
Biden, Joseph R.: as president, funding for marginalized victims, 177; as senator, VAWA passage facilitated by, 176

biopower: definition of, 237. *See also* necropolitics

BIPOC (Black, Indigenous, and People of Color): college education as inaccessible for, 107–8, 263–64n58; as disproportionately arrested, convicted, sentenced, and exonerated, 30, 158, 172, 173; mass migrations of, and housing and labor justice, 46–50; as more likely to be sexually assaulted, 3, *113*; RCC wage hierarchy chart with salary, race, and gender, *113*; Reagan "welfare reform" pathologizing, 97; sex offender registration as especially destructive for, 157. *See also* women of color

—ADMINISTRATORS: attrition and, 124; and the glass ceiling, 124, 266n86; and the glass cliff, 124, 266n88; promotion of white-acting BIPOC to, 94, 119–24

—ADVOCATES: attrition disproportionately high for, 7, 116–17, 118, 122–23, 215; quantification paperwork normalizing marginal survivors disproportionately falling to, 187; radical activism (outside carceral systems) advanced by, 9–10, 11, 12; restorative justice and, 12. *See also* Asian rape crisis advocates; Black rape crisis advocates; Indigenous rape crisis advocates; Latina/e/o/x rape crisis advocates; marginalized advocates; professional advocacy; Third World Women and Violence Conference (1980)

—SURVIVORS: as "excess Others," and culturally informed care as unaffordable, 78–83, 259n79; as percentage of all rape victims (82% by some estimates), *113*; vulnerability to racism by anti-rape advocates, 36–37, 72, 215. *See also* Black rape survivors; Indigenous rape survivors; marginalized survivors

Black church: as gathering place without white mob interference, 46–47; housing and labor justice, 47–50

Black communities: CCTs about, 70; college education as inaccessible for, 107–8; high prevalence of rape against, 70; imprisonment of Black men and effect on the family, 134; imprisonment of Black men and loss of generational knowledges and cultures, 134; incarceration statistics as disproportionate, 137; Oppression Pyramid, *135*; War on Drugs and law enforcement presence increased in, 137. *See also* anti-Blackness and anti-Black racism; Civil Rights Movement (1960s)

—BLACK MEN: anticrime rhetoric criminalizing the existence of, 134–38; and the death penalty, 30, 172–73; as disproportionately arrested, convicted, sentenced, and exonerated, 30, 158, 172, 173; post–Civil War convict leasing and imprisonment of, 134; "superpredator" myth, 156; War on Drugs and mass incarceration of, 137. *See also* lynching of Black men; racist rape myths used to target Black men

—BLACK WOMEN: dissemblance as self-protection, 25; housing and labor justice during industrialization, 46–50; as percentage of incarcerated women, 33; post–Civil War mass migration to the North and exploitation of, 47; socialist-like communes during industrialization, 48; and the Third World movement, 33. *See also* Black feminism; Black rape crisis advocates; Black rape survivors; enslavement—women

Black feminism: as methodology, 13, 25, 27, 59, 159, 189–90, 204, 206, 215–16; suppression of knowledge produced by, 189–90; and tensions following the 1980 Third World Women and Violence Conference, 38. *See also* intersectionality

Black Freedom activists, and anti-rape activism, 32–33

Black liberationists. *See* Baker, Ella; Bako, Yolanda; Beal, Frances; Chikoti-Bandua Estes, Valeriana; Cooper, Brittney; Crenshaw, Kimberlé; Davis, Angela Y.; Height, Dorothy I.; Malcolm X; Parks, Rosa; Ross, Loretta J.; Shakur, Assata; Touré, I. Nkenge; Wells, Ida B.

Black Lives Matter: abandonment of RCC or domestic violence shelter by community partners due to sign on front desk, 2–5, 205–6, 243n1; "defund the police," 3, 78; and hope for a better future, 209; as motivation for cultural competency trainings (CCTs), 70; and National Association of Social Workers' public apology for its contributions to racist practices, 97; racist police brutality as basis of protest, 2–3, 4, 91; resentment of advocates who call out racism, 8

Black Panther Party (BPP), 34–35, 37, 136

Black Power movement, 134

Black rape crisis advocates: and CCTs, 72; on the demographics of the offender, 196; racist abuse by survivors, 115–16; racist encounters in the workplace, expectation they will remedy their own, 260n4; on serving on a "minority board" of directors, 127; on taking a breath to slow down the precarity crisis, 84. *See also* marginalized advocates; professional advocacy

Black rape survivors: as alienated from RCCs lacking cultural competency, 75; as "excess Others," and culturally informed care as unaffordable, 78–83, 259n79; prosecutions for self-defense against rape, 34–35; vulnerability to anti-Black racism by anti-rape advocates, 36. *See also* marginalized survivors

Black social work movement: formation of NABSW, 97; on the intimate knowledge of communities as necessary, 96–97

Black Women's Liberation Committee (BWLC) of SNCC, 32–33. *See also* Civil Rights Movement (1960s)

Block, Sharon, 229

boards of directors of rape crisis agencies: overview, 99; "minority board" and local community needs, 127; as predominantly white cisgender people, 122, 127; RCC wage hierarchy chart with salary, race, and gender, *113*; sheriff board-member objects to Black Lives Matter sign and activates a mass withdrawal of community partners from SART, 2–5, 205–6, 243n1; systems professionals placed on, 4, 122

Boston Women's Health Collective, *Our Bodies, Ourselves* (1970), 33

Bourdieu, Pierre, 18, 254–55n14

Bromley, Harriet, et al., 75

Brownmiller, Susan, *Against Our Will*: Menachem Amir's (discredited) study used and disseminated widely by, 173; as anti-Black study, 136, 175; and carceral feminism, 136; and claim to be leader of the anti-rape movement, 36; Angela Davis's review of, 230; shared sentiment with Religious Right Citizens for Decency Through Law, 28

Building Movement Project, 124, 264n64, 266n88

Bumiller, Kristin, 10–11
Bureau of Justice Statistics (BJS), 177–78
Burgess, Ann W., 174
BYP100, 165

Campbell, Rebecca, 12
capitalism: anticapitalist resistance as necessary to success of anti-rape movement, 54–55, 71, 84; competition as logic of workplace, 49, 112, 119; deployed to disguise social oppressions, 56; normative social hierarchy of, 54, 55; rape frequency as higher under, 54; as sociocultural resource mobilization, 18, 56. *See also* cultural capitalism; industrialization; neoliberal normativity; production of rape survivors in the neoliberal rape crisis center
capital punishment, 30, 172–73
carceral agents: advocates as, 132–33; systems professionals as, 131–32, 267n2. *See also* carceral feminism
carceral creep: convict leasing, 47, 134; definition of, 133–34; as "stealth revolution," 132, 139–40. *See also* carceral feminism
carceral feminism: overview, 18–19, 141–42; overview of advocates as carceral agents, 132–33; alliance of liberal feminists and neoconservatives in rape law reform, 10–11, 27–32, 136–40; anticrime legislation supported, 139; authority of advocate ceded to systems professionals, 146–50, 161; as carceral advocacy, 133, 151; carceral coercive benevolence and, 153; complicity in surveillance and punishment of survivors, 133; as conditional support, 151; definition of, 141, 237; devaluation of the advocate in, 148–49, 158–59; expansion of rape laws and sentencing, 141–42, 156–57; harms of carceralism acknowledged without taking steps to address the violence, 132–33; mass incarceration fueled by, 156; and panopticon, the rape crisis center as, 155, 188, 238; racist anti-Black male myths as driving, 136, 137, 156; radicalism as displaced by, 132–33, 152; as recycling carceral violence, 156–59; and secondary victimization, advocates apologizing instead of stopping it, 153–55, 156; and secondary victimization, advocates' inability or refusal to intervene in, 11, 142–44, 150, 153–54; and secondary victimization of enormous socioeconomic costs to victims, 159; state funding as force in, 132; as "stealth revolution," 132, 139–40; and systems professionals, collusion with, 142–44; third-party policing by advocate, 150–55; as victimizing those who have already been victimized, 157–58; welfare funding slashed and rise of, 138–39; whiteness centered by, 36–37. *See also* SARTs (sexual assault response teams); secondary victimization
carceralism: anticrime rhetoric entangling antipoverty projects with, 135–38; as broad range of sociolegal activities of control, 131, 134, 136; collaboration as emboldening, 133; colonial captivity and enslavement as constructing legal system to control marginalized populations, 133; definition of, 133, 237; happy affect of doing advocacy disrupted by the feminist killjoy, in favor of awakening to the urgency for change, 8, 155–56, 160, 237; as invisible to the general public, 133, 136. *See also* carceral creep; carceral feminism
carceral professionalism (white cultural ideology), 145–46, 148–49
carceral systems, industrialism as, 46–47

care work: advocates as "service providers" and ambivalence toward or refusal to engage in, 21–22; as not altering the exchange of survivors for agency funding, 55; radical advocacy as widening emotional bandwidth, 10. *See also* affective advocacy; ugly emotions
Caringella, Susan, 161
Carruthers, Charlene, 1, 215
Castañeda, Antonia I., 43
Catholic Church: and colonial rape law, 43; hospitals run by, and secondary victimization, 183, 278n76
Çayir Burke, Ebru, et al., 124–25
CCTs. *See* cultural competency trainings (CCTs)
Cell 16, 33–34
Centers for Disease Control and Prevention (CDC), anti-rape task force, 176, 186
CETA (Comprehensive Employment and Training Act), 29
Charmaz, Kathy, 222
Chen, Mel Y., 188, 194
Chicana women: and the Third World movement, 33; vulnerability to racism by anti-rape advocates, 36
Chikoti-Bandua Estes, Valériana, 90–94, 125, 128–30, 135, 232, 260nn3–4; Necessary Interruptions (consulting business), 129, 260n3; and Social Justice Fund NW, 129, 260n3
Child Abuse Prevention and Treatment Act (1974), 30
childcare: Jane Addams's development of, 48; as the assumed responsibility of mothers, 59–60; as barrier to participation of marginalized advocates, 105–6; government assistance block grants, 186; mutual aid organizing, in the radical version of advocacy, 126; white women providing for Third World women's meeting, 37

child sexual abuse, 28, 103, 108–9, 157; high rate of people who are incarcerated and experienced sexual abuse, 157
Christianity: Catholic Church, 43, 183, 278n76; Christian welfare reform movement, 46–48; evangelical, in neoconservative movement, 27, 28, 31; evangelicalism, 46, 47–48, 69; Protestantism, 47, 95; rape survivor treatment by, and advocate rejection of, 46. *See also* Black church; religion and anti-rape advocacy; white Christian nationalism
Christie, Nils, 58. *See also* "ideal" or "perfect" victim
Civil Rights Act (1964), 134
civil rights added to rape law, then rescinded, 29, 30
Civil Rights Movement (1960s): anti-rape activism in, 32–33, 40, 229–30; historical narratives eliding the radical nature of, 23; and narratives of success or decline, 40; successes of, 134. *See also* Baker, Ella; Beal, Frances; Height, Dorothy I.; Jackson, Mae; King, Dr. Martin Luther, Jr.; Malcolm X; Parks, Rosa; Patton, Gwendolyn
Civil War aftermath. *See* post–Civil War years
class: college education accessibility and, 107–8, 110, 263–64n58; and disparities in care, 64, 66–67; and professionalization, 96, 107–8, 110–11; radical feminists of the 1970s and tensions of class and, 36–37, 38, 40; and vulnerability to rape, 3. *See also* middle-class and wealthy survivors; poor people
Cleaver, Eldridge, *Soul on Ice*, 136
Clinton, Bill: neoliberalization of welfare, 138–39; signing VAWA into law, 139
coercive benevolence (white benevolence), 42–43, 95–96, 100, 153, 158–59

cognitively disabled people, as high percentage of incarcerated population, 157
Coker v. Georgia (1977), 30, 172
college education and professionalization: overview, 107–11; archives assuming only credentialed academics can conduct research, 229; as barrier of entry for marginalized people to serve as advocates, 107–8, 111, 126, 263–64n58; cannot substitute for experiential learning to support marginalized victims, 68, 109–10, 111, 142; change of policy to allow trainees to replace mandatory in-house training with, 107; colonial history of the helping professions and development of credentialing, 95–96, 97, 108–9; as expensive or proxy for wealth, 107, 108, 111, 203–4; and ignorance of political roots of advocacy, 108–9; lack of preparation for anti-rape advocacy, 108–10, 119–20; rape crisis agency administrators and norm of credentials, 101, 110–11, 119–20; as "stepping stone" for white advocates, 108–10, 120; training to support college students, 74, 76
college students as survivors: drugged, and disparities in care, 64–65; Koss's "one in four" study of, 174–75, 275n35; VAWA expanding carceral authority over, 139
Collins, Patricia Hill, 189–90
colonial epistemicide, 24–25, 42
colonialism: Black women's spectrum of anti-rape advocacy activities, 44–46; of helping professions and development of credentialing, 95–96, 97, 108–9; Indigenous children forced into assimilationist boarding schools, 95, 108–9; Indigenous women's spectrum of anti-rape advocacy activities, 43–44, 45; myth that rape didn't exist in Indigenous communities prior to, 41–42; property law analysis elides rape of marginalized women and girls, 42–43, 59; rape as tool of, 41; white social work and the logics of (white benevolence/coercive benevolence), 42–43, 95–98, 100. *See also* enslavement
color of skin and colorism: and disparities in care, 66–67; and vulnerability to rape, 3
Combating Sexism, 34–35
commercial sex. *See* sex workers
community, as term, 131
community building: advocacy in relation and, 85–89; collaborative network for referrals, 86–89; definition of transformative justice community, 131, 165–66; by direct services advocates, 1–2; as fulfilling an aim of CCTs, 89; fundraising via networks in, 104; and hyperinstitutionalization of advocacy, 126–30, 197–99; identification of community in solidarity, 133; inviting conversations with abolitionist partners, 165–66; Latina advocates and, 126; "minority board," and local needs of, 127; as radical advocacy, 49–50, 89; trust building, 165–66; and the welfare reform movement/settlement house movement, 49–50. *See also* mutual aid
"community partners" as not our radical community, 131–32, 158–59. *See also* carceral feminism; rape crisis centers, neoliberal; SARTs (sexual assault response teams); secondary victimization; systems professionals
compassion fatigue and burnout, 117, 124, 183, 237; workplace organization and coping behaviors to alleviate, 124–25. *See also* attrition and alienation
Concilio Mujeres, 34–35
consciousness raising in advocacy, 237; as mutual aid principle, 49, 85–86

consent: coerced, for SAFE exam, 140; informed consent, difficulties obtaining, 192; and insufficiency of theorizing rape through property laws, 59, 60; as insufficiently obtained for quantified data collection, 19, 184–88, 191–93; paperwork presented if victim requests a service RCC is reluctant to supply, 62; rape reform instituting policy of, 28; for release of victim's information, 62; for SAFE exams, and paperwork required of victims, 191
convict leasing, 47, 134
Cooper, Brittney, eloquent rage, 207
Corrigan, Rose, 11, 39–40, 215
court advocacy/legal advocacy: CCTs for, 71; interfacing with systems vs. survivors' needs, 147–48; interpreters, 52; protection of victim's rights, 144; and the question: "Is this still advocacy?," 51–52
COVID-19, 121
Cree language, 195
Crenshaw, Kimberlé, 13, 159, 215–16
crime. *See* anticrime rhetoric; carceralism; criminal legal system; drugs; mass incarceration; rape crime reporting; welfare policies
Crime Victims Compensation. *See* Office for Victims of Crime (OVC)
criminal legal system: anticrime rhetoric labeling people of color "criminals," 135–38; constructed to control some people for the benefit of others, 133–40, 155–56; disabled people as more likely to be arrested and jailed than nondisabled, 157; as gateway into racial stigmatization and permanent marginalization, 156–57; police pressuring victim to withdraw her statement, then charging her with false reporting for withdrawing, 140–41; restorative justice and, as two sides of the same coin, 204. *See also* anticrime rhetoric; carceral feminism; carceralism; welfare policies
Crisis Text Line, 123
critical fabulation, 25–26, 42–46
critical quantification: as alternative to shunning quantification, 193–94; as collaborative network of mutual aid, 197–99; as community-driven quantification, 195–96, 198–99; competitiveness rejected under, 197–98; data about survivors not solely the product of one actor but are produced and continuously revised in movement, 195; and data sovereignty, 193–94; as hyperprofessionalized network, 197–99; as not data-driven policing nor administrative confinement, 196. *See also* radical rape crisis advocacy (outside carceral systems)
—ANIMACIES AND: accepting victims as they are, 194–95, 196–97; advocacy as flexible, constantly shifting form of forms (no single "real movement" or "right" way), 195; "bottom up" trans networked responses to sexual violence, 195; community-designed action plans, 195; definition of, 194; kinetic movement of, 198–99; as reconceptualizing the traditional taxonomy, 194; social identities as endlessly shifting forms, 194
critical quantitative scholarship, 193–94
cultural capitalism: overview, 18; definition of, 56, 57, 237, 254–55n14; multiplicity of forms of, 56; as part of economic capitalism, 254–55n14; race eliminated in discourses of, 255n15; social capitalism as part of, 254–55n14. *See also* ethnic capitalism; production of rape survivors in the neoliberal rape crisis center; racial

capitalism; victim commodity thesis (rape-as-theft argument)
cultural competency trainings (CCTs): overview, 70; advocates' investment in improving, 70–71; agencies not conducting, 73; as baseline or refresher for advocates, 77; cultural identities offered in, table summarizing, 75–76, 76; difficulty of training in the allotted time, 77; disparities in support for marginalized victims as motivation for, 69, 70; insufficiency of, and alienation of marginalized clients, 74, 75; model templates, 70–71; national organizations or state coalitions producing, 70–71, 74–75; normativity of "ideal victim" reinforced by, 71–72; and not locally specific, 75; as performance of diversity, 75; as reinforcing discrimination and stereotypes, 72, 74–75; superficiality of, 73–74; variable effectiveness of, 75–76. *See also* multiculturalism as neoliberal normativity
culturally humble advocacy. *See* radical rape crisis advocacy (outside carceral systems)—culturally humble advocacy
culturally specific rape crisis agencies: overview, 70; advocacy in relation and, 86–88; disparities in support for marginalized victims as motivation for, 69; funding as decreasing over time, 187; funding capped at small percentage of total grant award, 176; marginalized victims defined as "excess Others" and culturally informed care as unaffordable, 78–83; and methodology of text, 218; minority grants, 177–79, 187, 277n60; minority grants at risk, 179; quantification of victims as normative violence, 185–86; specific cultural capital offered to marginalized victims, 70; state-imposed market limitations absolving advocates of duty to respond, 63. *See also* cultural competency trainings (CCTs); radical rape crisis advocacy (outside carceral systems)—culturally humble advocacy; tribal agencies (rape crisis centers)

data sovereignty, 193–94
Davis, Angela Y.: on anticapitalist resistance as necessary for success of anti-rape movement, 54, 71, 84; and the Loretta J. Ross archive, 230; on professionalization of RCCs, 109; as radical forebearer of anti-rape advocacy, 22; review of Brownmiller's book, 230
Dawes, Anna L., 95–96
DC Rape Crisis Center: assassination of Yulanda Ward and, 38–39; as first rape crisis center in US, 35–36; formation by multiracial group (1972), 35; hotline, 35; "How to Start a Rape Crisis Center" (1972), 35; on the importance of in-service donations and volunteers, 35; network for mutual aid, building, 35, 37, 61; on number of RCCs, 36; professionalization of anti-violence advocacy challenged by, 36; on service professionals, place for, 35; survivor-advocates as prime authorities on rape, 35; systems professionals, decision to work with, 136–37; Third World Women and Violence Conference (1980), 37–39, 175, 190, 231. *See also* FAAR (Feminist Alliance Against Rape) (nationwide network); Touré, I. Nkenge
D'Cruze, Shani, 25
D/deaf survivors: as "excess Others," 79–80; interpreters, 80; low rate of accessing advocacy, 80; specific cultural capital needed by, 70
Deer, Sarah, 193, 211

Department of Corrections (DOC), funding violence and sexual assault coalitions, 144–45, 158–59. *See also* incarcerated population; mass incarceration; prison industrial complex

Dilts, Andrew, 155–56, 160

direct services advocates: advocate positions meant to prevent secondary victimization, 144; attrition disproportionately higher than administrative workers, 112, 114, 115–17, 122; community building by, 1–2; fissure of anti-rape advocacy into administration and, 98, 99; as increasingly not reflective of the community's demographics, 122; sexual violence currently experienced by, as stigma, 225; transforming into radical feminist, 160–66; volunteers considered "low skilled" in hierarchy of RCC, 99; the wage hierarchy as devaluing the work of, 112, 114, 116–17, 119, 122, 145; wage hierarchy between administration and, 112–14, 264nn62,64; wage hierarchy chart with salary, race, and gender, 113; wage hierarchy of the SART and state's judgment of rape response roles, 145; wage improvements in the radical version of advocacy, 126, 129. *See also* administration—hierarchy between direct services and; advocacy trainings; cultural competency trainings (CCTs); direct services advocates as service providers representing the state; marginalized advocates; professional advocacy; radical rape crisis advocacy (outside carceral systems)

direct services advocates as service providers representing the state: overview, 21–22, 54–55, 98; authorization from administrators for activities of, 99–100; as conditional advocacy, 63; as discourse manifesting reality of, 23; as dominant narrative erasing the history of radical anti-violence advocacy, 22–23, 26–27, 31–32, 39–40; emotional care work, ambivalence toward, 21–22; and fictitious hierarchy of rape victim needs, 82–83; gaslighting by systems professionals to keep advocates in line with, 205–6; paying money out of pocket, 100; technical knowledge required for, 22; unconditional positive regard expressed for victims, 61. *See also* production of rape survivors in the neoliberal rape crisis center; resource book (or binder)

disabled people: as excluded from Elizabethan welfare, 95; Fireweed Collective, 203; as high percentage of all incarcerated people, and as more likely to be arrested and jailed, 157

disabled rape survivors: advocates ceding authority to SAFEs for, 146; and CCTs, 73–74; and consent to quantification, 192–93; as "excess Others," 79–80; and informed consent, difficulties obtaining, 192; mandatory reporting requirement, 102; specific cultural capital to assist, 70; vulnerability to rape, 3; workshops about working with, 91. *See also* marginalized survivors

—AND ABLEISM: the intake form causing serious long-term harm, 184; RCC resentment of advocates who call out, 8

dissemblance, 25

domestic violence movement: advocacy training, 263n51; alliance of liberal feminists and neoconservatives and legal reform (carceral feminism), 28–29, 139; amount distributed to victim services has decreased since VAWA's inception, 186–87, 278n86; barriers to leaving, 99–100; child sexual abuse, 28, 103, 108–9, 157; civil rights law

reworked to support (and rescission of), 29, 30; funding for shelters and training programs, 29, 98, 186, 262n35; intimate partner violence, 15, 29, 142, 156; lethal retributive attacks against victims who report, 156; mandatory arrest policies, 29, 139; and methodology of the text, 16; number of attempts to leave before success (average), 66; professionalism of advocates, 101; and rape, 15–16; spousal/dating violence, 15; support for criminalized survivors of (#SurvivedAndPunished), 195. *See also* FAAR-NCN; National Communication Network (NCN)
double bind, definition of, 237
Down syndrome, 157
Dripps, Donald, 57–58
drugs: administrative violence on victims accused of using, 33, 138, 141; drugged survivors, 64–65, 116; racialization of poverty and drug use, 137–38; War on Drugs, 137–38
Duggan, Lisa, 31
Duster, Alfreda, 229–30
Dworkin, Andrea, 29

Edwards, Malik, 37. *See also* Black Panther Party
elderly victims, 102
Embrace (rape crisis center): overview, 1–2; advocates explain the intersectional framework in which eliminating police brutality against Black people can reduce sexual violence against marginalized victims, 2–3; Black Lives Matter sign placed on front desk, 2; board member–sheriff objects to Black Lives Matter sign and activates a mass withdrawal of community partners from SART, 2–5, 205–6, 243n1; financial withdrawal by community partners, 3, 5; kitchen table talk, 2; and methodology of the text, 232
emotion. *See* affective advocacy; care work; ugly emotions
English Elizabethan welfare projects, 95
English language: and white norms of professional advocacy, 102. *See also* limited English-speaking proficiency (LEP)
enslavement: as critical feature of US culture, 54, 56–57; as feudalist reinforcement of racial hierarchies, 56; the neoliberal RCC and similar valuation of victims and bodies under, 54–55, 60, 82. *See also* post–Civil War years; racial capitalism; racist rape myths used to target Black men
—ABOLITIONIST MOVEMENT: maroon communities, 44–45; white women serving in, 95
—ENSLAVED WOMEN: Black women's spectrum of anti-rape advocacy activities, 44–46; Indigenous women's spectrum of anti-rape advocacy activities, 43–44, 45; property law as negating rape of (white benevolence), 42–43, 59
erotic capitalism, 56
ethnic capitalism: and cultural capitalism, 56, 255n15; definition of, 255n17; distinguished from racial capitalism, 255n17
ethnicity: and vulnerability to rape, 3, 36–37, 72, 215. *See also* Asian communities; Black communities; color of skin and colorism; Hawai'i; Indigenous peoples; Latina/e/o/x communities; Pacific Islander communities
everywoman analysis myth, 5, 237. *See also* neoliberal normativity
executive directors: compensation of, 112, *113*, 264n64; as disproportionately identified as white non-Hispanic, 124. *See also* professional advocacy

FAAR (Feminist Alliance Against Rape) (nationwide network), 35–36, 98–99, 107; *FAAR Newsletter*, 35–36
FAAR-NCN, 36, 38; *Aegis* (periodical), 36
Facebook/Meta, Sexual Assault Advocacy Network, 228
Family Justice Center/One Place, 132
Family Violence Prevention and Services Act (1984), 29
farming communities: advocacy in relation and, 87–88; agricultural justice, 88, 104; as first for budget cuts, 83
FBI (Federal Bureau of Investigation): J. Edgar framing rape as product of BIPOC cultures, 172; quantification of crime statistics, 171–72; rape crime reporting as amplifying the racist rape myth used to target Black men, while erasing white racial terror from the public eye, 172; rape enforcement, 28; Uniform Crime Reports (UCRs), 171, 173–74, 274n18, 276n52; white criminal gangs, 171–72
federal laws: CETA (Comprehensive Employment and Training Act), 29; Child Abuse Prevention and Treatment Act (1974), 30; Civil Rights Act (1964), 134; Family Violence Prevention and Services Act (1984), 29; Law Enforcement Assistance Act (1965), 136; Omnibus Crime Control and Safe Streets Act (1968), 136; Prison Rape Elimination Act (PREA, 2003), 144, 159; Sexual Offender Registry and Notification Act (SORNA, 2006), 156–57; Title XX, 29; Victims of Crime Act (VOCA, 1984), 29, 144–45, 159, 188, 198; Victims of Trafficking and Violence Protection Act (2000), 30; Violent Crime Control and Law Enforcement Act (1994), 29–30, 139. *See also* Violence Against Women Act (VAWA, 1994)

feminism: "Sex Wars" split of, 31, 32. *See also* Black feminism; carceral feminism; Latine feminisms; liberal feminism; white feminism
feminist killjoy, disrupting the happy affect of doing advocacy in favor of awakening to the urgency for change, 8, 155–56, 160, 237
Feminist Law Collective, 38
feminist of color approach, 133
Fireweed Collective, 203–4
Floyd, George, 91
food justice, 134, 142
Foucault, Michel, 151, 153, 155; biopower, 180
Fraser, Nancy, 259n79
Freedman, Estelle, 229
free-market advocacy. *See* radical rape crisis advocacy
free-market advocacy transformed. *See* rape crisis centers, neoliberal
Friedman, Deb, "Rape, Racism—and Reality," 36
Fuentes, Marisa, 26
funding by government grants: overview, 54–55; amount distributed to victim services has decreased since VAWA's inception, 186–87, 278n86; competition for, and decreased funding, 186, 187; competition for, and normative quantification, 19, 181; competition for, critical quantification and rejection of, 197–98; competition for, the survivor discourse (empowerment model) and production of rape survivors, 63–64, 68–69, 78, 239; as contingent on advocate cooperation with systems professionals even when the victim doesn't want their presence, 4–5; dependence on, 4, 177; dependence on, and advocates as carceral agents, 132–33; difficulty of getting continuing grants, 187, 216; displacement of

victims' needs in favor of the NPIC, 4–5; foundation and individual donor contributions as small percentage of, 177; legal mandate for state spending, 98; loss of, due to anti-Black practices, 129; loss of, due to law enforcement disagreement with advocates' support of Black racial justice movement, 3–5; market limitations imposed by, 61–63; minority grants, 177–79, 187, 277n60; minority grants at risk, 179; "misuse of funds" as disciplining threat, 55; as neoliberalism, 4; as percentage of total funding, 117, 276n51; priorities and restrictions set by, 61; quantification of victims and, 169, 177–79, 180; SASP program, 98, 176–77, 262n35; from state Department of Corrections (DOC), 144–45; STOP program, 98, 176–77, 262n35; surveillance of antirape advocacy enabled by, 98; systems professionals granted nearly absolute power over advocates, 4; VAWA establishing, 31–32; VOCA, 29, 144–45, 159, 188, 198. *See also* direct services advocates as service providers representing the state; neoliberal normativity; nonprofit industrial complex (NPIC); production of rape survivors in the neoliberal rape crisis center; professionalization of the rape crisis center; Violence Against Women Act (VAWA, 1994)

funding, radical options for: community networks, 104; DC Rape Crisis Center and, 35; supporting survivors and generating funding as co-constitutive, 10. *See also* mutual aid

fungibility, 117–18, 186, 237

García, Inez, activism to free, 34–35
Garner, Margaret (from Gerda Lerner), 45
Gay Liberation movement, 134

gender: quantification and normalization of, 181; and vulnerability to rape, 3; wage hierarchy chart with salary, race, and gender, *113*

gender capitalism, 56
Ghanbarpour, Susan, 26
Gilmore, Ruth Wilson, 27, 204, 206
Ginsburg, Ruth Bader, 30
glass ceiling, 124, 237, 266n86
glass cliff, 124, 266n88
glass escalator, 266n86
grant writing: legal mandate for grants manager, 98; survivor discourse (empowerment model) in, 63–64, 68–69, 78, 239; "underserved" victims grant opportunities, 177–78, 276n52. *See also* quantifying rape victims in grant applications

grassroots social change, critical fabulation and the imagination of the other(ed) stories as propelling, 26

Great Depression, 48
Greer, Germaine, 31

Haitian survivors, 127
Hale, Sir Matthew, 42–43
Halley, Janet, 31
Hall, Jacquelyn Dowd, 23, 40
Hartman, Saidiya, 25, 59
Hawai'i: Native advocate on the burden of training her white colleagues, 109–10; rape and precolonial society, 41–42
hearing impaired. *See* D/deaf survivors
Height, Dorothy I., 229
helping professions: colonial logics of, 95–98, 100; educational credentialing, 95–96, 97
Hispanic communities: college education as inaccessible for, 107–8. *See also* Latina/e/o/x communities; Puerto Rican women
Hispanic rape crisis advocates, racist abuse by survivors, 118

Hispanic rape survivors: "minority board" of directors and increased comfort of, 127; prosecutions for self-defense against rape, 34–35; and rural transportation service cuts, 83; translation of materials for, 91; vulnerability to racism by anti-rape advocates, 36
Holland, Sharon P., 46
Holmstrom, Lynn L., 174
hooks, bell, "killing rage," 6–7, 206, 207
Hoover, J. Edgar, 172
hotline advocacy: overview, 217; collaborating closely with carceral actors, 144; DC Rape Crisis center and, 35; in the genealogy of anti-rape advocacy, 40; marginalized victims and disparities of care, 65–66; and methodology, 217; neoliberal normativity and, 217; outsourcing direct victim services to carceral professionals, 68; as volunteer-run, 35, 99; white-centered, 36–37
housing justice: coercive benevolence of housing workers, 153; industrialized labor and, 46–50; queer/ed communities of color (1960s), 134; socialist-like communes, 48. *See also* shelters; unhoused victims; welfare reform movement (settlement house movement)
Hsu, Vox Jo, 195
Hulsether, Lucia, 21, 191, 193
human trafficking, 86–87; sex trafficking, 29, 139, 159

"ideal" or "perfect" victim: all advocate-participants could describe at least one case involving, 227; attributes of, 58, 79; CCTs reinforcing normativity of, 71–72; as disproportionately receiving more services, 62, 69; funding reductions for marginalized survivors due to bifurcation with, 187; marginalized victims defined as "excess Others" in comparison to, and unaffordable to provide care, 78–83; multiculturalism and production of, 71–73; normativity of needs of, determining worthy vs. unworthy victims, 64–66, 67, 69, 100, 178; and the racist myth blaming the Black male stranger for rape, 58; rape victim-blaming of femmes of color and emergence of, 138; universal victim capital claimed to meet all victims' needs, 55; the victim commodity thesis assuming, 58–59. *See also* production of rape survivors in the neoliberal rape crisis center

immigrants: as alienated from RCCs lacking cultural competency, 74; Asian (typically Chinese) laborers, 47, 48; college education as inaccessible for, 107–8, 263–64n58; housing and labor justice, 46–50; as more likely to be sexually assaulted, 3; and mutual aid networks, 48–50; post-WWI mass migrations, 48; professional credentials recognized in EB2-National Interest Waiver visas, 92; and secondary victimization by advocates, 68–69; socialist-like communes, 48; southern Black women migrants to the North treated as, 47; as survivors, VAWA as expanding carceral authority over, 139; white Christian nationalist nativism and prejudice against, 47, 48. *See also* limited English-speaking proficiency (LEP)

incarcerated population: Black men as disproportionately arrested, convicted, sentenced, and exonerated, 158; disabled people as high percentage of, and as more likely to be arrested and jailed than nondisabled people, 157; high rate of individuals who experienced childhood sexual abuse suggests rape victims are being punished for being rape victims, 157; privatization and profiteering on the backs of, 158; trans and gender-diverse people, high rate of incarceration at least once in their lifetimes for nonviolent reasons, 157. *See also* mass incarceration

incarcerated women: accelerated rate of incarceration, 138; women of color as vast majority of, 33

incarceration and rape: Prison Rape Elimination Act (PREA) coordinators (reporting sexual assault), 144; radical multiracial coalitions challenging, 34–35, 63

—INCARCERATED SURVIVORS: advocate cedes authority to corrections officers, 146–47; corrections officers flexing power to manage victim capital, 147; the dangers of reporting often outweigh the violence, 159; extreme vulnerability to rape, 159; the neoliberal RCC and limited advocacy for, 63; PREA pays expenses for, 159; sex trafficked due to lack of recourse, 159

—INCARCERATION OF PERPETRATORS: recidivism for nonsexual crimes due to hardships of lifelong sex offender registration, 157; sex offender registration as lifelong punishment, 156–57. *See also* sentencing

indentured women, colonial rape negated by property law, 42–43

Indiana, anti-pornography laws, 29

Indigenous peoples: children forced into assimilationist boarding schools, 95, 108–9; college education as inaccessible for, 107–8; counting schemas as method of transferring knowledges, 171; critical quantitative studies, 193–94; data sovereignty, 193–94; on dispossession as arriving through the insemination of corporate values one tribe at a time, 205; and generational sexual victimization, 108–9; Indigeneity as political and legal identity, not solely a racial one, 181–82; on the kinetic movement of critical quantification, 198; and maroon communities, 45; myth that rape didn't exist prior to colonization, 41–42; Native identity and critical quantification, 198–99; prisons located in tribal lands, 137; quantification as dispossessing knowledges of, 193–94; restorative justice (peacemaking) originating with, 49; sovereignty movements, 45, 134; spectrum of responses to rape among, 44; spiritual reclamation, 44, 73. *See also* critical quantification; Two-Spirit people

Indigenous rape crisis advocates: on accepting victims as they are and refusing the capitalist production of survivors, 194–95, 196–97; on CCTs and lack of local specificity, 74; on the connection between boarding schools and generational sexual victimization, 108–9; on critical quantification, 196–97; on the need to stop working with systems, 155; observing and telling the story of the victim denied services based on her "non-Native" appearance and presentation, 167–69, 185–86, 273n2; on quantification's material consequences, 182–83; state coalition trainer's microaggression toward, 74–75; on systems professionals as erasing Native survivors as too small a sample, 180; tribal social media groups utilized for outreach by, 104. *See also* tribal agencies (rape crisis centers)

Indigenous rape survivors: quantification of victims has not changed the extremely high rates of rape, 193; secondary victimization by law enforcement, 162; VAWA expanding carceral authority over, 139; vulnerability to racism by anti-rape advocates, 36; woman denied services based on her "non-Native" appearance and presentation, 167–69, 185–86, 273n2; woman would not have been denied under critical quantification, 198–99

Indigenous women: colonial rape of enslaved and poor, spectrum of anti-rape advocacy activities, 43–44, 45; colonial rape of, negated by property law, 42–43, 59; and enslavement as critical feature of the US, 54, 56–57; Missing and Murdered Indigenous People/Women, Girls, and Two-Spirit People (MMIP/WG2S), 43, 91, 109, 193; prosecutions for self-defense against rape, 34; socialist-like communes during industrialization, 48; and the Third World movement, 33

industrialization: housing and labor justice, 46–50; laws enforcing exploitation and development of convict leasing, 47; and post–Civil War mass migrations to the North and West, 47

Interrupting Criminalization, 165

intersectionality: as absent in advocacy training, 72, 77; advocates' lack of awareness of, 66–67, 71; creation of social justice movement alliances, 42, 59; definition of, 238; framework of, as necessary to eradicate sexual violence, 3; as method, 60, 85; neoliberal gaslighting of advocates to scare them away, 205–6; standpoint as positionality within, 239; violence in legal reform, 37, 44, 49. *See also* secondary victimization—intersectional harm

intimate partner violence. *See* domestic violence movement; rape

inventorying resources. *See* production of rape survivors in the neoliberal rape crisis center

Jackson, George, 38
Jackson, Mae, 33
Jacquet, Catherine O., 212, 229
Johnson, Lyndon B.: Great Society programs, 134–35, 138; War on Poverty, 28, 135–37

Kanuha, Val Kalei, 11–12, 41, 246n47
Kendall, David E., 30
Kennedy, John F., antidelinquency programs, 134
Kim, Mimi E., 11–12, 39, 133–34, 152, 246n47
King County Sexual Assault Resource Center, 92
King, Dr. Martin Luther, Jr., 23, 38
kitchen table talk, 2
Koshy, Susan et al., 101
Koss, Mary P., 174–75, 275n35
koyama, emi, 126, 129
Kulkarni, Shanti, et al., 124

labor justice, 46–50, 126, 129–30, 134
Latina/e/o/x communities: college education as inaccessible for, 107–8; incarceration statistics as disproportionate, 137. *See also* Hispanic communities; Puerto Rican women
—Latina/e/o/x women: socialist-like communes during industrialization, 48; and the Third World movement, 33; vulnerability to racism by anti-rape advocates, 36
Latina/e/o/x rape crisis advocates: and carceral coercive benevolence, 153; and community building, 126; dismay

with advocacy training, 104; the pay gap and attrition of, 116–17; personal networks utilized by, 104; on the racialized labor disparity between white advocates and, 125; on secondary victimization by police, 141

Latine feminisms: agricultural justice, 88, 104; as anti-carceral, 141; as coalitional, 116–17; as coalitional, Third World Women's Alliance (TWWA) as change of name from Black Women's Liberation Committee, 33; housing and labor justice, 48; and networking, 125; and tensions following the 1980 Third World Women and Violence Conference, 38

law enforcement: abandonment of RCC or domestic violence shelter due to Black Lives Matter sign on front desk, 2–5, 205–6, 243n1; anonymous vs. identified rape reporting, 151; funding for rape response training and operations, 28, 29, 136, 139, 176–77; interview and paperwork process, 191; majority identify as white men, 145; mandatory arrest policies in domestic violence, 29, 139; militarization of local (1965), 136; professionalization pressure and RCC choice to collaborate with, 137, 146; as racialized and gendered hierarchy, 145; rape crime reporting, falsifying data to reduce numbers, 171, 274n18; VAWA and involvement in victim services, 30, 31, 139; wage hierarchy and state's judgment of rape response roles, 145, 270–71n67; wage hierarchy chart with salary, race, and gender, 113. *See also* SARTs (sexual assault response teams); systems professionals

—VIOLENCE AND BRUTALITY: Black Lives Movement in response to, 2–3, 4, 91; as intersectional, 2–3.

See also secondary victimization—by systems professionals

Law Enforcement Assistance Act (1965), 136

Law Enforcement Assistance Administration (LEAA, 1965): funding for law enforcement rape response training, 28, 29, 136; Prison Rape Elimination Act (PREA) coordinators, salary paid by, 144; RCCs opting to collaborate with, 137, 138

Law, Victoria, 131

legal advocacy. *See* court advocacy/legal advocacy

lesbians: as advocate, on direct services advocates increasingly not reflective of the community's demographics, 122; of color, and radicalism, 9–10; as survivor, and implicit biases of advocates with dominant identities, 127. *See also* marginalized advocates; marginalized survivors; queer people (inclusive of 2SLGBTQIA+ people and those who live outside of normative constructs)

LGBTQ+. *See* lesbians; marginalized advocates; marginalized survivors; queer communities of color; queer people (inclusive of 2SLGBTQIA+ people and those who live outside of normative constructs); trans and gender-diverse people; Two-Spirit people

liberal feminism: alliance with neoconservatives in rape law reform (carceral feminism), 10–11, 27–32, 136–40; and cooptation of the anti-rape movement, 39, 138–40; fictitious hierarchy of rape victim needs, 82–83; multiculturalism, 78; racial disparities not considered by, 9, 36–37; and redistribution of resources, 259n79; and white ascendancy, 122. *See also* carceral feminism; white feminism

liberalism, definition of, 238

limited English-speaking proficiency (LEP): of advocate, and carceral feminism, 154–55; advocate policing the boundaries of survivor's linguistic capabilities, 152; advocate's knowledge of language-appropriate resources, 22; community organizers teaching English, 48; and consent forms as not equatable to consent, 191–93; fungibility of advocates and, 117–18; lack of advocate preparation for, and alienation from seeking services, 74, 150, 192; translation of written materials for, 91; translators for, 83, 152; and vulnerability to rape, 3

Lipsky, Michael, frontline bureaucracy theory, 216

Little, Joan, 34

Lorde, Audre, 37, 126

lynching of Black men: Black Reconstruction activists falsely accused of rape and, 171; as extrajudicial murder, 134; George Floyd, 91; NAACP statistical reporting on, 172; the racist rape myth and false accusations in, 30, 134, 171, 172; as state-sponsored murder of Black men, 134, 172; Ida B. Wells's quantified antilynching campaign, 171, 172, 188; Marvin Wolfgang's study of rape prosecutions and, 172–73, 188. *See also* racist rape myths used to target Black men

McGuire, Danielle L., 23

MacKinnon, Catharine, 29

Maier, Shana L., 181

Maine Coalition Against Sexual Assault (MECASA), 41–42

mainstream advocacy histories: assassination of radical activists and appropriation by the neoliberal RCC, 38–40; call-out traditions, 34; caution against nostalgic erasure of tensions inherent among, 40; exposing the scope of harms against women of color, 32–33; FBI rape statistics used to awareness of rape as crime, 173–74; first formal anti-rape conference (1971), 34; incarceration and rape as issue for, 35, 63; interethnic coalitions, rise and eventual separation of, 37–39; multiracial coalitions, 34–35; networking connections for mutual aid, 35–36, 37, 61; organizing for release of women on trial for self-defense against rape (survivor justice), 34–35; racial and class tensions within the anti-violence movement, 36–37, 38, 40; Rape Prevention Month, 34; rape speak-out (1971), 34; on retributive justice after rape, 33, 34; self-defense against rape, 33–34; women's health, 33

mainstream rape crisis agencies, definition of, 218

Malcolm X, 38

Manhattan Women's Political Caucus, 34

marginalized advocates: attrition as disproportionately high among, 7, 116–17, 118, 122–23, 215; attrition rates from training, 106, 107; burden of educating peers about racism and normativity falling on, 109–10; college education norm as barrier of entry to, 107–8, 111, 126, 263–64n58; lived experience as basis of support for marginalized survivors, 104, 105; lived experience devalued in advocacy training, 104–5, 107; lived experience valued in the transformed RCC, 126–27; quantification paperwork normalizing marginal survivors disproportionately falling to, 187; RCC capitalizing on "diverse" identities of, 104; training as barrier of entry to, 104–7. *See also* Asian rape crisis advocates;

BIPOC—advocates; Black rape crisis advocates; immigrants; Indigenous rape crisis advocates; Latina/e/o/x rape crisis advocates; professional advocacy; queer people—advocates
marginalized survivors: absorption of independent agencies into larger, normative institutions unsuited for, 67–68; alienation of clients due to lack of culturally specific care, 67–68, 74, 75, 83, 87–88, 150, 192; defined as "excess Others," and unaffordable to provide care, 78–83; definition of, 227, 238; disparities in care received by, 62–63, 64–69, 70, 85; as disproportionately affected by sexual violence, 170; and the everywoman analysis as myth, 5, 237; funding for culturally specific services as decreasing, 187; fungibility and assignment of all to a non-Black advocate of color, 117–18; preferred over "underserved survivors" as term, 244n19; property law analysis elides rape of marginalized women and girls, 42–43, 59–60; racism experienced by, 36–37, 72; rape defined flexibly enough for inclusion of, 16; "underserved" minority grant opportunities, 177–79, 187, 277n60; the victim commodity thesis as preemptively negating cultural violence of, 59. See also BIPOC—survivors; Black rape survivors; cultural competency trainings (CCTs); disabled rape survivors; Indigenous rape survivors; multiculturalism as neoliberal normativity; production of rape survivors in the neoliberal rape crisis center; queer people—survivors; secondary victimization
marijuana, and mass incarceration, 137. See also drugs

maroon communities, 45–46
mass incarceration: Black and Latino Americans as disproportionately incarcerated, 137; carceral feminist expansion of rape laws as fueling, 156; number and types of prisons, jails, and institutions, 137; privatization, profiteering, and prison labor, 158; racist myths about incarcerated persons, 137; racist rape myths about Black men and, 136, 137, 156; US incarceration rate the highest in the world, 137; War on Drugs and, 137–38. See also incarcerated population; prison industrial complex
Mazurek, Terri L., 12
mc'duff, robin, 36
medical advocates, 144
medical-forensic exams (rape kit). See SAFEs (sexual assault forensic-medical examiners)—sexual assault or rape kits
medical industrial complex: criminalization of people on welfare via, 97; definition of, 238; and social work professionalization, 97
medicalization of care: advocacy coopted by, and advocate acquiescence to, 40, 97, 99, 102, 103, 144, 146, 147, 148; and advocates' ambivalence toward or refusal to engage in care work, 61–62; as amplifying the profit within the medical industrial complex, 55, 61, 64, 68, 76, 82, 86, 91; the enlarged role of SAFEs in anti-rape work, 35, 82, 131–32, 144, 146, 147, 148, 163, 267n2; policy changes that amplified the role of medical professionals, 39, 97; resistance by BIPOC advocates, 21, 33, 140, 147; SAFEs as carceral agents, 131–32, 267n2
Mehrotra, Gina, et al., 180
Melamed, Jodi, 255n15

methodology: anti-Black racism as highlighted in, 221; COVID-19 pandemic as context, 219–20, 224; and domestic violence, 16; Indigeneity as political and legal identity, not solely a racial one, 181–82; participants' personal experience of sexual violence, 201–2, 225, 226; rape, capacious definition of, 15–16; researcher bias, 219; "white" not capitalized; Black capitalized, 243n2. *See also* anti-rape movement history, recovering; archival research
  —METHODS: abbreviations used in text, 241–42; anonymity of participants preserved in the text, 14, 226–27, 233; coding: process coding and values coding, 222–24; concept map, 17–20; consent of participants and others, 220, 232, 260n4, 273n2; data privacy and security, 224–25; interviews, in-depth semistructured qualitative method, 13, 219–21, 227, 281n12; IRB approval and protocol, 217, 225; literature review, 10–13, 215–16; member checking, limited, 223–24; oral history interviews with Embrace and Valériana Chikoti-Bandua Estes, 232; participants not compensated, 219, 228; possible exclusions due to sample chosen, 216–17; pronouns, 225; recorded and unrecorded interviews, 220; recruitment of participants, 218–19; remote interviewing, 219–20; resource document shared with participants, 221, 227–28; sample, 13–14, 216–17, 226–28, 233–36; sampling, 217–19, 225–26; sampling bias, 218–19, 225–26; social identities as identification method, 14, 223, 225, 226–27, 233–36; survey of participants, 219; terminology list, 237–39; timeframe of, 216; transcriptions, 221, 224
  —THEORY: critical methodologies, 223, 230; data analysis: grounded theory and discourse analysis, 222–23; decolonial methodologies, 230; dissemblance, 25; frontline bureaucracy theory (Lipsky), 216; kitchen table talk, 2; listening for missing and fragmented voices, 223, 230; positionality of the researcher, 7, 201–9, 215, 228–29; as queered project, 16. *See also* queer of color critique

#MeToo, 156, 195
Mexico, Spanish colonialist settlers, 43–44
Michigan, Criminal Sexual Misconduct statute, 28, 29
Michigan Women's Task Force on Rape (MWTFR), 28–29
middle-class and wealthy survivors: and disparities within victim services, 64; the everywoman analysis and neoliberal normativity, 5, 237. *See also* "ideal" or "perfect" victim; poor people
migration within the US: housing and labor justice, 46–50; post–Civil War mass migrations, 47; socialist-like communes, 48. *See also* immigrants
Miller, Chanel, *Know My Name*, 227–28
Mingus, Mia, 131
Minnesota, anti-pornography laws, 29
minoritized survivors. *See* marginalized survivors
"minority board" of directors, 127
minors as victims, 103, 109, 141, 157, 192
MMIP/WG2S (Missing and Murdered Indigenous People/Women, Girls, and Two-Spirit People), 43, 91, 109, 193
Moraga, Cherríe, 37
Moral Majority, 31
moral wages, 117, 238
Morgan, Robin, 29

Mulla, Sameena, 277n67
multiculturalism as neoliberal normativity: definition of, 238; as devaluing cultural minority victims in need, 78; disparities in support for marginalized victims as motivation for, 69, 70; as exacerbating cultural capitalism problems in anti-rape advocacy, 77; as isolating marginalized victims, 72; as not locally culturally specific, 75; production of the "ideal/perfect" survivor via, 71–73; as redirecting capital without addressing market conditions, 71, 77–78; resource books lacking specific information for marginalized victims, 77–78; secondary victimization produced by, 72, 78; and stratification of anti-violence politics in the wake of the Third World Women and Violence Conference (1980), 38. See also cultural competency trainings (CCTs)
Muslim survivors, 68–69
mutual aid: advocacy in relation, 85–89; the Black social work movement and, 96; collaborative network of referrals, 86–89; consciousness raising as principle of, 49, 85–86; and the continuum of prevention, 86; creation of transformative justice organizations armed by practices of, 45; critical quantification as network of, 197–99; culturally informed referrals, 86, 87; definition of, 85, 238; FAAR (Feminist Alliance Against Rape) (nationwide network), 35–36, 98–99, 107; and hyperinstitutionalization of advocacy, 126–27, 197–99; industrialized workers and development of networks of, 48–50; of queer/ed communities of color, and seen as threat to the US state, 26–27, 134; as radical, 10; rape crisis centers (1970s) and networks for, 35–36, 37, 61; socialist-like communes, 48; Third World Women and Violence Conference (1980) and framework of, 37. See also abolitionist histories; anti-rape movement history, recovering; mutual aid; radicalism, reclaiming for advocacy; radical rape crisis advocacy (outside carceral systems); transformative justice; ugly emotions

NAACP, 30, 172
NAACP Legal Defense and Educational Fund (LDF), 30, 172–73
National Association of Black Social Workers (NABSW), 97
National Association of Social Workers (NASW): apology for its contributions to racist practices, 97. See also social work
National Black Feminist Organization New York Chapter, 34
National Black United Front, 38
National Coalition Against Domestic Violence National Day of United (1981), 37
National Communication Network (NCN), 36
National Conference of Puerto Rican Women, 34–35
National Network to End Domestic Violence, 278–79n86
national organizations: and cultural competency trainings (CCTs), 70–71, 74–75. See also state coalitions of rape crisis agencies
National Sexual Assault Coalition Resource Sharing Project, 93
National Sexual Violence Resource Center, 186, 278–79n86; "Cultural Competency" podcasts, 71. See also Pennsylvania Coalition to Advance Respect
Necessary Interruptions, 129, 260n3
necropolitics, 189–93, 194, 196, 199

neoconservatives: alliance with liberal feminists in rape law reform (carceral feminism), 10–11, 27–32, 136–40; attacks on diversity initiatives, 179, 193, 203; attacks on queers, trans, and anyone nonnormative, 203; evangelical Christianity in movement of, 27, 28, 31; rape as social problem, 190–91, 279n101; refusing to accept the numbers social scientists and anti-rape feminists had found, 175; refuting rape law reform entirely, 31; and spousal rape exception, 29. *See also* anticrime rhetoric; carceral feminism; multiculturalism as neoliberal normativity; welfare policies—welfare "reform"

neoliberalism: definition of, 4, 238; social ontology of fear under, 79. *See also* mass incarceration; neoliberal normativity; welfare policies

neoliberal normativity: academic research as imbricated in, 228–29; as buttressed by liberal feminist alliance with neoconservatives to mainstream anti-violence projects, 11; definition of, 5–6; everywoman analysis of, as myth, 5, 237; mutability of, in response to demands of radicalism, 15; radicalism as weapon against the binary of, 10, 13, 19–20. *See also* carceral feminism; multiculturalism as neoliberal normativity; production of rape survivors in the neoliberal rape crisis center; professional advocacy; race crisis centers, neoliberal; victim capital

neurodivergent people: advocates, 110; disabled, and informed consent, 192; disabled, high percentage of incarcerated population, 157; survivors, 91, 192

New York Radical Feminists (NYRF), rape speak-out (1971), 34

New York Redstockings: call-out traditions, 34; Rape Prevention Month, 34

New York Women Against Rape Inaugural Women of Color Caucus meeting, 37–38

Nixon, Richard, War on Drugs, 137–38

non-English speakers. *See* limited English-speaking proficiency (LEP)

nonprofit industrial complex (NPIC): overview, 54–55, 204; absorption of independent agencies into larger multi-service agencies, 31, 67–68, 278–79n86; care work as not altering the exchange of survivors for agency funding, 55; definition of, 238; government welfare spending cuts and rise of, 97–98; the hierarchization of RCCs and formation of, 98–99; "race to lead" rates, 124, 266n88; secondary victimization as exacerbated by capitalist logics of, 55, 66. *See also* direct services advocates as service providers representing the state; funding by government grants; professionalization of the rape crisis center; rape crisis centers, neoliberal; secondary victimization

normativity, definition of, 169, 238

NOW (National Organization for Women): National Task Force on Rape, 28, 174; New York, 34; support for government funding of anti-rape advocacy, 36

NPIC. *See* nonprofit industrial complex (NPIC)

Office for Victims of Crime (OVC): access to victim compensation requires survivors to cooperate with police and forensic-medical examiners, 4; reimbursement of victim's expenses, 4, 29, 159; Victim Assistance Training (VAT), 74, 75; Victims of Crime Act (VOCA), 29, 144–45, 159, 176, 188, 198. *See also* US Department of Justice (DOJ)

Office of Crime Victims Advocacy (OCVA), 92, 93, 129
Office on Violence against Women (OVW): mission and budget of, 176, 186–87; SASP (Sexual Assault Services Program), 98, 176–77, 262n35; STOP (Service, Training, Officers, and Prosecutors) program, 98, 176–77, 262n35; "underserved" minority grant solicitation, 177–79, 187, 277n60
Omnibus Crime Control and Safe Streets Act (1968), 136
One Place/Family Justice Center, 132
Oppression Pyramid, 135
organizational types: absorption of independent agencies into larger multi-service agencies, 31, 67–68, 278–79n86; dependence on governmental funding as affecting all, 4; for-profit, 4, 218, 278–79n86; public, 4, 169, 218, 278–79n86. *See also* culturally specific rape crisis agencies; nonprofit industrial complex (NPIC); tribal agencies (rape crisis centers)
OVC. *See* Office for Victims of Crime

Pacific Islander communities: college education as inaccessible for, 107–8; women of, and the Third World movement, 33. *See also* Asian communities—women; Hawai'i
Paglia, Camille, 30
Palotai, Ada, 26
panopticon: definition of, 238; rape crisis centers as, 155, 188
Parks, Rosa, 22, 23, 229–30
pathology, definition of, 238
Patton, Gwendolyn, 33
Pauly, Madison, 90, 91, 260n2
Pennsylvania Coalition to Advance Respect, "Cultural Responsiveness" bulletins, 71. *See also* National Sexual Violence Resource Center

perfect victim, definition of, 238
pernell, deanne, 36
perpetrators: Black people and non-Black racialized and gendered groups as disproportionately arrested, convicted, sentenced, and exonerated, 30, 158, 172, 173; female, 28; few held accountable, through legal or nonlegal measures, 156; lethal retributive attacks against victims who report, 156; RCCs refusing to respond to persons with criminal records, 157–58; sex offender registration as lifelong punishment, 156–57; as weaponizing their privilege through rape, 3, 15, 54; white cisgender heterosexual men as percentage of, 3, 243n3. *See also* incarceration and rape—incarceration of perpetrators; prosecutions for rape; racist rape myths used to target Black men; sentencing
police victim advocates, 144
police violence. *See* law enforcement—violence and brutality
poor people: colonized, spectrum of anti-rape advocacy activities by Indigenous women and allies, 43–44; criminalization of, 97, 134–38; declared to be the cause of crime, 135–36, 137–38; post–Civil War mass migrations to the North and industrialist exploitation of BIPOC and white women, 47; Reagan "welfare reform" and pathologization of, 97; white and white-acting, seen as "worthy" and "innocent," 135; white, colonial property law negating rape of (while middle- and wealthy white woman protected), 42–43. *See also* enslavement; housing justice; labor justice; marginalized survivors; welfare policies; welfare programs; welfare reform movement

pornography: alliance of liberal feminists and neoconservatives in anti-pornography laws (carceral feminism), 29, 31, 32; mass production and distribution of media, 29; and the "Sex Wars" split among feminists, 31

positionality of the researcher. *See under* methodology

post–Civil War years: Black liberationist calls for armed "self-help," 45; Black men falsely accused of rape and lynched, 134; Black Reconstruction activists falsely accused of rape and lynched, 171; convict leasing, 47, 134; mass migrations to the North and West, 47. *See also* immigrants; industrialization; lynching of Black men; racist rape myths used to target Black men; welfare reform movement (settlement house movement)

precarity crisis (fear there is a shortage of victim capital), 18, 64–69, 78, 83, 84, 238

predominately white institutions (PWIs), 238

PrEP, 57

prison industrial complex: Black people and non-Black racialized and gendered groups as disproportionately arrested, convicted, sentenced, and exonerated, 30, 158, 172, 173; as the capitalist system's feudalist reinforcement of racial hierarchies, 57–58; definition of, 238. *See also* incarcerated population; mass incarceration; welfare policies

Prison Nation, 6, 160–61, 166, 204, 238

Prison Rape Elimination Act (PREA, 2003), 144, 159

production of rape survivors in the neoliberal rape crisis center: overview, 18; as conditional advocacy, 63; multiculturalism and, 71–73; outsourcing direct victim services to systems professionals, 68–69, 69, 74, 82; the survivor discourse (empowerment model) of, in competition for funding, 63–64, 68–69, 78, 239; and system justification by advocates, 79. *See also* direct services advocates as service providers representing the state; "ideal" or "perfect" victim

—INVENTORYING AND DISTRIBUTION OF VICTIM RESOURCES: overview, 55; consent for release of victim's information, 62; consent/paperwork if victim requests a service the RCC is reluctant to supply, 62; enslavement's valuation of bodies as replicated in, 54–55, 60, 82; the "ideal/perfect" victim as disproportionately receiving services, 62, 69; "ideal victim" normativity of survivor's needs determining worthy vs. unworthy victims, 64–66, 67, 69, 100; judgments of who is a victim or not, 87; liability concerns of RCC and refusal to provide, 62; marginalized victims defined as "excess Others" and culturally informed care as unaffordable, 78–83, 259n79; marginalized victims' disparity in receiving services, 62–63, 64–69; market constraints imposed by administrator authorization for services, 99–100; market constraints imposed by funders, 61–63, 85; precarity crisis (fear there is a shortage of victim capital) and disparities of care, 18, 64–69, 78, 83, 84, 238; resistance to providing emotional care, 61–62; the resource book and, 77–78. *See also* multiculturalism as neoliberal normativity; victim capital professional advocacy: overview, 18; and belief that professionals are best suited to respond to rape victims, 101, 110–11; call to desist from, 125; "certification" of professional advocates by state coalitions, 128; as continuum, 101; lived experience of marginalized advocates devalued as legitimate knowledge, 104–5, 107, 109–10, 111, 117; "moral wages" paid marginalized advocates, 117; as racialized hierarchy, 101–2, 107, 119–23, 124–25; radical version of (hyperinstitutionalization), 126–30, 197–98; socialization as set of powerful social norms, 101; the wage gap of marginalized advocates as devaluing the specialized cultural skill sets of, 116–17, 119. *See also* advocacy trainings—and professionalization; college education and professionalization; direct services advocates as service providers representing the state; professionalization of the rape crisis center

—"UNPROFESSIONAL" PERCEPTION OF BIPOC ADVOCATES: abuse of power by advocate of color in response to violence experienced, 118–19; challenges in survivor acceptance and additional specialized cultural skill sets required due to, 115–16, 117; compassion fatigue and burnout due to, 117, 124–25; congregation of advocates of color in response to, 125; and the double bind, 115–16, 117–19, 124, 265n70; "fungibility" and overburdening of non-Black women of color, 117–18; harms experienced on the job, and risks of reporting, 118; hiring of diverse advocates, 123–25; the pay gap and attrition, 116–17, 122–23; racist abuse by survivors ignored by administration, 115–16, 118, 119; reorganization of workplace and labor norms to help alleviate, 124–30; as risk to promotions or higher wages, 102, 119, 124; tensions cast as "professional" conflicts, instead of acts of anti-Black racism, 90–94, 122, 128–29, 260nn2–4

—WHITE NORMS OF: overview, 94, 101–2; attire, 102; and COVID-19 provisions for direct services workers vs. administrators, 121; English usage, 102; policies negating identities as privileging, 104–5; promotion of white or white-acting BIPOC advocates over BIPOC, 94, 119–23, 124, 266nn86,88; white ascendancy (condition of being or acting white made to seem neutral and inclusive), 121–23, 124–25, 239; whiteness of advocate accepted as legitimate authority, 114–15

professionalization of the rape crisis center: overview, 97–99, 101; and the competitive workplace, 112, 114, 119; DC Rape Crisis Center challenging (1978), 36; FAAR warning about (1975), 98–99, 107; government funding and legal mandate for grants manager, 98; and hierarchization of advocacy into administration and direct services, 98, 99; and history of the "helping profession" and social work, 95–97; legitimizing the RCC to the state and, 98–99; paid administrators vs. volunteer and low-paid direct services advocates, 99; pressure for, and RCCs opting to collaborate with law enforcement, 137, 139; Reaganomic "welfare reform" budget cuts and the "nonprofitization effect," 97–98; systems professionals and demand for, 99;

professionalization of the rape crisis center (*cont.*)
professionalization of the rape crisis center wage hierarchy between administration and direct services, 112–14, 116–17, 119, 122, 264nn62,64; wage hierarchy chart with salary, race, and gender, *113*. See also administration; direct services advocates; grant writing; nonprofit industrial complex (NPIC); professional advocacy

Project NIA, 165

property rights, rape law theorized through: the consent paradigm and, 59, 60; and the "ideal" victim, 58–59; incommensurability of exchange and, 58–60; marginalized victims unaccounted for, 42–43, 59; state rape law reform and, 28; valuation of victim's worth as problem, 58–60

prosecutions for rape: attorneys forcing victims to relive their experience, 140; Black men disproportionately arrested, convicted, sentenced, and exonerated, 30, 158, 172, 173; less than 1% of cases make it to jury trial, 140; lethal retributive attacks on victims who report rape, 156; plea deals as routine to avoid sex offender registration, 156; quantified data collected for purposes of, 277n67; secondary victimization and, 140; victim's costs of travel and time in, 159

prostitution, ascribed to any single woman, 49. See also sex workers

Protestantism, 47, 95

Puar, Jasbir: paranoid temporality, 202; precarity crisis, 65

public assistance: food stamps, 138; public housing, 138. See also welfare policies

public health: CDC anti-rape task force and, 176; social problems called "epidemics," 97

Puerto Rican women: and abortion, 33; as advocates, and insufficiency of consent forms, 191–92; National Conference of Puerto Rican Women, 34–35; as percentage of incarcerated women, 33

Pulido, Laura, 120

quantifying rape victims in grant applications: overview, 19, 167–70; advocate resistance to, 179–80; amount of work conducted per victim, 168; assumed erroneously to be an objective "neutral" act, 168, 169–70, 174, 175–76, 177, 184, 189; biases and stereotypes imposed via, 168–69, 190; categorizing people, 168, 190; competition for grant funding and, 19, 181; consent as insufficiently obtained for, 19, 184–85, 191–93; critical quantification as alternative to, 193–94; definition of, 168; as dispossessing Indigenous knowledges, 193–94; "eligible" or "ineligible" victimhood relies on subjective interpretations of socially constructed identities, 168–69, 179; funding as dependent on compliance with, 169, 177–79, 180; fungible quantification, 186; minority grant funding, 177–79, 187, 277n60; minority grant funding at risk and social identity questions may change, 179; no improvement in victim services or rape rates achieved due to, 186–87, 193; number of victims seen, 168; panopticon, the rape crisis center as, 188; as political weapon defining the limits of a "normal victim," 169, 184; pressure on advocates to quantify survivors, 19, 178–79, 181; racist and colonialist history of development, 171–73, 184, 190; reporting/not reporting recorded, 168; specific social identities tracked, 177–79, 180–81, 190, 276n52; as subjective, 168, 184–85, 188–89; as subjective, women of color's

insistence ignored by white academics and advocates, 175, 189–90; systems professionals' reports, 277n67; taxonomies illustrate the composite numbers and their calculation, 168; taxonomies produced by advocates for the state serve no purpose, 170, 188–93; "zombie" taxonomies produced by, 190–91, 193
—NORMALIZATION OF SURVIVORS: overview, 169–70; as administrative violence, 169–70, 182–86, 190–91; advocates filling in the answers, and mischaracterizations, 180–82, 189, 190; advocates implicitly accept identities as the state sees them, as secondary victimization, 182–83; asking the victim to fill out the form or to give more consent is administrative violence, 191–93; as biopower, 169, 180, 191–92; clear guidelines not given on how to collect the data, 189, 190; denial of services on basis of, 167–69, 185–86, 273n2; disabled survivors, harm to, 184; done without their knowledge (carceral control), 169; funder priorities, and creating taxonomies that sustain normativity, 19, 169, 181, 188; gender normalization, 181; Indigeneity assumed to be a racial identity, eliding its political and legal import, 181–82; intersectional and fluid identities elided in, 169, 170; marginalized advocates fill out the majority of service forms normalizing survivors, thereby becoming the agent of their oppression, 187, 190, 193; as necropolitics, 189–93, 194, 196, 199; neoliberal normativity sustained by advocate, 170; normative analysis by grants officer, 179, 277n62; normative classification methods, 170, 179–85; radical advocacy displaced by, 19, 170, 188; services offered may be inappropriate based on mischaracterization and, 183, 184; as "speaking for" the advocate, 188; as "speaking for" the victim, 170, 180–81, 182–83, 184–85, 191, 278n75; systems professionals implicitly accept identities as the state sees them, and secondary victimization, 183, 278n76; trans survivors, harm to, 183, 278n76
—RISE OF RAPE VICTIM STATISTICS: Menachim Amir, anti-Black rape study (discredited), 136, 173, 175; Joe Biden (senator) leveraged the data to facilitate passage of VAWA, 176; and claim rape was one of the "fastest growing crimes," 174; FBI crime reporting, 171–72, 173–74, 274n18, 276n52; Mary P. Koss's "one in four," 174–75, 275n35; NAACP reporting, 172; Diana E. H. Russell, disseminated Amir's misinformation, 173; Ida B. Wells, quantification of lynching, 171, 172, 188; Marvin Wolfgang's study, 172–73, 188; women of color seeking to challenge the racist and misleading reporting, 175. *See also* Brownmiller, Susan, *Against Our Will*
queer communities of color: mutual aid conducted by, 26–27, 134–35; mutual aid networks seen as threat to US state, 134; rape victim–blaming of, 138. *See also* queer people
queer/ed or queer/ing, 16, 239
queer of color critique: overview, 15; and capacious definition of rape, 15–16; as genealogy of radicalism, 9–10, 13, 217; necropolitics, 189–93, 194, 196, 199; and production of rape survivors in the neoliberal rape crisis center, 60; queer methodologies, 223, 230

queer people (inclusive of 2SLGBTQIA+ people and those who live outside of normative constructs): CCTs about, 70, 71–72; critical quantitative studies, 193–94; definition of, 16, 237; quantification and mischaracterization of, 181, 189; queer liberationists and the feminist "Sex Wars," 31, 32; and queer methodologies of the text, 223; radical advocacy advancements by, 9–10, 11, 12, 126; radical organizations established by, 34–35, 165, 195, 203–4; and vulnerability to rape, 3. *See also* lesbians; queer communities of color; trans and gender-diverse people; Two-Spirit people

—ADVOCATES: and advocacy in relation, 88–89; on advocates increasingly not reflective of the community's demographics, 122; on intersectional violence of intake forms, 183; lived experience of, utilized in support, 104; on quantification and mischaracterization, 189; quantification paperwork normalizing marginal survivors disproportionately falling to, 187; radical activism (outside carceral systems) advanced by, 9–10, 11, 12; and restorative justice, 12; working conditions and attrition, 123, 187. *See also* marginalized advocates

—SURVIVORS: and implicit biases of advocates, 104–5, 127; not being willing to take the one pathway the neoliberal RCC offers, 204–5; queerphobic people portraying victims as sexual predators/offenders, 157; rape defined flexibly enough for inclusion of, 16. *See also* marginalized survivors

race: and disparities in care, 66–67; radical feminists of the 1970s and tensions of class and, 36–37, 38, 40; and vulnerability to rape, 3; wage hierarchy chart with salary, race, and gender, 113. *See also* Asian communities; Black communities; color of skin and colorism; Indigenous peoples; Latina/e/o/x communities

racial capitalism: overview, 56; the capitalist system as feudalist reinforcement of racial hierarchies, 56–57; the consent paradigm and rape-as-theft argument, 59; and cultural capitalism, 255n15; definition of, 56, 239; ethnic capitalism distinguished from, 255n17; knowledge about white European cultures can elevate wealth and social standing, 57; professionalization and, 101; white settler economic dispossession is anti-Black racial oppression of BIPOC, 57

racial disparities: liberal feminism and failure to consider, 9, 36–37; and social work, as serving white interests in, 96, 107–8

racial hierarchy: active dismantling of, 128; definition of, 239; enslavement as feudalist reinforcement of, 56; the prison industrial complex as feudalist reinforcement of, 57–58; professional advocacy as, 101–2, 107, 119–23, 124–25; in Third World movement, 120. *See also* racial capitalism

racial segregation, and professionalization of social work, 96

racism: advocates experiencing from survivors, as ignored in "professional" RCC, 115–16, 118, 119; advocates experiencing from survivors in workplace, 115–16; advocates experiencing in workplace, expectation they will remedy their own racist encounters, 260n4; apology by National Association of Social Workers for their contributions to racist practices, 97;

arrests, convictions, and sentencing as disproportionate, 30, 158, 172, 173; BIPOC survivors experiencing in the RCC, 36–37, 72, 215; educating white advocates about, as burden falling to marginalized advocates, 109–10; resentment of advocates who call out, 8; state coalition trainer's racist microaggression, 74–75; white advocates educating other white people about, 127. *See also* anti-Blackness and anti-Black racism; lynching of Black men; racist rape myths used to target Black men

racist rape myths used to target Black men: Susan Brownmiller's book premised on, 173; capital punishment for, 30, 172–73; capital punishment removed for rape, activism for, 30; carceral feminism as driven by false reporting, 136, 137, 156; convict leasing of Black men and effects on the family and community, 134; and disproportionate arrests, convictions, sentencing, and exonerations of Black men, 30, 158, 172, 173; false accusations of rape, and imprisonment, 30, 134, 171; false accusations of rape, and lynching, 30, 134, 171, 172; the FBI and J. Edgar Hoover framing rape as a product of BIPOC cultures, 172; FBI crime reporting statistics amplifying the myth while erasing white racial terror from the public eye, 171–72; and the "ideal" victim, construction of, 58; mass incarceration and, 136, 137, 156; protests of, 34; Reconstruction activists as threat to white socioeconomic power, lynched using imagery of, 171; Diana E. H. Russell's book premised on, 173; "superpredator" myth and, 156; welfare "reform" rationales using, 136, 137; Ida B. Wells's quantified antilynching campaign, 171, 172, 188. *See also* lynching of Black men

radical activists: Black Reconstruction activists lynched, 171; labeled as terrorists and criminals, 135; mutual aid networks of queer/ed communities of color seen as threat to the state, 134

radicalism, reclaiming for advocacy: overview, 23–24; as advocacy in relation with community, 85–89; as affective activism, 8, 66, 160; affinity groups, 126–27; as challenging neoliberal normativity in all its aspects, 7–8, 10, 13, 19–20; definition of, 8, 239; emotional bandwidth widened by, 10; feeling rape is radical advocacy, 24, 50–51, 84–85; as "feminist killjoy" disrupting the happy affect of doing advocacy in favor of awakening to the urgency for change, 8, 155–56, 160, 237; and hyperinstitutionalization of advocacy, 126–30, 197–99; implicit biases, addressing, 126, 127; lived experience, valuing, 126–27; outreach, prevention, and intervention as well-oiled wheel, 86; queer of color critique as genealogy of, 9–10, 13; as shifting attention from the binary toward diverse transformative possibilities, 10, 84; slowing down and taking a deep breath, 84; supporting survivors and generating funding as co-constitutive, 10; "The master's tools will never dismantle the master's house" (Audre Lorde), 126; as weapon against the binary of neoliberal normativity, 10, 13, 19–20; white "radical feminism" as appropriation of radicalism, 9. *See also* abolitionist histories; anti-rape movement history, recovering; mutual aid; radical rape crisis advocacy (outside carceral systems); transformative justice; ugly emotions radical rape crisis advocacy (outside carceral systems): advocates becoming radical, 160–66; community-advocate relations (advocacy in relation), 85–89; decor and attire to make survivors comfortable, 166; as free-market advocacy, 61, 67; given scant scholarly attention, 11; marginalized advocates and survivors as advancing, 9–10, 11, 12; "minority board" of directors, 127; new labor norms, 129–30; as resisting the "no future" imposed by systems, 12–13; restorative justice as "fatal strategy" embedding carceral normativity, 11–12; trust building, 87–88, 127, 165–66. *See also* abolitionist histories—imagined future histories; critical quantification; culturally specific rape crisis agencies; mutual aid; radicalism, reclaiming for advocacy; transformative justice; tribal agencies (rape crisis centers)

—CULTURALLY HUMBLE ADVOCACY: alienation of clients due to lack of, 67–68, 74, 75, 83, 87–88; fungibility and assignment of a non-Black advocate of color to all marginalized survivors as attempt at, 117–18; neoliberal normativity defining the victims as "excess Others" and care as unaffordable, 78–83

—NEOLIBERAL ADVOCACY AS FORGOING: overview, 55; advocacy training as eliding, 103–4; carceral feminism as displacing, 132–33, 152; college education norms and ignorance of political roots of advocacy, 108–9; early determination of RCCs to stick with, 35, 136–37; gaslighting by systems professionals, 205–6; the pay gap as financial incentive to abandon, 114; quantification of victims and, 19, 170, 188

rape: advocates as survivors of, 14, 160, 201–2, 205, 225, 226; definition of, 15–16, 239; as issue of interlocking power and oppression, 15, 54; spousal rape, 29; as weaponization of privilege, 3. *See also* perpetrators; racist rape myths used to target Black men; rape crisis centers; rape law; victims

Rape, Abuse, and Incest National Network (RAINN), 123, 243n3

rape crime reporting: and claim rape was one of the "fastest growing crimes," 174; FBI statistics Uniform Crime Reports (UCRs), 171, 173–74, 274n18, 276n52; law enforcement falsifying data to reduce numbers, 171, 274n18; NAACP's reporting, 172; no reporting required if "evidence" produced by victim witness is "unfounded," 274n18. *See also* quantifying rape victims in grant applications—rise of rape victim statistics

rape crisis centers: first in the US (DC Rape Crisis Center, 1972), 35; number of, 36, 186–87, 278–79n86. *See also* radical rape crisis advocacy (outside carceral systems); rape crisis centers, neoliberal

rape crisis centers, neoliberal: absorption of independent agencies into larger multi-service agencies, 31, 67–68, 278–79n86; and carceral lock-in, path dependence toward, 139; as carceral panopticon, 155, 188, 238; outsourcing direct victim services to systems professionals, 68–69, 69, 74, 82; wage hierarchy, 112–14, *113*, 116–17, 119, 122, 264nn62,64; wage hierarchy chart with salary, race, and gender, *113*. *See also* administration; attrition and alienation; boards of directors of rape crisis agencies; cultural competency trainings (CCTs); direct services advocates; direct services advocates as service providers representing the state; executive directors; funding by government grants; "ideal" or "perfect" victim; mainstream advocacy histories; nonprofit industrial complex (NPIC); production of rape survivors in the neoliberal rape crisis center; professionalization of the rape crisis center; rape law reform; Violence Against Women Act (VAWA, 1994)

rape law: based originally in property rights, 28, 42–43; carceral feminism and expansion of, 141–42; originally applied only to white women, 43; victim commodity thesis (rape-as-theft argument), 57–60, 78. See also property rights, rape law theorized through; rape crime reporting; rape law reform

rape law reform: alliance of liberal feminists and neoconservatives and (carceral feminism), 10–11, 27–32, 136–40; antipornography laws, 29, 31, 32; civil rights law added, and rescinded, 29, 30; coercion/force, 28; consent, 28; feminist "sex wars" split between antipornography activists and queer liberation activists supporting sexual freedom and sex workers, 31, 32; as gender-neutral crime, 28; model rape law proposed by MWTFR, 28, 29; and property rights as original basis of rape law, 28, 42–43; racist myths blaming Black men, and removal of capital punishment for rape, 30; racist myths, protests of, 34; rape shield laws, 28; spousal rape not covered under, 29. See also federal laws; Violence Against Women Act (VAWA, 1994)

Rape Prevention Month, 34

rape trauma syndrome, 174

Reagan, Ronald, "welfare reforms" pathologizing the poor, 97–98, 138

Red power movement, 134

religion and anti-rape advocacy: advocacy in relation and collaborative networks, 86; lack of training in diversity of, 75; minority faiths, and expanded grants, 177; RCC policies preventing advocates from sharing their own identities, 104–5; and recognition of implicit biases, 104–5, 127; and secondary victimization by advocate, 68–69

Religious Right Citizens for Decency Through Law, 28

resource book (or binder): as alienating marginalized clients from RCC, 87–88; the collaborative network as radical alternative to, 86–89; lack of specifics needed for marginalized victims, 77–78

resource mobilization. See mutual aid; production of rape survivors in the neoliberal rape crisis center

restorative justice: in advocate's fantasy RCC, 208; and carceral justice, as two sides of the same coin, 204; defined as response seeking to resolve violence outside of the harmful carceral state, 11–12, 239; as "fatal strategy" embedding carceral normativity, 12, 246n47; Indigenous American origin of (peacemaking), 49; nonviolence as response to violence, 49; transformative justice compared to, 11–12, 49, 204. See also transformative justice

Richie, Beth E., 39

Robinson, Cedric, 18, 56. See also racial capitalism

Roiphe, Katie, 30

Roosevelt, Franklin D., New Deal, 134

Ross, Loretta J.: Angela Davis and, 230; and DC Rape Crisis Center, 37; and Third World Women and Violence Conference (1980), 37–38

rural advocacy, among first to be cut from budgets, 83. *See also* farming communities
Russell, Diana E. H.: and Brownmiller, 173; *The Politics of Rape from the Victim's Perspective*, 173
Rutherford, Alexandra, 175

SAFEs (sexual assault forensic-medical examiners): as carceral agents, 131–32, 267n2; consent and paperwork, 191; demand for professionalization of RCCs, 99; forcing a victim to undergo exam, 140; identifying primarily as white cisgender women, 145; quantified reports written by, 277n67; secondary victimization by, 140, 150; wage hierarchy and state's judgment of rape response roles, 145; wage hierarchy chart with salary, race, and gender, *113*. *See also* SARTs (sexual assault response teams); secondary victimization; systems professionals
—SEXUAL ASSAULT OR RAPE KITS: coerced consent for, 140; definition of, 239; funders' priorities and medicalization, 61; police investigator asking advocate what to do with (the evidence), 151; as victim capital, 82. *See also* secondary victimization
SAMFEs (sexual assault medical-forensic examiners), 239. *See also* SAFEs
Sanctified Sisters Woman's Commonwealth (Texas), 50
SANE (sexual assault nurse examiner), 239. *See also* SAFEs
Santa Cruz Women Against Rape (SC-WAR), 36, 37
SARTs (sexual assault response teams): overview, 131–32, 161; abandonment of RCC or domestic violence shelter due to Black Lives Matter sign on front desk, 2–5, 205–6, 243n1; additional labor of advocates to fill in for carceral actors, 151–52; advocacy positions structured to protect victim from secondary victimization, 144–45; advocate cedes authority to systems professionals, 146–50, 160–62; advocates affirming themselves as powerful actors, 162–64; advocates as radical feminists, claiming of, 163–64, 166; advocates interfacing with systems vs. survivors' needs, 147–48; anonymous vs. identified rape reporting, 151; definition of, 239; devaluing of the advocate in, 148–49, 158–59; helpful if survivors wish to seek legal recourse or protective orders, 132, 161; housed in a single building, 132, 161; as multidisciplinary teams (MDT), 132; racialized and gendered hierarchy within, 145–46; as reflection of the larger US culture, 161; third-party policing by advocate, 150–55; VAWA as formalizing, 132; wage hierarchy and state's judgment of rape response roles, 145, 270–71n67; wage hierarchy chart with salary, race, and gender, *113*; white cultural ideology (carceral professionalism) as legitimating authority in, 145–46, 148–49. *See also* carceral feminism; systems professionals
saunders, karen, 36
Schenwar, Maya, 131
Schlafly, Phyllis, 31
Scottsboro Boys, 172
secondary traumatic stress (STS), definition of, 239
secondary victimization: by industrialization, 49; the nonprofit industrial complex as exacerbating, 55, 66; by perpetuating dominant/hegemonic histories, 41

—BY ADVOCATES: consent and paperwork, time and attention required, 191–93; due to displacement of victims' needs in favor of the agency's funding needs, 5, 66; and the everywoman analysis (only one "normal" way to advocate for one "normal" victim), 5, 237; multiculturalism and, 72, 78; and neoliberal normativity, 5–6; quantification (intake form) as administrative violence, 169–70, 182–86, 191–93; responsibility for lifetime costs experienced by rape victims, 159; survivor's fear of Islamophobic therapy, 68–69; white advocates denying support to BIPOC victims, 215. *See also* carceral feminism

—BY SYSTEMS PROFESSIONALS: overview, 5, 11; advocate positions specifically meant to prevent, 144; advocates apologizing instead of stopping it, 153–55, 156; advocates' inability or refusal to intervene in, 11, 142–44, 150; attorneys in prosecutions, 140; consent and paperwork, 191; deadnaming a trans survivor, 183, 278n76; law enforcement, 140–41, 147, 150, 162, 164; police pressuring victim to withdraw her statement, then charging her with false reporting for withdrawing, 140–41; SAFEs, 140, 150

—INTERSECTIONAL HARM: advocates' refusal to actively dismantle the carceral complex as, 159–60; studies focusing on the administrative staff as perpetuating, 215–16; white-centered agencies as perpetuating, 9, 36–37

second rape, 5, 239. *See also* secondary victimization

sentencing: capital punishment removed from rape law, 30; carceral feminists lobbying for harsher punishments, 142; mandatory convictions and minimum sentencing guidelines, 137, 142; plea deals to avoid sex offender registration, as routine, 156; sex offender registration as lifelong punishment, 156–57. *See also* incarceration and rape—incarceration of perpetrators

settlement house movement. *See* welfare reform movement

settler-colonial capitalism, 56; dispossession as arriving through the insemination of corporate values one tribe at a time, 205

sex trafficking, 29, 139, 159; human trafficking, 86–87

Sexual Assault Advocacy Network (Facebook/Meta), 228

sexual assault. *See* rape

sexual capital, 56; rape as theft of (victim commodity thesis), 57–58, 59–60

sexual intercourse, positive, and victim commodity thesis (rape-as-theft), 57–58, 59–60

Sexual Offender Registry and Notification Act (SORNA, 2006), 156–57

sexual orientation (sexuality): as form of transformational knowledge, 195; as increased vulnerability to rape, 3, 168; as intersectional social identity, 121; and methodology, 223; quantification of, 189; RCC policies preventing advocates from sharing their own identities, 104–5. *See also* lesbians; queer communities of color; queer people (inclusive of 2SLGBTQIA+ people and those who live outside of normative constructs); trans and gender-diverse people; Two-Spirit people

sexual violence. *See* rape

sex workers, queer liberation feminists and, 31, 32
Shakur, Assata, 38, 230
shelters: for abused unhoused women, 35, 65–66; coercive benevolence of housing workers, 153; of DC Rape Crisis Center, 35; for domestic violence victims, 29, 98, 186, 262n35; funding restrictions and limited housing support, 61, 85; as victim capital, 57. *See also* welfare reform movement (settlement house movement)
Simpson, Leanne Betasamosake, 167, 198
social capital. *See* cultural capitalism
socialization, definition of, 239
Social Justice Fund NW, 129, 260n3
social ontology of fear, 79
social work: apology by NASW for their contributions to racist practices, 97; class and racial disparities serving white interests in, 96, 107–8; colonial helping professionalism and, 95–98, 100; educational credentialing, 95–96, 97, 108; hierarchy of administration and direct services in, 96; and the medicalized "nonprofitization effect" in anti-rape advocacy, 97–98; and pathologization of people on welfare, 97; poverty wages and social stigma of, 108
—MARGINALIZED SOCIAL WORKERS: the Black social work movement, 96–97; National Association of Black Social Workers (NABSW), 97; social workers who don't live in the community lack critical knowledge, 96–97, 104
sovereignty: data sovereignty, 193–94; movements for, 45, 134
Spanish colonialist settlers, 43–44
standpoint, definition of, 239
state coalitions of rape crisis agencies: overview, 90–91; boards of directors of, as predominantly white cisgender people, 122; "certification" of advocates as professionals, 128; and cultural competency trainings (CCTs), 70–71, 74–75; hours of advocacy training specified by, 263n51; trainer's racist microaggression, 74–75. *See also* national organizations
state laws: anti-pornography, 29, 31, 32; Michigan's model law and reform of, 28, 29; rape law originally based on property rights, 28, 42–43. *See also* rape law reform
storytelling: conventional, 24–25; patterned or scenic storytelling, 27
Strunk, Kamden, 190
Student Nonviolence Coordinating Committee (SNCC), 32–33. *See also* Civil Rights Movement (1960s)
substance abuse disorders, rape victims with, 64–65
Suina, Michele, 193–94
surveillance: gaps in the law and, 134; prisons and, 134
#SurvivedAndPunished, 195
survivor discourse (empowerment model), 63–64, 68–69, 78, 239
survivor justice, 34–35
survivors. *See* victims
Sweet, Paige L., 63, 259n79
system justification, 79
systems professionals: authority of RCC grants manager legally mandated on par with, 98; DC Rape Crisis Center and, 35, 136–37; definition of, 239; early resistance of RCCs to working with, 35, 136; gaslighting to keep advocates as service providers, 205–6; helpful if survivors wish to seek legal recourse or protective orders, 132, 161; memorandums of understanding (MOUs), RCCs with, 132; multiculturalism and neoliberal burdens placed on, 77–78; on nonprofits' board of directors, 4, 122; pressure to professionalize and RCC

decision to collaborate with, 136–37; and professionalization of RCCs, 98, 99; quantified reports written by, 277n67; RCCs outsourcing advocacy-related tasks to, 68–69, 69, 74, 82; wage hierarchy chart with salary, race, and gender, 113. *See also* SARTs (sexual assault response teams); secondary victimization—by systems professionals
—EMPHASIS ON WORKING WITH: and advocates as carceral agents, 132–33; advocates must legally ensure involvement of, even where the victim doesn't want their presence, 4–5; survivors victimized by the carceral state are pushed out of access to rape responses, 36

taxonomy, definition of, 239
technical assistance, in advocates' work, 22, 239
therapeutic state: overview, 5; elevation of advanced credentials, 111; and funder priorities, 5, 61; wage hierarchy chart with salary, race, and gender, *113*
therapy: advocacy equated with, 110–11; importance of therapy assumed for survivors, 102–3; and secondary victimization by advocate, 68–69
third-party police: advocates as, 150–55; definition of, 239
Third World movement: promotion of whites or white-acting BIPOC over Black women, 94, 119–23, 124, 266nn86,88; racial hierarchy in, 120
Third World Women and Violence Conference (1980), 37–39, 175, 190, 231
Third World Women's Alliance (TWWA): early theorizing about intersectional nature of violence, 33; organizing against the punitive carceral state, 32–33, 34–35; *Triple Jeopardy* (magazine), 33
Thirteenth Amendment, 134

Thompson, Becky, 9
Thuma, Emily L., 37
Tillman, Korey, coercive benevolence, 153
Title XX, 29
Touré, I. Nkenge: archival research on, 231; on building the anti-rape movement from the messy range of advocacy, 38, 42; as first African American rape crisis center director, 37; and Third World Women and Violence Conference (1980), 37–38, 231
Toypurina, 43
trans and gender-diverse people: as advancing radical advocacy, 126; as advocates, 71–72, 126; CCTs about, 71–72; definition of, 245n32; incarceration at least once in their lifetimes for nonviolent reasons, 157; quantified data collection as misrepresenting, 180–81; white trans-exclusionary "radical" feminists and, 9. *See also* queer communities of color; queer people
—SURVIVORS: deadnamed by SAFE in the hospital, 183, 278n76; provision of gender-affirming attire for, 83; sexual assault experienced by more than half of, 157; and the trans networked responses to sexual violence, 195
transformative justice: in advocate's fantasy RCC, 208; carceral liberalism and inability to engage with, 132–33; critical quantification and, 196; definition of community, 131, 165–66; early radical feminist theorizing of, 37; hyperinstitutionalization of advocacy, 126–30, 197–99; as multiplicity of actions, 44, 45–46; organizing mutual aid collectives, 45; radicalism as shifting attention away from the binary and toward diverse possibilities of, 10, 84; restorative justice compared to, 11–12, 49, 204. *See also* abolitionist histories;

transformative justice (*cont.*)
critical quantification; radicalism, reclaiming for advocacy; radical rape crisis advocacy (outside carceral systems)
transient victims, 83, 91
transnational feminists of color, 37
tribal agencies (rape crisis centers): advocacy in relation and, 86–87; authorization by administrators for advocates' activities, 99–100; and critical quantification, 196–97, 198–99; decor and attire to make survivors comfortable, 166; and methodology of text, 218; outreach and, 86–87, 104; victim denied services based on her "non-Native" appearance and presentation, 167–69, 185–86, 273n2; victim would not have been denied services under critical quantification, 198–99; white advocate on her professional legitimacy in, 114–15. *See also* culturally specific rape crisis agencies; radical rape crisis advocacy (outside carceral systems)
tribal lands, prisons located in, 137
Trump, Donald, and administration, 179, 193, 201–2
Truth, Sojourner, 265n70
Two-Spirit people, 16, 91, 181, 237. *See also* Indigenous peoples; lesbians; marginalized advocates; marginalized survivors; queer communities of color; queer people (inclusive of 2SLGBTQ-IA+ people and those who live outside of normative constructs); trans and gender-diverse people

ugly emotions: and crisis conceptualized as moment of change, 202–4, 208; eloquent rage, 207; fear of what could happen if we claim radical feminism, 164–65; fear, ontology of, 79; fear there is a shortage of victim capital (precarity crisis), 18, 64–69, 78, 83, 84, 238; feeling rape is anti-rape work, 24, 50–51, 84–85; "feminist killjoy" disrupting the happy affect of doing advocacy in favor of awakening to the urgency for change, 8, 155–56, 160, 237; paranoid temporality, 202; as reshaping advocacy into a "killing radicalism," 6–7, 13, 19–20, 89. *See also* affective advocacy; care work
Ujima: National Center on Violence Against Women in the Black Community, 70
underserved/underrepresented survivors. *See* marginalized survivors
unhoused victims, and disparities of care, 64–66, 85. *See also* shelters; transient victims
United Farm Workers, 34–35, 88
United States v. Morrison (2000), 30
United Way, 4, 67
University of Alabama conference (1975), 173, 229
US capitalist-carceral settler state: enslavement as critical feature of, 54, 56–57; as erasing histories of anti-rape work, 22–23. *See also* colonialism; enslavement; federal laws; funding by government grants; neoliberal normativity; racial capitalism; rape law reform; welfare policies—welfare "reform" (neoconservative)
US Department of Justice (DOJ): anti-rape task force, 176. *See also* Law Enforcement Assistance Administration (LEAA, 1965); Office for Victims of Crime (OVC)
US Office of Justice Programs (OJP), 176, 186
US Supreme Court: *Coker v. Georgia* (1977), 30, 172; Ruth Bader Ginsburg, 30; *United States v. Morrison* (2000), 30

VAWA. *See* Violence Against Women Act (VAWA, 1994)
victim capital: care work, 61–62; defined, 57; differential value of (assets and liabilities), 57; gender-affirming attire for trans victims, 83; hearing aids, 70; housing, 99–100; incarcerated survivors and, 146–47; interpreters, 52, 70, 80, 83; medical-forensic exams (rape kits), 82; medicine access, 57; pet deposit, 99–100; Plan B contraception, 65; public transportation tickets, 57; relocation within prisons, 63; sage, 73; shelter connections, 57, 61; therapy and counseling, 68–69, 82; translation of materials into other languages, 91; transportation, 62, 83; visa assistance, 73
victim capitalism. *See* production of rape survivors in the neoliberal rape crisis center; victim capital; victim commodity thesis (rape-as-theft argument)
victim commodity thesis (rape-as-theft argument): as incommensurable exchange, 58–59; marginalized victims unaccounted for, 59–60, 73; multicultural capitalism repeating the problem with, 73, 78; positive sexual intercourse as capital, 57–58, 59–60; valuation of victims as problem, 58–60, 78
victims: BIPOC as percentage of all victims (82%), *113*; lifetime cost to, *113*, 159; reimbursement of expenses related to rape, 4, 29, 159. *See also* BIPOC (Black, Indigenous, and People of Color)—survivors; disabled rape survivors; "ideal" or "perfect" victim; marginalized survivors; queer people—survivors; secondary victimization

Victims of Trafficking and Violence Protection Act (2000), 30
video games, 29
Violence Against Women Act (VAWA, 1994): overview, 29–30, 176; civil rights protection, and rescission of, 29, 30; Clinton signing into law, 139; as formalizing carceral presence in rape responses, 139; law enforcement involvement in victim services, 30, 31, 139; and neoliberal feminist cooptation of the anti-rape movement, 39, 138–40; prison program funding, 144–45; rape crisis centers established by, 30, 139; reimbursement of victim's costs, 4, 29, 159; SARTs formalized through, 132. *See also* Office for Victims of Crime (OVC); Office on Violence against Women (OVW)
Violent Crime Control and Law Enforcement Act (1994), 29–30, 139. *See also* Violence Against Women Act (VAWA)
Viva García campaign, 34
Voth Schrag, Rachel J., et al., 125

Wachter, Karin, et al., 125
Walter, Maggie, 193–94
Wanrow, Yvonne, 34
Ward, Yulanda: activism for justice for, 39, 230; assassination of, 38–39, 40; and the DC Rape Crisis Center, 38
War on Drugs, 137–38
War on Poverty, 28, 135–37
Warrior, Betsy, 34
War, Yulanda, and DC Rape Crisis Center, 37
Washington, Forrester B., 96–97, 104
WCSAP (Washington Coalition of Sexual Assault Programs), 90–94, 102, 123, 128–29, 232, 260nn2–4
Wegrzyn, Annie, 70
Weisenfeld, Judith, 48

Weiss, Benjamin, 139
welfare policies: antidelinquency programs (Kennedy), 134; Great Society programs (Johnson), 134–35, 138; mutual aid networks of queer/ed communities of color seen as threat to the state, 134; rape survivors finding temporary respite in, 135
—WELFARE "REFORM" (NEOCONSERVATIVE): anticrime rhetoric entangling carceral approaches with antipoverty projects, 135–38; and mass incarceration for petty crimes, 137; neoliberal privatization and slashing of benefits (Clinton), 138–39; pathologizing poor people, 97–98; racialization of poverty and drugs, 137–38; racist rape myths about Black men, 136, 137; rape victim–blaming casting women of color as deserving of punishment, 138; Reagan administration, 97–98, 138; reduction of spending to "incentivize" marginalized people, 138; slashing, and rise of carceral feminism, 138–39; slashing, and rise of nonprofit industrial complex (NPIC), 97–98; "welfare queen" labels, 138
welfare programs: English Elizabethan Protestant projects, 95; Indigenous children forced into assimilationist boarding schools, 95, 108–9
welfare reform movement (settlement house movement): Jane Addams's Hull House (1889), 47–48; and community building, 49–50; as consciousness-raising space, 49; housing and labor justice, 46–50; mutual aid collectives, 48–49; Sanctified Sisters Woman's Commonwealth, 50. *See also* immigrants

Wells, Ida B.: admiration of Jane Addams, 48; calling for armed "self-help," 45; quantification of lynching, 171, 172, 188; as radical forebearer of anti-rape advocacy, 22; in research methodology, 230
West, Robin, 59–60
white: as term in reference to race, 243n2
white ascendancy, 121–23, 124–25, 239
white benevolence (coercive benevolence), 42–43, 95–96, 100, 153, 158–59
white Christian nationalism, nativism and prejudice against immigrants, 47, 48
white criminal gangs, 171
white cultural ideology (carceral professionalism), 145–46, 148–49, 239
white feminism: as addressing structural gender inequities, 9; advocating for state funding, 36; alliance with neoconservatives to mainstream anti-rape law and policy (carceral feminism), 10–11, 27–32, 136–40; essentialism and trans-exclusivity of, 9; as formalizing advocacy, 9; gender as the hegemonic form of oppression (denial of intersectionality), 9; intersectional violence as unrecognized and perpetuated by, 9, 36–37; leadership of the anti-rape movement claimed by, 9, 36; "radicalism" as appropriated by, 9. *See also* direct services advocates as service providers representing the state; rape law reform
white men (cisgender and heterosexual): belief that they are the true Americans, 48; as creators of Anglo-American rape laws, 42–43; discrepancies with Black men's rates of incarceration and exoneration, 158; as dominant storytellers, 24–25; as members of RCC board of directors,

122; as owners of enslaved people, 54, 60; as percentage of perpetrators, 3, 243n3; as percentage of systems professionals, 145, 172; as primary lynchers, 171
white rape crisis advocates: and Black victims as "excess Others," 80–81; and CCTs, 74–75, 77, 86; ceding authority to SART colleagues, effect on marginalized victims, 149–50; on community-driven quantification, 196; on the hiring of formally educated white people with no experience to supervise BIPOC advocates, 119–20, 122; implicit biases, awareness of, 104–5, 127; as motivated by morally sound desire to reduce white supremacy, 81; and normative victims, 82; on obtaining informed consent, 192; on position of power of the advocate, 185; racism education of, falling to marginalized advocates, 109–10; reliance on advocacy trainings, 104; therapy as focus of, 102–3; whiteness creates professional legitimacy, 114–15; willingness to talk with other white people about racism, 127. *See also* professional advocacy—white norms of
white rape survivors: anti-Black racist abuse of advocates, 115–16; and the everywoman analysis, 5, 237. *See also* "ideal" or "perfect" victim; middle-class and wealthy survivors
white supremacists and white supremacy: Indigenous and Black women's anti-rape advocacy of raiding towns of, 43–44, 45; knowledge about white European cultures as racial capital among, 57; white Christian anti-immigrant nationalism, 47, 48. *See also* anti-Blackness and anti-Black racism; racism

—VIOLENCE AGAINST PEOPLE OF COLOR: assassination of Yulanda Ward, 38–39, 40; the Black church as refuge from, 46–47; FBI crime reporting as amplifying the Black male rapist myth, while erasing white terror from the public eye, 172; racially terrorizing and lynching Black and Brown communities, 46–47, 171–72; Wells's and Wolfgang's quantified studies intending to counteract white racial terrorism, 171, 172–73. *See also* lynching of Black men; racist rape myths used to target Black men

white women: childcare provided by, for Third World Women and Violence Conference (1980), 37; in the enslavement abolitionist movement, 95; and forcing Indigenous children into assimilationist boarding schools, 95; the "ideal" or "perfect" victim as assumed to be mythical, 227; and Protestantism, 47, 95; rape laws originally applied only to, as property of white men, 43; and social work, educational credentialing of, 95–96. *See also* Addams, Jane; poor people; welfare reform movement (settlement house movement); white rape crisis advocates; white rape survivors

Wies, Jennifer, 101
Wilkins, David B., 101–2
Wilson, Alex, 195
Winnubst, Shannon, fungibility, 186
Wolfgang, Marvin, 172–73, 188. *See also* Amir, Menachim
women of color: and abortion, 33; anti-violence activism narrowing focus with the rise of neoliberal RCCs, 39; dissemblance as self-protection, 25; forced sterilization and, 33; medical discrimination against, 33;

women of color (*cont.*)
as percentage of incarcerated women, 33; publications and gatherings for, inspired by the Third World Women and Violence Conference (1980), 37–38; rape victim–blaming of, 138. *See also* Asian communities—women; BIPOC (Black, Indigenous, and People of Color); Black communities—women; Chicana women; Hawai'i; Indigenous women; Latina/e/o/x communities—women; marginalized advocates; marginalized survivors; Pacific Islander communities

Women of Color anti-violence conference (1983), 37–38

Women of Color Network, 124; in author's resource document, 227–28

Women's Anti-Rape Coalition, 174

Women's Crisis Center (Ann Arbor), 36–37

Wong, Nellie, 37

Wood, Leila (Wachter, et al.), 125

Woods, Dessie, 34

World War I, mass immigrations to the US, 48

Wrenn, Mary V., 79

Yosso, Tara J., 18

Yung, Corey Rayburn, 274n18

YWCA (Young Women's Christian Association): and absorption of smaller anti-violence collectives, 31, 67–68; housing and labor justice, 46–50

Zelnick, Jennifer, 206

"zombie" taxonomies, quantification producing, 190–91, 193

ABOUT THE AUTHOR

MELINDA CHEN is an Assistant Professor in the Department of Women's and Gender Studies at the University of Oklahoma.

www.ingramcontent.com/pod-product-compliance
Ingram Content Group UK Ltd.
Pitfield, Milton Keynes, MK11 3LW, UK
UKHW042141040226
467712UK00002B/85